Russian Foreign Policy

Russian Foreign Policy

The Return of Great Power Politics

Second Edition

Jeffrey Mankoff

A COUNCIL ON FOREIGN RELATIONS BOOK

ROWMAN & LITTLEFIELD PUBLISHERS, INC.
Lanham • Boulder • New York • Toronto • Plymouth, UK

The Council on Foreign Relations (CFR) is an independent, nonpartisan membership organiza-tion, think tank, and publisher dedicated to being a resource for its members, government offi-cials, business executives, journalists, educators and students, civic and religious leaders, and other interested citizens in order to help them better understand the world and the foreign policy choices facing the United States and other countries. Founded in 1921, CFR carries out its mission by maintaining a diverse membership, with special programs to promote interest and develop expertise in the next generation of foreign policy leaders; convening meetings at its headquarters in New York and in Washington, DC, and other cities where senior government officials, members of Congress, global leaders, and prominent thinkers come together with CFR members to discuss and debate major international issues; supporting a Studies Program that fosters independent research, enabling CFR scholars to produce articles, reports, and books and hold roundtables that analyze foreign policy issues and make concrete policy recommendations; publishing *Foreign Affairs*, the preeminent journal on international affairs and U.S. foreign pol-icy; sponsoring Independent Task Forces that produce reports with both findings and policy prescriptions on the most important foreign policy topics; and providing up-to-date information and analysis about world events and American foreign policy on its website, www.cfr.org.

The Council on Foreign Relations takes no institutional positions on policy issues and has no affiliation with the U.S. government. All views expressed in its publications and on its website are the sole responsibility of the author or authors.

Published by Rowman & Littlefield Publishers, Inc.
A wholly owned subsidiary of The Rowman & Littlefield Publishing Group, Inc.
4501 Forbes Boulevard, Suite 200, Lanham, Maryland 20706
http://www.rowmanlittlefield.com

Estover Road, Plymouth PL6 7PY, United Kingdom

British Library Cataloguing in Publication Information Available

Library of Congress Cataloging-in-Publication Data
Mankoff, Jeffrey, 1977–
    Russian foreign policy : the return of great power politics / Jeffrey Mankoff. — 2nd ed.
       p.   cm.
    Includes bibliographical references and index.
    ISBN 978-1-4422-0824-7 (cloth : alk. paper) — ISBN 978-1-4422-0825-4
(pbk. : alk. paper) — ISBN 978-1-4422-0826-1 (electronic)
    1. Russia (Federation)—Foreign relations—21st century.   I. Title.
JZ1616.M36   2011
327.47—dc23

                                                            2011025307

∞™ The paper used in this publication meets the minimum requirements of American National Standard for Information Sciences—Permanence of Paper for Printed Library Materials, ANSI/NISO Z39.48—1992.

Printed in the United States of America

Contents

Acknowledgments

This second edition would not have been possible without the first edition, and all those who contributed to making it possible. The origins of the book lie in a smaller research project conducted under the auspices of Yale University's Studies in Grand Strategy, on the basis of research conducted during the summer of 2005 at the Carnegie Moscow Center. In a sense, this is a book about grand strategy, or the grand strategy of one particular country. Intellectually and materially, it owes much to the Studies in Grand Strategy program, to International Security Studies (ISS), to Yale University, and to the individuals who made it possible. In this category, thanks are due above all to John Lewis Gaddis, who encouraged me to write the book and provided an academic home to work on it during my time as a fellow and then associate director of ISS. Paul Kennedy, the director of ISS, along with ISS senior fellow Charlie Hill, provided valuable advice and criticism. So too did Keith Darden of Yale's political science department. Ann Carter-Drier, Susan Hennigan, Igor Biryukov, Minh Luong, Ted Bromund, and Kathleen Murphy truly made ISS feel like home for three years, while ISS, the Henry Chauncey Fellowship, and the Smith Richardson Foundation provided valuable financial support.

When I first began working on the project that would lead to this book at Carnegie Moscow, Natalya Bubnova welcomed me and helped me make the most of my time in Moscow. Dmitry Trenin provided valuable input at key moments. After taking a break from this project to focus on completing my dissertation, I returned to write the bulk of the first edition during my year as a John M. Olin National Security Fellow at Harvard University. Once again, I would like to express my gratitude to Stephen Peter Rosen, then head of the Olin Institute, to my colleagues Terence Lee and Dima

Adamsky, to Carol Saivetz who read and commented on an early draft of two chapters, to Mark Kramer who gave unstintingly of his time and encouragement, and to Lt. Gen. Kevin Ryan, Charles Cogan, Paige Duhamel, and Ann Townes.

The Council on Foreign Relations (CFR), where I was first an adjunct fellow and then an International Affairs Fellow, has also played a crucial role in both editions of this work. Former CFR Vice President, Director of Studies, and Maurice R. Greenberg Chair Gary Samore; George F. Kennan Senior Fellow for Russia and Eurasia Studies Ambassador Stephen Sestanovich; Assistant Director of Studies Melanie Gervacio Lin; Director of Publishing Patricia Dorff; and research associate John Elliott all contributed in their own ways to the first edition. For the second edition, thanks are due as well to current Vice President, Director of Studies, and Maurice R. Greenberg Chair James Lindsay; and once again to Trisha Dorff and Steve Sestanovich.

At Rowman & Littlefield Publishers, I am grateful to Jessica Gribble, Alden Perkins, and Carrie Broadwell-Tkach. A special note of gratitude goes to my editor Susan McEachern, whose persistence in keeping after me to complete the revisions played an important role in ensuring that the second edition appeared in a timely fashion.

Finally, thanks as ever to my family, and the friends who helped keep me sane through the long, often lonely process of writing and revising. You all know who you are. Thank you.

Prologue

Producing a new edition of an existing work is quite different from writing a wholly new work. When a book engages with current events, part of the work that goes into a subsequent edition entails merely updating the narrative. Yet if all that goes into the revision process is the addition of new facts, it is a fair to ask why anyone would go to the trouble and expense of buying the new edition when the older one remains perfectly serviceable and distinguished solely in the inclusion of details and anecdotes that have taken place since the original edition's appearance. What I have tried to do in the revision process is not merely to update the narrative, but also to use the more recent historical record to test and refine the underlying theme of the whole book.

In the case of this particular book, such a process of testing and refining has been the more necessary because of significant developments in and outside of Russia since the publication of the first edition in late 2008–2009. When the first edition appeared, Dmitry Medvedev had just settled into the Kremlin, and much about his outlook and priorities—and their consequences—remained in the future. As I write this in mid-2011, Medvedev has served the better part of a presidential term, and is close to declaring his intentions with regard to the next election scheduled for March 2012. His mentor, prime minister, and grey cardinal Vladimir Putin remains very much on center stage, albeit as part of a strange two-headed executive split between the Kremlin and the Russian White House (seat of the prime minister and cabinet). Medvedev's presidency has also coincided with a serious economic crisis, exacerbated by the political fallout of Russia's pyrrhic military victory in Georgia in the summer of 2008.

The war, the ensuing economic crisis, and the emergence of Medvedev (even if his power remains constrained by his seemingly subordinate relationship to Putin) have altered certain elements of Russian foreign policy. The hubris that led Russia into Georgia has largely gone, as has the reflex to blame most domestic and foreign problems on the ill will of the United States. Rather, Russia has increasingly focused on getting its own house in order, albeit with mixed success. In the process, it has pursued a more cooperative relationship with the major Western powers, above all the United States, which has itself been led by a new sort of president since January 2009. The U.S.-Russia "reset" has been an important foreign policy success for both Moscow and Washington, and one that looked all but impossible during the dark days of August and September 2008. The success of the reset in many ways seems to vindicate one of the major themes of this book, namely that Russian foreign policy, whatever its excesses, has never been explicitly anti-American, and indeed that Russian leaders from Yeltsin to Putin to Medvedev have sought good relations with the United States to the extent that doing so was compatible with their broader aim of establishing and protecting Russia's role as one of the major global powers. In Barack Obama, the Kremlin has finally found an American leader with whom it can do business, and the results after two and a half years have been encouraging.

Nevertheless, the reset remains fragile, because the basic Great Power worldview underlying Russian foreign policy has not gone away. Whatever its domestic troubles and whatever the state of its relations with the United States, Russia will continue to insist on having a seat at the table in addressing threats and challenges across the world. To the extent that the United States is willing to accommodate that desire, the perpetuation of the reset (or ultimately the development of a genuine partnership) remains possible. However, U.S. leaders, including those who follow Obama, will need to remember that while Russia has a direct interest in having good relations with the United States, it remains unlikely in the near-medium term to pursue a path of Western integration, joining a U.S.-led collective security community founded on liberal-democratic values. Historically, the United States has done poorly at building partnerships with powerful states that insist on carving out their own path (think of U.S. relations with de Gaulle's France). Whatever else has changed in Russia since the 2008 war, the underlying desire to act and be treated as one of the world's Great Powers remains intact. With this second edition, I hope to show how that underlying premise remains intact, and will continue to shape Russia's international behavior under Medvedev, as well as whoever sits in the Kremlin after 2012.

Abbreviations

ABM	antiballistic missile
APEC	Asia-Pacific Economic Cooperation organization
ASEAN	Association of Southeast Asian Nations
BRICs	Brazil, Russia, India, China
BTC	Baku-Tbilisi-Ceyhan oil pipeline
BTE	Baku-Tbilisi-Erzurum gas pipeline
CACO	Central Asian Cooperation Association
CDC	Community of Democratic Choice
CDU	Christian Democratic Union (Germany)
CFE	Conventional Forces in Europe (Treaty)
CFP	Common Foreign Policy (EU)
CIS	Commonwealth of Independent States
CNPC	Chinese National Petroleum Company
CPC	Caspian Pipeline Consortium oil pipeline
CSTO	Collective Security Treaty Organization
DPNI	Movement Against Illegal Immigration
EEC	European Economic Community
ENP	European Neighborhood Policy (EU)
ESDP	European Security and Defense Policy (EU)
ESM	Eurasian Union of Youth
EU	European Union
EurAsEc	Eurasian Economic Association
FSB	Federal Security Service (*Federal'naya Sluzhba Bezopasnosti*)
G8	Group of Eight
GDP	gross domestic product
GU(U)AM	Georgia-Ukraine-(Uzbekistan)-Azerbaijan-Moldova group

IAEA	International Atomic Energy Agency
ICBM	intercontinental ballistic missile
IMEMO	Institute of International Economics and International Relations
IMF	International Monetary Fund
IMU	Islamic Movement of Uzbekistan
IRI	International Republican Institute (U.S.)
KGB	Committee on State Security (*Komitet Gosudarstvennoi Bezopasnosti*)
KPRF	Communist Party of the Russian Federation
LDPR	Liberal Democratic Party of Russia
LNG	liquefied natural gas
MAP	membership action plan (NATO)
MED	International Eurasian Movement
MGIMO	Moscow State Institute of International Relations
NATO	North Atlantic Treaty Organization
NDI	National Democratic Institute (U.S.)
NGO	nongovernmental organization
NPT	Non-proliferation Treaty
NRC	NATO-Russia Council
NSC	National Security Council (U.S.)
OSCE	Organization for Security and Cooperation in Europe
PCA	Partnership and Cooperation Agreement
PfP	Partnership for Peace (NATO)
PJC	Permanent Joint Council (NATO)
PSA	Production Sharing Agreement
RATS	Regional Anti-Terrorist Structure (SCO)
SCO	Shanghai Cooperation Association
SLBM	submarine launched ballistic missile
SORT	Strategic Offensive Reductions Treaty
SPS	Union of Right Forces (*Soyuz Pravykh Sil*)
START	Strategic Arms Reduction Treaties
SVOP	Council on Foreign and Defense Policy (*Sovet vneshnei i oboronoi politiki*)
UK	United Kingdom (of Great Britain and Northern Ireland)
UN	United Nations
U.S.	United States of America
USSR	Union of Soviet Socialist Republics
WEU	Western European Union
WTO	World Trade Organization

Introduction

The Guns of August

With the world's attention focused on the opening of the Beijing Olympics on August 8, 2008, Russian tanks suddenly poured across the border into the breakaway Georgian province of South Ossetia, launching the first large-scale use of Russian military power abroad since the collapse of the Soviet Union. In a matter of days, the Russians had smashed the Georgian military, seized South Ossetia, and threatened the Georgian capital of Tbilisi. On August 26, Russia announced its recognition of South Ossetia and another separatist province of Georgia, Abkhazia, as independent states, all while dismissing the protests and threats of a West shocked by this reversion to what seemed like old-fashioned Russian imperialism. Less than two decades after the implosion of the Soviet Union, the invasion of Georgia was a stunning announcement that Russia had again become a force to be reckoned with, one that did not feel itself constrained by international institutions—or other countries' opinions.

While Russian troops lingered in Georgia throughout the autumn in violation of the ceasefire agreement they signed on August 16—demonstrating the impotence of outside powers to stop them—the Russian economy began spiraling rapidly downward. Perceiving increased political and economic risk, foreign investors began withdrawing large amounts of capital from Russia, precipitating a run on the stock market. Russia's economic difficulties were only beginning, however, as the implosion of a massive housing bubble in the United States set off a worldwide freeze in credit markets and a flight to safety by investors. Facing the prospect of a full-scale economic meltdown, the Kremlin intervened to orchestrate a bailout of several leading banks, prop up the ruble, and repeatedly halt trading on the stock market to prevent further slides. With a global recession in the offing, oil prices fell from a high of $147 per barrel in July to less than $50 a barrel in late November. Russia—its economy heavily dependent on sales of oil and gas abroad—was hit extremely hard. Following years of rapid growth, the Russian economy contracted by 4.2 percent in the fourth quarter of 2008, and continued falling for much of 2009. When the dust had settled, Russia's economy had shrunk by 7.9 percent in 2009, one of the worst results among industrialized countries during the global economic crisis.[1]

The war and the economic crisis highlighted one of the central dilemmas confronting modern Russia, namely, the tension between a tradition of relying on the ability to project power abroad as a means of asserting influence and a desire to harness the forces of globalization and integration to create a more competitive, respected state. This tension, based on competing narratives on the nature and identity of the Russian state, is central to the making of Russian foreign policy. It is also clearly reflected in the man nominally in charge of the country throughout both the war in Georgia and the financial crisis, President Dmitry Medvedev. A lawyer, blogger, and fan of Western rock music, Medvedev appeared the most liberal and reform-minded of the potential successors to former president Vladimir Putin. While Medvedev has repeatedly emphasized the need for Russia to become a fully modern country enjoying the fruits of globalization, he, as well as those who still wield power behind the scenes, continues to advance the notion that Russia remains very much a traditional Great Power, one of a handful of powerful, fully sovereign states whose interactions collectively define the nature of international politics.

Medvedev and his allies have, however, helped shape the way Russia conceptualizes what it means to be a Great Power in the twenty-first-century world. Above all, Medvedev's Kremlin has focused on the economic underpinnings of power, recognizing that Russia's economic vulnerabilities growing out of its need for foreign technology and expertise create an opportunity for positive-sum interactions with other major powers, above all the United States. Medvedev has also accelerated the process of burying the post-Soviet neuroses that have at times hijacked Russian foreign policy, promoting widespread acceptance of the fact that the United States is no longer obsessed with containing Russian power. To the extent that this recognition has penetrated the upper echelons of the Russian government, Moscow has been able to pursue deeper and more sustained cooperation with the U.S. than in previous eras. It has done so, however, even as the Russian elite continues to emphasize Russia's aspiration to be a central player in an increasingly fluid international order, that is, to be a Great Power.

The basic premises of Russian foreign policy have been indelibly shaped by historical experience. Consolidation at home and expansion abroad were always the keys to securing Russia against its marauding neighbors, whether Tatars, Turks, Poles, or more recently, Germans. Without defensible frontiers, Russia historically fell back on the establishment of buffer zones between itself and its rivals. Ukraine played this role against the Turks and Tatars for centuries; Poland played it against Germany in the nineteenth century and again after the 1939 Nazi-Soviet Pact. During the Cold War, it was the USSR's Eastern European satellites (again with Poland at the forefront) that served to insulate the Russian heartland against foreign aggression. To keep control of the massive bureaucratic and military apparatus needed to administer the territories it continued to accumulate, Russia developed a strong and heavily centralized state, with vast power concentrated at the top and local autonomy heavily constrained.

When the Soviet Union collapsed in December 1991, the rump Russian Federation was a shadow of its Soviet predecessor. The country's frontiers were pushed back farther than they had been since the seventeenth century, while the once-mighty Red Army simply collapsed in disarray. Stripped of its superpower role and the bloc of like-minded states it had supported during the Cold War, post-Soviet Russia ceased being an object of fear among its neighbors or the central preoccupation of its onetime superpower rival. When Russia was no longer feared, its interests were increasingly ignored by other states. Moscow's objections were brushed aside as NATO attacked close Russian ally Serbia in 1999 and swallowed up many of Russia's neighbors, including the post-Soviet Baltic states in 2002.

This period of foreign policy drift coincided with domestic turmoil that followed in the wake of the Soviet collapse. Inside Russia, law and order broke down, crime surged, civil war broke out in Chechnya, and politics at the top often appeared dangerously adrift under the erratic rule of Boris Yeltsin. This weakness at home and abroad masked the Russian elite's continued emphasis on maintaining Russia's leading global role, even if the country that actually existed in the early to mid-1990s possessed few of the attributes of a major power, apart from a crumbling nuclear arsenal and the seat on the UN Security Council it inherited from the USSR.

It took Russia's political and economic recovery during the decade between the 1998 and 2008 financial crises to provide a foundation for a reassertion of old patterns in foreign policy. This decade largely coincided with the presidency of Vladimir Putin, who was widely blamed (or praised) for placing Russian foreign policy on a new, more confrontational path. While Putin's influence was significant, the roots of Russia's more assertive foreign policy during these years run deeper. Putin merely embodied a worldview and a set of policy preferences that much of the elite continued to favor, even though Russia was too weak to actually pursue them for much of the 1990s.

Even the battering of the country's economy after 2008 did not dampen Russian leaders' aspirations to play a greater role on the world stage. It did however force them to confront the limitations that "hard power" faces in a globally networked, economically interdependent, and media-saturated world. Russia's challenge therefore remains figuring out how to graft its historically determined identity as a Great Power onto the reality of a world moving beyond old notions of balance of power and spheres of influence, long staples of Russian geopolitical thinking.

Many Russians continue to see a hostile world, now comprising not just the old bogeyman of NATO, but newer threats such as jihadism and a rising China lapping at their borders. The response has been to fall back on the tried and true—a strong state backed by a strong military, and a foreign policy that emphasizes strategic depth and autonomy on the world stage. Complicating this picture is the fact that the world of the twenty-first century is not the world of the nineteenth, and the old certainties of Russian foreign policy are not entirely suited to addressing new threats and challenges, many of which cross state borders and cannot be solved with the kind of hard power Russia brought to bear in Georgia. A major underlying tension in contemporary Russian foreign policy discourse is consequently between past and future, autarky and integration.

Whatever difficulties it continues to face (including a shrinking population and massive levels of corruption), Russia in the second decade of the twenty-first century is a much more consequential international actor than the chaotic Russia of the 1990s. The war between Russia and Georgia consequently provides the backdrop for this book's fundamental theme: the resurgence of Russia's power and autonomy as an actor in the international system and the impact of that resurgence on the conduct of Russian diplomacy.

The upsurge in Russian power since 1998 has many sources: most important has been the general trend of rising prices for hydrocarbons and other commodities of which Russia is a major exporter (though oil prices collapsed during the 2008 crisis, by early 2011 oil was again trading at more than $100 per barrel). Russia's energy-fueled economic growth allowed Moscow to begin reversing the precipitous decline of its military forces, freeing itself from dependence on foreign creditors, and exerting pressure on customers of its oil and gas. Less quantifiably, Russia's energy boom contributed to a new sense of confidence among the country's elite, which became in consequence less reticent about standing up for what it believes to be Russia's national interests. The wars in Iraq and Afghanistan, moreover, fed into a perception that the United States is tied down elsewhere and that the era of U.S. hegemony in the world is past—a sentiment that the global financial crisis that began in 2008 only strengthened. Thanks to these developments, the Russian Ministry of Foreign Affairs was able to boast that "the main accomplishment of recent years is Russia's newly attained foreign policy autonomy."[2]

Russia's greater coherence, stability, and confidence all contributed to Moscow's willingness to use force in the dispute with Georgia. Power, however, is only one factor driving foreign policy. A state's identity in the international system—whether it sees itself as a satiated or a revisionist power, a nation-state or an empire—provides the intellectual framework that shapes decisions about how power is employed. The same is true for how a country and its leadership articulate their national interest, which is less an objective goal than a subjective understanding of what will benefit different actors in the state. In short, recognizing that the Russia ruled by the Putin-Medvedev "tandemocracy" is a stronger, more stable state than the Russia Putin took over on the last day of 1999 is necessary but not sufficient to understanding the evolution of Russian foreign policy during the intervening period.

Ideas, that is, the worldviews and policy preferences of the Russian elite, matter as well.

Understanding the nature of Russia's interactions with the rest of the world in the second decade of the twenty-first century (and after) is therefore impossible without at least appreciating the continuities between Medvedev's Russia and the rapidly changing, often unpredictable country that emerged from the breakup of the Soviet Union in 1991. The central contention of this work is that the frequently assertive, narrowly self-interested foreign policy that has characterized Russia during the Putin-Medvedev years is the culmination of a process that began over a decade earlier, during the presidency of Boris Yeltsin, at a moment when the bulk of the Russian elite came to recognize that integration with the West and its institutions was neither possible nor desirable, at least in the short-to-medium term. With Russia's own instability and the West's mounting frustration over its inability to remake Russia in its own image, Kremlin leaders began laying the foundation for Russia to return to its accustomed international position as an independent pole in a system of shifting, competitive states. Arguments in the 1990s over NATO expansion or the West's response to ethnic cleansing in Kosovo thus merely foreshadowed the more serious disputes a decade later over the war in Georgia.

The years of Vladimir Putin's presidency saw Russia's reemergence as a global power with interests—and the capacity to pursue them—across much of the world. Such a position as one of a handful of major powers is something many Russian elites have long wanted for their country, but only with the economic and political recovery of the Putin years did that ambition start to seem attainable. Medvedev came into office in the summer of 2008 just as that recovery was being called into question, by both the pyrrhic victory in Georgia and the economic crisis that ensued. Medvedev has had the difficult task of adjusting Russian foreign policy to fit that new reality, while balancing—as Putin and Yeltsin did—Russia's engagement with the West against the need to contain the arc of instability around Russia's borders while simultaneously managing relations with an increasingly vibrant East Asia.

Medvedev also confronts the not-inconsiderable foreign policy legacy of his predecessor. Under Putin, Moscow's approach to dealing with challenges as diverse as instability on its borders, the rise of China, and the expansion of NATO became notably pricklier and more assertive.[3] The actual process of making Russian foreign policy also changed. The chaotic pluralism of the 1990s gave way to a system dominated on the surface by the president and his staff, though characterized by an ongoing, if submerged, struggle for influence among actors within the security services, the military-industrial complex, and large state-owned companies. During the 1990s, fundamental debates about the direction of Russia and its role vis-à-vis the West were a staple of public discourse within the elite. The power struggles under Putin, in contrast, often appeared less about ideology than about control of and access to resources.

Medvedev's invocation of modernization as the lodestar for Russian foreign policy has to a degree reopened many of the debates of the 1990s, exacerbating the split between those seeking to reestablish Russian supremacy within the borders of the former USSR at the expense of ties to the outside world, and those who see modernization and globalization as the only realistic paths to restoring Russia's major power status.[4] These debates, however, are in a sense more tactical than strategic. Medvedev's supporters and opponents are largely agreed that Russia ought to remain a fully sovereign international actor pursuing a foreign policy dictated by a narrowly defined national interest and eschewing integration with international institutions that impose intrusive behavioral norms; they differ on the question of how to achieve that goal given the many challenges Russia continues to face.

This quest for autonomy on the international stage is hardly a new theme in Russian foreign policy. After the collapse of the westernizing strategy pursued in the early 1990s by Yeltsin and young reformers such as acting prime minister Yegor Gaidar, head of the State Property Committee and privatization guru Anatoly Chubais, and foreign minister Andrei Kozyrev, the Russian governing class turned its back on the idea of seeking integration with the West and its institutions. In foreign affairs, the transition from Kozyrev to Yevgeny Primakov as foreign minister symbolized (but did not cause) the shift to a new approach emphasizing Russia's role as a sovereign Great Power in an anarchic, self-help international system where power, rather than international norms or institutions, remained the ultima ratio in international relations.

This new approach found broad support within the Russian elite of the mid-1990s and has continued to inform Russian foreign policy ever since. Putin succeeded in mastering the Byzantine world of Russian bureaucratic politics by embodying and adhering to this wide-ranging elite consensus emphasizing Russia's historic Great Power role; a balance between Russia's western, southern, and eastern flanks; and an active diplomacy in pursuit of what most of the elite perceived as Russia's interests as a state. Though Medvedev's emphasis on modernization and cooperation with the West has sparked renewed debate, Medvedev's Kremlin has embraced the general outlines of this consensus much as Putin's did, concentrating on the need to restore Russia to its leading international role in a world dominated by powerful states, self-interest, and (to a degree) geopolitics.

Following years of post–Cold War irrelevance and decline, Russia during the Putin years went to great lengths to prove to the rest of the world that it mattered internationally—at times in ways other powers perceived as aggressive, nationalistic, and threatening. Whether supporting separatist groups in neighboring states, cutting off gas to Belarus and Ukraine, or standing up for Iran at the UN Security Council, Russian foreign policy often appeared dangerously anachronistic in the West—even before its invasion of Georgia in support of the South Ossetian separatists. Actions that Moscow portrayed as justified by its greater strength and confidence seemed in the West aggressive and malevolent. The editor-in-chief of *Russia in Global Affairs*, Fyodor Lukyanov, aptly likened the foreign policy behavior of Putin's Russia to that of the infamous "new Russians" of the early 1990s, a nouveau riche whom others perceive as arrogant and lacking refinement and who will continue his escapades "until he runs into someone even richer or smarter, or else manages to offend just about everyone."[5]

The war in Georgia, the subsequent economic crisis, and the transition to Medvedev's presidency helped curb these excesses. The war highlighted the limits of Russia's ability to translate its renewed confidence into either military power (while Russia was victorious, the war highlighted the Russian military's many technical and organizational shortcomings) or diplomatic leverage (tellingly, none of Russia's allies assented to the Moscow-sponsored independence of South Ossetia and Abkhazia). The economic crisis proved that the Russian economy was inextricably linked to the outside world, and that foreign perceptions could have an appreciable effect on Russia's political and economic standing. The more difficult internal and external circumstances Russia faced after 2008 provided the context for Medvedev's efforts to recast Russia's emphasis on international power and autonomy for a changed world. In grasping the Obama administration's outreached hand and turning away from aggressive foreign adventures to focus on rebuilding Russian power at home, Medvedev sought to challenge the widespread perception of Russia as merely a spoiler, rather than a constructive member of the international community. That transformation remains partial at best, and Russian foreign policy can at times appear as contradictory and baffling as ever.

Of course, the changing priorities of Russian foreign policy affect more than just the West. Russia's neighbors, including both the former Soviet republics and nearby countries such as China, Iran, and Turkey also have a direct stake in how Russia chooses to interact with the outside world. China, another rapidly rising state uncomfortable with a world order in which Western norms dominate, has been at times a useful partner but also a worrisome rival for the Kremlin. Chinese traders have kept the economy of the vast Siberian and Far Eastern border regions afloat as their Russian population has shriveled. Beijing's purchases of Russian military equipment propped up the Russian military-industrial complex at a time when orders from Russia's own military were negligible. In geopolitical terms, China's discomfort at the constraints imposed by U.S. power has at times encouraged Beijing and Moscow to seek common cause on a range of issues, from the war in Iraq to the presence of U.S. forces in Central Asia.

Such cooperation, however, has not eliminated the deep-seated fear many Russians feel about their giant neighbor with its huge population, booming economy, and history of Sino-Soviet and Sino-Russian border disputes. China's emphasis on economic integration and a peaceful rise have also at times put it at odds with a Russia less invested in the persistence of the status quo, notably during the Georgian conflict, when Beijing refused to endorse Moscow's recognition of the breakaway republics. The U.S.-Russia "reset" and the growing power disparity between Russia and China have also forced Russian diplomats and analysts to rethink at least some of their enthusiasm for embracing China as an alternative to the West.

The states most directly impacted by Russia's assertive foreign policy are those immediate neighbors who were once also members of the Soviet Union. Since the collapse of the USSR in 1991, the successor states have sought to establish (or reestablish) a new identity for themselves out of the shadow of Russia. Some, like Belarus, have renounced little of their Soviet past, while others, particularly Georgia, have sought to maximize the cultural, political, and historical distance between themselves and Moscow. For the Kremlin, keeping the former Soviet republics from becoming jumping-off points for hostile forces has been the dominant theme. The fall of the USSR turned the areas around Russia's borders into a contested zone for the first time since the Russian Civil War of the early 1920s, and Russia's leaders saw the incursion of foreign forces (including both NATO and foreign NGOs) in the worst possible light.

Russia's sometimes manic approach to the former Soviet Union is thus part of the larger dynamic of Great Power competition that has characterized Russian foreign policy for the past decade-plus. Russia has long viewed the post-Soviet region as a special case, an area where Russia has unique rights and responsibilities to which other major powers should defer, even if Moscow has had little appetite for actually reabsorbing its onetime dependencies (notably, Russia made no attempt to annex South Ossetia or Abkhazia in 2008). This emphasis on the post-Soviet space has at times constrained Russia's ability to maintain positive relations with other large powers, including the U.S. and China, which have their own interests in the former USSR. For some Russians (particularly members of the so-called Eurasianist school), reintegration of the post-Soviet space provides an alternative to integration with the global, Western-dominated economy and international institutions. Whether it can reconcile or triangulate its interests in the former Soviet Union with its outreach to the West in particular will be a major test of whether Russia can achieve its Great Power aspirations in the long run, or whether it will remain a largely regional actor.

During the late 1990s, Russia appeared to have been so weakened by political, economic, and military collapse as to be finished as a shaper of world affairs. Even as analysts and diplomats in the West dismissed Yeltsin's Russia as a prickly but ultimately irrelevant nuisance, Russia's elites chafed at what they saw as their country's temporary eclipse. No matter Yeltsin's affinity for the West and no matter Russia's continued dependence on foreign assistance, most of Russia's ruling class continued to think of their country as destined by history and geography to be one of the principal guardians of world order. It took Yeltsin's departure, along with the consolidation of state power and skyrocketing energy prices, to give substance to such ideas. Putin and Medvedev's Russia has not embarked on a new, more threatening path in the world but has merely recovered enough to act in a way that even most Yeltsinites desired. The changed tone of Russian diplomacy under Putin at times masked the continuity of these aims. That new tone, however, resulted more from changed circumstances than changed goals. These circumstances—state consolidation, high energy prices, the waning of U.S. supremacy—will not end anytime soon.[6] Nor did the recession into which Russia was thrust during the second half of 2008 force a retreat from some of Russia's Putin-era hubris, any more than previous economic disasters in 1991–1992 and 1998 did.

Regardless of Medvedev's ability to truly shape foreign policy (Putin retains significant influence as prime minister, particularly given the possibility that he will return to the presidency in 2012), Russia's international behavior will continue to operate on the basis of the same considerations that have driven it since the implosion of Kozyrev's integration strategy around 1994–1995. These include a desire to have a seat at the table in major international and regional security institutions even while standing aloof from Western-dominated organizations that emphasize shared values (i.e., remaining outside the collective known as the West), to be consulted on all decisions affecting international peace and security, to cooperate flexibly with other major powers to the extent that doing so advances Russian national interests, and to maintain a special role in the post-Soviet space. Given the enduring nature of the Russian elites' preferences as well as the external environment confronting it, Russian diplomacy will continue to strive in this direction for the foreseeable future, regardless of who sits in the Kremlin.

1

Contours of Russian Foreign Policy

Since the collapse of Communism, Russia has endured a confusing, often torturous process of self-definition. Stripped of the geopolitical and ideological certainties of the Soviet era, contemporary Russia has been forced to answer a series of fundamental questions about its own identity as a state and role to the post–Cold War international order. No longer controlling an imperial hinterland in Europe and freed from a zero-sum relationship with the United States based primarily on the logic of mutually assured destruction, Russia in the early twenty-first century is in many ways a state in search of itself.

This process of self-definition is in many ways central to the ongoing debates about the nature of Russia's national interests, and hence its approach to foreign policy in a world of emerging and evolving threats. The debate over the basic principles underlying Russian foreign policy has continued unevenly since the last days of the Soviet Union, when Mikhail Gorbachev first evoked the vision of a "common European home" stretching from the Atlantic to the Urals—or from Vancouver to Vladivostok. In the early 1990s, President Boris Yeltsin presided over a country that appeared to be moving rapidly to join its onetime Cold War enemies in an expanded democratic West. Before long, this rush toward integration with the West foundered on the rocks of domestic opposition and foreign skepticism. By the middle of the 1990s, it had been replaced by a determination to restore Russia as an independent international actor whose interests remained distinct from those of the liberal capitalist West. This new approach to foreign policy rested on a deep-seated consensus among the Russian elite about the nature of the post–Cold War world and about Russia's role in it.

Strongly rooted in Russian history, this consensus emphasizes Russia's destiny to be one of the shapers and upholders of the global order, and a dominant force in its own region—in other words, to be a Great Power. Russia's interaction with the outside world has long owed much to the peculiarities of culture and geography. From the earliest days of recorded history, Russia has been in Europe but not wholly of it. Kievan Rus', the early medieval predecessor of all the modern East Slavic states (Russia, Belarus, and Ukraine), was intimately involved in European diplomacy; the eleventh-century grand prince Yaroslav the Wise married off his three daughters to the kings of Norway, Hungary, and France, respectively, and sent his navy against the Byzantine Empire. The Byzantines' most lasting impact on Russia, however, was Orthodox Christianity, which Kievan Rus' adopted in 988. Over the subsequent millennium, Orthodoxy gave Kievan Rus' and its successors an identity distinct from the Catholic/Protestant countries to its west, particularly as Europe underwent the intellectual upheavals of the Renaissance, the Reformation, and the Enlightenment. When Kievan Rus' fell to the Mongols in 1241, much of what is now Russia was further cut off from developments taking place farther west, its politics and culture increasingly oriented toward the steppe regions to the south and east.

Geography has also contributed to Russia's sense of distinctness. Lacking natural barriers such as major mountain ranges, Russian history is littered with attacks by foreign armies, including those of Genghis Khan and his Mongol-Tatar descendants, the Ottoman Turks, the French in the nineteenth century, and the Germans (twice) in the twentieth—not to mention numerous conflicts with marauding Poles, Lithuanians, Swedes, and others. Meanwhile, the Russian heartland around Moscow and the various medieval principalities (such as Vladimir, Suzdal, and Tver) it absorbed in the process of "gathering the lands of Rus'" lie far from the coast and far from global trading routes in the age of maritime commerce. Territorial expansion beyond this core region, toward the Baltic and Black Seas and the Pacific Ocean, provided Muscovy—and later Russia—with access to trade, technology, and ideas, while enmeshing it in the international diplomacy of surrounding regions in both Europe and Asia. Expansion, and the need to administer Russia's vast territory, encouraged the development of a powerful state, which became at once the driver of Russia's ambitious diplomacy and its principal beneficiary. In contrast to England or the United States, tsarist Russia's emergence as an imperial power was driven not by traders and merchants, but through military conquest in pursuit of power, security, and prestige.

Following the Napoleonic Wars, which concluded with the soldiers of Tsar Alexander I marching down the Champs-Élysées, tsarist Russia became one of the linchpins in the Concert of Europe, the association of powerful states that maintained the European balance of power for the next century. Russia's entente with France and Britain, coupled with the rapid growth of its economy before 1914, contributed to the weakening of the concert and helped spark World War I. Soviet Russia's isolation from Europe during the 1920s and 1930s made possible Germany's bid to throw off the restraints imposed by the Treaty of Versailles and once again threaten the European balance. When war came again in 1939, it was Soviet troops who played the central role in defeating the Wehrmacht and destroying Nazi Germany. As it marched toward Berlin, the Soviet Union's Red Army overran the bulk of eastern and central Europe, staying until 1989, dividing Europe's eastern and western halves and sparking the four-decade Cold War with the United States.

While Russia was long a major player in European diplomacy, under Soviet rule it increasingly sought a global role, as the self-proclaimed head of the international Communist movement and as a direct participant in the affairs of countries as diverse as Cuba, Vietnam, and Afghanistan. As the leader of the so-called Eastern bloc and owner of the largest nuclear arsenal, the Soviet Union was also one of the two global superpowers whose ideological and geopolitical standoff extended across the globe and provided the principal framework for global politics in the second half of the twentieth century. Russia's identity as a Great Power, in other words, has a deep historical resonance that did not evaporate when the Soviet Union collapsed at the end of 1991.

While it is possible to overstate the influence of this history on the foreign policy of today's Russian Federation, Russia's security and global influence have always been linked to the state's ability to defend itself from attack and to overcome its geographic and economic isolation. Expansion, militarization, and search for secure frontiers have been hallmarks of Russian foreign policy for centuries, as Russian leaders have pursued their quest for international power and influence. Despite the changes that Russia has undergone since 1991 (not to mention since 1917 or 1815), foreign policy is not made in a historical vacuum, and these traditions continue to color strategic thinking—for instance in Russia's sensitivity about NATO military assets near its borders and its reluctance to seek integration with Western-dominated institutions. While the emphasis on these factors has shifted over time, they make up at least a framework for the general consensus about foreign policy that continues to operate within the elite.

Upon his emergence from obscurity in the late 1990s, Vladimir Putin pursued a strategic design that both reflected basic elements of this consensus and used it to shape Russia's restoration as a major global power in the post–Cold War world. Strengthened by high oil prices and a booming economy, Russia under Putin achieved many of the goals to which the

Russia of the 1990s merely aspired. The rapid growth of Russia's economy laid the foundation for a more active, assertive foreign policy, as Russia pushed back against what its elites increasingly saw as the West's proclivity for ignoring and patronizing it. This process culminated in Russia's August 2008 invasion of Georgia, whose pro-Western government had been seeking to join NATO and reassert control over the Russian-backed separatist regions of Abkhazia and South Ossetia.

While the war succeeded in its immediate objectives—putting Georgia's NATO ambitions on hold and serving notice to the West that Russia retained the ability to forcefully assert its interests (at least in its own region)—it also had some unexpected consequences for Russia's position as a global actor. The war sparked a run on the Russian stock market and a new round of capital flight, particularly on the part of foreign investors who had flocked to Russia as the economy had boomed during Putin's second term as president. Meanwhile, even close Russian allies resisted Moscow's calls to recognize South Ossetia and Abkhazia as independent states, serving notice that Russia's influence had not recovered to the extent that many in the elite had hoped. The war also coincided with the beginning of the worst global economic downturn since the 1930s, in which Russia's economy plummeted rapidly in tandem with energy prices. While the crisis in Russia was relatively short, it highlighted serious vulnerabilities and punctured the hubris of those who saw Russia's rise as an established fact.

These experiences provided the background for a reassessment of Russia's foreign policy priorities, if not the fundamental principles underpinning them, under Dmitry Medvedev, who became president in May 2008. During Medvedev's presidency, Russia has not abandoned its claim to major power status. It has though undergone a process of rethinking what, precisely, it means to be a Great Power in the twenty-first century, while acknowledging that no matter how impressive its Putin-era recovery, Russia's influence remains far below what it was during the Cold War. Russia lacks the economic dynamism of China, the military power and global influence of the United States, or the even the robust institutions of rapidly developing states such as Brazil or South Korea. Russia no doubt enjoys many advantages, including a well-educated population and vast natural resources (not to mention a shrunken but still massive nuclear arsenal). Yet in a world where economic growth, trade, and investment are the main drivers of international influence, Russia remains outside the top league. This recognition lies at the heart of Medvedev's so-called modernization agenda, which aims at overhauling Russia's economy, encouraging competition, breaking up monopolies, and promoting the development of high technology and high value-added industries, all of which require good relations with the technologically advanced countries of both the West and Asia.

This emphasis on modernizing the economy goes beyond what Putin sought. Yet Medvedev appears to have assimilated his mentor's understanding of Russia's basic strategic objectives—above all the need to restore Russia's position among the major global powers—while recognizing both that Russia must first get its own house in order, and that factors other than sheer military might will determine Russia's sway on the world stage in the twenty-first century. Modernization, then, is both about improving living standards for ordinary Russians, and tied to the widely shared ambition to restore Russia's international position. A 2011 report by the influential Institute for Contemporary Development (*Institut sovremennogo razvitiya*, INSOR), which Medvedev himself nominally chairs, describes conditions inside Russia and the country's international role as mutually reinforcing:

> A country's greatness [*velichie*] is above all determined by what it can offer the world, [and] the extent of its attractiveness to foreign partners. Russia's basic position as a state with significant natural resources hardly exhausts our role in the world.
>
> International influence is above all a function of [a state's] internal condition. . . .
>
> Russia can exist as an active world power while taking innovative approaches to politics [at home]. But it should not be active merely for the sake of external effect, divorced from consideration for . . . the domestic potential of its foreign policy.[1]

As with Putin, Medvedev's ability to shape Russian foreign policy to a large extent depends on his adherence to the general strategic consensus long prevailing within the Russian elite. The foundation of this consensus is the enduring belief that Russia is a Great Power, albeit a weakened one, with interests in many corners of the globe and a responsibility to look out for itself in a dangerous, indifferent world. Russia's elite is therefore inclined to envision its country playing a role in the world analogous to that of the United States, rather than integrating with the less realpolitik-inclined European Union (EU), even though many of its closest diplomatic and economic partners are in Europe.[2]

Consequently, Russian foreign policy continues to focus on upholding (or creating) a system of international relations in which large states are the primary guardians of global order, free to pursue their national interests as they deem fit, respecting one another's primacy within a circumscribed sphere of influence, maintaining a general balance of power among themselves, and rejecting the applicability of "universal" norms in favor of respecting states' sovereignty within their own borders. Despite the chaos of the 1990s, Russia's leaders never ceased regarding their own country as one of these major powers. The implication, as Russian diplomats and policy makers have repeatedly emphasized, is that Russia must therefore have an independent foreign policy, rather than function merely as an appendage of the West or a supplier of natural resources to the world market.[3]

THE "OFFICIAL MIND" OF RUSSIAN FOREIGN POLICY

Official strategy documents provide some basic insight into this worldview. Although the importance of these documents should not be overemphasized—they are the work of bureaucratic horse trading and are often left deliberately vague in order to satisfy competing constituencies—the language they use does provide some insight into how officials responsible for Russian national security view the world. More a guide to the broad principles behind policy than a catalogue of responses to specific challenges, the Foreign Policy Concept and similar documents (including the National Security Strategy and the Military Doctrine) define the mental universe within which policy decisions are made.

Particularly instructive in this regard are differences between the Foreign Policy Concept adopted in December 2000, almost a year into Putin's presidency; its replacement, which was approved by Medvedev barely a month into his term in office in 2008; and a draft concept leaked by the Foreign Ministry in the spring of 2010. The first, Putin-era document, lists as the top priority of Russian foreign policy:

> Promoting the interests of the Russian Federation as a great power and one of the most influential centers in the modern world [by] ensuring the country's security, preserving and strengthening its sovereignty and territorial integrity and its strong and authoritative position in the world community [in order to promote] the growth of its political, economic, intellectual, and spiritual potential.[4]

This statement, along with the Concept's subsequent priorities ("shaping a stable, just, and democratic world order . . . [based] on equitable relations of partnership among states") is notable for the attention it gives to notions such as sovereignty, Great Power, and partnership among states.[5] The language is that of geopolitics—a world of states seeking power and pursuing their national interests while balancing against other large states. Such language, and such a worldview, would be unthinkable in official statements from the United States, much less the European Union.

The 2008 version, which Medvedev signed shortly after taking office, copies about 80 percent of the text of its predecessor verbatim.[6] The differences, however, are significant. The term *Great Power* (*velikaya derzhava*) is gone, replaced by a reference to Russia as "one of the leading centers of the contemporary world" and repeated mention of a "new Russia." Russian analysts argue that the changes reflect a greater emphasis on Russia's position as a rising power, a work in progress with lingering socioeconomic weaknesses that belie the blustery tone of the Putin-era document, although the notion of striving for Great Power status remains an important subtext.[7] In addition to repeating the above paragraph, the top priorities of Russian foreign policy under Medvedev are described as:

> Creating favorable external conditions for the modernization of Russia, transformation of its economy through innovation, enhancement of living standards, consolidation of society, strengthening of the foundations of the constitutional system, rule of law and democratic institutions, realization of human rights and freedoms and, as a consequence, ensuring national competitiveness in a globalizing world.[8]

The focus on innovation and modernization—not to mention political reform—represents a significant departure, at least rhetorically. The Russia of the 2008 Concept is one that is still struggling to meet its potential, and fully cognizant of the obstacles it faces. One final important difference is that the 2008 document also specifies that the cabinet, which is headed by the prime minister, carries responsibility for implementing Russia's foreign policy. This addition allowed Putin, who became prime minister immediately on stepping down from the presidency, to maintain a hand in foreign affairs, though previous prime ministers were largely denied this role.

Given the war with Georgia that broke out barely a month after Medvedev signed the 2008 Concept, it is difficult to square that document's emphasis on development, the rule of law, and other liberal reforms with the hard-line response to mounting tensions with Tbilisi. To be sure, the 2008 Concept dropped its predecessor's almost ritualistic reference to the need for a belt of good neighbors around the Russian Federation's borders. Still, the contrast speaks to a certain confusion, or, more likely, a still unresolved debate about how to prioritize the competing desires for a leading role in the post-Soviet space and a cooperative relationship with major outside powers that have their own interests in the region.

That debate has only intensified over the course of Medvedev's presidency, with some calling for economic modernization in partnership with the West and others (especially among the *siloviki*, or members of the security and intelligence services) continuing to favor a more autarkic approach to development combined with a foreign policy that prioritizes Russian influence in the post-Soviet space over relations with the wider world. The leaked 2010 draft concept, whose authenticity the Foreign Ministry has never denied, attempts to square this circle by simultaneously calling for "modernization alliances" with leading economic powers in the West and Asia, and reaffirming Russia's commitment to playing a dominant role in the post-Soviet space. On the one hand, it focuses on "securing access to external sources of modernization" and suggests that Russia draw lessons from other countries' experiences of creating modern economies—in line with Medvedev's focus on foreign policy as a tool for domestic development. This focus on modernization, particularly the establishment of modernization alliances, implies prioritizing good political relations with economically advanced and rapidly developing countries—including the U.S., EU, Russia's BRIC partners (i.e., Brazil, China, and India, later joined by South Africa to create BRICS), and some of the technologically advanced states of East Asia.

Within the Commonwealth of Independent States (CIS), the draft foreign policy concept calls for taking advantage of the global economic crisis that broke out in late 2008 to consolidate Russia's leading position, while nonetheless keeping the door to cooperation with the U.S. in the region open. In line with long-standing Russian views, it also calls for constructing a "just and democratic world order based on collective principles and the supremacy of international law," while strengthening the role of organizations like the BRICS and the Shanghai Cooperation Organization as counterweights to the dominant position of the West.[9]

The various incarnations of Russia's Foreign Policy Concept, drafted by the Ministry of Foreign Affairs, largely reflect the views of the professional diplomats. The National Security Concept (and its successor, called the National Security Strategy to 2020) also includes input from the military and security services and provides a broader perspective on how Russian officialdom views the international security environment around Russia. The 2000 National Security Concept identifies two mutually contradictory trends shaping the future international order: "the strengthening economic and political positions of a substantial number of states and their integration in a complicated mechanism of multilaterally directed international processes" and "attempts to create structures of international relations founded on the world community's domination by the developed countries of the West led by the U.S. and predicated on the unilateral—especially in the power-military sense—resolution of the key problems in world politics."[10] The focus on states and power generally, coupled with the belief that Russia's position in the world is threatened by the formation of a world order from which it is excluded, are the basic tenets of the essentially geopolitical understanding of world politics that prevailed during Putin's presidency.

The National Security Strategy to 2020, which was confirmed in May 2009 after several years of drafting and revision (reflecting deep disagreement among various departments and factions of the elite), downplays the threats posed by Western attempts to dominate international structures while highlighting the importance of Russia's integration into global economic processes as a means of improving socioeconomic conditions in the country. Instead of demanding that the international community treat Russia as an equal of the most powerful states, it merely notes that "conditions have developed for overcoming the internal and external threats to national security [and for] the Russian Federation's dynamic development and transformation into one of the leading powers in terms of its technological progress, standard of living, and influence on global processes."[11] In its focus on the security and well-being of the Russian population as well as its aspirational (rather than hectoring) tone, the 2009 strategy eschews much of the hubris that drove its predecessor, even if the underlying goal of ensuring Russia takes its place as one of the world's leading powers remains.[12]

The understanding of how the world works contained in these documents has important implications for the way Russian foreign policy is actually conducted. Russian diplomacy is focused on bilateral relations with other states, especially large states such as the U.S., China, and India, rather than on multilateral pacts based on commitments to shared values. Moscow largely even prefers to deal with transnational problems such as terrorism within the framework of bilateral relations. At the same time, the focus on bilateral relations means that Russia has lagged behind other major powers as a provider of global public goods. Russia's contribution to discussions on topics such as developing an international regime for addressing climate change or overhauling global financial regulation in the aftermath of the 2008 banking crisis has been modest at best. Unlike multilateral forums, bilateral state-to-state relations have the advantage, from the Russian perspective, of avoiding the creation of intrusive behavioral norms while preserving (at least for the major powers) states' sovereign equality. The Russian government prefers to work through those multilateral organizations that, like the UN Security Council, the BRICS forum, or the G8/G20, are essentially clubs of equals that do not limit Russia's sovereignty over its domestic affairs, and where the United States (or the West more broadly) do not occupy a dominant position.[13]

Worry about the overarching role of the U.S. in international affairs has been a major factor in Russia's promotion of the concept of multipolarity (*mnogopolyarnost'*) as the key to international stability. In its most basic form, this term simply refers to a kind of concert arrangement among the Great Powers, akin to the nineteenth-century Concert of Europe or an idealized version of Franklin Roosevelt's "Four Policemen." It is at once an attempt to negate the continued dominance of the United States and a broader framework for thinking about the nature of modern international relations, where knowledge, technology, and power are more widely distributed than at any previous moment in history, yet where sovereign states rather than norm-based international institutions continue to play the leading role.[14]

Multipolarity implies a world of states more or less equal, if not in their inherent power capabilities (few Russian officials are rash enough to claim that Russian "hard power" will match that of the United States anytime soon), then at least in their capacity to shape the international order. A multipolar order was largely something Russian officials in the 1990s, such as former foreign minister Yevgeny Primakov, sought to create.[15] In the early twenty-first century, they increasingly see it as an existing phenomenon thanks to the rise of China, the blunting of U.S. military power in Iraq and Afghanistan, and the economic difficulties of the West in the context of the global financial crisis.

If the world in the twenty-first century is destined to be multipolar, the Russian elite is largely unanimous in believing Russia must be one of the poles. For all the talk of integration with the West in the aftermath of the September 11, 2001, terrorist attacks, there was never any real belief in Russia's giving up its identity as an autonomous actor in world affairs. During Putin's presidency, much of this discussion turned around the concept of "sovereign democracy," whose popularizer, Kremlin ideologist Vladislav Surkov, described as a state whose goals and methods—both at home and abroad—are made solely on the basis of calculations of national interest, rather than because of external pressure to conform to behavioral norms. The focus on sovereignty as a value, coupled with the revival of Russia's economic fortunes during the Putin years, greatly enhanced Moscow's ability to conduct an independent foreign policy. Foreign Minister Sergei Lavrov underlined the importance of this newfound autonomy in a September 2006 address in Los Angeles:

> And for us, this autonomy [*samostoyatel'nost'*] is a key issue, and we will continue to act on this basis both within the country and in the international arena. . . . I think that the rapid revival of Russia's foreign policy autonomy is one of the issues which is complicating relations between us, since far from everyone in the U.S. has gotten used to this. But they must get used to it.[16]

In the more parlous economic circumstances of Medvedev's presidency, Russia has dropped the concept and rhetoric of sovereign democracy (which Medvedev himself criticized), but continues to pursue a foreign policy designed to maximize both Russia's freedom of maneuver and its international influence. The existence of a multipolar world order requires, in the Russian analysis, the strengthening of those international institutions and laws promoting the sovereignty and equality of the world's major states.[17] Consequently, the Kremlin continues to favor a system of international relations in which large states are the primary shapers of global order, with their intramural relations dictated by calculations of national interest.[18] Russian diplomats are wont to argue that the cause of stability is best served by upholding those norms and institutions (above all, the UN Security Council) that formalize the existence of a Great Power concert. According to Putin, "We must clearly recognize that the critical responsibility . . . for securing global stability will be borne by the leading world powers [*vedushchie mirovye derzhavy*]—powers possessing nuclear weapons [and] powerful levers of military-political influence."[19] In a world dominated by Great Powers, smaller states are left to fend for themselves as the large states jockey for influence over them, while international norms are merely tools that states manipulate in pursuit of their own national interests.

Despite its emphasis on power, geopolitics, and the importance of remaining apart from the West, Russian foreign policy is not—as many of its critics charge—aimed at overthrowing the international order that emerged at the end of the Cold War. Nor is it animated by a desire to weaken, divide, or undermine the West. For the most part, it is conservative and inward-focused, emphasizing above all the need to maintain an international environment conducive to the domestic reforms most of the elite believes are necessary for reestablishing Russia as a major global player. As the authors of a major 2006 Trilateral Commission report judiciously caution:

> Russia is essentially defensive and independent rather than aggressive and expansionist. Russia will use pressure of many kinds on less powerful neighboring states and use leverage with the major powers where it has it . . . but it does not seek confrontation with them. . . . The ambition of the present leadership, supported by the majority of the electorate, is to re-establish Russia as a strong, independent, and unfettered actor on the global stage.[20]

THE WEST IN RUSSIAN FOREIGN POLICY

Relations with the West constitute the primary frame of reference for Russian foreign policy. Moscow's interactions with other parts of the world, including the former Soviet states around its borders, are conditioned upon the state of relations with the Western community and especially the leading member of that community, the United States. The Cold War legacy of bipolarity is a major reason for the ingrained Western-centrism of Russian foreign policy; Russia's ruling elite grew up during an era when Moscow and Washington largely directed the fate of the world. Besides, given the United States' continued predominance, it is hardly surprising that Russia's leaders should think of their relationship with Washington as central to their country's international position since "there is almost no regional or global policy issue that Russia could presently decide without taking into consideration the 'American factor.'"[21] Europe, meanwhile, is Russia's most important economic partner as well as a region whose culture and history are closely intertwined with those of Russia.

The West's importance as a frame of reference for Russia has not generally been reciprocated by Western leaders since the end of the Cold War. In part, the West's lack of attention has to do with the realization that today's Russia is in many ways a weaker, less threatening power than was the Soviet Union. In a world containing al Qaeda terrorists, financial institutions with global reach, rogue states seeking nuclear weapons, and a rapidly developing China, Russia does not normally figure in the top rank of problems competing for the attention of Western statesmen.

The United States, as the remaining superpower and the mirror to which many Russians hold up their own country, occupies a special place in the elites' thinking about Russia's place in the world.[22] At the same time, the European Union, which is closer geographically and more closely intertwined in social and economic terms, offers Russian elites an alternative more critical of Russia's internal failings, but also at times uncomfortable with America's global hegemony. For this reason, some Russian thinkers have (especially in the run-up to the Iraq war and in the aftermath of the war with Georgia) reanimated the old Cold War idea of trying to play Europe off against the United States. Nonetheless, the West as a collective abstraction remains the key reference point for the conduct of foreign policy.

The debate about Russia's relationship with the West centers in particular on the degree of institutional and ideological convergence between Russia and its former Cold War enemies, that is, about Russia's interest in and ability to "join the West." Although Russia's convergence with the West seemed somewhat inevitable in the last days of Soviet power, the deep-seated differences between Russia and even its immediate neighbors in East-Central Europe have repeatedly intervened.[23] And while there has been much debate over the past two decades about Russia's ability and interest in "joining the West," there has never been a comparable level of interest in the idea of Russia "joining the East." Consequently, a Russia that is not firmly anchored in Western institutions is one that is largely on its own internationally, maneuvering between East and West or pursuing what Russian diplomats since Primakov have referred to as a "multivector" foreign policy.

For much of the 1990s, even as then-President Yeltsin was shelling his recalcitrant parliament and presiding over a corruption-ridden privatization scheme, most observers in the U.S. and Europe operated on the assumption that Russia had made some kind of fundamental choice about joining "Western civilization"—even though major disagreements on issues such as the war in Chechnya and the Kosovo crisis perpetually complicated relations.[24] Somewhat ironically given later developments, the ascension to power of Vladimir Putin in 1999 (first as prime minister, then as president, then again as prime minister) was welcomed in Western capitals for reversing the slide toward kleptocratic decay taking place under Yeltsin and for confirming Russia's generally Westward course.[25] Putin, a former KGB operative in East Germany who had been a key adviser to the reformist mayor of St. Petersburg, Anatoly Sobchak, was initially praised for steering Russia back toward integration with the West. In contrast to the ill and erratic Yeltsin, Putin appeared the calm professional who would bring competence and stability back to the Kremlin after the drift of Yeltsin's last years in power.

The September 11, 2001, attacks in the United States reinforced this newfound faith in Russia's turn toward integration with the West. Putin was widely praised for the alacrity with which he declared his country's readiness to assist the United States and to put aside old suspicions about U.S. intentions. This decision to cooperate in the U.S.-led war on terror appeared to confirm Putin's fundamentally Western orientation and Russia's unshakable determination to recast its identity as a Western rather than a global or a Eurasian power.[26]

Yet even during the post–September 11 rapprochement between Russia and the U.S., there were warnings that the era of good feeling should not mask the fact that Putin's vision of foreign policy was an expansive one. Despite Putin's acceptance of U.S. initiatives during this period, there were signs of more difficult times to come; as early as 2002, Russia's quest for greater influence in the former Soviet states—in particular an apparent attempt to wrest control of the strategically and economically valuable Kerch Strait from Ukraine—was causing unease in Western capitals.[27]

Moscow saw the attacks of September 11 as the culmination of trends that had been under way for many years (Russia's experiences in Chechnya and Central Asia had awakened Moscow to the dangers of Islamist terrorism well before 2001). The events of that day, and even more, the muscular U.S. response to them—invading not only Afghanistan but Iraq as well—reinforced Russia's interest in a world of many powerful states, rather than a single hegemon. So too did Washington's willingness to ignore strenuous Russian objections to policies such as extending NATO membership to countries Russia considered critical to its own security or withdrawing from the Antiballistic Missile (ABM) Treaty.[28] Objections to the fruits of U.S. unilateralism only fed skepticism within Russia about whether Russia could, or indeed should, aspire to join the Western community of nations. Such skepticism was reinforced by the outbreak of apparently pro-Western "colored revolutions" in several post-Soviet states in the years 2003–2005. Moscow viewed the overthrow of corrupt, largely pro-Russian autocrats as part of a concerted U.S.-led campaign to roll back Russia's influence in its own backyard, and increasingly began to push back, both within the post-Soviet region and at the global level.

Since Medvedev became president in mid-2008, relations between Russia and the West have largely swung back from the confrontational posture characterizing the last years of Putin's presidency toward greater collaboration. To a significant extent, the change is the result of a renewed effort on the part of Western leaders (especially U.S. president Barack Obama) to reengage Russia. To the extent that the West has been willing to take Russian preferences into consideration, Moscow has been less inclined to seek limits on Western influence. At the same time, the legacy of the war with Georgia and the subsequent financial collapse have shifted the terms of Russia's own foreign policy debate. While the Medvedev-era elite continues to talk about Russia's destiny to be a Great Power, the emphasis has been much more on transforming Russia so that it can fulfill that role, rather than merely demanding that others treat it as a major power regardless of its relative weakness.

Medvedev has made modernization the central component of his strategy for strengthening Russia as an international actor. In Medvedev's characterization, modernization implies creating a high-tech, knowledge-based economy while reducing Russia's dependence on resource extraction. This emphasis grows out of the recognition both that Russia cannot hope to become a truly global power without foreign assistance to address its economic and social limitations, and that the challenges it will face in the twenty-first century are increasingly transnational and will require cross-border collaboration to solve. A corollary of this focus on modernization has been the need to maintain good relations with the West, which possesses the capital, knowledge, and technology that Russia needs if it is to ever achieve the kind of modernity Medvedev envisions. Notably though, the discussion is not any longer about joining the West; rather it is about lowering tensions with the West in order to allow Russia to develop its own intrinsic potential and itself play a leading role in responding to common challenges.[29]

Of course, the view that technological modernization is the central task of Russian foreign (and domestic) policy remains controversial both in and outside of Russia. Skeptics question whether Russia's overly centralized political system and rickety institutions are capable of bringing about—much less operating—a truly modern, knowledge-based economy. Given the number of officials and other elites who derive personal benefits from the status quo, it is also unclear whether Medvedev will be able to overcome the deeply entrenched forces of inertia. Moreover, given the seemingly insatiable demand for Russia's oil and gas, some critics doubt that the costs associated with moving to a knowledge-based economy would offset the benefits Russia continues to derive as a supplier of raw materials to the global market. These obstacles mean that Medvedev's modernization agenda faces uncertain prospects (the more so given the possibility that Medvedev will be sidelined following the 2012 presidential election). Even if modernization à la Medvedev succeeds, it is unlikely to overturn the basic premises underlying Russian foreign policy and bring Russia fundamentally into the political-moral community of the West, given the breadth of support for the notion of Russia maintaining an autonomous role on the world stage throughout the elite.

In the West itself, perceptions of Russian foreign policy since 1991 have been characterized by a dialectical process of expectation and disappointment about Moscow's integration with the institutions collectively composing the West. In the early 1990s, many Western analysts assumed, in line with Francis Fukuyama's then-popular "end of history" thesis, that Russia would shed its superpower aspirations and link its fate to the institutional structure of the liberal democratic West—much as many of the USSR's onetime satellites in Eastern Europe, such as Poland and Hungary, did.[30] With the alcohol-fueled decline of Boris Yeltsin and the rise of illiberal groups such as Vladimir Zhirinovsky's ironically named Liberal Democratic Party of Russia (LDPR), along with Russia's more aggressive policy toward its neighbors in the middle to late 1990s, pessimism about Russia became the norm in Western capitals. By the end of the decade, Russia looked dangerously close to becoming a failed state, one whose weakness created a temptation for extremist groups, organized crime, and more dynamic neighbors to seize its assets (including potentially pieces of its nuclear arsenal), and whose dangerous unpredictability rendered it a menace against which the West needed to guard itself.

With the rise of Putin in the early 2000s, the pendulum swung back, and many in the West—notably George W. Bush—again saw Russia as an aspiring member of the Western family, especially after the 9/11 attacks created a community of interests between Moscow and Washington that had not existed for close to a decade. Yet the U.S. took advantage of Russia's more accommodating stance to take steps, such as pulling out of the ABM Treaty and conducting another round of NATO expansion, which Russia had long opposed. The Bush administration assumed that a Russia truly inclined to the West would not object to these actions, since the whole idea of a conflict between Russia and the West was outdated—if NATO had no intention of attacking Russia, why should Russia care which of its neighbors joined?

Most Russians, of course, did not see U.S. actions in the same light, and in any case Putin's Russia was never as pro-Western as the U.S. assumed it to be in 2001–2002—nor as anti-Western as many in the U.S. subsequently assumed. By the end of Putin's term as president, Russia's energy-fueled economic recovery and the United States' misadventure in Iraq had created a sense in Russia that the era of U.S. hegemony was passing and that Russia would be one of the principal beneficiaries. The more assertive Russia of Putin's second term renewed fears in the West about Moscow's alleged desire to weaken and divide the West, and even about the possibility of a new Cold War breaking out—especially after Russia's invasion of Georgia.[31]

As Russian analyst Dmitri Trenin observed in 2006, "Until recently, Russia saw itself as Pluto in the Western solar system, very far from the center but still fundamentally a part of it. Now it has left that orbit entirely: Russia's leaders have given up on becoming part of the West and have started creating their own Moscow-centered system."[32] This desire to remain apart from the West is not, however, a recent development, but rather a historically conditioned principle that has animated Russia's foreign policy for most of the post-Soviet period. It is worth remembering that after a brief flirtation with Western integration in the early 1990s, Yeltsin's Russia was also subjected to harsh criticism both for its turn away from democracy and for its resistance to Western foreign policy initiatives (especially in the Balkans). It was Yeltsin, after all, who used tanks to defeat his parliamentary opposition in 1993, and it was under Yeltsin's watch that Russian troops seized the airport in Priština, Kosovo, in 1999, nearly causing a firefight with NATO soldiers in the process. As early as 1994, some observers noted that for the foreseeable future Russia's foreign policy would be driven by "the championship, above all, of Russia's own national interests" and self-perception as one of the world's Great Powers rather than by partnership with the West.[33] Or, as the analyst and then-Duma deputy Alexei Arbatov also pointed out in 1994, "There is an overwhelming consensus on the main goal of strategic and national security: that Russia should remain one of the world's great powers."[34]

The September 2001 terrorist attacks in New York and Washington were a searing moment for the United States, and for a U.S. administration that saw them as heralding nothing less than a war between civilization and barbarism. Russia and its leaders sympathized with the U.S., but also saw the attacks as an opportunity to advance their own long-standing strategic objective of enhancing Russia's power and autonomy on the international stage, deliberately positioning Russia as an indispensable player in the unfolding "global war on terror." Russia's offer of a partnership in the aftermath of the attacks was designed to enhance Russia's leverage vis-à-vis the United States and to collaborate with Washington against the common threat of Islamic extremism. It was not a decision to subordinate Russia's long-standing geopolitical interests to those of the West, or to associate

Russia itself fully with the West, as several East European countries had done after the end of the Cold War.

Failure to appreciate the motives guiding Russian behavior after 9/11 no doubt contributed to the disappointment many Western leaders expressed when relations with Russia became increasingly fraught in subsequent years (particularly following the U.S. invasion of Iraq and the outbreak of the "colored revolutions" in the post-Soviet space). The point is that the desire to remain outside of the West as a political (and moral) grouping is a deep-seated one among the Russian political class that has less to do with a particular configuration of power in the Kremlin than with Russian political and cultural elites' understanding of their country's own history and role in the international system. Even under the seemingly liberal Medvedev, Russian foreign policy is less about integration with the West than about improving relations with the West as a means of securing Russia's development as an influential, fully sovereign international actor. The difference is crucial: if Medvedev's outreach to the West is based on this sort of strategic calculation, it is—like Putin's outreach after 9/11—reversible if the context of U.S.-Russian relations were to change as it did following the invasion if Iraq and the colored revolutions.

While Russia's foreign policy priorities did not undergo a fundamental transformation during the Putin years, the functioning of the political system did, with consequences at least for the way Russia was perceived beyond its borders. Though Yeltsin's Russia was hardly a paragon of democracy (Yeltsin, after all, had ordered tanks to fire on his rebellious parliament, and his 1996 reelection was marred by corruption and manipulation of the electoral system on a massive scale), it was a more open, tolerant place than today's Russia. Under Putin and Medvedev, elections have been tightly controlled, as opposition figures such as former prime minister Mikhail Kasyanov, former deputy prime minister Boris Nemtsov, and one-time chess champion Garry Kasparov all discovered when they sought to challenge the Kremlin's tightly managed succession process.[35] Much of the independent media have been swallowed up by the state or its proxies (such as natural gas monopoly Gazprom), and a not inconsiderable number of independent journalists, such as Anna Politkovskaya of *Novaya Gazeta*, have turned up dead or severely injured following attacks that many observers have linked to the Kremlin or its proxies in the security services. Even big business has been forced to adhere to the government's line, and the Kremlin has shown no hesitation in going after obstreperous oligarchs such as Vladimir Gusinsky, Boris Berezovsky, and Mikhail Khodorkovsky with the entire coercive apparatus of the state. Though Medvedev has called for greater openness and respect for the law, his actual accomplishments in this area have been sparse.

Given the importance of democratic values and practices in the West's self-perception, Russia's lack of democracy cannot but have consequences for Russia's relationship with the Western world. Of course, Western powers have managed to have cooperative, even close, relations with a variety of nondemocratic states such as Saudi Arabia, Hosni Mubarak's Egypt, and even (at times) China. Russian observers, especially those sympathetic to the West, thus sometimes complain that Russia is being held to a double standard on the issue of democracy.[36] The state of democracy in Russia has important consequences for foreign policy but does not, in and of itself, determine the extent to which Moscow can find common cause with the United States and Europe.

Among Russians, perceptions about governance and democracy have foreign policy consequences because of a persistent link between attitudes toward Russia's domestic political development and toward interactions with the West. On the one hand, polls continually show that most Russians would prefer the government to be more socially oriented, even at the expense of Russia's leading global role. Meanwhile, the sociologist William Zimmerman showed in the 1990s that Russians who favored a market economy and democratic politics also supported close cooperation with the West, while supporters of a Soviet-style political and economic system were equally consistent in advocating a more confrontational approach to dealing with the West.[37]

The split between an elite committed to Russia becoming a major international power and a public favoring at least some of the tenets of social democracy is in part the result of the fact that Russia's fundamental identity, including its degree of belonging to the Western/European community, remains poorly defined.[38] This confusion about Russia's identity should hardly come as a surprise; one of the persistent historical patterns in Russian life has been the debate between Westernizers (including Peter the Great, nineteenth-century intellectuals such as Aleksandr Herzen and Ivan Turgenev, and perhaps Mikhail Gorbachev) on the one hand and their nationalistic, often Orthodox-centric, opponents on the other. The latter's ranks include nineteenth-century Slavophiles like Fyodor Dostoevsky, twentieth-century nationalist philosophers such as Ivan Ilin and Nikolai Berdyaev, and Soviet hard-liners who would reject their predecessors' Orthodox mysticism but share their suspicion of the West and sense of Russia's special mission in the world.

With the Soviet collapse, the process of scripting a new national identity out of the collective memory of the populace has been one of the most challenging tasks for all post-Communist states in Eastern Europe and Eurasia. In a rather short span of time, these states have had to free themselves from the shackles of Communist orthodoxy, reintegrate their pre-Communist pasts into collective memory, and work out a new relationship with a European Union that was itself busy undermining the traditional foundations of national distinctiveness. Some formerly Communist states have moved more thoroughly than others to establish an identity that allows them to pursue a stable, collective security-focused foreign policy in the context of a vastly changed European landscape.[39] Russia has been notably less successful than states such as Poland in doing so, and the lure of the West continues to compete for attention with Russia's autarkic, imperial past as a model for future development.[40]

A Russia that is firmly anchored to Western institutions is one that, like Germany and Japan after 1945, has decided to trade its foreign policy autonomy for prosperity and security within an increasingly integrated community of nations whose priorities are economic rather than political. Yet the analogy with postwar Germany and Japan has never been widely accepted in Russia. While many average Russians would be willing to see their country relegated to the role of a medium-sized regional power if such a diminution resulted in greater prosperity, Russia's elites are largely wedded to the idea of their country as a major power.[41] Given the top-heavy configuration of the Russian political system, it is mainly the elites' priorities that matter, especially on questions of foreign policy—even if Medvedev has made improved living standards one of the major goals of his modernization agenda and his foreign policy.

Whatever their other political and ideological differences, Russia's elites are generally in agreement that Russia is, and should remain, a power with global interests and global reach. To be sure, Putin and Medvedev have often spoken of Russia as being part of Europe.[42] On the other hand, officials and diplomats have made no secret of their interest in Russia playing a truly global role, analogous to that of the United States or, indeed, of the Soviet Union during the Cold War. As then-foreign minister Igor Ivanov cautioned (before the September 11 attacks), neither Russia's jettisoning of Communist ideology, its halting democratization, nor hope for better relations with the West would cause the country to "narrow the scope of its foreign policy interests."[43]

The fact that Russia's ambitions are global does not by itself determine the nature of Moscow's relations with other countries. A Russia that operates outside the institutional and normative bounds of the West can set itself up as a rival and a spoiler if it so chooses. However, it is worth remembering that despite its impressive growth in the years leading up to 2008, Russia remains significantly behind the truly major powers in economic and military terms. Russian GDP in 2010 was approximately $1.48 trillion, less than one-tenth that of the United States and behind its BRIC partners Brazil and China (Russia's GDP was slightly ahead of India's, though India's growth far outstripped Russia's).[44] Military spending, despite a decade of large increases, was roughly $61 billion in 2009, compared to more than $660 billion in the U.S. and almost $100 billion in

China.[45] This financial reality acts as a constraint on Russia's foreign policy ambitions, particularly its ability to act as a rival to the West.

PUTIN'S LEGACY

Russia's return as a major international player, as well as its increasingly frosty relationship with the Western world, largely coincided with Vladimir Putin's term in the Kremlin (2000–2008). This worsening of relations with the West, not to mention Putin's background in the KGB and the consolidation of authoritarianism on his watch, eventually made Russia's second president a rather reviled figure in Western capitals and (especially) in the Western press. Though initially hailed in much of the West as a capable, energetic modernizer, by the time he stepped down to become prime minister for the second time in 2008, Putin carried with him a decidedly sinister reputation only exacerbated by the appearance of him upstaging Medvedev in prosecuting the Georgian war.[46] Given the highly centralized nature of the Russian political system, Putin's direct impact on foreign policy was considerable, and remains so since his move from the Kremlin to the White House (seat of the Russian prime minister and his cabinet). Yet despite significant Western criticism, his actual legacy as a statesman is quite complex. Putin's emphasis on rebuilding Russian power led him to approach the West in different ways at different times, depending on the needs of Russia's international position. Underlying his entire approach though was a commitment to the restoration of Russia as a major power.

Putin, of course, did not originate the Great Power aspirations at the heart of Russia's interactions with the rest of the world. On the other hand, and to a much greater degree than his predecessor Yeltsin, Putin succeeded in translating those aspirations into a concrete reality. His ability to position Russia as one of the indispensable pillars of the international system owes much to fortuitous circumstances (above all the sustained rise in global prices for Russia's major export, energy, that took place during his presidency). At the same time, Putin's success was in part the result of his ability to pursue a clearly articulated vision of the world and Russia's place in it and to mobilize the resources necessary to achieve his ends.[47]

Putin was also careful to operate within the broad elite consensus about Russia's role as one of the world's leading powers. In this way, he managed to neutralize opposition and give himself substantial freedom to maneuver at the tactical level. By positioning himself as a defender of Russia's international prerogatives, Putin largely managed to defuse opposition to individual initiatives, above all when he sought to avoid fruitless quarrels with other major powers. Just as only Nixon could go to China, only Putin could sell a rapprochement with the West to Russia's still-powerful hard-liners, both after 9/11 and during Medvedev's presidency (though he and Medvedev have appeared to clash on a handful of occasions, it is clear Putin has largely supported the warming of relations with the U.S. and Europe of which Medvedev has been the public face). For the first half of Putin's presidency, the most notable fact about Russian foreign policy was its generally passive, reactive nature—a development that led some analysts to argue that a historic turning point had been reached, bringing an end to the era of confrontation between Russia and the West once and for all. In Putin's second term, such optimism gave way to a new round of philippics about the resurrection of Russia's imperial instincts that reached unprecedented levels during the war in Georgia.

The changing nature of Russia's international behavior during the course of Putin's presidency makes sense as part of a broader strategy aimed at restoring Russia's ability to play the global role preferred by its elites. In bandwagoning with the United States after 9/11, and seeking to minimize quarrels with the West thereafter, Putin made a strategic calculation that international cooperation—along with restoring the domestic bases of Russian strength—was the most effective means of recapturing Russia's lost global influence. When the external and internal environments changed as a result of rising energy prices, the war in Iraq, and the colored revolutions in the CIS, so, too, did the Kremlin's strategy for attaining its geopolitical goals.

During Putin's second term, the pattern of deferring to Western initiatives, notably in connection with the war in Afghanistan, gave way to a much more determined assertion of Russian power, at times in direct contravention of U.S. and EU aims. Russia's increased oil and gas wealth underpinned a sense of power and independence that shocked observers used to a Russia whose menace lay in its weakness rather than its strength. One example of Russia's suddenly assertive international behavior was the January 2006 decision to shut off gas supplies to Ukraine, ostensibly to force Kyiv[48] to pay market price for deliveries of Russian energy. The subtext to this dispute over energy prices, however, centered on the 2004 Orange Revolution, which brought to power a strongly pro-Western Ukrainian president, Viktor Yushchenko, who had campaigned on a platform of reducing Ukraine's dependence on Russia and seeking membership in Western institutions (including NATO). It seemed that Moscow was using its dominant position in Ukraine's energy market as a way of forcing Kyiv to hew to a more pro-Russian foreign policy. Ukraine, like other former Soviet republics still dependent on Russian gas, was in essence given a choice: "Either loyalty . . . or independence, at the highest [possible] price."[49]

While 2006 began with a crisis over gas, the end of the year was marred by the assassinations of Anna Politkovskaya, the investigative journalist gunned down in the lift of her Moscow apartment building, and of the ex-KGB agent and political dissident Aleksandr Litvinenko, who was poisoned in London with the rare radioactive element polonium. Whatever the motivation for these and similar high-profile killings, they had a chilling impact on relations with the Western world. Critics of Putin—including a dying Litvinenko—blamed the Kremlin for complicity in the assassinations. Officials in the U.S. and Europe claimed that the assassinations were part of "the steady accumulation of problems and irritants [that] threatens to harm Russia's relations with the West."[50]

Nor were Russia's relations with the U.S. and Europe helped by the fact that the Kremlin was then busy launching assaults on some of the biggest and most influential Western energy companies. Moscow sought to take control of massive extraction operations on Sakhalin Island and at the Shtokman field in the Far North that had been ceded to firms like Royal Dutch Shell and BP in the 1990s. Similarly, Putin's Russia seized and dismantled the largest private oil company in the country, Mikhail Khodorkovsky's Yukos, in mid-2003. The nationalization of Yukos (and the jailing of Khodorkovsky) not only sent a chilling message about Russia's commitment to the rule of law, but also affected Western interests directly, insofar as Yukos' existing U.S. and European shareholders were wiped out by the nationalization. Khodorkovsky had also been negotiating the sale of a major stake in his company to ExxonMobil or Chevron Texaco, which lost out when the bulk of Yukos' assets were transferred to Russia's state-owned Rosneft at a cut-rate price.

The assassinations of Politkovskaya and Litvinenko, along with the Kremlin's response to the colored revolutions, the nationalization of Yukos and arrest of Khodorkovsky, the gas cutoffs to Ukraine, reluctance to end Russian participation in Iran's nuclear program, the 2007 suspension of the Conventional Forces in Europe (CFE) Treaty, attempts to block the independence of Kosovo, hostile response to the planned deployment of NATO antimissile systems in the Czech Republic and Poland, and the invasion of Georgia all contributed to the perception that Putin's Russia was bent on aggressively promoting its exclusive interests at the expense of partnership and cooperation with the West. For many Russians, though, that partnership as originally constructed had been a failure, and Russia's international resurgence under Putin was merely a sign that Moscow had had enough of being alternately hectored and ignored by its alleged partners in the West. Western support for anti-Russian regimes like that in Georgia, the relentless expansion of NATO, U.S. scorn for arms control agreements, the deployment of weapons systems close to Russia's borders, the dismemberment of Russian ally Serbia—all seemed incongruous with the rhetoric of partnership too when viewed from Moscow.

In the context of these disputes, Putin pointed at specific policies and decisions taken by the West, while continuing to argue that partnership as such remained a realistic goal if Washington and its allies would only take Russian interests seriously. With the election of Barack Obama, who called on the U.S. and Russia to "reset" their relationship, Washington effectively acknowledged that its own policies had played at least some role in the souring of relations with Russia. At the same time, Russia's economic difficulties and Medvedev's campaign to reshape the Russian economy forced Moscow to place more emphasis on cultivating the U.S. and Europe after 2008. The result was a rapid, if still uncertain warming in ties, cemented when Medvedev traveled to Washington in June 2010 for a highly productive summit meeting that culminated with the U.S. and Russian presidents chatting casually over hamburgers, and with the signing of an agreement later that year to cooperate on missile defense. Yet uncertainties remained. Medvedev's modernization agenda focused on accessing Western investment and technology, but the West continued to struggle to articulate what, precisely, it wanted either from or with Russia, and indeed whether it could trust Medvedev's Russia sufficiently to pursue a deeper and more enduring partnership. The absence of a strategic vision for the future of the relationship means that the rapprochement pursued by Medvedev and Obama remains tenuous, subject as ever to the shifting of political winds.[51]

RUSSIA AND THE NON-WEST

How Russia defines itself in relation to the West is in many ways the country's key foreign policy question. That relationship will continue to play the central role in determining the nature of Russia's interactions with other countries and with international institutions. Even if Russia's leaders do not see their country as belonging to the West in some fundamental way, their foreign policy has nonetheless inevitably been Western-centric. Moscow's relations with the other former Soviet republics, with Asia (especially China), and with the rest of the world have largely been a function of its position with respect to Europe and, more fundamentally, the United States.

The global financial crisis, which affected the West much more severely than Asia, has however pushed Moscow to place a higher priority on the "Asian vector" of its foreign policy. Medvedev's modernization program identifies wealthy Asian states such as South Korea and Singapore as sources of modernization in their own right, and as representatives of an alternative to the Western model of development that holds lessons for Russia too. Moscow has consequently sought a larger role for regional organizations such as the BRICS and RIC (Russia, India, China) groups and an enhanced presence for itself in established groups such as ASEAN (Association of Southeast Asian Nations)—albeit with limited results. Compared to its interactions with both the West and the former Soviet states though, Russia starts from a significant disadvantage in its attempts to become a major economic and security player in East Asia, given the small size of Asian Russia's economy and Moscow's long history of pursuing a Western-centric foreign policy.

Like Russia, China and India remain committed to the notion of absolute sovereignty, at least for themselves, and opposed to what they perceive as Western attempts to impose a single system of values and practices onto the world. Moreover, the disproportionate impact of the financial crisis on the West strengthened the conviction of many in Beijing, Delhi, and elsewhere in Asia that the global balance of power was undergoing a long-term shift.[52]

The most important non-Western, non-CIS country for Russia is China. China is a power in some ways analogous to Russia, and Moscow's relations with Beijing have, like its role in the CIS, often served as a reflection of the state of relations with the West. Russian statesmen sometimes portrayed China as a kind of alternative to the West, whether as a model for economic development without political liberalization or as a geopolitical pole toward which Russia can align in opposition to the West. China is moreover one of the major customers for Russian energy and was for many years also a principal buyer of Russian military technology. Russia and China have also maintained a wary partnership (formalized in the Shanghai Cooperation Organization, or SCO) based on economic cooperation, an uneasy détente in Central Asia, and a shared commitment to checking the expansion of U.S. influence in the region, even if the two powers' emphasis has often differed.[53]

A large, rapidly growing country uneasy with Western hegemony in the world, China is in a sense a natural partner for a Russia keen on the establishment of a multipolar world. On the other hand, Russo-Chinese relations suffer from a long history of mistrust and rancor. Territorial disputes, immigration (especially in sparsely populated Siberia and the Far East), and competing ambitions in Central Asia mean that while Beijing and Moscow often found it expedient to cooperate in checking the exercise of U.S. power, they remain wary partners, as indeed they were for much of the past half century. Russian leaders have at times also expressed real worry about China's future plans and ability to dominate the Russian Far East.

At the same time, Medvedev's modernization agenda nonetheless aims to harness East Asia's growth for the development of Asian Russia.[54] Belatedly recognizing the degree to which global dynamism has shifted to Asia in the aftermath of the post-2008 financial crisis, it also seeks to create a foundation for Russia to assume a larger role in Asian security affairs.[55] Despite the complexity of political relations, China remains critical to both these schemes.

Moscow's relations with its former dependencies in the CIS, meanwhile, provide something of a test case for how Russia's evolving post-Soviet identity has shaped its external relations, with Moscow's atavistic imperial instincts vying with a newer and narrower conception of the Russian Federation's national interests. After a decade of neglect and selective engagement, Putin's Russia sought to play a much more active role in the so-called Near Abroad, in part as a way of pushing back against what it perceived as Western encroachment, while forcing the West to take its demand for a seat at the table seriously. Medvedev's declaration, shortly after Moscow recognized the independence of Abkhazia and South Ossetia, that Russia would regard the area around its borders as "a region in which it has privileged interests" is a clear indication that the CIS remains a primary object of Russia's more active foreign policy.[56]

In part, this increased activity was merely a consequence of Russia's more vigorous approach to foreign policy, as the former Soviet republics are in many ways the natural sphere of influence for a Great Power Russia, much as Latin America was long considered the strategic backyard of the United States. Moreover, given the strategic location and extensive oil and gas reserves of many CIS states, Moscow's stepped-up activity in the region also gave it a strong card to play in relations with energy-consuming countries in both Europe and Asia. If Russia's more active international stance has been the main factor "pushing" Moscow into the CIS, then instability within several of the former Soviet republics (including the rise of Islamic radicalism and terrorism in the Caucasus and Central Asia) has simultaneously served to "pull" Russia into the region.[57] Russia's growing interest in Central Asia as well as its open intervention in the politics of states including Belarus, Georgia, Azerbaijan, Moldova, and Ukraine have been a source of continuing discord with the West. The Medvedev-era rapprochement between Russia and the West has benefited both from a warier approach to the region on the part of the West (a consequence of the global economic crisis and the war in Georgia), as well as from the confluence of interests created by the worsening situation in Afghanistan and Pakistan. None of these factors is likely to be permanent, however, and a renewed struggle for influence in the post-Soviet space remains the greatest threat to continued cooperation between Russia and the West.

PAST, PRESENT, AND FUTURE

To place the Putin-Medvedev era into its proper context, it is necessary to understand how Russian foreign policy evolved and changed before Putin came to power in 2000. The country Putin took over, of course, was not a tabula rasa, and while his term in office saw the displacement of Yeltsin's ruling circle (the so-called Family, led by Yeltsin's daughter Tatyana Dyachenko and the now-exiled oligarch Boris Berezovsky), Putin did not completely displace either Russia's ruling elite or the basic assumptions underlying Russian foreign policy. Indeed, in the realm of foreign policy, the change was less pronounced than in domestic affairs.

Medvedev, meanwhile, was not only Putin's hand-picked successor, but his presidency has remained to a considerable degree in Putin's shadow, since Putin remains a kind of gray cardinal in his role as prime minister and many Putin loyalists continue to hold important positions throughout the presidential administration and government. Indeed it is questionable whether Medvedev would have much of a political constituency without Putin's support—apart perhaps from a coterie of liberal intellectuals and lawyers. Given the unusual symbiosis between Medvedev and Putin, it is difficult to argue that Medvedev has been responsible for any tectonic shift in Russian foreign policy, even if his emphasis on economic development and improving relations with the West go beyond what was openly discussed during the Putin years.

To make sense of the origins of the consensus underlying much of Russian foreign policy, it is worth recalling the career of Yevgeny Primakov, foreign minister from 1996 to 1998, later prime minister and then rival of Putin for the presidency. Despite the vitriol Primakov encountered from Putin's circle when the two men were rivals for the 2000 presidential nomination, Putin followed several of the foreign policy prescriptions laid out by Primakov during (and before) his tenure as foreign minister. Primakov continues to matter because if anything, the real turning point for Russian foreign policy came not in 2000, when Putin became president, but earlier, around 1992 or 1993, when it became clear that then-foreign minister Andrei Kozyrev's call for Russia to join the Western community of nations was not sustainable, either domestically or internationally. Primakov, who would replace Kozyrev in 1996, embodied the newly assertive tenor of Russian foreign policy that has, more recently, coexisted uneasily with a desire for a productive, equal partnership with the West.[58]

Russia's foreign policy "revolution" (such as it was) was the result of the mounting frustrations evinced by the Russian population over the course of the country's reforms in the early 1990s, the failure of the West to step in to rescue the Russian economy or integrate Russia into Western security structures, and the perception that Kozyrev was kowtowing to the West without achieving anything appreciable in return. For a Russian elite (especially the new elite that had come to prominence in the early Yeltsin administration from positions in the middle ranks of the bureaucracy or the provincial leadership) that never ceased to think of the country as a major world power, Kozyrev's approach was both humiliating and counterproductive. A number of influential economic players in the military-industrial complex and other large state-owned industries likewise felt their own interests threatened by Kozyrev's desire to open up the Russian economy to outside competition.[59]

Resistance to Kozyrev's ideas also stemmed from the fact that the external world confronting Russia continued to look much as it had during the Cold War. Institutions such as NATO had not themselves undergone sufficient transformation since the end of the Cold War and were in the mid-1990s torn between attracting Russia and containing it in the event that Russia's experiment with democracy failed. With no formal institutional mechanisms for managing Russia's integration with the West, Moscow often felt itself faced with a series of faits accomplis that it had no ability to influence, above all in connection with the expansion of NATO. Resentment over the West's perceived double standards and attachment to zero-sum thinking has since the mid-1990s been a constant complaint among Russian politicians and academics, who charge that the end of the Cold War merely gave Western powers an opportunity to roll back Russian influence, seize Russian markets (especially in the arms trade), and establish a semicolonial economic relationship in which Russia exports raw materials and imports advanced technology.[60]

Even worse, Russia during the Yeltsin-Kozyrev years had difficulty articulating a convincing justification for deferring to Western leadership since it had not yet developed a coherent vision of its own interests. To many observers inside Russia, the pursuit of integration with the West in the early 1990s was less a strategic decision than an indication that Russia lacked a strategy entirely.[61] In one now infamous and symptomatic exchange, Kozyrev asked former U.S. president Richard Nixon, "If you . . . can advise us on how to define our national interests, I will be very grateful to you" (Nixon wisely declined to tell the Russian foreign minister what his own country's interests were).[62]

The pursuit of integration under Kozyrev and acting Prime Minister Yegor Gaidar in the early 1990s did not bring improvement to the lives of most ordinary people, who were suffering from the economic and political chaos that followed the Soviet collapse. In the mind of the Russian electorate, democracy increasingly came to be associated with poverty and instability. The almost inevitable result was a backlash against the idea of the West as well as against Russia's own "artificial Westernization."[63] The fault was not entirely that of Gaidar or Kozyrev, or of Yeltsin himself, but nonetheless they and the ideas they represented took much of the blame. As a result, notions of convergence and integration with the West lost their appeal, and Russia's leaders began shifting back onto a more Westphalian, Great Power course.

It was not long before the mounting opposition to Kozyrev began having an effect on the actual conduct of Russian foreign policy. As early as August 1992, opposition from hard-liners in the Supreme Soviet and the military forced Yeltsin to cancel a visit to Japan because of the territorial dispute over the Kuril Islands (which the USSR seized from Japan in the last days of World War II). With Kozyrev still in office, the Kremlin adopted a document called "Russia's Strategic Course toward Members of the Commonwealth of Independent States" (*Strategicheskii kurs Rossii s gosudarstvami-uchastnikami Sodruzhestva Nezavisimykh Gosudarstv*) in September 1995. This document argued that Russia had a vital stake in ensuring that its post-Soviet neighbors adopted policies congenial to Russian interests, that Moscow should take the lead in establishing a new Russia-focused system of interstate relations within the CIS, and that bilateral relations with members of the CIS should be predicated on these states' willingness to pursue regional integration on Russian terms. This decree served notice that Moscow would not lightly accept the rollback of its influence over its neighbors.[64]

In the meantime, Yeltsin had bombarded the Supreme Soviet in October 1993 to oust the coalition of nationalists and Communists intent on deposing him, but the elections that followed left Vladimir Zhirinovsky's protofascist Liberal Democrats as the largest party in the new State Duma. Then, in 1994, Russian troops entered Chechnya to crush an uprising by the restless population of that region, committing widespread and well-publicized atrocities in the process. Both the rise of Zhirinovsky and the war in Chechnya reflected the depth of hostility to the post-Soviet status quo that had emerged between 1991 and 1994. They also helped create a more defensive tone in Russia's interactions with an outside world that looked on with incredulity at what was transpiring.[65]

Primakov, who took over at Smolenskaya Ploshchad (headquarters of the Ministry of Foreign Affairs) when Kozyrev was finally ousted in January 1996, inherited the reins of Russian foreign policy at a time when developments were already pushing Russia in a more assertive direction. He pursued a course that was at once more consensual domestically and more confrontational internationally. It sought to establish Russia as one of the leading states in the international system (commensurate with its position as a permanent member of the UN Security Council) and to limit the influence of the United States in the area of the former Soviet Union. Primakov at times also toyed with the idea of building a counterhegemonic bloc among countries hostile to or distrustful of the United States, including Iran, Libya, North Korea, Cuba, and China, albeit without result.

Primakov declared that under his watch Russia would reject both the strident anti-Westernism of the Soviet Union and the naïve romanticism of the early 1990s in favor of an approach that would emphasize Russia's "status as a great power" and an "equal, mutually beneficial partnership" with the United States and Europe.[66] What these concepts meant in practice was not always clear. Primakov and his backers rejected a subservient relationship to the West but were less clear as to what other principle would serve as the foundation for their strategy, leading one Western analyst to lament that Russian foreign policy under Primakov "is difficult to define. It is difficult even to detect."[67] Primakov sought to overcome the domestic political rifts opened by Kozyrev's strategy of integration as a prelude to Russia's reemergence as an active, autonomous international player, but lacked a grand strategic vision about the role this new Russia would play. Some alarming incidents soon occurred, most notably the near-firefight between Russian and NATO troops over control of the Priština airport in 1999.

Serious clashes between post-Soviet Russia and its partners in the West are thus nothing new, even if the consequences of such clashes became more serious during the 2000s. Nor for that matter is the elite's general set of priorities a recent development. What has changed since the mid-1990s is Russian power (economic, military, and soft) relative to the West, along with the Kremlin's growing ability to dominate the foreign policy–making process. Though the post-2008 economic crisis took some of the wind out of Russia's sails—and some of the hubris out of its diplomacy—the fact remains that Russia in the second decade of the twenty-first century is a much wealthier, more cohesive, and more confident country than the Russia of the early 1990s, and this transformation continues to affect the way Russia interacts with the outside world. In relative terms, Russian power has also been aided by the United States' preoccupation since 9/11 with the wars in Afghanistan and Iraq, and more recently by the worst economic crisis since the Great Depression. Russian observers and politicians continue to cite the rising demand for energy, diminution of U.S. power, and rise of new global actors such as India and China to assert that a multipolar world order, which for Primakov was an aspiration for the future, already exists.[68]

The continuity between past and present becomes still clearer in Medvedev's articulation of Russian foreign policy priorities. In an interview shortly after the end of hostilities in Georgia, Medvedev summarized the five overriding positions guiding Russia's foreign relations (what at the time was termed the "Medvedev Doctrine"): (1) "Russia recognizes the supremacy of the basic principles of international law"; (2) "the world must be multipolar," since a world dominated by one power "is unstable and threatened by conflict"; (3) "Russia does not desire confrontation with any country"; (4) "protecting the lives and dignity of our citizens wherever they are located"; and (5) "Russia, like other countries of the world, has regions in which it maintains privileged interests."[69] These principles were sharply criticized in the West, especially the fourth and fifth points.[70]

After all, it was in defense of Russian "citizens"—residents of South Ossetia who had received Russian passports—that the Kremlin justified its
invasion of Georgia. And the notion that Moscow would explicitly claim
a region of privileged interests appeared a needless throwback to the days
of balance-of-power politics, spheres of influence, and other seemingly
anachronistic concepts.

Despite its poor reception in the West, the Medvedev Doctrine was on
the whole less revolutionary than it seemed at first glance. Indeed, the
creation of a multipolar world governed by international law, with the
major powers working among themselves to solve problems, has been a
basic aim of Russian foreign policy for close to two decades and has been
widely expressed in other contexts. Protecting Russia's privileged interests
in the former Soviet Union has also been central to Russian foreign policy
ever since the USSR collapsed, even if Medvedev's declaration was somewhat more explicit than what Moscow had stated openly in the past. The
claim to protect Russian citizens "wherever they are located" was more of
a departure, though tensions over the status of ethnic Russians in the Baltic states have long been an irritant in Russia's relationship with Europe.
In any case, Medvedev's fourth point aside, the tenets of the Medvedev
Doctrine could just as easily have been made by a Primakov or a Putin
(even if Primakov would not have systematized them). Only the fact that
the doctrine was elaborated in the wake of a war that took the West badly
by surprise made it seem like some sort of basic reversal.

Nor has the rapprochement with the West over which Medvedev presided in the years after 2008 fundamentally changed these assumptions.
The "reset" between Moscow and Washington stems from a number of
sources, but one central factor has been increased U.S. deference to Russian interests in the post-Soviet region. The Obama administration has
shown little of its predecessor's inclination to regard the former Soviet
Union as a target for democracy promotion (often viewed in Moscow as
promotion of anti-Russian regimes). And while the invasion of Georgia
may have had negative repercussions on Russia's international reputation
and economy, it did stop the process of NATO expansion in its tracks,
thereby removing one of the major bones of contention in relations between Russia and the West. By at least tacitly accepting the Medvedev
Doctrine and acknowledging that maintenance of its leading role in the
post-Soviet space is a redline for Russia, the West has made possible a
much higher degree of cooperation with Moscow both in the region and
globally, particularly given the more cautious approach Russia itself has
pursued in the aftermath of its 2008 debacles. This mutual restraint has
facilitated more sustained cooperation, including within the former Soviet
Union. Examples include cooperation to transport supplies to Afghanistan by way of the so-called Northern Distribution Network (NDN)

through the Caucasus and Central Asia, and the adoption of a coordinated response to the instability that rocked Kyrgyzstan in the summer and fall of 2010.

ECONOMICS AND FOREIGN POLICY

Part of the reason Russia under Putin and Medvedev became more effective at pursuing an independent foreign policy was its rapid economic growth following the end of the 1998 financial crisis. At least until the implosion of the Russian stock market a decade later, Russia's leaders no longer felt themselves economically dependent on the West, thanks in particular to persistently high prices for oil and gas. The resultant windfall allowed the Kremlin to pay off its debts to the International Monetary Fund (IMF) and other Western creditors ahead of schedule—while strengthening Russia's hand in dealing with Europe, much of which remains dependent on Russian energy. Moscow consequently felt it had a greater degree of autonomy in foreign affairs and the freedom to engage in balancing against the West where it served Russian interests to do so. Likewise, the onset of a new economic crisis in 2008 forced Russian leaders to confront the limitations of their ambitions, and helped facilitate a new rapprochement with the West and a more restrained pursuit of Russian aims.

One element of the Russian approach to foreign policy particularly characteristic of the Putin-Medvedev years was precisely the increased attention given to economic factors as a component of national power.[71] In a major departure from Soviet days, Russia's leadership has been very explicit about the connection between economic success, prosperity, and the ability to project power in the world. In its last years, the Soviet Union was an economic basket case—"Upper Volta with Rockets," as the *Economist* famously described it in 1988. The Russia of the 1990s was not much better off, particularly after the financial crisis of 1998 derailed Russia's tentative recovery and fed an atmosphere of political upheaval.[72]

Putin was initially appointed prime minister in August 1999 in part to provide new leadership in resolving this financial emergency. As both prime minister and president, Putin has been very cognizant of the importance of the economy for Russian politics and diplomacy, while Medvedev's call to use foreign policy as a tool of modernization is in some ways the culmination of this shift. While Russia's leaders worked during Putin's first years in office to close the gap between their country and the rapidly developing economies of the Far East, an assertive, expensive foreign policy was a luxury Moscow simply could not, in Putin's estimation, afford. This realization set Putin apart not only from many others in the leadership during his first term, but also from members of the Yeltsin-era foreign policy establishment like Primakov, who were much less attuned to the economic and financial elements of their foreign policy.

In contrast, Putin told the Security Council in mid-2006 that "the level of military security depends directly on the pace of economic growth and technological development."[73] Putin's annual addresses to the Federal Assembly (Duma and Federation Council) repeatedly emphasized the importance of social and economic recovery as a prerequisite for the more active foreign policy he and much of Russia's elite favored. In his first such address, in July 2000, Putin warned that "the growing gap between ourselves and the leading states is turning Russia into a Third World country."[74] Likewise, in his final address to parliament, in April 2007, Putin listed his economic accomplishments and told the assembled representatives, "Contemporary Russia, in restoring her economic potential and recognizing her possibilities, is striving for a relationship of equality with all nations."[75]

Putin's government also made conscious policy choices designed to stimulate and harness economic growth for the purpose of enhancing state power, though results were mixed. Despite impressive economic growth for most of Putin's presidency, the Russian economy remained dominated by the extraction and refining of hydrocarbons, and the state increasingly became a major economic player in a way that limited opportunities for private investors. And though Russia benefited from high oil prices during most of Putin's presidency, he left office with the economy still facing significant structural problems, including too many unprofitable factories propped up by state assistance and an underreformed banking sector. Oil and gas production also began leveling off (significant expansion would require massive investment to increase extraction from remote, inaccessible fields in places such as the Barents Sea and the Yamal Peninsula in the Far North), while capital flight remained substantial.[76] Still, Russia's GDP experienced consistent, rapid growth throughout Putin's presidency, reaching 7.6 percent in 2007, his last full year in the Kremlin.

It was Medvedev's fate to become president just as this boom was coming to an end. Much of the world was already tipping into recession when Medvedev replaced Putin in May 2008. The next few months saw the collapse of the U.S. housing bubble and the largest Wall Street panic in generations. Russia's economy was not, as many had argued, decoupled from this turmoil abroad. Nor did the August 2008 war with Georgia and now-Prime Minister Putin's menacing allegation that the Mechel Steel Company was overcharging its Russian customers (setting off fears of a Yukos-style nationalization) soothe foreign investors. During the second half of 2008, Russia's stock market lost more than 90 percent of its value, while the economy soon plunged into a serious recession. For 2009 as a whole, the economy shrank 7.9 percent, foreign direct investment dropped 45 percent, and the government was forced to run a deficit for the first time since 1999 in order to cope with a rise in unemployment and prevent a run on the ruble.[77]

With the global downturn in demand, energy prices also plummeted, as oil declined from a high of $147/bbl in July 2008 to a low of $32/bbl only five months later. Since oil sales account for by far the largest single component of Russian GDP, the rapid plunge in energy prices exposed Russia's vulnerability to events entirely beyond its control. This energy price shock also provided the backdrop for Medvedev to make his case for modernization, the crux of which is overhauling a commodity-driven economy that leaves the country vulnerable to exogenous price swings while doing little to promote indigenous technology and sustainable growth. As Medvedev remarked to a gathering of Russian ambassadors in July 2010, the essence of Russian foreign policy under his watch would therefore be to promote the transition to a high-tech, knowledge-based economy. To succeed, this strategy would require the reversal of many Putin-era initiatives—including liberalizing the investment climate to attract foreign investors (especially in the energy industry), winding down state corporations that crowd out private investment, and ultimately opening up the political system as well.[78]

All of these steps provoked significant resistance from within the Putin-era establishment, which remained concerned both for Russia's international standing and for their own financial positions. While they disagreed about which course to follow, both Medvedev and his opponents agreed that the future shape of Russia's economy would determine whether Russia would succeed in restoring its status as a key pillar of the international order. Either Russia would be open to the liberal, rules-based global economy while maintaining good relations with the Western states that were its principal trading partners and sources of foreign investment, or it would pursue statist autarky with its field of vision largely restricted to the former Soviet Union while holding the outside world largely aloof.

That Russia could afford such debates was in part a testament to how far its economy had come since the nadir of 1998. The Putin-era economic growth bequeathed the state a greater degree of foreign policy autonomy than it had previously enjoyed, especially because Putin took advantage of the improved circumstances accompanying his presidency to reduce Russia's foreign debt and modernize the military. Putin used the boon of higher oil revenues (transferred to the government by way of a windfall tax on high oil prices) to pay off Russia's international debt burden early, reducing foreign leverage over Russian policy. Moscow's debt payments to both the IMF and the Paris Club of sovereign creditors proceeded ahead of schedule; by 2003 Moscow had discharged all of its sovereign debt to the IMF.[79] By the end of Putin's presidency, the country had accumulated foreign reserves totaling over $476 billion, behind only Japan and China internationally (though it was forced to spend several tens of billions of dollars to prop up the economy in the latter part of 2008 and early 2009). Windfall profits from the energy sector also allowed Moscow to establish a massive stabilization fund, designed to cushion the domestic economy against future price shocks as well as to guard against so-called Dutch disease, where capital inflows push up the value of the currency, crowding out investments and raising the price of exports in foreign markets.[80]

In keeping with its view of the world as an arena for Great Power rivalry, Russia also moved to take advantage of its newfound wealth to upgrade the military. The early months of Putin's presidency were marred by the sinking of the *Kursk* submarine, an event that showcased both the decay of the Russian military machine and the president's seemingly poor grasp of military matters. After years of neglect and decline under Yeltsin, who remembered the coup against his predecessor and feared the dangers of a too-powerful military to Russia's democratic experiment, the armed forces became a major beneficiary of state largesse under Putin and Medvedev. Military spending grew steadily throughout the 2000s, doubling from $26 billion in 2000 to more than $53 billion in 2009 (before falling slightly in 2010 in consequence of the recession).[81]

A new procurement plan, announced in February 2011 called for the armed forces to spend more than $650 billion on new equipment over the coming decade, much of it for the navy and air forces. New submarines, frigates, amphibious assault ships, helicopter gunships, and fighter planes would enhance Russia's ability to project power and, by building a credible conventional capability, reduce its dependence on nuclear weapons. Given the chaotic state of the defense industry, many analysts were skeptical that the planned expenditures would have much of an impact on Russia's military effectiveness, but the decision to spend such sums on upgrading the military's power projection capability was itself a signal of the Kremlin's commitment to maintaining an independent global role.[82] (See figure 1.1.)

Despite the Kremlin's efforts to boost military spending, the Russian military remains a shadow of its Soviet-era self, which in turn constrains Moscow's ability to project power, and hence its claim to be a truly global actor. Still, as Putin cautioned in 2006, "We must not repeat the mistakes of the Soviet Union, the mistakes of the Cold War era. . . . We must not solve the problem of military construction at the expense of the development of the economic and social spheres. This is a dead end that will only lead the country to waste its resources."[83] Medvedev's focus on foreign policy as a tool for development has only strengthened this caution.

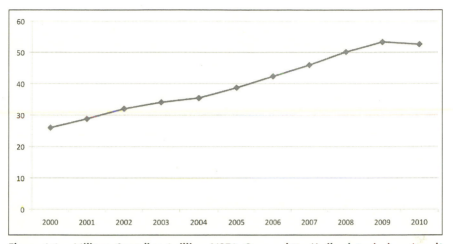

Figure 1.1. Military Spending (million USD). *Source:* http://milexdata.sipri.org/result .php4

Although Russia has largely eschewed integration with Western political institutions, one of its most urgent yet challenging priorities has been to take advantage of economic globalization, particularly by joining the World Trade Organization (WTO). Though Putin generally backed WTO membership, it only became a top priority under Medvedev, both because Russia's exclusion undermines its aspiration to play a leading role in global financial affairs, and in connection with Medvedev's modernization strategy (WTO membership would be especially harmful for the uncompetitive state companies that Medvedev's supporters see as the main impediments to modernization). As of early 2011, Russia remained by far the largest economy outside the WTO, and its exclusion continues to rankle an elite that places great stock in Russia's having a seat at the table in leading global institutions. WTO membership would also force Russia to address many of its problems in areas like contract enforcement and intellectual property rights that Medvedev and his backers argue impede technological development and modernization.

Russia's gradual movement toward WTO accession (negotiations were opened in 1993) seemed to stall in the aftermath of the conflict in Georgia, as several Western countries began rethinking their support, while Moscow itself suspended implementation of a number of agreements that had already been reached. Medvedev made a renewed push for WTO membership, and indeed appeared to be on the verge of reaching an agreement in the summer of 2009 when Moscow suddenly announced that it was putting membership on hold while it pursued a customs union with Belarus and Kazakhstan under the auspices of the Eurasian Economic

Community (EurAsEC). Once the customs union was up and functioning, the three countries would then apply for joint WTO membership (this procedure also implied significant delays, since Russia would only be able to join once the Belarusians and Kazakhs qualified for membership). A few weeks later, Moscow reversed course again, after being informed that WTO rules contained no provision for such a trilateral accession. It was only with the U.S.-Russia "reset" that the perpetual logjam over WTO membership appeared to give way, as the Kremlin effectively browbeat recalcitrant bureaucrats to resolve the issues holding up accession agreements with the U.S. and EU, while the Obama administration also identified Russian WTO membership as a priority in its relationship with Moscow.

Despite Medvedev and even Putin's (intermittent) support for economic integration and WTO membership, economic nationalism remains strong inside Russia. Consolidation of state control over the oil and gas sectors was one of the key ways Putin's Kremlin amassed power at home and exerted influence abroad. Russia's natural resource monopolies Gazprom (which Medvedev chaired before his elevation to the presidency) and, to a lesser degree, Rosneft were tools with which the Kremlin pursued its diplomatic ends through economic means. Putin himself described Gazprom as "a powerful political and economic lever of influence over the rest of the world," and Russian attempts to gain control of downstream assets in Europe and the former Soviet states attest to the reach of this and similar levers.[84] They also provided a steady revenue stream for members of the political elite and a source of large-scale corruption. For this reason, the state-and-resource-dominated economy that emerged in Russia after 2000 underpinned the restoration of authoritarianism under Putin and stands as an impediment to Russia's membership in the WTO.

The Russian government portrayed its reassertion of state control over the economy in terms of rectifying the abuses of the corruption-riddled privatization of the early to mid-1990s. The opening bell in the government's struggle for control of the energy sector was sounded with the campaign to seize control of Yukos in 2003. The seizure of Yukos was part of a larger pattern of state-driven consolidation in the energy sector and other pieces of the economy's "commanding heights."[85] The surge in oil and gas prices following the 2003 U.S. invasion of Iraq drastically increased the value and importance of energy worldwide. The rapid increase in oil prices was a boon in particular to Russia, then the world's second largest oil producer after Saudi Arabia. Not only did oil revenues facilitate Putin's policy of asserting Russia's financial independence, fears of shortages in consuming countries enhanced Russia's diplomatic bargaining power in line with arguments made by Putin and many of his *silovik* backers even in the 1990s.

Seen in this light, the Russian government's campaign against Yukos is of a piece with other attempts to establish control over energy resources for geopolitical purposes. The price wars that broke out between Moscow and a number of former Soviet states (most damagingly with Ukraine) make sense in the context of realizing that control of oil and gas supplies confers greater leverage than possession of unreliable satellite states. Demanding market prices from Kyiv and other post-Soviet capitals allowed Gazprom to realize higher revenues and to sow political chaos in countries seen as turning their backs on Russia.

Nor was control of energy supplies and transit routes merely a regional concern. Before its nationalization, Yukos had been heavily involved in lobbying the Kremlin over the route of a pipeline to supply gas to East Asia and was engaged in discussions with ExxonMobil and Chevron Texaco that would have opened the way for significant Western investment in the Russian energy sector. By seizing control of Yukos, the Kremlin ensured that it would have the final say over the pipeline route and that foreign investors would be prevented from grabbing hold of an industry it considered strategically vital.[86] For similar reasons, the Kremlin blocked attempts by a Chinese oil company to buy a stake in Yukos after its seizure.[87] The Kremlin has also made little secret of its interest in acquiring downstream assets inside Europe as part of its quest for energy security. As a supplier, Russia's definition of energy security focuses on having guaranteed, predictable demand. Its European customers, on the other hand, worry about having a secure supply. These competing perspectives have long been an impediment to an agreed framework for regulating the energy trade.

Still, Moscow's attitude to foreign investment has rarely been straightforward, resulting in a kind of economic schizophrenia. While aggressively keeping foreign investors out of controlling positions in the oil and gas sector, the Kremlin has sought to attract foreign investment and expertise elsewhere. The quest for foreign investment became even more of a priority in the aftermath of the 2008 economic crisis and its attendant capital flight, and with the launching of Medvedev's modernization agenda. Trade and investment also have political consequences. They promote economic interdependence and give business a stake in maintaining good relations. The relative paucity of trade and investment flows is consequently an important factor in the volatility of U.S.-Russian political relations, while Russia's deep economic ties with Germany underpin an increasingly close political relationship between Moscow and Berlin.

The common denominator uniting the closed nationalistic and liberal integrationist strands of Russian economic policy has been the preoccupation with geopolitical power. Controlling its neighbors' access to strategic oil and gas supplies is a blunt form of power, while the wealth generated from foreign investment and through increasing exports (as a result of eventual membership in the WTO) is a subtler but no less important aspect of enhancing the state's strength in order to play a larger geopolitical role. Which approach ultimately prevails will depend on a range of factors, including the long-term trend of oil prices, the outcome of Russia's WTO bid, and the country's political future after 2012. Relations with the West will also have an impact; a more durable political rapprochement will make it easier for supporters of integration to make their case within the Russian political elite.

CONCLUSION

It remains to be seen whether Russia's assertive foreign policy remains viable in the longer term, particularly if Medvedev's campaign to modernize and diversify the economy does not succeed and if Russia fails to adapt to a rapidly shifting world order in which power is increasingly economic, broadly diffused, and based on the ability to generate consensus for multilateral action.[88] To be sure, the preferences of Russia's elites are unlikely to change in any substantial way in the near future. Yet even they are aware that the tightly controlled political system Putin created is increasingly incapable of resolving the economic and social challenges Russia continues to face, and that some kind of political change is— eventually—inevitable.

Compared to the relatively narrow foreign policy elite, the general public is more concerned with bread-and-butter issues and less focused on boosting Russia's status on the world stage. Political change that truly empowers citizens may well result in a less confrontational foreign policy. Such change, however, would require displacing a ruling class that derives significant benefits from the status quo. While change is likely, therefore, it will take time. In the interim, long-established approaches to foreign policy will continue to prevail—particularly if energy prices continue their upward trend, since a new energy boom fueled by a global economic recovery and continued demand growth in East Asia would reduce the pressure on Moscow to move away from its commodity-dependent economic model.

Yet a foreign policy based on the revenues from high energy prices is necessarily hostage to fluctuations in the global energy market, as indeed it was during the Soviet Union's economic boom of the 1970s and the subsequent bust of the 1980s.[89] Moreover, Russia's economy is still inflexible and uncompetitive. Despite increased spending and attempts to reform the outdated system of conscription, the military remains deeply corrupt and inefficient.[90] Xenophobia is rampant and growing, even though Russia's shrinking population will make immigration increasingly important to sustaining economic growth in the coming decades.[91] All of these factors are structural, and will continue to limit Russia's ability to actually pursue the Great Power role its elite desires.

As it stands, Russia's unfavorable demographic situation in particular could limit the country's power projection capabilities over the long term. The population has already declined from 148.7 million people at the start of 1992 to an estimated 142.9 million according to preliminary results of the 2010 census.[92] The decline would have been even more severe if not for large-scale in-migration from the other post-Soviet republics—initially of ethnic Russians who found themselves in a foreign country when the USSR collapsed, and increasingly of non-Russian labor migrants from the Caucasus and Central Asia.[93] High rates of immigration notwithstanding, the decline of the Russian population is among the most severe in percentage terms in history for a country not in the throes of war or famine.

While some of the decline is attributable to couples' reluctance to have children amidst the disastrous economic conditions of the 1990s, other contributing factors appear more intractable. Rates of premature death, especially for Russian men, remain among the highest in the world—largely as a result of lifestyle choices (drunkenness, smoking, poor diet, homicide/suicide). Rates of HIV infection are high and growing, particularly among the country's large number of intravenous drug users. Nor is the demographic decline spread evenly among regions of the country or ethnic groups. On the whole, the birthrate among traditionally Muslim peoples was notably higher during the 1990s—with a range of potential consequences for the social cohesion of a country increasingly roiled by Slavic-Russian nationalism.[94]

These weaknesses are real, and will limit the effects of Russia's attempt to reassert itself globally. At the same time, their impact should not be overstated. Even in its still-troubled state, Russia's military can be used to intimidate and bully neighboring states—as Georgia discovered to its cost—while the possession of a large nuclear arsenal and a permanent seat on the UN Security Council will continue to assure Russia some degree of world power and deference even from Washington and Beijing. The demographic crisis is a more serious impediment, but apart from its impact on the armed forces (which partially in consequences are seeking to move away from conscription), its impact will primarily be regional. Russia's population decline is being felt most in Siberia and the Far East, that is, along the border with China. Managing relations with Beijing will therefore be among the most critical tasks of Russian foreign policy in the next century, and the demographic disparity is only one component of the complex relationship between a relatively diminished Russia and a rapidly growing China.

To the extent that Russia over the past two decades has pursued a consistent, grand strategic approach to foreign policy, that approach has been predicated on seeking the reemergence of Russia as a major power capable of pursuing what it perceives as its national interests in a still-anarchic world order. What exactly it hopes to achieve with that power has often been less clear, and two decades since the Soviet collapse, Russia still lacks a coherent vision of its global aims beyond merely ensuring it has a seat at the table. Of course, following seventy years of Communist messianism and centuries of Orthodox-nationalist messianism before that, the rest of the world might welcome the Kremlin adopting a more restrained vision of its role in the world.[95] Yet unlike its East European neighbors, and unlike Germany and Japan at the end of World War II, Moscow has not embraced integration, collective security, and pooled sovereignty as an alternative, a development that continues to limit the prospects for real integration with Western institutions even as political relations improve.[96]

While Russian foreign policy is global in scope, it also remains constrained by domestic political considerations and the unfolding struggle to define a post-Soviet, postimperial identity. Strengthening the state, the economy, and the military are all prerequisites for Russia's eventually living up to the expansive vision of its role in the world that has emerged in the two decades since the Soviet collapse. Russia's foreign policy long emphasized tactical flexibility and caution as its leaders (including Putin and Medvedev) sought a breathing space to recover the country's strength. This strategy of pursuing global stability and internal regeneration has many precedents in Russian history. It was adopted by Tsar Alexander II and Aleksandr Gorchakov after the Crimean War, and again by Sergey Witte and Pyotr Stolypin following the Russo-Japanese War and the 1905 Revolution. These men and their ideas have been consciously adopted as models by a number of current Russian statesmen who see their own task in equally stark terms.[97]

Gorchakov (whose portrait hangs on the wall of Sergey Lavrov's office at Smolenskaya Ploshchad) termed his approach *sosredotochenie*, "reconcentration," while Stolypin used the term *peredyshka*, or "breath catching." In both cases, the underlying principle was that the country should focus on resolving its domestic problems—such as serfdom and labor unrest—before embarking on an expansive foreign policy. In post-Soviet Russia, too, the scope of the country's domestic problems was such that the kind of global, Great Power foreign policy advocated by Primakov (and much of the Russian elite) was largely unattainable. Still, Yeltsin's Russia tried, even confronting the U.S. directly on a handful of occasions, particularly over Kosovo and Chechnya. The first years of Putin's presidency, by contrast, were marked by a much greater degree of deference to Western initiatives, even ones that the Russian establishment strenuously opposed (such as the inclusion of the Baltic states in NATO).

In contrast to the Gorbachev and Yeltsin-Kozyrev years, however, this deference appears to have resulted less from any basic convergence between Russian and Western policy goals or any attempt to appease the Western powers than from a recognition of Russia's weakened position in the international system and of the need for domestic consolidation. Before the August war and financial crisis of 2008, Russia's leaders seemed to believe that the period of consolidation was over, and that Moscow was again strong enough to stand up to the rest of the world. In subsequent years, Russian leaders have become more circumspect, and the idea of downplaying conflicts with the outside world (especially the West) has again become fashionable. Medvedev in particular has argued that the upheavals of 2008–2010 are not a blip, but indicative of structural weaknesses that Russia must address over the span of a generation or more. Less clear is how widely his diagnosis is shared across the political spectrum, or how much opportunity he will have to push through his ideas for turning Russia into a truly modern country that benefits from close relations with both the advanced democracies of the West and the rapidly developing states of East Asia.

In political science terms, both neorealist and constructivist approaches to international relations have some relevance in explaining the twists and turns of Russia's post-Soviet foreign policy.[98] Neorealists emphasize the existence of international anarchy, where states' behavior is conditioned by the distribution of power among them.[99] A state like Russia that experiences a precipitous decline in relative power (as when the USSR collapsed) would be expected to retract its geopolitical ambitions commensurate with its reduced standing in the world, while a state whose relative power is increasing should pursue a more expansive international role as it tries to assert influence and defend its security. This pattern seems to hold reasonably well for Putin's Russia—seeking security through retrenchment when weak and through assertion when strong—but is less helpful in explaining why Yeltsin's Russia refused to scale back its ambitions in the late 1990s, even as the war in Chechnya and the 1998 financial collapse revealed the depth of Russia's decline.

Here, constructivist theories provide some insight, which is also applicable, albeit in a different way, to the Putin-Medvedev era and beyond. Constructivists emphasize that states' international behavior is above all a function of their self-perception and the identity constructed by their elites.[100] Russia's insistence on acting and being treated like a Great Power remains widely shared among policy makers and thinkers. Politics continues to matter, and Russian foreign policy continues to be determined as much by its leaders' choices and domestic constraints as by objective international factors.[101] While post-Communist Russia has struggled to define itself culturally and politically, there has been much greater agreement about Russia's international role. Russian elites have long viewed their country in Great Power terms, with interests that stretch around the world and with a right to be consulted on a wide variety of international issues that do not necessarily affect Russia's interests in any direct way. Liberals like Kozyrev have been no less forthright than their political foes in propounding the thesis that Russia remains a Great Power whose interests must be taken into account by others, including more powerful states like the U.S.[102]

While this conception of Russia as a Great Power has been critical in setting the course for Russian foreign policy, it does not explain the vacillations and inconsistencies that have characterized that policy since 1991. It is possible to argue, as Andrei Tsygankov does, that these vacillations are the result of different identity coalitions having power at different times over the past decade and a half.[103] To be sure, Kozyrev embodied a radically different set of values than did Primakov or Putin (Medvedev is a more complicated case). Yet one of the key discontinuities in Russia's recent diplomatic history is between the interest in cooperation with the West evinced by Putin in 2001–2002 and the more confrontational attitude adopted by the same Putin a few years later. Moreover, under Kozyrev, Primakov, Putin, and Medvedev—despite a host of other disagreements—officials have not questioned Russia's fundamental identity as an autonomous Great Power and key actor in the international system. Identity and identity coalitions thus do not explain the full range of variation over time, and it is necessary for this reason to turn back to neorealist thinking about power and the search for security.

The consensus surrounding Russia's role as a fully sovereign Great Power is so secure that Medvedev will have little choice but to pursue the creation of a multipolar world dominated by Great Powers pursuing their respective national interests, even if his own approach to foreign policy suggests that Russia should first lay the foundations at home for this broader vision of its activities abroad. Whoever is president following Russia's 2012 presidential election will face a similar set of constraints. His success in carving out a space for Russia to act as one of the world's major powers will therefore be determined above all by Russia's ability to resolve its domestic difficulties and retain the economic capacity to force others to take its concerns seriously.

2

Bulldogs Fighting under the Rug

The Making of Russian Foreign Policy

In any country, establishing precisely who makes foreign policy is difficult. The challenge is even greater in a country like Russia with weak formal institutions and a political system that has been in more or less constant flux for two decades. The collapse of the Soviet Union and the Communist bloc left the Russian Federation awkwardly balanced between its imperial-authoritarian past and what was hoped by many to be a democratic future. Yet even as the Russian political system has evolved under presidents Yeltsin, Putin, and Medvedev, it has failed to develop the sturdy institutions that would lend a degree of regularity to its international behavior. Russia's failure to institutionalize has resulted in a highly centralized ruling apparatus, with enormous power concentrated at the top and few of the constraints that exist in the pluralistic countries of the West such as free elections, a free press, or a loyal opposition. Still, Dmitri Trenin's observation that, despite the centralization and authoritarian tendencies of modern Russia, "the Russian political system rests on the acquiescence of the governed" remains valid.[1] A narrow elite may make foreign policy, but the wider public constrains the range of choices available to that elite.

The centralization of decision making means both that foreign policy in Russia is the preserve of an elite and that the elite itself is smaller and more directly connected to the regime than in the 1990s. Of course, in most countries, foreign policy is the province of a fairly select intellectual and economic elite. Moreover, even in a country as politically regimented as Russia, the elite is far from homogeneous, and various strands of opinion on the nature of Russia's national interest are clearly visible, even within the Kremlin itself. The recentralization of authority that occurred primarily under Putin did not re-create the political structure of the Soviet Union, which, with its ideological underpinnings and rigid *nomenklatura* system of appointments, had a much narrower group of individuals capable of influencing foreign policy.[2]

In institutional terms, foreign policy decision making in contemporary Russia is concentrated inside the presidential administration and, since Putin's move from the Kremlin to the Russian White House, in the office of the prime minister—not, it should be noted, in the Ministry of Foreign Affairs (*Ministerstvo Inostrannykh Del*, MID), the Security Council (*Sovet Bezopasnosti*), or the cabinet. Constitutionally, the presidency completely overshadows the prime minister in the realm of foreign policy. Under the Medvedev-Putin "tandemocracy," however, at least some of the de facto responsibility for foreign policy (particularly within the former Soviet Union) followed Putin to the prime ministership. Putin's ability to carry authority with him in spite of the Russian constitution's clear formulation that the president alone shall "administer the foreign policy of the Russian Federation" is a clear example of the weakness of formal institutions.[3]

Though some of its members are true experts in foreign affairs and occasionally fill diplomatic roles as well, the Russian parliament has never played a major role in the making of foreign policy. The Federation Council (the upper house) was made purely appointive in 2003, and its role has been increasingly subordinated to the presidential administration that is indirectly responsible for choosing its members.[4] Although the lower house, the State Duma, remains elective, the Kremlin's manipulation of the electoral system and political parties has drastically reduced the Duma's ability to act autonomously. With the progovernment United Russia (*Yedinaya Rossiya*) Party controlling 70 percent of the seats in the Duma (315 out of the 450 total as of mid-2011) and dominating election campaigns with the aid of the state's administrative resources, the legislature has become a reliable ally of the Kremlin rather than an independent force.[5]

While theoretically responsible for playing the lead role in defining and implementing foreign policy, the Foreign Ministry has also become rather peripheral in terms of setting a strategic course. Its eclipse stems from a number of sources. Upon becoming foreign minister in 1991, Andrey Kozyrev dismissed many high-ranking officials (including all the deputy ministers) left over from his Soviet predecessor. Among those who remained, most were extremely skeptical of Kozyrev's attempts to build a positive-sum relationship with the United States.[6] At the same time, the Foreign Ministry was not ready for the more pluralistic policy-making environment of the early 1990s. Accustomed to a more hierarchical system, the Foreign Ministry's post-Soviet leadership was caught off guard by the emergence of alternative power centers and ceded much of the initiative to groups such as the military-industrial complex, the Ministry of Defense, and the armed services, as well as large businesses and regional leaders with their own set of foreign policy priorities.[7]

With the strong-willed Yevgeny Primakov as foreign minister and President Yeltsin weakened both personally and politically, the Foreign Ministry became more visible and influential in the late 1990s. Primakov came to embody a consensual approach to foreign affairs that encompassed most of the players in the unfolding foreign policy debate. With the rise to power of Vladimir Putin, the post of foreign minister has been held by men—Igor Ivanov (1998–2004) followed by Sergei Lavrov—from the ranks of career diplomats lacking strong political connections or strongly articulated views about the direction of Russian foreign policy. Thus while it makes sense to speak of a Kozyrev foreign policy or a Primakov foreign policy, one cannot in the same way speak of a Lavrov foreign policy, since Lavrov's role has been principally to implement the concepts developed by his political superiors in the Kremlin. Under both Putin and Medvedev, a few close associates, such as Sergei Ivanov (former chairman of the Security Council, defense minister, and first deputy prime minister), former ambassador to Washington Yury Ushakov, and presidential aide Sergei Prikhodko have been key foreign policy advisers despite not holding ministerial portfolios.

The Security Council, whose importance has ebbed and flowed over time, is mainly a forum for drawing up broad conceptual documents and an advisory group for the president, designed to resolve competing bureaucratic priorities. Under Sergei Ivanov's leadership the Security Council played a key coordinating role within the administration, thanks to the close personal ties between Ivanov and President Putin. A similar dynamic operated under Yeltsin, when the Security Council's importance varied directly with the level of trust its chairman enjoyed with the president.[8] From 2004 to mid-2007, when Igor Ivanov, the technocratic former foreign minister, served as the council's chairman, its foreign policy role was much diminished.[9]

Medvedev's appointment of the *silovik* (i.e., a member of one of the various internal security forces descended from the Soviet-era KGB) and former FSB director Nikolai Patrushev as head of the Security Council, and of retired general staff chairman Gen. Yury Baluevsky as deputy chairman, was interpreted by Russian analysts as an attempt to give the council renewed authority—or alternatively to banish potential rivals to prestigious but irrelevant posts.[10] Ultimately Patrushev did restore the Security Council to a central coordinating role (codified in the National Security Concept which the council released in April 2009), with responsibility for overseeing the work of the entire national security bureaucracy on behalf of the presidential administration and serving as the main forum for strategic planning among the various ministries and commissions working on national security issues.[11] Much as with the National Security Council (NSC) in the United States, the Russian Security Council is thus an adjunct of the presidency more than an independent bureaucratic actor.

The transformation of the Federation Council into a purely appointive institution and the creation of seven super-regions overseen by presidential appointees also deprived regional governors of much of their power, including the power to freelance in foreign policy (until 2000, when they were forced to appoint representatives in their place, regional governors simultaneously served on the Federation Council; following the 2004 Beslan massacre, Putin ended the direct election of governors—today governors are appointed by the Kremlin and in turn they appoint members of the Federation Council).

The state's growing role in the economy has had more mixed results. On the one hand, the nationalization of Yukos (and the example it set) means that the top officials of major companies have become state employees subject to discipline from above.[12] On the other hand, given its size and concentration in strategic industries like energy, the state sector of the economy has become a powerful actor in its own right, potentially acting as a veto player on foreign policy decisions affecting its interests directly; the gas industry in particular retains the ability to frustrate the center's initiatives if its interests are at stake while the protracted nature of Russia's negotiations to enter the World Trade Organization (WTO) owes much to the opposition of state corporations and oligarchs who benefit from Kremlin-backed protectionism.

Despite this success in centralizing the foreign policy decision-making process within the Kremlin, Putin's Russia was not a monolith, and Medvedev's duopolistic Russia is even less so. While the role of the legislature and regional leaders may have been greatly circumscribed, other groups remain important players in the policy process. Two in particular deserve mention: large energy companies and the security services (including the military).[13] The Russian economy's dependence on oil and gas exports for foreign exchange earnings, along with the symbiotic relationship between big business and the state have all limited the government's ability to rein in major corporations such as the natural gas monopoly Gazprom. If nothing else, the "great recession" that began in 2008 at least appears to have curbed the extremes of corporate power, since state behemoths like Gazprom as well as major oligarchic-owned firms such as RosAl (Russian Aluminum, owned by the oligarch Oleg Deripaska) saw their financial position deteriorate and their dependence on state handouts rise.

Still, big business can at times and in certain areas impede the implementation of the government's foreign policy agenda. The directors of inefficient, state-owned companies, especially natural resource monopolies, worked hard to block Russia's WTO ascension, which both Medvedev and Putin identified as a priority.[14] As Gazprom is the country's principal cash cow, it will no doubt continue to exert substantial pressure on foreign policy, though the Kremlin has tried at times to limit its power by replacing its leadership (Aleksey Miller for Rem Vyakhirev) and stocking its board with Kremlin insiders, including Dmitry Medvedev himself, who served as Gazprom's chairman before his elevation to the presidency. As president, Medvedev repeatedly called for scaling back and ultimately dismantling many state corporations, whose outsize influence and access to government funds have proven a drag on Russian competitiveness. In April 2011, Medvedev demanded that high-ranking officials step down from corporate boards in an effort to make business more efficient—in effect recognizing that the symbiosis of the state and business that Putin promoted had become a drag on the economy and a major source of corruption. Coupled with the decline in oligarchic fortunes during the economic crisis, unwinding the state corporations and weakening the link between large firms and the state could do much to curb corporate power over foreign policy, if these reforms are not blocked by the beneficiaries of the essentially corporatist status quo.

The security services are another institution with strong views on foreign policy not entirely subject to Kremlin control. Much of the military command advocates prioritizing the former Soviet Union in Russia's foreign policy and adopting a more confrontational approach toward the United States; the war with Georgia thus found strong backing among this constituency. The debate over Russia's new Military Doctrine, which was finally released in February 2010 after years of delay, is indicative of how the high command understands the world and the threats facing Russia. One notable aspect of the new doctrine is the emphasis it continues to place on state-based threats, and particularly on the danger that continued NATO expansion poses to Russian security. The focus on NATO and the West more generally is in line with the views of the military leadership; former chief of the general staff and later Security Council deputy chair Yury Baluevsky argued that "the struggle for spheres of influence among the developed countries claiming for themselves world and regional leadership" is among the chief destabilizing factors in the post–Cold War world.

These views, however, do not seem to have been widely shared among the civilian leadership in the Kremlin, which has been keen since the end of the war with Georgia to reverse Russia's growing isolation from the developed West (a trend that accelerated with the election of Medvedev and Barack Obama to the presidencies of Russia and the U.S., respectively) and which is fully aware of the security services' repeated failure to prevent catastrophic terrorist attacks inside Russia. Sergey Ivanov, Putin's right-hand man on national security, directly criticized Baluevsky's focus on

state-based threats, claiming that "Russia has no military or political enemies."[15] When the Military Doctrine was finally released, it ended up
splitting the difference between the uniformed and civilian leadership.
The document termed NATO's continued expansion and attempts to assign the alliance a global security function (but not its existence per se)
threats to Russia's security, while also acknowledging that "the spread of
international terrorism" constituted a threat.[16]

Under Putin, the *siloviki* increasingly spread their influence throughout
the state and the economy. While much of their activity has been connected to sewing up lucrative economic fiefdoms, their power cannot but
have an impact on the making of foreign policy. The Soviet-era KGB was
considered something of an intellectual elite (and unusually cosmopoli-
tan in its outlook). To the extent that the foreign policy preferences of
leading *siloviki* can be known, they generally have a strongly Eurasianist,
anti-Western undertone. Igor Sechin, a former military intelligence officer,
Putin's deputy chief of staff, and later deputy prime minister, has long
been reputed to be one of the Kremlin's leading hard-liners.[17]

Under Medvedev, the impact of these ideological preferences has been
diluted by a broadening of the political elite, with various groups of pro-
Western economists, lawyers, and other so-called *civiliki* taking on important positions in the power structure. Yet because much of what passes for
politics inside the Kremlin walls has to do more with securing access to
rents than advocating particular policy positions, pragmatic alliances between hard-line *silovik* and moderately pro-Western *civilik* factions and
individuals are not uncommon.

Some elements of the security services are less ideological—much of the
defense industry, for example, favors improved relations with the West in
large part as a way to open new markets for Russian military technology.[18]
Moreover, given the scale of Russia's military collapse in the years since
the end of the Cold War and the sheer cost of full-scale rearmament, the
newer generation of military leadership has softened to some degree on
the nature of the threat from the West. By downplaying the likelihood of
confrontation with the U.S. or NATO even as the armed forces continue to
focus on the West as the principal threat to the country, the Kremlin has
emphasized economic development as the basis for Russia's international
restoration. Putin and Medvedev's success in downsizing the military (especially the ground forces), along with the extremely bitter debate over
moving toward contract service in place of the draft are good indications
of the struggle among different bureaucratic and ideological factions that
continues behind the façade of Kremlin unity.[19]

Indeed, the cause of military reform has been held back in large part
because of the continuing distrust between the Kremlin's inner circle,
drawn heavily from the nonmilitary components of the national security

bureaucracy (mainly the intelligence services) and the military leadership in the Defense Ministry and General Staff. In early 2007, Sergey Ivanov was promoted to first deputy prime minister and replaced as defense minister by Anatoly Serdyukov, a former furniture salesman and tax inspector with no background in defense issues. It is notable that neither Ivanov, a career intelligence officer and close associate of then-president Putin, nor Serdyukov are from the career military ranks, as Yeltsin's defense ministers had been. The appointment of such complete outsiders signaled how little trust the Kremlin had in the upper ranks of the military.[20]

Serdyukov's role as defense minister has been to preside over a shift to a smaller, more professional, and better armed military—a move that the officer corps has bitterly opposed. The brass's opposition is based on several factors, including the loss of income that would accompany an end to the practice of officers hiring out troops under their command as cheap labor, and the fact that Serdyukov's reform would drastically cut the number of officers in the Russian military (while the reform bill promises that cashiered officers would receive housing and pensions, few are confident that the state will be able to follow through on these promises). Opposition from within the officer corps, as well as a lack of funding, have repeatedly delayed the move to a fully professional military, but with strong backing from both Medvedev and Putin, Serdyukov has retained his position in the face of almost universal opposition from the military leadership. Serdyukov's plan to downsize the military runs counter to the emphasis placed ever since the Napoleonic Wars on a mass conscript army. It would instead create a military designed to fight small wars across the former Soviet Union and address the asymmetric challenges of separatism and terrorism, in the process abandoning Russia's historic claim (in practice already long eroded) to be a global military superpower. The amount of political capital Putin and Medvedev have spent on the military reform—and the extent of opposition to it from within the ranks—testify to the potential impact the reform package could have not just on the Russian military, but on Russian foreign policy more broadly.

The reformers around Serdyukov and the political leadership that continues to back him recognize that Russia no longer has the capacity to act as a geopolitical counterweight to the West, and that a military whose only raison d'être is to fight a pitched battle on the plains of Central Europe cannot cope with the real security challenges Russia faces in the twenty-first century. Yet acknowledging the loss of conventional military superiority to the West is a bitter pill for many Russians to swallow, particularly in light of the widespread belief that Russia must remain a major power in the modern world. The success or failure of the military reform project will therefore say much about whether Russian elites can divorce their Great Power ambitions from traditional military measures of power and recognize that power in the twenty-first century is less dependent than ever on military force.

THE CONSTRAINTS OF MASS OPINION

On balance, the Russian state under Putin and Medvedev has much greater autonomy in foreign affairs than it did during the 1990s, when not only business and the military, but also local governors and the legislature often pursued their own foreign policy agendas. Yeltsin's Kremlin was often completely unable to coordinate the activities of the Security Council, Foreign Ministry, Defense Ministry, and a plethora of short-lived bureaucratic actors (the Foreign Policy Council and Defense Council, created and later abolished by Yeltsin) nominally under the president's control.[21] Yet much of that autonomy remains dependent on the president's ability to balance competing interests and factions within his administration, a task Putin and Medvedev have managed by never identifying too closely with any particular group or clan—though many observers note that competition among the various bureaucratic factions represents the greatest danger to the stability of Russia's hybrid tandemocracy government.

The Kremlin's domination of the foreign policy-making landscape extends to public opinion as well. While it may be true that, even more so than in most Western democracies, foreign policy in Russia is the preserve of a narrow elite, the role of public opinion in setting Russia's external course cannot be entirely discounted. True, with elections to the Duma and for the presidency largely ritualistic, the traditional avenues for the public to influence foreign policy are blocked. Even in the Yeltsin years, though, the Russian public had a low sense of what political scientists term "external efficacy"—or the belief that their preferences can have an impact on public policy.[22] Yet Russia is far from a closed society, and the intensity of debates played out in the media (especially print media and the Internet) reflect the degree to which public opinion is engaged in discussions of foreign policy. Opinion polls show that the public at large continues to have strong preferences on issues of international politics and national security policy—though these often diverge from the views of the political-military elite.

Moreover, even if Russian elections are not entirely free or fair, neither are they completely meaningless as under Communism. So far, at least, the votes in national elections appear to have been fairly tallied (albeit after the authorities have sharply limited which names may appear on the ballot or have access to the media). The outcomes of Russian elections at the federal level therefore offer at least an approximation of public sentiment; in contrast to the Soviet era, ballots are generally cast in secret and overt compulsion to vote a particular way is limited (though voting in some regions, most notably Chechnya, has stronger Soviet overtones). Putin claimed, plausibly enough given his persistently high approval ratings, to base his rule on the consent of the governed; the fact that Medvedev received close to 70 percent of the vote in the March 2008 presidential election allowed him to effectively claim the mantle of public legitimacy from Putin. In mid-2011, despite the lingering impact of Russia's economic crisis, both Putin and Medvedev enjoyed approval ratings above 60 percent.[23]

Even without real elections, maintaining consent requires adhering to at least a minimum level of accord with the sentiments of the public. The public in Russia thus acts as a constraint, limiting the range of policy options the government can adopt—at least in a range of high-visibility policy areas such as relations with the former Soviet republics. The Kremlin makes foreign policy, but it depends on the acquiescence of the public in doing so, and its range of choices is constrained to a certain degree by what the public will accept.

That public opinion does not actually drive foreign policy in Russia can be seen in the divergence between public and elite sentiment and between public opinion and the government's actual policy choices. Repeated polls have shown that, on the whole, Russian public opinion is more isolationist and less confrontational than elite opinion.[24] Typical is a poll taken in October 2008 showing 47 percent of Russians believing that the military should only defend Russian territory, while only 30.4 percent believed it should intervene abroad (see table 2.1).[25]

Thus the elite consensus based on Russia's role as a Great Power does not necessarily hold at the level of public opinion, suggesting that a more democratic Russia with better institutions might embark on a rather different course in the world than the one pursued by the current semiauthoritarian regime.[26] Still, Russian citizens are aware of their government's efforts to enhance Russia's global role and are largely appreciative of the successes the Kremlin has achieved.[27] A majority of Russians believe that their country should be either a superpower or at least one of the ten to fifteen leading world powers—though when asked what being a superpower actually entails, most respondents list high living standards, rather than

Table 2.1 Should the Russian army defend the country on the territory of other nations or should it defend Russia alone on its own territory?

The Russian army should defend a country only on its own territory	46.9%
The Russian army should defend a country on the territory of other nations	30.4
Don't know	22.7

Source: Bashkirova & Partners, http://www.angus-reid.com/polls/34521/russians_reject_armys_intervention_abroad/.

Note: Telephone interviews with 500 Russian adults, conducted in October 2008. Margin of error 3.4 percent.

Table 2.2   In your opinion, what goal should Russia strive for in the twenty-first century?

	2003	2005	2007	2008	2010
Regain superpower status as in Soviet times	34%	34%	34%	37%	33%
Become one of the ten to fifteen most economically developed and politically influential countries in the world	35	38	47	45	42
Achieve leadership in the post-Soviet space	16	14	9	8	8
Russia should not strive for any global role	7	7	5	5	9
Difficult to say	8	7	5	5	8

Source: VTsIOM, 7 Sep 2010, http://wciom.ru/index.php?id=268&uid=13799.
Note: Asked of 1,600 respondents in 140 population centers, August 2010. Margin of error 3.4 percent.

any measure of political or military power, as the main criterion of that status (see table 2.2).[28]

On the whole, the Russian public tends to be less interested in the Great Power ambitions of its leaders and more interested in the quotidian details of everyday life. The public does seem to appreciate the fact that, over the past several years, the country has become more prominent and respected around the world. Yet appreciating what has been accomplished at relatively little cost is not the same as actually demanding a more assertive international posture.

IDEAS AND IDEOLOGIES OF THE ELITE

If public opinion at most sets the bounds of what is acceptable, elite opinions matter more in shaping the state's foreign policy agenda. The overall direction of elite opinion about the scope and content of Russia's national interest has changed substantially since the early 1990s. Calls for full-scale integration with the West, which were a staple of public discourse in the late 1980s and early 1990s, have become rarer. Cooperation with the West (especially on security issues and as a means for promoting modernization) remains important to many Russian leaders, but few elites still believe in using integration with Western institutions as a means of anchoring Russia's domestic political transformation, or in Russia pooling its sovereignty with the democracies of the West. In other words, many Russian leaders—including, it should be noted, both Putin and Medvedev—largely advocate cooperation with the United States and Europe against common threats (such as Islamic terrorism) but do not support the creation of a partnership based on shared values and institutions or actually "joining the West."[29]

Under Medvedev, Moscow has elaborated a new framework governing relations with the West, one that continues to respect Russia's self-proclaimed position as one pole in a multipolar world order but at the same time pursues a high degree of economic integration with Western states and institutions. The watchword for Medvedev's approach is modernization, which in the Russian context means overcoming the country's dependence on energy as the foundation of Russia's economy and international influence. Achieving such economic transformation is not possible, Medvedev and his supporters argue, without access to Western capital and technology, which in turn requires good political relations with the United States and the technologically advanced states of Europe and Asia. At most, these "modernization alliances" represent a half-step toward integration with the West, insofar as they focus almost exclusively on the economic side of the relationship. The major unanswered question is whether economic integration can succeed absent political reform at home, without which deeper political integration with the West will remain limited.

Russia's reluctance to pursue full-scale integration with the West is at least in part the result of the disappointments it experienced in the 1990s, when the perception developed that Russian overtures to the West were not being reciprocated. At the same time, the pervasiveness of Great Power ideology—*derzhavnost'*—in the thinking of Russia's political elites has to do with long-standing traditions of conceptualizing the world and Russia's place in it dating back to the tsarist era. The Russia of 1991, of course, was not a tabula rasa, and the influence of ideologies left over from the Soviet period remains strong today, even if only an extreme fringe would actively seek to restore the Soviet Union as such.

While the notion of Russia as an independent Great Power in an anarchic world has long existed within the elite, the ascension of Primakov to the post of foreign minister in 1996 marked something of a watershed. In constructivist terms, the transition from Kozyrev to Primakov reflected the emergence of a new consensus about Russia's identity as a state and its role in the global system. This identity is characterized by etatism (or *gosudarstvennost'*)—namely the idea that the state should play a leading role in the economic and political life of the country, and that the national interest in foreign policy should be defined in reference to the well-being of the state itself (rather than the protection of its citizens or the provision of global public goods, for instance). This identity also entails an emphasis on power as the principal criterion by which to judge the state's health. *Gosudarstvennost'* and *derzhavnost'* are the two major components of the geopolitical worldview that has predominated among the Russian elite since the 1990s, and in many ways grow out of a much older, even pre-Soviet intellectual tradition. Within that worldview, however, are many shades of emphasis, and it is the interplay among these shades that forms the substance of the Russian foreign policy debate.

The contours of that debate have changed to some extent since the mid-1990s, and have continued evolving since the ascension of Medvedev and the economic crisis that began in 2008. Medvedev's contribution has been to reframe, at least in rhetorical terms, the debate about what it means for Russia to be a Great Power. With his focus on modernization, Medvedev has essentially acknowledged that Russia is not at present on par with the United States (or even China) in terms of its global weight. Only by strengthening the economy, Medvedev argues, will Russia be able to have its voice heard by the other major powers. Moreover, in this formulation, foreign policy itself ought to be a tool for modernization. Economic integration with the United States and Europe is designed precisely to attract Western capital and technology to develop the Russian economy. While Medvedev has argued that the success of Russian foreign policy should be judged solely on "whether it contributes to improving living standards in our country," his conception of modernization is equally about strengthening Russia as an international actor—through enhancing the state's financial power, improving the military, and enhancing social cohesion.[30]

Medvedev's approach has revived a foreign policy debate that, during the latter years of Putin's presidency, had become somewhat stale. Even under Putin though, a spectrum of views continued to exist, despite the Kremlin's success in consolidating the process of decision making.[31] Scholars often identify a number of camps or schools of foreign policy thinking among the Russian elite.[32] While it is no doubt true that a few well-defined ideologies exist (particularly on the extremes), what is striking about the Russian elite is the size of the political spectrum's center and the range of opinions within the general consensus about Russia as a Great Power. During the Putin years, this *derzhavnost'-gosudarstvennost'* consensus was all but ubiquitous, which is one reason Putin's foreign policy generated so little controversy. A range of opinions continues to exist within this geopolitical framework, but the differences are, for the most part, about emphasis or particular policy choices rather than about overall strategy. Even Medvedev's focus on modernization and modernization alliances exists within this broader consensus; the president, after all, does not advocate Russia giving up its ambitions to be a major power with an autonomous global role, even as he seeks more cooperative relations with other major states.

For this reason, while the notion of distinct camps or schools remains a useful heuristic device, given the size and breadth of the mainstream, thinking about the center as a continuum rather than as a series of discontinuous units offers greater insight into the interplay of forces. Many of the most influential foreign policy thinkers and practitioners in Russia do not fit neatly in any of these boxes anyway. Certainly Medvedev, and even Putin, who at the same time tried to reestablish Russian dominance within the CIS and sought a cooperative, at times even close, relationship with the United States, defy easy categorization.

Some of the more salient and visible approaches include extreme Russian ethnonationalism, imperialistic Eurasianism, a kind of centrist *derzhavnost'*, and liberal Atlanticism. Actual policy, especially since the fall of Kozyrev, has been a sometimes uncomfortable balance among these trends.[33] Given the general stability of this consensus, there is reason to think that the foreign policy of early twenty-first-century Russia will look fairly similar for the immediate future. Of course, if Medvedev's push for economic integration, especially with Europe, gains traction, Russia may find itself hard pressed in the future to resist the pull of political integration, and with it, liberalization. That prospect is among the major reasons why Medvedev's still rather modest attempt at revising the foundations of Russian foreign policy remains so controversial within the elite.

Still, Russian foreign policy is for the most part fairly pragmatic and nonideological. Particularly influential is the centrist tendency, which is characterized by an eclectic borrowing of ideas and initiatives from the other, more ideologically coherent camps. Less an ideological movement than an attempt to synthesize the competing priorities of the other camps and an attempt to promote the private interests of certain well-connected officials, a type of centrism has remained the dominant approach since around 1993–1994, precisely because of its success in appealing to a broad constituency among the elite.[34] Within this broad middle, different individuals and groups have different shades of emphasis (Primakov tilted more toward the Eurasianists, for instance) but are united by a shared belief that Russia should play a pivotal role in world affairs, that it should maintain a sphere of influence around its borders, and that a relationship of equals with the other large powers (especially the United States) provides the basic foundation for the country's international behavior. Individuals such as Primakov, and indeed Putin and Medvedev themselves, have in practice largely appealed to a centrist constituency, if only by default.[35]

Russian Nationalism

On one extreme is a loose collection of activists and groups espousing racially tinged Russian nationalism, the most prominent of which has been the Movement Against Illegal Immigration (*Dvizhenie protiv nelegal'noi immigratsii*, DPNI), which, despite its name, has also played an important role in Russia's policy toward its southern neighbors in the CIS.[36] The

DPNI and others in the nationalist camp, including groups such as Slavic Union (*Slavyanskii soyuz*, conveniently abbreviated SS) and Russian National Unity (*Rossiiskoe natsional'noe edinstvo*, RNE) are essentially in favor of a smaller, more homogeneous Russia—in contrast to the "Red-Brown" alliance of the 1990s, when the far right embodied at the time by Vladimir Zhirinovsky's Liberal Democrats advocated an expansionist foreign policy. Rather than promoting integration within the post-Soviet space, the DPNI and its acolytes support a kind of "fortress Russia" mentality—particularly against the Muslim republics in the Caucasus and Central Asia—but also against China, which is rapidly becoming a major source of new immigrants to the Russian Far East and the source of much xenophobic angst along the Russo-Chinese border.

Since their enmity is directed primarily at the former Soviet republics to the south, the nationalists are, in comparison with the Eurasianists, relatively sanguine about the West despite their illiberalism and overt racism. Telling was a rhetorical spat that broke out between the DPNI and the Kremlin-supported Eurasian Union of Youth (*Yevraziskii soyuz molodezhi*, YeSM) after they had jointly participated in a march in St. Petersburg in November 2005. DPNI leader Aleksandr Belov (a nom de guerre from the Russian *belyi*, meaning "white") told journalists that his group had essentially hijacked the march from the Eurasianist group. "We marched against migrants, not against the expansion of Western influence, as YeSM had planned," he said.[37]

The DPNI rapidly became one of Russia's largest mass political organizations, in large part by tapping into a well of discontent and anxiety about the future among the Russian Federation's ethnically Russian population. The group's emphasis has been on combating what it portrays as ethnic gangs (mostly comprising Caucasians and Central Asians) who had allegedly taken over the commercial trade in Russian markets in the late 1990s and early 2000s. As it has become larger and more prominent, the DPNI has increasingly forged ties with far right and neo-Nazi parties across Europe, taking on in the process their hostility to parliamentary democracy, NATO, and the EU.[38]

It was also prominent in the confrontation with Georgia that culminated in the August 2008 war. During the years of tension between Moscow and Tbilisi following the Rose Revolution, the DPNI became one of the loudest proponents of the Kremlin's aggressive tactics targeting not only the Georgian state but members of Russia's Georgian diaspora as well. During the war, the DPNI all but advocated mob violence against the Georgian diaspora.[39] The symbiosis between the DPNI's calls to target ethnic Georgians in Russia and the Kremlin's increasingly heavy-handed campaign of intimidation led to much speculation that the DPNI was in fact a Kremlin creation designed to channel discontent away from the regime and toward a vulnerable ethnic minority.[40] Indeed, the Kremlin appears to have deliberately cultivated a variety of nationalist movements (including the DPNI, the *Rodina* party that took 9 percent of the vote in the 2003 Duma elections, and Zhirinovsky's Liberal Democrats—not to mention the pro-Kremlin youth group *Nashi*, which at one time helped fund the DPNI) in order to channel nationalist sentiment away from still more extreme, more violent far right groups.[41] This attempt to co-opt nationalist sentiment has at times backfired, as when *Rodina* appeared poised to become an independent political force capable of challenging the dominant United Russia party, or when several thousand youths inspired by the DPNI and other groups rampaged through central Moscow in December 2010 following the killing of an ethnic Russian soccer fan by a migrant from the North Caucasus—an event that led the government to outlaw the DPNI even as it sought to assuage nationalist rage by talking of restricting migration to the Russian capital.

While the nationalist camp is not primarily interested in foreign policy, its preferences do have an impact, particularly with regard to countries with substantial numbers of immigrants in Russia (like Georgia) or with significant populations of ethnic Russians. Rampant racism and xenophobia discourage many would-be migrants from moving to Russia, despite the country's demographic problems and labor shortages. Russia's fraught relationship with the Baltic states is also in part the result of attempts to appease nationalist opinion outraged by Latvia and Estonia's treatment of their Russian minorities. Since the Baltic states are now also members of the EU and NATO, Moscow's vigorous campaign on behalf of Russian speakers has broader implications for its relationship with Europe. Moreover, insofar as the illiberalism and racism promoted by groups like the DPNI is incompatible with the fundamental values of the West, the growth of extreme nationalism in Russia is an impediment to closer relations with the U.S. and the EU.

Eurasianism

The worldview generally termed Eurasianism (*Evraziistvo*) has a long pedigree in Russian academic and political circles, dating back in its original incarnation to the years immediately after the Russian Revolution. The meaning and significance of Eurasianism is much debated by scholars of Russian politics and international relations. At the most literal and basic level, Eurasianism simply means the belief that Russia's fundamental identity, and hence foreign policy priorities, are linked to its geographical position at the crossroads between Europe and Asia. Eurasianism ranges from the imperial and aggressive to various attempts at synthesizing the traditional antipodes of Westernizers and Slavophiles into a kind of Third Way.[42]

Eurasianist thinkers of all stripes are fond of employing the language of traditional geopolitics, particularly the theories of Sir Halford Mackinder, who spoke of Eurasia as the world's "Heartland" and the "pivot of history," the control of which would give a country the resources and transportation routes to exercise global dominance.[43] The anti-American strain in much Eurasianist writing also receives a boost from the attention given to traditional geopolitical principles in much American foreign policy writing. Russian strategists of a Eurasianist bent frequently cite former U.S. national security adviser Zbigniew Brzezinski, who has referred to the post–Cold War world as a "grand chessboard," in order to justify their own aggressive impulses.[44]

Extreme Eurasianism (sometimes termed Neo-Eurasianism), associated especially with the ideologist and Moscow State University professor Aleksandr Dugin, is a bizarre, occasionally paranoid philosophy that bears more than a whiff of Nazism.[45] It has roots in a variety of West European antiliberal movements, especially the Franco-Belgian *Nouvelle Droite* (or New Right, a group that encompasses groups like the Le Pens' French National Front and the Flemish nationalist *Vlaams Belang*) and post–World War II West German conservatism. Its pedigree in Russia goes back to a variety of thinkers among the White Russian émigrés of the 1920s and 1930s, who were themselves influenced by the late nineteenth-century pan-Slav movement.[46] Eurasianism in contemporary Russia is in many ways a recipe for the reconstruction of a state looking very much like the USSR, both in terms of frontiers and in terms of its authoritarian political system, which is allegedly the only appropriate one for Eurasia's unique civilization.

At the same time, by virtue of its expansive geographic vision, Eurasianism for the most part rejects the narrow racial focus of groups like the DPNI, though it is equally illiberal. Its proponents advocate a statist version of Russian patriotism in which adherence to their ideas of a great Russian Empire transcends ethnic boundaries. In this essentially Hegelian worldview, the state is the embodiment of the people's characteristics and the focal point of the people's loyalties. Because the Russian state encompasses a wide array of racial, ethnic, and religious groups, most Eurasianists hold that all groups sharing a common Eurasian history and identity are part of the larger Eurasian "super-ethnos," which is more expansive than the DPNI's Russian nation (*russkii narod*). Consequently, Eurasianists see the ethnically based Russian nationalism of the DPNI as a danger to Russia's coherence as a civilization and to its role as a force for integrating the Eurasian landmass. Dugin and others have been sharply critical of the nationalists' role in precipitating violence against other Eurasian peoples, especially the Caucasians, who have become the focal point for the DPNI's campaign against illegal immigrants.[47]

This focus on the Russian state as a force for integrating various ethnicities into a common front does not mean that the Eurasianists are committed to the idea of ethnic or racial tolerance per se. While accepting that the indigenous peoples of Eurasia (Slavs as well as the various Turkic and Finnic inhabitants of central Russia, Siberia, and Central Asia) are constituent parts of a Eurasian "super-ethnos," Dugin and his ilk see a large gap between native Eurasians and the peoples of the West, particularly the Jews, who supposedly are compelled by biological and cultural factors to oppose the Eurasians' communalistic values. Extreme Eurasianism thus combines aspects of Nazi-style biological racism and anti-Semitism with a kind of geographic and cultural determinism lacking among the small-Russia nationalists of the DPNI.

In terms of foreign policy, the more extreme version of Eurasianism essentially sees the West as a direct geopolitical competitor to Russia, much as it was during the Cold War. Adherents of Eurasianism urge Russia to act as the nucleus for a new bloc of states able to stand up to what Col.-Gen. Leonid Ivashov, one of its most outspoken publicists, termed the global "military dictatorship of the United States."[48] The competition between Russia and the West is at times cast in crude racist terms, as in the writings of the philosopher and historian Lev Gumilev, who, with Pyotr Savitsky and others, was responsible for adapting the Eurasianist ideals of the 1920s White émigrés to the circumstances of the disintegrating USSR of the 1980s. Gumilev (son of the well-known Acmeist poets Nikolai Gumilev—executed by the Cheka in 1921—and Anna Akhmatova) charged that the Soviet Union failed because it was a bastardized version of Russian statehood that incorporated the foreign ideology of Marxism and fell under the sway of Jewish leaders who were alien to the Russian national psyche; this scapegoating of the Jews for the failures of the Soviet Union was (and remains) common among a variety of Russian extremist groups. In this way Gumilev imparted the biological-genetic determinism of the Nazis onto the cultural and geographic theorizing of earlier Eurasianist thinkers such as Savitsky.[49]

The most important contemporary Eurasianist thinker though is Dugin, author of *Foundations of Geopolitics* (*Osnovy geopolitiki*), which may be the most widely read work on strategy and foreign policy in post-Communist Russia. Dugin is also a frequent commentator in the Russian media on politics and foreign policy.[50] His underlying message is the need for Russia to reemerge as a great empire, dominating the Eurasian space and challenging the United States and the West more generally for world supremacy. Dugin rejects the historic and cultural legitimacy of all the post-Soviet states except Russia itself and Armenia (a Christian state with a history stretching back thousands of years), believing that for historical, cultural, and geopolitical reasons, they should return to Russian control.

As the pivot between East and West, a restored Russian Empire must, according to Dugin, act as the central component of a broad alliance stretching from Western Europe to Japan. In Dugin's view, constructing a Eurasian empire of this sort requires the reabsorption of states like Ukraine and Kazakhstan into a new Russia that has recommitted itself to the supremacy of the collective over the individual and to the leading role of the Orthodox Church. The emphasis on winning over Europe for an anti-U.S. coalition (a policy Moscow briefly attempted during the period leading to the U.S. invasion of Iraq in 2003) rather than seeing the West as a cohesive bloc is another distinguishing feature of the Eurasianist approach. Such an alliance of European and Asian states is necessary in order to isolate the U.S. Stripped of its connections to Europe and to its major ally in the Far East, the United States' geopolitical position would thus be fatally undermined. As the nerve center for an all-out assault on U.S. global dominance, Dugin even mentions pulling Latin America from under U.S. influence and fomenting unrest within the United States on the basis of racial and economic discontent.[51]

These geopolitical reveries would be little more than armchair philosophizing if not for the close connections Dugin, and the Eurasianist movement more generally, has developed with key figures in the Russian national security bureaucracy. As John B. Dunlop has shown, leading military figures, including Lt.-General Nikolai Klokotov of the General Staff Academy as well as Ivashov, formerly of the Defense Ministry's International Department, participated in the drafting of *Foundations of Geopolitics*, which thus reflects at least in part the thinking of the Russian high command about the nature of the post–Cold War world. Dugin himself served as a consultant to former Federation Council speaker Gennady Seleznev and, more importantly, managed to forge links between his Eurasianist movement and the powerful FSB (*Federal'naya sluzhba bezopasnosti*, Federal Security Service) domestic intelligence agency. Through contacts with well-connected political operator Gleb Pavlovsky and former defense minister Col.-Gen. Igor Rodionov, Dugin also gained access to the inner circle of Putin's Kremlin. As a result of these connections, Dugin played a central role in drafting the 2000 National Security Concept. Many Russian observers also saw Dugin's hand behind the declaration Medvedev gave at the culmination of the 2008 war with Georgia, declaring the post-Soviet space a zone of "privileged interests" for Moscow.[52]

Moreover, Dugin's thirty thousand member International Eurasian Movement (*Mezhdunarodnoe evraziiskoe dvizhenie*, or MED), which has branches in countries from Vietnam to Chile, is funded in part by the Russian Presidential Administration, as well as the Moscow Patriarchate and the Central Spiritual Administration for Russian Muslims.[53] Adherents of the Eurasianist philosophy continue to hold influential positions in the bureaucracy as well as inside the Kremlin itself (examples include Pavlovsky and Sechin).

At times Dugin nonetheless criticized Putin for peddling a lukewarm version of Eurasianism while continuing to pursue good relations with the West—though his overall evaluation of Putin's presidency was largely positive, thanks to Putin's decision to "stop blindly following the West" and reassert Russian power in the post-Soviet space. His appraisal of Medvedev has been much more critical, accusing Putin's technology-loving, seemingly pro-American successor of acting like a "caricature" who has lost his way.[54]

Despite his prominence and connections, Dugin's actual influence on state policy is limited by a recognition that implementing his ideas could have disastrous consequences for Russia. Putin, who at times borrowed from Dugin's rhetorical toolbox, was well aware that Russia had nothing to gain—and much to lose—from an actual confrontation with the West. Medvedev's push to reconcile with the West following the war in Georgia runs directly counter to Dugin's prescription to use the conflict as a template for restoring Russian hegemony throughout the CIS and intensifying the confrontation with the United States. As with the DPNI, the Kremlin's flirtation with Dugin and the MED appears in part driven by a desire to co-opt a potentially dangerous movement to prevent it from becoming a threat to stability at home.

Centrism: Between Eurasia and the West

A combination of the Eurasianists' emphasis on Russia's leading role in the former Soviet space with a desire for productive, nonconfrontational relations with the West is the foundation for the centrist tendency in Russian geopolitical thought and practice. While paying significant attention to the territory of the former USSR, the centrists reject some of the mistier notions of Russia's special identity and civilizational affinities with the peoples of Eurasia.[55] Instead, the centrists have a more traditional conception of Russia's national interests, reject confrontation with the West for its own sake, and merely suggest that Russia pursue a balanced foreign policy that pays as much attention to its interests and obligations in the East as it does to those in the West. In the words of a leading sinologist at the Foreign Ministry's Moscow State Institute for International Relations:

Russians are Europeans who were carried to and left in Asia by history and fate. So conclusions should be made[,] but not the conclusions after exotic Eurasian theories about Asian essence of Russians. It is necessary to understand that Russia's future depends a lot on the relations with Asian neighbors and on Russia's approach to them.[56]

Other thinkers with good connections to the Putin-Medvedev leadership are also supporters of this approach—with Russia as the central pillar of a bloc of states encompassing more or less the frontiers of the Soviet Union, but not necessarily in direct opposition to the United States and Europe. They tend to hold that, while productive relations with the West are essential for Russia's future (particularly its economic future), Moscow cannot neglect the fact that its hinterland is in Asia. Consequently, Russian foreign policy must be active in Asia as well as in Europe, Moscow has a special responsibility for the territory of the CIS, and Russia should never put itself in a position where it must choose between the West and its neighbors to the south and east. Moscow's work on the Iranian nuclear program and decision to sell high-tech weapons to China over Western objections, even while pursuing close cooperation with the Obama administration on missile defense and other sensitive security issues, are manifestations of this multivectoral approach to foreign policy. Other centrists—especially those associated at one time with the Yabloko Party—tilt more toward the West, arguing that while Russia cannot escape its responsibility for upholding order in Eurasia, its long-term interest is in a strategic rapprochement with the liberal Western powers.

Similarly, in an analysis of Russia's foreign policy options following the September 11 attacks and the U.S. decision to invade Iraq, the centrist Council on Foreign and Defense Policy (*Sovet vneshnei i oboronoi politiki*, SVOP) warned against full-scale security integration with the Western powers, a course that would be rejected by a wide range of Russian politicians and would result in Russia's playing a subordinate role to the economically more powerful states of the United States and the European Union. A more realistic alternative, the council argued, was for Russia to press for the formation of a "security alliance of the leading powers" that would continue to respect the distinct interests of each partner.[57] Such a course, which would allow Russia to play an independent role apart from the West, would be more in keeping with the country's unique Eurasian identity. As SVOP head Sergei Karaganov wrote in 1997:

> Russia is returning [to] its historic, Janus-like position—looking east and west simultaneously. Neither Asian, nor European, this middle ground is not mere compromise, it is the authentic Russia.[58]

Despite his belief in Russia's Janus-like identity, Karaganov has also supported improved relations between Russia and the West. In the aftermath of September 11, he called for full-scale cooperation with the West against the common threat of Islamic terrorism.[59] Today, the SVOP continues to favor close relations between Russia and the U.S., even more so than with the EU.[60] This relationship, however, must be a partnership of equals, where the U.S. will have to respect the rights of the other Great Powers, which, in the Russian case, means allowing Moscow to seek further political and economic integration with the other states of the CIS and pursue its own path of political development.[61]

Among the centrists are other thinkers who emphasize the overall importance of the United States and the West generally, even while accepting that Russia must continue to play the leading role in the former Soviet space. A good example is Vladimir Lukin, one of the founders of the Yabloko Party (whose name, meaning "apple," was derived from its three founders' surnames—Grigory Yavlinsky, Yury Boldyrev, and Lukin—hence YABL-oko), former ambassador to Washington, deputy speaker of the Duma, and Russia's human rights ombudsman. Lukin, a committed democrat for whom good relations with the United States is one of the core principles of Russian security, is nonetheless wary about the notion that Russia is essentially a Western country. Shortly after the fall of the Soviet Union, during the high point of Kozyrev's strategy of pursuing Russia's integration with the West, Lukin warned that it was a mistake to ignore Russia's unique identity as a civilization, as he argued many well-meaning Western politicians and academics had done:

> Any attempts to force Russia solely into either Asia or Europe are ultimately futile and dangerous. Not only would they cause a serious geopolitical imbalance, but they would also undermine the historically established social and political equilibrium within Russia itself.[62]

Following the calamity of September 11, Lukin came to increasingly emphasize the importance of close ties between Russia and the major Western powers. Yet he also insisted that rapprochement take place in such a way as to ensure the preservation of Russia's unique attributes as a society. Russia should adopt, Lukin argued, those fundamental European values such as respect for human rights that are not inimical to its own unique identity, and should in time seek to join European structures on a fully equal basis while also seeking close cooperation with the United States. The key to the success of such a strategy, according to Lukin, was for Russia's Western partners to recognize that Russia is in many ways unique. "I am pro-Europe and think Russia should be part of Europe," Lukin wrote, "but not in the sense that Russia should cease being Russia."[63]

This approach also has advocates among the "patriotic" opposition, including now the Communist Party of the Russian Federation (KPRF) and Vladimir Zhirinovsky's Liberal Democratic Party of Russia (LDPR). To be sure, the KPRF and the LDPR both advocated a much more aggressive, confrontational approach to the West in the early 1990s. However, for opposite reasons—in the Communist case to appeal to a broader range of voters, and for the LDPR, to take advantage of the Kremlin's patronage—these groups moved toward a less confrontational position during the

Putin administration. They now argue in favor of a more forward policy in the CIS as a defensive maneuver, a way to protect Russia and its allies against foreign encroachment, rather than as a step toward sparking a confrontation with the West. As KPRF chairman Gennady Zyuganov wrote in 2006:

> Russia is the heir to the Russian Empire and the Soviet Union. The Belovezha Accords [dissolving the USSR in December 1991] were illegal and criminal. Russia must strive intently but peaceably to overturn them, in full accordance with international law and in full agreement with those former republics and territories of the USSR ready for the restoration of a fraternal union with Russia in the framework of a unified statehood.[64]

Understanding the depth and breadth of such sentiment is one key to grasping why Russia has been unable and unwilling to bring itself fully into the Western camp as men like Kozyrev advocated, and why even Medvedev's Russia continues to think of itself as a separate piece of the international order. Medvedev, with his emphasis on using rapprochement with the West as a means of attracting foreign capital and technology to Russia, has not reverted back to the Kozyrev-era strategy of seeking political integration with the West as much as he has sought to create a Russia that is both powerful and respected internationally—much as Lukin and other pro-Western centrists long advocated.

Indeed, the economic crisis that engulfed the first years of Medvedev's presidency gave some momentum to this impulse. While the West remains the source of the technology and investment capital necessary for the success of Medvedev's modernization strategy, the crisis exposed the West's own vulnerability and the shift of economic dynamism to Asia. While modernization in the short run therefore required access to Western capital and technology, in the longer term, it would, as the Foreign Ministry acknowledged in a major 2010 policy review, benefit from more extensive economic ties with the booming East as well.[65] Economic engagement with China and other major Asian economies is particularly important for the development of Siberia and the Far East, which have been condemned by geography and demographics to lag far behind European Russia in development terms and would benefit from Asian investment and the development of transportation links to the booming markets of China and Southeast Asia. Deepening economic ties between the Russian Far East and Asia will of course have political effects as well, but most centrist thinkers are keen to emphasize that Russia cannot develop these ties at the expense of good relations with the West, which in any case remains more important for Russia's overall economic health.

Atlanticism

Even after the fall of Kozyrev and the installation of a new, more state-centric and more Eurasianist foreign policy under Primakov, the influence of pro-Western sentiment remained substantial. This sentiment, associated largely with the liberal Right Cause (*Pravoe Delo*) party and its predecessors (especially the defunct Union of Right Forces, *Soyuz Pravykh Sil* or SPS), some economic officials in Putin's and Medvedev's governments, and a variety of academic specialists, emphasizes above all Russia's need to cooperate with the highly developed countries of the U.S. and Europe as part of an overall strategy of transforming Russia itself into a liberal democratic state and member of the "democratic world community."[66] For the most part, support for integration with the Western world and its institutions is accompanied by support for liberal—that is, democratic and market-oriented—domestic priorities. The connection, of course, lies in the fact that supporters of an Atlanticist foreign policy believe that only adherence to international norms will allow Russia to achieve integration with Western institutions. In this way, the Atlanticists emphasize the similarities rather than the differences between the United States and Europe and believe Russia should cooperate with both more or less equally.

A number of officials with liberal leanings remained in prominent positions even under Putin—especially in positions related to economic policy.[67] Of course, their tenure was rarely secure (some, such as former prime minister Mikhail Kasyanov and economic adviser Andrei Illarionov eventually became outspoken opponents of Putin). Medvedev himself made his name as a prominent economic liberal. His frequent calls during his transition to the presidency for Russia to become a rule-of-law state and to overcome its culture of "legal nihilism" grew out of an understanding that the country would be unable to achieve its full economic, and hence geopolitical, potential as long as investors remained distrustful of Russian institutions.[68]

As president, Medvedev has made Atlanticism respectable again in the upper reaches of the Russian government. Yet Medvedev's Atlanticist credentials are qualified by his continued support for Russia as an independent geopolitical player and the failure of his administration to make good on many of the political and economic reforms it has backed rhetorically (not to mention lingering questions about Medvedev's actual ability to drive Russian foreign policy). Indeed, it is the recognition that without democratization Russia will never be a full partner, much less a member of the West, that sets the true Atlanticists off from those around Medvedev who favor a rapprochement with the U.S. and Europe but are content to leave Russia's political system to evolve independent of foreign policy considerations.

Outside the Kremlin, liberal and Atlanticist ideas remain well represented among the Russian intellectual elite. Intellectual liberalism in its
Russian context is above all defined by its focus on the economic component of foreign policy, its emphasis on good relations with the West (including in some cases support for Russia truly becoming a Western country
with all that implies), and support for democratization at home. These
priorities are fairly consistent throughout the liberal camp, despite the
deep divisions that exist among different liberal thinkers and movements.[69] Former privatization guru Anatoly Chubais, for example, advocated an assertive foreign policy on liberal lines, with a democratic Russia
leading a campaign to unite the world's democracies into a bloc that
would be responsible for upholding order and promoting liberal values
worldwide.[70] Dmitri Trenin of the Carnegie Moscow Center, meanwhile,
favors a Russia that is closely associated with Europe, ultimately joining
European institutions on a fully equal basis. What unites them is a belief
that the era of geoeconomics has replaced the era of geopolitics, that Russia is historically and culturally a European power, and that political democratization at home is necessary both for its own sake and as a means
of tying Russia's fate to the most advanced states of the West.

In contrast with even the softer Eurasianists who would prefer to move
closer to Europe while keeping a respectful distance from the U.S., Atlanticist thinkers tend to focus on both the United States and the European
Union as an essentially unified West that Russia must, eventually, join. In
the Atlanticist narrative, Russia has little choice but to pursue integration
with the network of institutions that collectively make up "Europe" (even
if never formally joining the EU or NATO), on the basis of historical affinities as well as the growing economic linkages between Russia and the
EU. Meanwhile, Atlanticists look toward the United States, a country that
still exists very much within history, as a strategic partner and a model for
the role that a restored Russia can play in the world.

Political figures, many once associated with SPS or Right Cause (including Boris Nemtsov, Leonid Gozman, and Georgy Bovt), and Yeltsin-era
officials such as former prime minister Sergei Kirienko are also prominent
members of the Atlanticist camp. Before his untimely death, Yeltsin's first
acting prime minister Yegor Gaidar particularly emphasized the need for
Russia to moderate its international ambitions on economic grounds, arguing presciently that the record oil prices that fueled Putin's assertive
foreign policy would not last.[71] A handful of major newspapers and web-
sites, particularly those focusing on business and finance such as *Kommersant*, *Vedomosti*, *Gazeta.ru*, *Tochka.ru*, and to a lesser degree *Nezavisimaya
Gazeta*, have also promoted Russia's deepening involvement in the Euro-
Atlantic world.

Russia's Atlanticist foreign policy intellectuals are principally associated with a handful of Moscow-based research institutes and think tanks, including the Carnegie Moscow Center, the Gorbachev Foundation, and the Institute of World Economics and International Relations (*Institut mirovoi ekonomiki i mezhdunarodnykh otnoshenii*, IMEMO) at the Russian Academy of Sciences. Under Medvedev, the Institute of Contemporary Development (*Institut sovremennogo razvitiya*, INSOR) led by the businessman Igor Yurgens has been a major source of Atlanticist foreign policy thinking and has benefited from its close ties to the president. Despite his election to the Russian presidency, Medvedev continues to chair INSOR's advisory board, which also includes leading economic officials, including deputy prime minister Igor Shuvalov and minister of economic development and trade Elvira Nabiullina.

In January 2010, INSOR released a major report on Russia's future that emphasized many of Medvedev's pet themes, including the connection between modernization and security. The report argued not only that Russia had to overcome its dependence on natural resources to fuel its economy, but also that a modern economy could not function without full-scale democratization of Russia's politics and "constructive cooperation with all neighbors and leading global powers." Such cooperation would lay the foundation for increased trade and investment with developed Western countries, while making Russia respected abroad for its economic strength as well as its military might. Most strikingly, the report called for Russia to eventually aspire to full membership in NATO and a close strategic partnership with both the EU and the United States. At the same time, Russia's economic modernization would enhance its "soft power" within the CIS, allowing Moscow to dispense with the need for bluster and threats in its relations with neighboring countries.[72] Of course, INSOR's public statements go well beyond what Medvedev himself has called for, and the basic relationship of the institute to the president's policy remains unclear. While INSOR's recommendation might be trial balloons for major foreign policy shifts, they might also be little more than academic exercises designed to bolster Medvedev's reputation among liberal intellectuals (and the West) with little prospect of implementation.

KREMLIN, INC.

While Medvedev's presidency has reopened a debate about Russian foreign policy that seemed relatively subdued under Putin, the ability of any faction to impose its will remains limited by what may prove to be Putin's most lasting legacy—the state's outsize hold on the economy.[73] The creation of national champions along with the cross-fertilization between the Kremlin's inner circle and the boards of major companies such as Gazprom,

Rosneft, and Transneft has given a new class of officials and managers an extraordinary degree of influence. This bureaucratic-oligarchic elite largely stands outside the ideological debate, instead pressing for policies that merely enhance its own wealth and power. It is also deeply divided, with various factions or "clans" supporting and benefiting from their ties to Putin or Medvedev respectively. While several members of these clans (like the Eurasianist and Putin acolyte Igor Sechin) have strong ideological preferences, self-interest often trumps the more abstract notions of ideology, to the extent that Sechin is reportedly a bitter rival of the equally hardline Eurasianist Viktor Cherkesov, a close adviser to the comparatively liberal Medvedev.[74]

Wealth and power were linked even in the Yeltsin years, as oligarchs like Boris Berezovsky and Vladimir Gusinsky used their riches to buy political access. Under Putin, members of the bureaucratic elite like Sechin, presidential administration economic adviser Arkady Dvorkovich, minister of industry Viktor Khristenko, and Medvedev himself were installed by the Kremlin on the boards of major state-owned enterprises such as Gazprom (Medvedev and German Gref), Rosneft (Sechin), and Transneft (Khristenko, Dvorkovich).[75] Moreover, many of the individuals placed by Putin's Kremlin in key positions in the economy were *siloviki*, and hence also have extensive ties to the security services, which became something of a state within a state under Putin. Medvedev also appointed many of his own colleagues from the legal profession (the *civiliki*) to important positions in the state, the judiciary, and at Gazprom. In the process, he essentially created another bureaucratic clan, or clans, engaged in jockeying for power and resources, even if their instincts on economic and foreign policy questions differ from those of leading *siloviki* such as Sechin.

Putin's Kremlin portrayed the presence of state officials on the boards of corporations such as Gazprom as ensuring that Russia's largest corporations behaved in the public interest, even if one side effect was worsening corruption.[76] Meanwhile, Russia's private sector saw its power and access to leading officials diminish during the Putin years, with the Yukos case being only the most dramatic example of business's reduced influence.[77] To be sure, Putin did not "liquidate the oligarchs as a class" as he had promised to do, and favored businessmen such as Roman Abramovich and Oleg Deripaska continued to have good access to Putin's Kremlin. Yet the economic crisis that savaged Russia beginning in late 2008 did much to reduce the power of the private sector oligarchs, particularly Deripaska, who had to be bailed out by the state after being dressed down by Putin on national television for his plan to close factories in the town of Pikalevo. Medvedev, in contrast, became increasingly convinced that Russia's version of state capitalism was both a drag on Russia's economic growth and potentially a check on his own political ambitions, leading him to call for state officials to step down from corporate boards in April 2011.

The nexus between wealth and power—a situation some analysts have termed "Kremlin, Inc."—means that many well-connected individuals have their own very lucrative fiefdoms to protect. If, to paraphrase Calvin Coolidge, the business of Russia is business, then the philosophical and ideological argument about the relative importance of the West and Eurasia in Russian foreign policy matters less than does ensuring that Russia's commodity reserves continue to bring the state and its servitors as much revenue as possible.[78]

Yet the existence of Kremlin, Inc., does have foreign policy implications, especially insofar as national champions in industries such as shipbuilding, nanotechnology, and other sectors—not to mention energy—have largely crowded out private business. Since these companies' role is more cash cow for management than engine of development, they are for the most part inefficient and uncompetitive on global markets, relying instead on handouts from the state to stay afloat (and to keep workers employed). The prospect of opening Russia to the outside world and exposing these firms to foreign competition could have disastrous consequences for state corporations as well as private firms owned by well-connected oligarchs such as Deripaska, who has consequently been a firm opponent of Russia joining the WTO. The members of Kremlin, Inc., tend to downplay the importance of global economic integration in favor of an essentially autarkic development plan that focuses on the former Soviet Union as a source of raw materials and a more or less captive market for Russian goods. The more Russia remains outside the increasingly global world order, the smaller its stake in the preservation of the status quo.

A foreign policy wholly driven by the narrow economic interests of Kremlin, Inc., is one that would in consequence be largely inimical to the West's aim of maintaining an open, rules-based, liberal international order—another reason it appears incompatible with Medvedev's reform program. Early in his presidency, Medvedev called for turning Moscow into a major global financial center, on par with Shanghai, Dubai, or Hong Kong—a step incompatible with domestic preferences and protectionism. Likewise, Medvedev's emphasis on modernization would require making it easier for uncompetitive companies to fall into bankruptcy, along with easier access for foreign investors. Medvedev himself seems to recognize the extent of the changes to Russia's socioeconomic model that his vision requires, but skepticism about his actual authority and concern that Putin and others will act from behind the scenes to block overly radical reform create uncertainty whether Medvedev will have much lasting success, as do questions about the future of Russia's dual power structure following the presidential elections scheduled for 2012.

THE KREMLIN UNDER PUTIN AND MEDVEDEV

As for Russia's second and third presidents themselves, gauging the influence of different ideologies is difficult. Putin was a bureaucrat and (to a limited extent) a politician, while Medvedev was a lawyer by training; neither is an ideologue as such. The Kremlin has also been, especially since 2004 or so, quite closed and difficult to penetrate. In practical terms, the Putin government gave something to members of each ideological camp—the Russian nationalists got an assault on illegal migrants, especially Georgians, and increased rhetorical concern for ethnic Russians in the Baltics and Central Asia; the Eurasianists got increased military spending and a concerted campaign to bring Ukraine and Georgia back into the Russian orbit following their colored revolutions; and the liberals got a push for Russian membership in the World Trade Organization and a strategic partnership with the United States following the attacks of September 11, 2001. Overall, the Putin government's approach to foreign policy focused on enhancing Russia's power and influence (both within Eurasia and globally) while as much as possible preserving productive working relations with the United States and Europe.

Medvedev has proven slightly more complex. His rhetorical approach to foreign policy has at times sounded suspiciously like that of the repudiated Kozyrev, calling for alliances (of a type) with the leading Western powers and perhaps less fixation on the post-Soviet space.[79] He has also called for radically overhauling the economy, a step that, if implemented, would undermine Kremlin, Inc., and bring Russia more fully into the global economy. Medvedev has gone far beyond Putin in calling for global economic integration and close political partnerships with the West. Yet it was also Medvedev who referred to Russia's zone of privileged interests following the war with Georgia, and who publicly denounced cooperation with Ukraine as long as Viktor Yushchenko remained in power. Medvedev sometimes sounds like a true-believing Atlanticist, while at others he comes across as a nationalist firebrand to rival Putin.

Unlike Putin for most of his presidency, Medvedev does not appear to exercise anything like complete control over the Russian ship of state. Not only does he have to contend with the corruption and inertia of much of the bureaucracy, his own complicated relationship to Putin limits his authority in practice, even on foreign policy where the Russian constitution assigns the president a dominant role. Putin, who left the Kremlin as relations with the West reached their post-1991 nadir, is associated in the public mind (both in Russia and abroad) with a different style of foreign policy than that heralded by Medvedev's invocation of modernization alliances. As prime minister, Putin's approval ratings generally outstrip those of Medvedev, and the perception among most observers both at home and abroad is that Putin's voice is still decisive. Speculation that Putin will seek to return to the Kremlin in 2012, pushing Medvedev aside, further weakens Medvedev's claim to be the authoritative voice of Russian foreign policy.

Still, Putin and Medvedev have mostly appeared to be on the same page when it comes to foreign policy. One seemingly significant quarrel broke out in the spring of 2011 when Putin compared the West's invocation of humanitarian motives in its bombing of Libya to a "medieval crusade," a remark Medvedev pointedly deemed unacceptable. This quarrel was more about Russia's long-standing opposition to the U.S. and its allies deploying military power abroad in situations not affecting international peace and security, and the question of whether the U.S.-Russia reset had changed the impact of such deployments on Russian interests. Most disagreements that have emerged though have centered on the organization of Russia's economy and its position in the world. Putin was a leading proponent of national champions in so-called strategic sectors of the economy, essentially walling off large parts of the economy from foreign investment while using the Kremlin's control of oil and gas supplies as a tool of foreign policy. Medvedev in contrast has emphasized the need for Russia to attract more foreign investment to fund modernization, and has called for dismantling the state-owned behemoths created under Putin.

Similarly, the two men have often appeared to differ on the question of Russia's membership in the WTO. Though Putin spoke of WTO membership as a priority during his presidency, in his capacity as prime minister Putin announced in June 2009 that Moscow would only join the organization as part of a customs union with Belarus and Kazakhstan—even though no precedent for such a joint membership existed and even though Belarus and Kazakhstan were much farther from meeting the criteria for membership than Russia itself. Putin's announcement directly undercut assurances Medvedev had given just days before that Russia was on track to join the trade body. A month later, Medvedev repudiated Putin's stance, announcing that Russia would join the WTO independently, but in parallel with Belarus and Kazakhstan. Some observers saw the confusion as the result of a struggle between Putin and Medvedev—or at least their supporters.[80] Another possibility is that Moscow simply backtracked when it realized that joining the WTO as part of a customs union was unworkable in practice.[81]

To get a sense of the Putin-Medvedev team's "official" ideology, it is also helpful to look briefly at the pronouncements of the man often referred to as the Kremlin's ideologist, Vladislav Surkov. While Surkov has long been close to Putin, who first brought him to prominence, his pronouncements on foreign policy in particular have typically supported the modernizing, moderately pro-Western course now publicly associated with Medvedev

(Medvedev became Putin's chief of staff in 2003; Surkov was at the time deputy chief of staff).[82]

Surkov's main contribution has been in providing a relatively consistent theoretical underpinning for both Putin's efforts at consolidation and Medvedev's modernization agenda, on whose behalf Surkov has been one of the principal mouthpieces. The crux of Surkov's argument is that at the end of the day, Russia can only rely on itself, and must therefore be strong and unified enough to look out for its interests in a rapidly changing world. According to Surkov, in order for Russia to be a truly sovereign state, capable of standing up for its own interest in the world, it cannot be under the influence of foreign companies, foreign investors, or foreign NGOs—and its native elite has to come to regard itself as intrinsically Russian. As part of this process, Surkov argued during the Putin years that Russia had to regain control over its most valuable strategic resources, namely its oil and gas reserves, from foreign companies that acquired stakes in them for a song when Russia was desperate for foreign cash in the mid-1990s (interestingly, Surkov worked for Yukos's now-exiled chairman Leonid Nevzlin in the mid-1990s).

Yet Surkov has also been a leading ideologist of modernization, and his views appear to have informed much of Medvedev's own rhetoric on the subject, especially on the link between economic modernization and state power. Once again, his emphasis is on ensuring that Russia can stand on its own feet internationally. Establishing control of Russia's natural resources was the first step; with that achieved, Surkov began propounding the notion that oil and gas were not enough to keep Russia in the first rank of major powers. Instead, Surkov argued that Russia had to be competitive with leading powers such as the U.S. and China, especially in those fields where mastery has allowed Washington and Beijing to pull ahead of other countries: information technology, communications, nanotechnology, and so on. Surkov's vision of modernization remains a heavily statist, top-down process in which the Kremlin plays the leading role in setting priorities and marshalling resources. Surkov is not hostile to the private sector or civil society as such, but he argues that at Russia's current stage of development, the state must remain in the lead to prevent the upheavals associated with modernization from sowing chaos.[83]

Surkov's belief in the reassertion of Kremlin authority is driven by a desire to enhance Russia's international standing and ability to stand up for its interests on the global stage. These interests are not necessarily those of the West, but nor are they driven by the Eurasianists' inveterate hostility to the West. Eurasianist thinkers like Dugin, who have similarly supported the idea of a foreign policy that emphasizes Russia as a sovereign power, focus on sovereignty as the factor necessary for balancing against the U.S. For Surkov and his supporters in the Kremlin, however, sovereignty is more about allowing the Kremlin to have freedom of action—supporting or opposing Washington as Russian national interest dictates without allowing international institutions or norms to act as constraints. Since the West remains the main repository of wealth and technology that Russia needs to effect its own modernization, Surkov largely supports good relations with the U.S. and Europe, precisely as Medvedev's notion of modernization alliances emphasizes (along with Obama's top adviser on Russia, Michael McFaul, Surkov cochairs the civil society working group within the U.S.-Russia Bilateral Presidential Commission). The problem with the West, from Surkov's point of view, is not that it is incorrigibly hostile to Russian interests, but that its interests are not Russia's (in this view, Surkov has much in common with some of the more moderate Eurasianists).

Ideology, of course, is far from the only factor driving Russian foreign policy, which at times seems far too confusing and contradictory to admit of simple ideological explanations. Certainly, given the existence of Kremlin, Inc., the naked pursuit of profit cannot be dismissed as a factor motivating Russian foreign policy either. Nonetheless, ideas about the nature of the world continue to matter in a fundamental way. Given the influence of Eurasianist thinking in many parts of the Russian national security bureaucracy (including among *siloviki* such as Sechin) and the general consensus of *derzhavnost'* and *gosudarstvennost'*, actual policy often seems to follow Eurasianist prescriptions, especially within the borders of the CIS.

The war in Georgia in particular exposed the limits of the corporatist de-ideologizing of foreign policy. The economic impact of the war was severe, with the Russian stock market getting pummeled by investors suddenly worried that Russia had become a force for regional instability. Between May and September 2008, Russia's benchmark RTS index lost over 46 percent of its value, a decline of $700 billion on paper, and following the war, trading had to be shut down for several days in mid-September to prevent a complete collapse.[84] The rest of 2008 was no better.

To be sure, Russia could stand to benefit economically in the long run if the instability in the South Caucasus ends up shelving Western plans for an energy corridor bypassing Russia. By dramatically heightening the perception of political and economic risk, the war and its aftermath greatly complicated this strategy. Still, if Russian foreign policy were only about making money, the war would never have happened or would have been completely wound down as soon as the financial consequences for the country and its elite became clear (given the concentration of wealth in Russia and lack of widespread investment in securities, the brunt of the initial economic plunge fell on members of the elite, including a number of oligarchs with close Kremlin connections, most notably Deripaska). The war seemed much more about Russia's long-standing interest in controlling a sphere of influence around its borders and sending a message to the Western powers about its renewed capabilities. Indeed, it was Eurasianists in the military and security services, not Kremlin-connected magnates, who appeared to be the driving force behind the conflict.

At the same time, the relatively nonconfrontational approach Putin typically tried to adopt with regard to the United States (not to mention the emphasis on outright rapprochement pursued by Medvedev) is indicative of the fact that the broader influence of Eurasianists is limited. Rhetorically, Medvedev took up Putin's definition of Russia as a fundamentally Western country, telling an audience in Berlin in June 2008 that "the end of the Cold War created conditions for building truly equal cooperation among Russia, the European Union, and North America as three branches of European civilization."[85] Even Medvedev's controversial proposal for a Euro-Atlantic collective security organization was likewise predicated on the notion of Russia belonging fundamentally inside Europe and in the West.

Putin gave contradictory utterances about Russia's location in the West/ Europe or Eurasia (of course, the former Russian president's ability to tailor the message to the audience was hardly limited to this issue).[86] In 2000 at the Asia Pacific Economic Cooperation (APEC) summit in Brunei, Putin declared, "Russia always felt itself a Eurasian country."[87] In his 2005 address to the Federal Assembly, he simultaneously spoke of Russia's "civilizing mission on the Eurasian continent" and his conviction that Russia "was, is, and always will be a leading European nation."[88] On other and more frequent occasions, Putin made reference to Russia's European identity. In his 2003 annual address, Putin said that integration with Europe "is our historical choice."[89] In his first meeting with U.S. secretary of state Madeleine Albright (two years before September 11, 2001), Putin "categorically insisted" that Russia was part of the West.[90]

Putin and Medvedev also pursued a rather active policy in Asia, and in doing so sought to emphasize the commonalities and shared interests between Russia and major Asian states like China, India, and Iran. Where Putin—and especially Medvedev—departed from the true Eurasianists was in the search for cooperation with the United States, even within the territory of Eurasia (e.g., in dealing with threats emanating from Afghanistan).[91] Despite the heated rhetoric that the war in Georgia generated, even then Moscow remained officially committed to partnership with the Western powers—as long as they accepted Russia's claim to a sphere of influence that included Georgia.

Equally important, Putin and Medvedev's focus on raising Russians' standard of living through economic growth was somewhat at odds with the Eurasianists' emphasis on traditional "hard" measures of security and autarky. The emphasis on economic integration (e.g., joining the WTO, signing trade agreements with Europe) is directly counter to the Eurasianists' call for regional consolidation within the CIS and rejection of the global capitalist order.[92] Moscow continues to pursue an Atlanticist, integrationist economic policy at the global level, while trying to uphold the Eurasianists' preference for creating a zone of Russian geopolitical influence across the territory of the former USSR.[93]

CONCLUSION

Foreign policy under Putin achieved a kind of balance between the prescriptions of the Eurasianists and the Atlanticists, while Medvedev has tried dragging the country in a more Atlanticist direction without repeating Kozyrev's (and Gorbachev's) mistake of outstripping domestic support for such a shift. Like Gorbachev, Medvedev is not a rebel, but a creature of the system that brought him to power. Moreover, he seemingly shares Gorbachev's recognition that that system he inherited is incapable of coping with the external challenges Russia faces. Medvedev is no doubt aware of the reasons for Gorbachev and Kozyrev's failures. Both underestimated the depth of opposition that their policies generated, not least from among those in the security services who thought they were abandoning Russia's traditional claim to major power status and its ability to stand up for its interests. In this context, Putin in his capacity as prime minister provides Medvedev a degree of political cover that Gorbachev and Kozyrev lacked. Even though Putin's own legacy is more nuanced than is often realized, his stature among the security services and with most of the Eurasianists insulates him from the criticism that drove both Gorbachev and Kozyrev from office.

Eurasianism meanwhile remains an important undercurrent in Russian political life, but it is far from the major organizing principle of Russian foreign policy. True, the Kremlin has attempted, at times quite forcefully, to limit the foreign policy autonomy of states like Ukraine and Georgia, but even within the CIS it has pursued a rather narrowly defined national interest rather than any expansive vision of imperial restoration, as evidenced by its refusal to continue providing gas subsidies to close ally Belarus or to seek the annexation of South Ossetia and Abkhazia. Empire is expensive, and the Soviet Union's need to subsidize its allies and dependents around the world proved to be a major strain on the state's budget. The economic crisis that attended the first few years of Medvedev's presidency only reinforced that tendency, as Russia cut back on its financial commitments even to other countries inside the CIS, while actively seeking to attract foreign investment and even returning to international bond markets after paying down all of its foreign debt during the Putin years.

The August 2008 Georgian war was no doubt a Eurasianist venture, despite Moscow's unwillingness to annex South Ossetia or Abkhazia as the first step in a plan of imperial restoration. Its timing was also significant, coming less than three months after Medvedev took office and while the functioning of the Putin-Medvedev tandemocracy was still being worked out. Medvedev came into office publicly favoring an improvement to the frigid relationship between Moscow and Tbilisi.[94] When the war started following Georgian president Mikheil Saakashvili's ill-advised attempt to seize the breakaway regions by force, Medvedev initially spoke of the conflict's limited nature and Russia's willingness to abide by a ceasefire negotiated by French president Nicolas Sarkozy (Putin, in contrast, flew to the combat zone and made a show of directing the troops in the field). Over time, Medvedev's statements became more menacing, laced with the kind of rough language for which Putin was famous, referring, for instance, to Saakashvili as a "political corpse" whom the West should jettison.[95]

The strange evolution of Medvedev's role during the crisis hints at the jockeying for influence taking place below the surface of Russian politics. It is doubtful the war was Medvedev's brainchild. Putin's own role in the crisis is no clearer, although his personal antipathy for Saakashvili was long known. Without a doubt, an aggressive streak of Eurasianism and nostalgia for the Soviet Union exists among many members of the Russian military and security services. It appears that these groups took advantage of Medvedev's uncertain grip on power (plus Saakashvili's poor judgment) to precipitate a crisis and leave the new Russian president little choice but to be the instrument of their aims.

Even if they succeeded in precipitating a war with Tbilisi, the Eurasianists' emphasis on the CIS as Russia's natural sphere of influence at the expense of relations with the West is somewhat unrealistic, as the postwar economic crisis showed. Despite its chastening experiences in Iraq and Afghanistan—not to mention the post-2008 economic crisis—the United States remains the most powerful state in the world, while Europe is crucial for the Russian economy. Russia's ability to achieve its goals of economic modernization and geopolitical influence cannot be attained without the development of close relations with both.

With his focus on economic integration and geopolitical aloofness, Putin seemed to be charting a course between a moderate version of Eurasianism and the more liberal Westernism of the early 1990s. Though the basic assumptions underlying Russian foreign policy have not much changed since Medvedev took over, the international context has, as Russia has lost some of the hubris that allowed it to shrug off outside criticism during the economic boom of the Putin years. Strengthening Russia as a major international player, pursuing a dominant position inside the CIS, and seeking pragmatic cooperation with the West is a course whose very expansiveness ensures its acceptance by the majority of influential political actors. To be sure, controversies will arise. In the aftermath of the Georgian conflict, relations with the other CIS states, especially those still burdened by "frozen conflicts" left over from the collapse of the Soviet Union, will be a prime source of discord. Their own economic difficulties have already opened them up to foreign influence, from both the West and the East (China has become a major player in Central Asia and even provided a loan to the Moldovan government when Moscow could not come up with the funds in the depths of the crisis).

Relations with the United States will, as always, also remain a prime subject for debate. For all his talk of Russia becoming a Great Power and looking out for its own interests internationally, Putin on the whole pursued cooperation with the U.S. to a significant degree. Whether offering a strategic partnership and the right to base troops in the CIS following September 11 or calmly swallowing American withdrawal from the ABM Treaty, the Putin administration was about as pro-American as a Russian government could have afforded to be, given the political configuration then prevailing in Moscow. When Moscow started to believe that the U.S. was taking advantage of this accommodating attitude to strengthen its own position relative to Russia, it began pushing back, culminating in its invasion of U.S. ally Georgia in August 2008. As U.S.-Russian relations improved in the context of the Obama-Medvedev reset, which provided Russia the recognition and seat at the table for which it had long clamored, cooperation between the two countries rapidly expanded into new areas, including sensitive ones such as missile defense and security assistance in Central Asia.

The legacy of the war and the economic crisis, though, gave ammunition to Medvedev and his allies to argue that Moscow overreached. Energy-fueled autarky, in their view, was proven inadequate as a basis for restoring Russia's global significance. In a networked, economically integrated twenty-first-century world, Russia needs new tools for getting what it wants. Above all, they argue, it needs a cutting-edge economy that will both bolster its ability to project "hard" power and restore the "soft" power that it lost with the collapse of Communism and the jettisoning of Marxism-Leninism. The Russia they seek is still one that is powerful and influential in the world. They recognize however that the nature of power and influence themselves have evolved since the Cold War, and that Russia too must evolve—or risk being left behind in a rapidly changing world.

3

Resetting Expectations

Russia and the United States

After decades of nuclear-tipped animosity, the end of the Cold War ushered in a previously unthinkable level of cooperation between Washington and Moscow. During the first years of the 1990s, the former rivals worked together to reverse Saddam Hussein's occupation of Kuwait, facilitate German reunification, dismantle the Soviet occupation of Eastern Europe, and secure the collapsed USSR's nuclear arsenal. The prospect of an enduring U.S.-Russian partnership was at the heart of U.S. president George H. W. Bush's vision of a "new world order" and Soviet leader Mikhail Gorbachev's invocation of a common security community stretching from Vancouver to Vladivostok. Yet the partnership to which both sides aspired in 1990–1991 unraveled with remarkable rapidity thereafter, leaving behind feelings of bitterness in both Moscow and Washington that only compounded the mistrust inherited from the Cold War era.

This rapid shift between expectation and disappointment has been a frequent theme in post–Cold War U.S.-Russian relations. As in the early 1990s, a close partnership between the United States and Russia emerged as one of the first, unexpected, fruits of the September 11, 2001, terrorist attacks, as Moscow rallied behind Washington in the unfolding "global war on terror" and provided significant assistance in the fight against the Taliban. Once again, it appeared that the U.S.-Russian rivalry that had darkened much of the twentieth century would be replaced in the twenty-

Adapted from Jeffrey Mankoff, "Russian Foreign Policy and the United States After Putin," *Problems of Post-Communism*, 55, 4 (July–August 2008): 42–51. Copyright © 2008 by M. E. Sharpe, Inc. Used by permission.

first with enduring cooperation between the world's largest nuclear powers. Yet just two years after 9/11, the relationship again descended into
confrontation as U.S. troops marched into Iraq over howls of protest from
Moscow (and other European capitals) while Russian president Vladimir
Putin was busy reversing much of the cautious liberalization that had
taken hold in Russia over the previous decade and increasingly intimidating Russian neighbors. By the time pro-American leaders rode waves of
popular discontent to power in Georgia and Ukraine in 2004–2005, talk
of partnership between the United States and Russia had been replaced by
fears of a new Cold War, fears that reached a new level of intensity when
Russian troops marched into U.S.-allied Georgia in August 2008.

The war in Georgia brought U.S.-Russian relations to their lowest point
since the collapse of the Soviet Union. Only months later, however, following presidential transitions in both countries, Washington extended
an olive branch (or a reset button) that new Russian president Dmitry
Medvedev eagerly seized. With this "reset" in bilateral ties, U.S.-Russian
relations entered an extremely productive period, filled with accomplishments in fields from arms control to economic cooperation to collaboration against transnational threats. The rapid improvement was further
evidence that U.S.-Russian relations are not based on a common strategic
outlook; rather, they remain largely transactional.

The success of the reset, consequently, did not banish fears that the new
era of U.S.-Russian cooperation remained dependent on a particular con-
junction of personalities and events in both countries, and was therefore
subject to reversal—much like the periods of reconciliation in the early
1990s and after the 9/11 attacks. While the United States and Russia may
have again become partners after 2008, their partnership remained fundamentally different from that between the United States and close allies
such as the UK or Japan. The difference is partially due to the continuing
legacy of the Cold War and the mistrust it spawned in both countries, but
is also connected to Russia's distinct role in global politics. As a country
that has not abandoned its claims to play an autonomous role on the
world stage and with a fundamentally different set of political and social
values, Russia continues to view itself as a (near) peer of the United States
whose ties with Washington are governed by calculations of national interest—rather than by the commitment to shared values and collective
security that binds Washington to London or Tokyo. Consequently, while
Russian leaders (including Putin and Medvedev) have generally viewed
cooperation with the United States as desirable, they do not see a U.S.-
Russian partnership as their only option.

Moreover, the popular narratives about the end of the Cold War that
prevail in the United States and Russia are strikingly different, leading to
a gap in perceptions about the nature of the threats the two countries face

in the modern world. Americans have long tended to see the end of the Cold War as a triumph of the U.S. political and economic system that justified the expansion of U.S. power into areas formerly subject to the defeated Soviet empire. In this view, as a defeated power, Russia should accommodate itself to the new, U.S.-dominated global order as its one-time East European satellites did by embracing democracy and reorienting its foreign policy toward confronting the transnational threats of the twenty-first century such as climate change, Islamic extremism, and pandemic disease (as well as the challenge of a rising China) rather than remaining obsessed with allegedly old-fashioned notions like geopolitics and spheres of influence.

Successive U.S. administrations have consequently been wary of going too far down the road toward an institutionalized partnership (rather than sporadic cooperation on issues of common interest) as long as Russia remained an outlier to the post–Cold War wave of democratization and collective security that swept the former Eastern bloc and is increasingly being felt in Asia, Latin America, and even the Middle East. The Obama administration's reset policy appears different in this regard precisely because it accepts Russia as it is—not a country in transition toward the Western political model or membership in Western security institutions, but as something sui generis that nevertheless remains vital to U.S. security interests around the world. At the same time, the Obama administration continues to stress the long-term goal of a more durable partnership, but without sacrificing the opportunity for more immediate cooperation based on the transactional logic that has long governed U.S.-Russian relations.[1]

The Russian narrative, unsurprisingly, is rather different, and this different understanding of the recent past has profound consequences for present-day U.S.-Russian relations. Russians do not generally speak of their "defeat" in the Cold War, and many resent the implication that Russia should merely become a junior partner of the United States in a post–Cold War world centered on Washington. Despite the Soviet collapse and the turmoil of the 1990s, Russia remains a major power. Its Putin-era economic recovery sustained the belief that Russia should remain an autonomous international player, and while the post-2008 economic crisis has reopened a discussion about what, precisely, autonomy and power mean in the modern world, it did not weaken the widespread belief that Russia must be more than merely an appendage to a U.S.-dominated world order. Moreover, Russian analysts argue that, as a postimperial power with a combination of instability and rising states around its borders, Russia confronts many traditional security challenges that remain alien to the United States—even though some threats, like terrorism, affect both.

Diverging narratives are not the only cause of difficulties in the U.S.-Russian relationship. As Russia has recovered from the weakness and chaos of the 1990s, it has been increasingly capable of pursuing the independent, Great Power role to which its elites continue to aspire. This more powerful Russia has been less dependent on the United States and more willing to stand up for what it perceives as its own interests—interests that do not always coincide with those of the United States or the West more broadly. Insofar as Russia has rejected the German–Japanese–East European model of trading autonomy on the global stage for inclusion in a U.S.-led collective security mechanism, its recovery and rise have made it a more difficult partner for the United States. While it remained weak, Russia saw a special partnership with the United States as the most effective route to power and influence in the world, while the stronger Russia that emerged in the 2000s developed a greater capacity to act autonomously and felt itself less in need of a United States that never seemed to take Russia's interests seriously anyway. Or, as the Russian Ministry of Foreign Affairs put it in a 2007 report, crises in the relationship emerge when "the Americans embark on a quest to build [relations with Russia] on the basis of a leader and a follower."[2]

Another challenge remains the difference between Russia's importance for the United States and the United States' importance for Russia. While the United States remains the central reference point for Russian foreign policy, Russia is no longer the main preoccupation of U.S. policy makers and diplomats. The collapse of the Soviet Union, along with the emergence of new threats like international terrorism and an increasingly powerful China, have all contributed to Russia's eclipse as the United States' top foreign policy priority.[3] This demotion continues to rankle many Russian leaders, for whom acceptance of a subordinate international role seems out of keeping with Russia's superpower legacy and Great Power aspirations.

Failure to formulate a new agenda for the relationship or an overarching framework in place of bipolar confrontation and containment has also contributed to the mutual disappointment. Even though the Cold War is over, U.S.-Russian relations remain dominated by "hard" security issues such as strategic arms control and the geopolitics of energy pipelines. Economic and institutional links between the two countries are sparse; when Russia has been an American ally, as in Afghanistan, it has done so only as part of an ad hoc "coalition of the willing."[4] For most of the post–Cold War era, the United States has been reluctant to seek deeper integration with a Russia that had not appeared to shed all the vestiges of empire, preferring to wait for Russia to move further down the path toward its own "end of history" moment. The paucity of economic linkages between the two countries, meanwhile, has deprived the relationship of stakeholders with an interest in better political relations. This overall lack of institutional ballast has made U.S.-Russian relations vulnerable to political shifts in either country. Without deep societal or economic connections, few people outside political-diplomatic-academic circles have a stake in maintaining good U.S.-Russian relations.

Nonetheless, U.S.-Russian relations since the inaugurations of Dmitry Medvedev and Barack Obama have been more substantive and more productive than in perhaps any previous era. The more cautious Russia that emerged following the war in Georgia and the late 2000s financial crisis, coupled with the Obama administration's persistent engagement founded on acceptance of Russia as it actually is (rather than as most Americans would like it to be) offer reason for hope that the two countries are ready to effectively normalize their relationship—agreeing and disagreeing as their interests dictate, but free from the overheated expectations and disappointments that have characterized earlier periods. It remains too soon, however, to declare that this rapprochement will succeed in building a lasting partnership where those of the Clinton-Yeltsin and Bush-Putin eras failed. The fundamental challenge for both countries remains entrenching cooperation and providing enough ballast to the relationship to weather the inevitable disagreements that will occur.

THE UNITED STATES IN RUSSIAN
FOREIGN POLICY THINKING

For Moscow, the state of relations with Washington at a given moment says a vast amount about the assumptions and capabilities underlying Russia's international behavior more broadly. The debate between the various ideological groups among the Russian elite centers to a great extent on the nature of Russia's policy toward the United States, while Russia's actions in much of the rest of the world—from Iran to China to Africa—can be understood only in the context of Moscow's strategy for dealing with Washington.[5]

Though relations between the United States and Russia have gone through a range of peaks and troughs since 1991, what is notable has been the degree to which Russia's priorities in the relationship have remained essentially stable for most of that period. To be sure, the debate between Eurasianists and Westernizers over Russia's U.S. policy is real enough, but its impact on the actual conduct of Russian foreign policy in this particular area is less than might be expected. The *derzhavnost'* consensus has its greatest hold precisely on this aspect of foreign policy primarily because it is the United States—the remaining *sverkhderzhava* (superpower)—of which Russian *derzhavnost'* is a mirror. Russia's need to act like and be accepted as a major power in its own right is a legacy of the country's historical international role, principally (though not entirely) during the course of the Cold War, when Soviet foreign policy was essentially Soviet policy toward the United States writ large. Hence, even today, Russia's ability to match the United States is a critical gauge of its international standing, even though the bipolar confrontation between capitalism and Communism is no more.[6]

At the same time, Russian statesmen argue that the very idea of a superpower as it existed during the Cold War no longer has any meaning (given the transnational nature of most major security threats and the emergence of new power centers in the modern world).[7] For this reason, instead of one or two states dominating the rest of the world and shaping its choices, the dominant Russian paradigm emphasizes the responsibility of all the leading states to uphold global security, working through clubs of major states, including the UN Security Council and the G8/G20.[8]

As for Russia itself, the proliferation of security threats to the east and south means the country is condemned to pursue a multivectoral foreign policy in the context of the emerging multipolar world order. Relations with the United States are one major vector, but Russia's security situation is such that the country cannot afford to rely on its relationship with Washington alone to defend it. This recognition is at the foundation of a strategy that Russian foreign minister Lavrov calls "network diplomacy [*setovaya diplomatiya*]," eschewing formal alliances and the ideologizing of foreign policy in favor of pragmatic, issue-based cooperation with all interested states.[9] Under Medvedev, this strategy has evolved to focus primarily on economic issues as Russia seeks to place its energy-focused economy on a more durable footing. In this context, the paucity of U.S.-Russian economic ties is a liability that leaves the relationship focused on many of the same security issues that have characterized it since the days of the Soviet Union.

Since the mid-1990s, Moscow's approach to the bilateral relationship has emphasized selective cooperation in keeping with the preservation of Russia's role as an independent Great Power; this framework remains central in the Medvedev government's thinking about the United States as well. Even during the days of Primakov and the conflict over Kosovo or the war in Georgia, Russian policy has rarely, despite what many U.S. strategists are wont to perceive, been directed at countering U.S. interests as such. To be sure, most Russian policy makers and intellectuals are smart enough to realize that their country has little to gain from an openly antagonistic stance toward Washington—though domestic criticism for seeking accommodation at the expense of Russian interests has at times driven more confrontational rhetoric. Rather, they lament Washington's penchant for ignoring Russia and not reciprocating gestures of cooperation.[10] Even in the fevered weeks and months following the war in Georgia, a period that represented a post–Cold War nadir for U.S.-Russian relations, Moscow appeared eager to wall off the impact of its intervention from the broader scope of bilateral relations (or, seen differently, hoped to force the United States to abandon Georgia as the price of preserving its relationship with Moscow). That the warming of U.S.-Russian ties in the context of the Obama "reset" developed without any change to the status quo in Georgia and its breakaway territories seemingly vindicated this calculation.

Much Russian frustration with the United States also has to do with unmet expectations—particularly the perceived lack of financial and diplomatic reciprocity—dating back to the first flush of post–Cold War cooperation. Certainly the lack of reciprocity contributed to Russians' disaffection with the aid they received from the United States in the first years after the Soviet collapse, when many expected a new Marshall Plan in return for throwing off the yoke of Communism and ending the Cold War. Instead, post-Soviet Russia got large quantities of advice about the virtues of a free market, accompanied by comparatively meager quantities of Western assistance. When that free market ended up leaving millions of Russians cold, hungry, and unemployed for the better part of a decade, the fault was laid at the door of the United States—whose representatives at times appeared more interested in making their own names and fortunes than in aiding the Russian transition—and those Russians who had advocated closer ties with Washington such as Kozyrev, acting prime minister Yegor Gaidar, and privatization architect Anatoly Chubais.[11]

Even today the perception lives on that Washington failed to adequately compensate Moscow for the sacrifices it has made over the course of the post–Cold War era., as well as in the post-9/11 era.[12] A particularly sore point is the fact that, as late as 2011, Washington still had not even gotten around to graduating Russia from the provisions of the Jackson-Vanik amendment prohibiting permanent normal trade relations. Passed in the 1970s to punish the Communist countries for their refusal to allow citizens freedom of movement (particularly preventing Soviet Jews from emigrating to Israel), many Russians see the continued application of Jackson-Vanik as evidence that the United States continues to treat Russia as a rival to be contained and pressured rather than a partner, especially as China and most of Russia's post-Soviet neighbors were graduated long ago.

Of course, the U.S. president can (and typically does) grant an annual waiver to Jackson-Vanik, rendering it more a symbolic irritant than a real impediment to cooperation. A more substantive example of U.S. failure to reciprocate was the Bush administration's unilateral overhaul of the foundations of the nuclear relationship between the two countries—refusing to ratify the START II agreement, discussions of allowing START I to lapse, withdrawal from the ABM Treaty, and the decision (since modified by Obama) to place an antiballistic missile system in Eastern Europe. The various nuclear agreements between Moscow and Washington are, like

Russia's membership on the UN Security Council, part of the country's superpower legacy that Russian leaders value precisely because they symbolize a relationship of equality with the United States, and Washington's cavalier attitude toward them in the Bush years was seen as an attempt to prevent Russia's reemergence as a major global power.[13]

Since Russia is no longer the United States' central foreign policy concern and is much weaker than its Soviet predecessor, Washington has simply been more willing to bypass Russian objections than it was during the Cold War. This problem is hardly unique to Russia: the United States' often unilateral approach to foreign policy under both presidents Bill Clinton and George W. Bush contributed to a perception in many countries that the United States no longer felt constrained by an international system it had come to dominate. As a former superpower itself though, Russia appeared more offended than most by Washington's reversion to unilateralism. Even on issues not directly affecting Russian security, such as the decision to invade Iraq, Washington's willingness to downplay and ignore Russian opposition fed a perception in Moscow that the rhetoric of partnership was a fig leaf for the unilateral extension of U.S. power at Russian expense. These experiences helped nurture a sense of resentment among the Russian political class toward the United States that overlay the residual mistrust left over from the days of the Cold War.[14]

At the same time, of course, regardless of specific actions on the part of the United States, Russian leaders (like leaders in most countries) have an incentive to resist U.S. pressure as a means of appealing to their own nationalists and showing that Russia still matters. In this regard, it is notable how broad the criticism of U.S. policy toward Russia has been, with even pro-Western politicians (such as the leadership of the liberal Yabloko Party, not to mention Dmitry Medvedev himself) criticizing America's perceived tendency to act without regard for Russian interests.

While it is primarily the views of elites that matter in shaping Russian policy toward the United States, public opinion helps shape and constrain the options available to policy makers. Given the omnipresence of the United States in Russian public discourse (including the press), few Russians are indifferent about the United States, and many share the sense of disappointment that dominates the elite narrative of the post–Cold War era. Public opinion polling confirms that assessments of the United States largely track the ups and downs of the bilateral relationship. Thus on the eve of the Iraq invasion in 2003, only 38 percent of Russians viewed the United States in positive terms, a figure that had risen to 62 percent by the end of 2010 when the reset was in full bloom (see table 3.1). Such volatility, of course, is indicative of the uncertainty that continues to dog the overall relationship, suggesting that Russian society has not come to view the United States as a natural or permanent partner.

Table 3.1   How on the whole do you feel about the United States?

	Mar 2003	Mar 2004	Jan 2009	Jan 2010	Mar 2011
Very good	3%	5%	2%	4%	5%
Mostly good	35	48	36	50	49
Mostly bad	37	26	34	25	26
Very bad	18	10	15	6	7
Don't know	7	11	13	15	13

Source: Levada Center/University of Aberdeen, 2001–2011, http://www.russiavotes.org/security/security_trends.php?S776173303132=fe556934f3931f7b343c88784415e348#126.

And of course, unmet expectations in the relationship cut both ways. If Russians too often see the United States as an arrogant power that ignores their interests, the United States tends to see the Russian Federation as a country that has not completely broken with its imperial past and refuses to play the role of a responsible stakeholder in the international system.[15] As a result, Washington has often pursued a dual policy toward Russia, working to limit the expansion of Russian influence (especially around Russia's borders) even while proclaiming its interest in a more cooperative relationship, for instance, in the fight against international terrorism. Russia's own actions have often made things worse, but on the most basic level, the United States' leadership has not figured out how to define the nature of its relationship with today's Russian Federation.

THE ELUSIVE STRATEGIC PARTNERSHIP:
FROM YELTSIN AND CLINTON TO PUTIN AND BUSH

In 2000–2001, when Vladimir Putin and George W. Bush were both settling into office, U.S.-Russian relations appeared to be headed for improvement following years of tension. The dangerous drift in both domestic and foreign policy of the late Yeltsin years had done much to damage relations with Washington—despite the close personal relations that existed between Yeltsin and Clinton and the repeated, if vague, invocations of a U.S.-Russian strategic partnership dating from the mid-1990s. The Clinton administration had tried to institutionalize the partnership through a variety of mechanisms, including a strategic stability group and a joint commission headed by U.S. vice president Al Gore and Russian prime minister Viktor Chernomyrdin, whose writ gradually expanded from energy and space to cover the whole range of bilateral problems. The early 1990s saw a number of genuine accomplishments, including agreement on removing nuclear weapons from Belarus, Ukraine, and Kazakhstan and the withdrawal of Russian troops from the Baltic states.[16] These concrete achievements however did not solve the fundamental problem that the United States no longer saw Russia as a foreign policy challenge of the first rank, while Russia increasingly resented that lack of U.S. attention and aid as it slipped further into crisis at home.

Despite the rhetoric of partnership, difficulties continued to amass as Russia's transition away from Communism proved complicated and the United States found itself confronting other problems that put it at odds with Moscow. U.S. support for NATO expansion, the first wave of which culminated in the admission of the Czech Republic, Hungary, and Poland to the alliance in 1999, significantly complicated relations with Moscow, as the Russians continued to see NATO as a fundamentally hostile force whose raison d'être remained the containment of Russian influence in Europe. Meanwhile, U.S. interest in ending the bloodshed engulfing the former Yugoslavia, first in Bosnia and then in Kosovo, clashed with Russian support for its client, Serbian strongman Slobodan Milošević, while the first war in Chechnya fed worries about Russia's potential disintegration—and unmitigated horror at the brutality of Russian forces sent to pacify the breakaway republic.[17]

In the fall of 1998, a financial collapse of epic proportions left Russia impoverished and unstable at a moment when the United States was beginning to adopt an increasingly forceful policy toward Serbia over Milošević's campaign of ethnic cleansing in Kosovo. Clinton's decision to launch airstrikes led to then-Russian foreign minister Primakov's notorious decision to turn his plane around over the Atlantic, cancelling a planned meeting with the U.S. president.[18] For the first time since the Cold War, the prospect of U.S. and Russian forces shooting at one another seemed possible when, without authorization from NATO, a detachment of Russian soldiers seized and held the Priština airport in June 1999.

What the conflict in the Balkans seemingly proved was that even under a committed internationalist like Clinton, the United States would not hesitate to act outside the framework of international law or the United Nations if doing so were deemed to be in the United States' national interest. This resort to unilateral application of military power (against a close Russian ally, no less) was evidence to many in Russia that, notwithstanding the end of the Cold War, international politics continued to be based on national interest and power rather than on multinational cooperation or the international legality embodied in the United Nations—which had refused to authorize the use of force in the Balkans in the face of a Russian veto.[19]

In Moscow, the attack on Serbia was further viewed as giving the lie to the notion that a common European security community had emerged with the end of the Cold War. It also convinced much of the Russian elite that Moscow needed to develop a more cohesive view of its own interests— along with the capability to pursue them independently of the West. While many in the military argued that the war gave Russia license to break from the one-sided dependence on the West that Yeltsin had forged, Yeltsin's newly appointed prime minister, Vladimir Putin, and Foreign Minister Igor Ivanov were more nuanced. They criticized the United States' invocation of humanitarian intervention and limited sovereignty as justifications for the use of force as contrary to international law, but insisted Russia would nonetheless continue to cooperate selectively with the United States.[20] They also criticized the United States for applying a double standard, and hinted that Washington's use of force on behalf of separatists in Kosovo could constitute a precedent—a theme to which Moscow would return during its invasion of Georgia nine years later.

Nonetheless, the idea of a strategic partnership with Washington remained important to the Russian leadership, helping to prevent a serious rupture over the crisis in Kosovo. This seemingly privileged relationship allowed Moscow to continue thinking of itself as central to U.S. security concerns (although Washington used the term *strategic partnership* to describe its relations with a number of countries of varying size and importance). Even in the midst of the Kosovo crisis, Ivanov pressed U.S. secretary of state Madeleine Albright to reaffirm that Washington remained committed to maintaining a strategic partnership with Russia.[21] Describing the relationship in these terms mattered to Russia precisely because of the country's post–Cold War decline, which made Russian pretensions to a global role increasingly tenuous. Since U.S. unipolarity appeared the dominant paradigm in international relations at the end of the 1990s, it flattered Russia's amour propre and enhanced Russian influence to be considered a strategic partner of the lone superpower. This dynamic would continue to inform Russian policy toward the United States after the September 11 attacks, when the decision to move closer to Washington was taken in large measure to enhance Russia's role as one of the principal states in the reshaped global order.

While the Kosovo crisis remained unresolved and civil war stalked the North Caucasus, a series of suspicious bombings led Russian leaders to authorize a new invasion of Chechnya, from which they had exited in 1996. This second Chechen war renewed international condemnation of Russian brutality and catapulted Russia's unknown prime minister, Vladimir Putin, who had argued for dealing forcefully with Chechnya, into the spotlight.[22] When Putin ascended to the presidency following Yeltsin's retirement at the end of 1999, many Russia watchers in the United States breathed a sigh of relief, despite continued unease over Russian actions in Chechnya.

In contrast to the ill and increasingly erratic Yeltsin, Putin was initially seen in the United States as a sober, responsible leader who would conduct foreign policy on the basis of Russian national interests rather than the extremes of emotion that had characterized Yeltsin's diplomacy in the last years of his rule. Putin appeared to recognize early on that the major dangers to Russia's security were instability around its borders and the threat of being sucked into futile small wars (akin to the USSR's disastrous Afghan adventure). By focusing on the threats from terrorism and small wars rather than on a large-scale conflict between Russia and NATO, Putin's initial rise to power actually helped reduce tensions with the United States.

Putin also gave concrete demonstrations of his interest in better relations with Washington. Almost immediately after becoming president and in the face of strong opposition from the General Staff, Putin cancelled plans to upgrade the Strategic Rocket Forces (whose main role was to fight a ballistic missile duel with the United States) and persuaded the Duma to conditionally ratify the START II agreement, which had been languishing since its signing in 1997. Soon thereafter, and again over the military's objections, Putin signed a new, if limited, arms control pact with Washington, the Strategic Offensive Reductions Treaty (SORT) or Treaty of Moscow, which also contained language committing the two sides to the establishment of a "new strategic relationship."[23]

Besides reducing tensions with the United States, the decisions to ratify START II and sign SORT also strengthened Russia's bargaining position in future arms control negotiations. New U.S. president Bush had already made clear his interest in withdrawing from the ABM Treaty. For that reason, the Duma's ratification of START II was made conditional on Washington's continued adherence to the ABM agreement and ratification of an additional protocol to START II reaffirming the ban on antiballistic missile systems. Since Washington pulled out of the ABM agreement shortly thereafter and never did ratify the additional protocol, Moscow's affirmation of START II had few practical consequences apart from casting U.S. policy in a negative light—though it also offered a path to deeper cooperation if the United States chose to reciprocate.[24]

The dual effect of Russia's arms control policy in 2001–2002—lowering tensions with Washington while enhancing Russian bargaining power—was typical of Putin's approach to dealing with Washington, leveraging relations with the United States to achieve Russia's broader power-political aims. Russia's arms control initiatives were not merely symbolic, as the opposition of the country's General Staff shows. At the same time, they were hardly a unilateral concession to the United States either. Since the size of the Russian arsenal had already dropped precipitously since the end of the Cold War (mainly due to budget constraints), SORT in effect ensured the maintenance of rough strategic parity by limiting the United States' ability to build new offensive weapons.[25] Meanwhile, START II ratification gave Moscow a card to play should Washington become serious about building an ABM system. In general, Putin's early appetite for arms control both put pressure on the United States to follow suit and, if successful, would have allowed Russia to cut back spending on its nuclear arsenal to focus on local threats.

These actions, while improving for a time U.S.-Russian relations, also helped promote Russia's global role and influence, which had also been a central goal of Russian foreign policy under Yeltsin. The main difference was that now, cooperation with the United States, rather than confrontation with it, appeared the most effective way for Russia to assert its global relevance, since fighting fruitless battles with Washington over, for instance, the ABM Treaty would have done little for Russia's image as a powerful, responsible member of the global community.[26] At the same time, the emphasis on avoiding conflict with the United States allowed Putin to focus on his domestic agenda, which remained the central component of his strategy for reviving Russia as a major global power.[27]

Notwithstanding its distaste for arms control, the Bush administration responded with cautious optimism to the initial Russian push for cooperation. After meeting Putin for the first time at a summit in Ljubljana, Slovenia, in June 2001, Bush famously and inopportunely remarked that he had "looked [Putin] in the eye" and "got a sense of his soul."[28] Despite this positive appraisal of Putin and his soul, in the first years of his presidency, Bush downplayed the overall importance of relations with Moscow.[29] National security adviser (and later secretary of state) Condoleezza Rice, an old Russia hand, had been particularly critical of the way the Clinton administration had dealt with Russia. She argued that Clinton had been too quick to rush to the aid of Yeltsin and Russia on account of Clinton's friendship with the Russian president and out of a now-misplaced fear of a Communist revival. Rice firmly believed that the Clinton team had turned a blind eye to Russian malfeasance—in Chechnya and elsewhere—while pandering to Yeltsin's vanity by pressing for Russian inclusion in the G8 despite its economic weakness and lack of democratic credentials.[30]

Under Rice's guidance, Bush came into office determined to recast the United States' policy toward Russia, rejecting what he saw as the naïve optimism of the Clinton administration in favor of a skeptical realism. Of course, given the legacy of the 1998 financial collapse and Russia's apparent international weakness, a policy of realism was easy to turn into a policy of neglect. To many Russians, the U.S. interest in abrogating the ABM Treaty and continuing to expand NATO was merely proof that Washington had decided it could proceed without taking Russian preferences into consideration even on issues Russia deemed central to its own security.

Russia's leaders also remained cautious regarding the degree of intimacy with Washington they were willing to accept. Moscow might have been ready to see Washington as an ally, but not to docilely fall in line behind it. As early as mid-2001, Foreign Minister Ivanov warned that Russia would "[combine] the firm protection of national interests with a consistent search for mutually acceptable solutions through dialogue and cooperation with the West."[31] On a more fundamental level, while Russia might have an interest in seeking cooperation with the United States on a range of issues where their interests overlapped, what was lacking, in 2001 and later, was an overriding interest on the part of either country in seeking deeper integration, given their different threat perceptions and different value systems.

In the past, issues such as a common external threat (e.g., Nazism), mutually assured destruction, or (in the mid-1990s when Yeltsin was casting around for legitimacy) an allegedly shared commitment to democracy pushed the two countries closer. By the start of the twenty-first century, though, no such overwhelming imperative existed, and so cooperation, while real, was doomed to remain sporadic unless the underlying needs of both states changed.[32]

The attacks of September 11, 2001, seemed to provide precisely the impetus needed for cementing U.S.-Russian cooperation into a more enduring partnership—in part thanks to the genuine and public outpouring of sympathy in Russia for the victims of the attacks, and in part because the attacks appeared to align the two countries' interests to a degree that had been lacking in previous years.[33] Both countries had now suffered grievously from Islamist terrorism and had a direct interest in ridding themselves of the Taliban regime in Afghanistan, which, along with its al Qaeda confederates, was playing an increasingly prominent role in aiding and training Chechen rebels and spreading Islamic radicalism throughout Central Asia.[34]

Aware of Russia's own history of confronting terrorism as well as its continuing problems with ensuring the security of its nuclear arsenal, Putin noted in late 2003 that terrorism—especially nuclear terrorism—is "the main threat to peace in the twenty-first century."[35] This position represented an important departure in Russian foreign policy, both for downplaying the threat of conventional military assaults against Russia (on the part of NATO, for instance) and for recognizing that Russia and the United States found themselves on the same side of an important historical watershed. This issue continued to unite the United States and Russia throughout the Bush-Putin era, with the two countries announcing at the 2006 G8 summit in St. Petersburg (a meeting otherwise notable for the other countries' criticism of Russia's human rights record) the formation of the new Global Initiative to Combat Nuclear Terrorism.[36] Cooperation in the sphere of counterterrorism continued even after the start of hostilities between Russia and Georgia in August 2008. And when Obama shifted the emphasis of U.S. policy from an open-ended war on terrorism to defeating the Taliban and al Qaeda in Afghanistan, he found in Moscow a willing partner capable of offering significant intelligence and logistical support.

Because of the war in Chechnya and the resulting wave of terrorist attacks in Russian cities, Moscow had focused on terrorism, especially Islamic terrorism, as the most immediate security challenge facing the country long before September 11, 2001. Until 9/11, the United States routinely condemned what it termed Russia's use of excessive force in waging what was essentially a counterinsurgency campaign in Chechnya—while Moscow responded that Washington lacked a proper frame of reference because it did not face the terrorist threat directly. With the attacks in New York and Washington, Islamic terrorism suddenly became the top security threat for the United States as well. To many Russians, September 11 had proven that Moscow had been right about terrorism all along and that now the United States would come to see the problem in the same light. As Igor Ivanov put it, the September 11 attacks "opened many people's eyes about the reality of terrorism [and] forced a rethinking of approaches to international cooperation . . . in the struggle against this evil."[37]

In the weeks and months after the attacks, Russian hopes for closer coordination with the United States were not to be disappointed. Dealing with Afghanistan had already been a major topic in U.S.-Russian negotiations in the months before September 11, though some U.S. observers were skeptical about the substance behind Moscow's professed hostility to the Taliban.[38] Four months before 9/11, a delegation to Moscow led by U.S. deputy secretary of state Richard Armitage agreed with its Russian hosts that the main issue in Afghanistan was that "the Taliban regime continues to sponsor terrorism, which has spread beyond the frontiers of Afghanistan."[39]

When Armitage returned to Moscow a week after the attacks in September, he asked the Russians directly for assistance in fighting the Taliban and al Qaeda, including the possibility of Russian military intervention in Afghanistan. While deciding to avoid direct military involvement, Putin was receptive to the American request for aid, offering intelligence cooperation, overflight of Russian territory, diplomatic pressure on the Central Asian states to cooperate with the antiterrorist campaign, participation in search-and-rescue missions, and military aid to the anti-Taliban Northern Alliance in Afghanistan, as well as (eventually) agreement to the placement of U.S. bases in Central Asia.[40] Russian leaders realized that, for perhaps the first time since the end of the Cold War more than a decade earlier, the United States needed Russian help. With its extensive ties to Central Asia (including a large intelligence presence) and experience in Afghanistan dating to the Soviet invasion of that country in 1979, Russia was ideally positioned to help the U.S. mission.

Moscow had also been a long-standing patron of the Northern Alliance, the predominantly Uzbek and Tajik force of former mujahideen now struggling to keep Afghanistan from falling to the mostly Pashtun Taliban. In addition to bringing about the demise of the Taliban and muting U.S. criticism of its activities in Chechnya, Putin—much like British prime minister Tony Blair at the same time—hoped that by becoming an indispensable partner in the newly proclaimed war on terror, Russia could position itself as a crucial player in the postwar reconstruction of the world while also directly influencing how the United States conducted its campaign against the Taliban and al Qaeda.[41] This campaign, after all, could result in serious consequences for Russia (with a Muslim population of around twenty million), not to mention its immediate neighbors in Central Asia.

Russian aid in the campaign was significant. It included detailed intelligence sharing on the part of both civilian and military intelligence agencies as well as acquiescence to Bush's request to station American troops in Uzbekistan and Kyrgyzstan.[42] Even the political leadership in Muslim regions of Russia generally supported the campaign against the Taliban and Russia's participation in it, though Muslim spiritual leaders were mostly opposed to what one influential mufti called "the destruction of [Afghanistan's] peaceful population and the division of the world by the global gendarme."[43] Despite the alacrity with which Putin offered to aid the U.S. mission, the Russian security establishment—the military in particular—remained uneasy about turning over Russian secrets to the Americans and, even more, to countenancing the presence of U.S. troops on the territory of the former Soviet Union. To prevent the United States from becoming too established in the region, the Russian military urged the Northern Alliance to drive the Taliban out of Kabul before U.S. forces arrived, and attempted to establish its own presence in Afghanistan ahead of the Americans.[44] Despite this unease, Putin's support for cooperation with the United States was decisive in keeping Russia's reluctant civilian and military bureaucracies on board.

Even Putin was clear though that the presence of U.S. troops in Central Asia would have to be temporary. Since the Russian leadership remained convinced that the United States still operated according to the same geopolitical calculations as the Kremlin, it saw a U.S. presence in Central Asia as a step in expanding Washington's sphere of influence uncomfortably close to Russian borders. For the time being, a U.S. presence in Uzbekistan and Kyrgyzstan was the price to be paid for giving Russia a central position in the unfolding war on terror and for finishing off the Taliban. Once these aims were achieved and the usual wariness crept back into U.S.-Russian relations, the U.S. forces in Central Asia would come to represent a check on Russian power in its own neighborhood.

Russian fears were especially pronounced because of how the September 11 attacks removed whatever constraints had previously existed on the use of U.S. military power. Washington's newfound readiness to use force and its willingness to act without seeking agreement among its allies renewed the criticisms emanating from Russia during the Kosovo war in 1999.[45] The United States may have considered Russia an ally in 2001–2002, but for the time being, Washington was not in the mood to defer to even its closest allies' sensibilities. Russian leaders also continued to worry about the impact of an expanded U.S. presence in Central Asia. With the United States ensconced in the region, Moscow feared losing its ability to dictate the routes for new oil and gas pipelines running from Central Asia and the Caspian region to global markets.[46] It also worried about the strategic consequences of a permanent U.S. military presence, which had the potential to undermine Russia's leading role in upholding the regional balance. Fearing that, once deployed, U.S. forces would not leave, Russian officials pushed the Central Asian governments to take a harder line on the U.S. military presence. Moscow was also instrumental in the adoption of the Shanghai Cooperation Organization's so-called Astana Declaration calling on the United States to set a timeline for the withdrawal of its forces from Central Asia. And when Uzbek president Islam Karimov, with the backing of China and the SCO, ordered U.S. troops to leave in mid-2005 after Washington had criticized his indiscriminate use of force against a popular uprising in the city of Andijon, the Kremlin stood firmly behind him, and subsequently conducted its first ever joint exercises with Uzbek forces as a show of solidarity.[47]

This opportunistic rush to embrace Karimov after the United States had rejected him was typical of the way Moscow, at least until the invasion of Georgia, had generally avoided initiating disputes but not hesitated to take advantage of Washington's difficulties to advance its own geopolitical agenda—all the while temporizing over whether a Taliban victory or an extension of U.S. power into Central Asia represented a greater long-term threat. Similarly, Moscow continually exerted pressure on the Kyrgyz government to expel U.S. forces from their base at Manas Airport near Bishkek. This pressure to shut down bases in Central Asia generally coincided with a waning of the Taliban threat in Afghanistan, which allowed Moscow to see the prospect of a long-term U.S. presence as a greater threat to its interests than the spread of Islamism. As Washington's focus shifted to Iraq and the Taliban gradually regained strength, Moscow began reconsidering this assumption.

The Kremlin's initial decision to aid the United States in Afghanistan was the centerpiece of a deliberate policy of cooperation with Washington, whose high point came in 2001–2002. In the eighteen months after the September 11 attacks, Moscow also supported U.S. initiatives against the

Iranian and North Korean nuclear programs and agreed to the launch of a "strategic energy dialogue" with the United States and EU in June 2002. Even as late as mid-2004, Russia signed on to the U.S.-devised Proliferation Security Initiative (PSI) to combat the spread of fissile material and other components of weapons of mass destruction.[48] All of these developments helped change the general climate in U.S.-Russian relations and created expectations for ongoing cooperation.[49] The accumulation of good feeling that resulted overshadowed the fundamental reality that cooperation on problems like the Iranian and North Korean nuclear programs was relatively easy to achieve because, as with Afghanistan, Washington and Moscow had largely the same aims, regardless of where their overall relationship was headed.

For the Russians, the goals of cooperating with the United States in the Afghan campaign were clear: elimination of Afghanistan as a source of Islamic radicalism, enhancement of Russia's claim to a role as a global power and an indispensible ally in Afghanistan, and a free hand in Chechnya. Unfortunately, many in the United States misunderstood the nature of Russia's cooperation. Rather than perceiving a calculated diplomatic maneuver, U.S. observers, including some in the Bush administration, saw Putin's decision to back the Afghan campaign as a signal that the Kremlin had made a fundamental strategic, even civilizational, choice to ally with the West, in the way that Poland and other East European countries had done after the Cold War.[50]

To be sure, Putin's decision to aid the United States in Afghanistan was a major decision, one that took substantial political courage to make in the face of opposition from the Russian military and security services. Yet it was only one piece of a larger and more complex Russian diplomatic strategy that was basically instrumental in nature. Russian rhetoric at the time was notably devoid of the kind of sweeping, epochal language used by many American observers keen to praise Putin's willingness to make common cause with the West. In his first address to the Federal Assembly following the September 11 attacks, Putin noted that, while the era of confrontation with the United States was over, the post-9/11 world order was still based on "fierce competition—for markets, for investment, for political and economic influence," and that Russia had to be "strong and competitive" in this world.[51] Putin was sincere in wanting partnership with the United States after 9/11, but not partnership at any price.

DISILLUSIONMENT, 2003–2008

The post-9/11 rapprochement, like its early 1990s predecessor, did not last. Another round of NATO expansion in 2002 brought the post-Soviet Baltic states into the Atlantic Alliance, placing NATO's frontiers less than 100 kilometers from St. Petersburg. The U.S. invasion of Iraq in 2003 renewed Russian criticism that the unilateral projection of U.S. power was a threat to international stability—even as the Taliban's apparent eclipse made cooperation in Afghanistan appear less vital. Meanwhile, a sustained rise in global energy prices reversed the long decline of Russia's economy, filling Moscow's coffers, paying down its foreign debts, and imbuing Russian leaders with a confidence that Russia was strong enough to stand up to the United States when its interests were threatened. The nature of the Russian government itself was changing as well, in ways that fed into existing fears and stereotypes in the U.S. Putin's moves to create a "power vertical" did away with elected governors and increasingly subjected the Duma and Federation Council to Kremlin control. The expropriation of Yukos and jailing of Mikhail Khodorkovsky likewise fed the perception that Putin was rolling back democracy and reversing Russia's development into a basically Western state. Shortly thereafter, the first of the "colored revolutions" broke out in Georgia, leaving Moscow and Washington on opposite sides of what appeared to be a struggle for the political soul of the post-Soviet space.

The U.S.-Russia partnership—always more an entente than a true alliance—came into being primarily because the two sides shared a common interest in Afghanistan and because Putin realized that overt opposition to the West (which at times had been the defining characteristic of Primakov's diplomacy) was counterproductive to his aim of restoring Russia's international credibility and influence. The partnership began to crumble because Washington and Moscow perceived themselves to have widely diverging interests in parts of the world other than Afghanistan and because the post–September 11 understanding between the two sides was never formal enough to manage their diverging strategic priorities the way NATO, for example, can iron out differences between its members. It may well be true that Putin made a fundamental decision early in his term to seek good relations with Washington as a major element of his foreign policy.[52] Nonetheless, the vagaries of politics and the persistence of national interests have meant that cooperation with the United States was only one component of Russian foreign policy, and often not the decisive one.

Even though Russia was not a central player in the drama, the war in Iraq badly undermined the foundation of U.S.-Russian cooperation laid after 9/11. Russia's main interests in Iraq were twofold. On the one hand, Moscow had an economic interest in the pre-2003 status quo, since Saddam Hussein's government owed Russia billions of dollars, much of it Soviet-era debts for weapons purchased during Iraq's war with Iran in the 1980s.[53] The more important reason for Russia's opposition was that, as with the assault on Serbia in 1999, Moscow believed the United States was usurping the legitimate authority of the UN Security Council to launch an invasion that much of the world saw as illegitimate and destabilizing. It feared that the U.S. invasion would weaken the authority of the Security Council, and with it, Russia's own ability to shape the international agenda. Washington largely ignored this broader critique of its policy, preferring instead to focus on Russia's economic interests as the main reason for its opposition. The belief that, in contrast to its close European allies who also opposed the war, Russian opposition was largely driven by economic self-interest made it easy for the United States to, as Condoleezza Rice put it, "punish France, ignore Germany, and forgive Russia."[54]

Because Russia did not seek to make trouble after the invasion had begun, and because it continued to be helpful in Afghanistan (where Moscow was capable of playing a more substantive role), Washington found it fairly easy to forgive the Russians. Many Russian observers meanwhile welcomed the diplomatic fallout Washington endured in the aftermath of the invasion as forcing the United States to recognize both the limits of its power and the importance of a multilateral foreign policy. Moscow argued that "in the [U.S.] administration's transition to a more sober evaluation of its capacities lies the potential for new and expanded cooperation with the USA within the framework of multilateral institutions—above all the UN."[55]

Meanwhile, although Congress and the White House had expressed their gratitude for Russian aid in Afghanistan, concrete concessions were few: restrictions on economic and technical cooperation as well as stringent visa requirements for travel to the United States remained in place, while Washington gave no indication it was willing to reconsider its opposition to the existing arms control regime or to abandon its support for NATO expansion. Putin's September 2003 visit to the United States, when the Russian president's advisers urged him to establish an enduring alliance with Washington, was a kind of symbolic turning point. Two years after the September 11 attacks, it was clear to observers in both countries that the strategic partnership was not living up to expectations. Both sides remained interested in preserving that partnership, but failed to articulate a framework for overcoming their continued disagreements—over Iraq, Yukos, and other problems.

Much of the difficulty lay in trying to define what such a partnership really meant in practice. Russian politicians and diplomats eager to preserve good relations with Washington argued that the partnership had hitherto been far too one-sided and that the United States would have to start making concessions to Russian *derzhavnost'* in order to preserve Russian support for the partnership arrangement. Russia's decision to close overseas military facilities in Cuba and Vietnam, acceptance of U.S. military installations in Central Asia, and muted response to both the demise of the ABM Treaty and NATO expansion were justified to a skeptical elite as a kind of down payment on the strategic partnership with the United States.[56] That down payment, however, ended up buying Moscow little in the way of enhanced influence with the Bush administration or concessions on issues of surpassing importance to Moscow. As then-Russian ambassador to the United States Yury Ushakov argued, much of the difficulty in bilateral relations stemmed from the fact that Washington believed "Russia can be used when it is needed and discarded or even abused when it is not relevant to American objectives."[57]

A crucial report drafted by a group of pro-Kremlin analysts for Putin before his September 2003 Camp David summit meeting with Bush argued, "It is the American approach to formulating and manipulating the bilateral agenda in the U.S. interest that continues to dominate."[58] The report suggested that Russia dedicate itself to establishing a full alliance relationship with the United States, urging Putin to pledge his cooperation in building the liberal democratic world order at the heart of the Bush doctrine and promise active assistance in resolving such major issues as the Israeli-Palestinian conflict and the Korean nuclear standoff.[59] As a privileged ally of the U.S., Russia would request a special responsibility for protecting the post-Soviet space from terrorism and instability. Putin took the proposal seriously and apparently raised the issue of a special U.S.-Russian partnership verging on an alliance with Bush at Camp David.[60]

The proponents of such an alliance stressed that, in exchange for Russia's friendship, the United States would have to accept Moscow's right to police its own neighborhood, albeit on the basis of a shared commitment to liberal democratic values. Even in late 2003, however, Putin's commitment to liberal democratic values appeared shaky at best, and the idea of Russia acting as a gendarme within the CIS looked, from Washington, too much like accepting Russia's claim to an exclusive sphere of influence— although the idea of a full alliance had its supporters in the United States as well.[61] In his statement to reporters after the Camp David summit, Bush called the United States and Russia "allies in the war on terror" and stressed their growing cooperation on arms control and in bringing stability to Afghanistan but made no mention of the proposal for a generalized U.S.-Russian alliance.[62]

The September 2003 Camp David summit represented perhaps the last serious attempt to create a substantive foundation for the U.S.-Russian strategic partnership until the announcement of the Obama administration's more limited reset policy more than five years later. In the twelve months following the Camp David summit, U.S.-Russian relations entered a period of significant tension. With the war in Iraq already roiling relations, electoral campaigns in both countries in 2004 encouraged nationalistic posturing. In Russia, this posturing was accompanied by turnover in Putin's team of advisers, with the replacement of pro-U.S. liberals by Eurasianists and *siloviki* in a number of key positions.[63] The campaign to seize control of Yukos, which began in the summer of 2003, threatened planned investment in the Russian energy sector by several U.S. firms and fed mounting skepticism in the United States about Putin's commitment to the rule of law. The Yukos drama also heralded the beginning of a much more nationalistic approach to Russia's energy riches on the part of the Kremlin, one that imperiled vast amounts of foreign investment in the energy sector, much of it dating from the early 1990s.[64] By the end of 2004, the Rose Revolution in Georgia and, even more, the Orange Revolution in Ukraine had found the United States and Russia on opposite sides of a major political and ideological struggle taking place throughout the former Soviet Union.

Russia opposed the colored revolutions both because of a (somewhat exaggerated) fear that they could serve as a template for regime change within Russia itself, but also because Moscow saw them not as legitimate expressions of popular will, but as a U.S.-inspired challenge to Russia's interests and influence in the post-Soviet space. The United States though saw the colored revolutions as a manifestation of the democratic spirit that the Bush administration argued lurked within all peoples. Washington embraced Mikheil Saakashvili and Viktor Yushchenko as embodiments of the democratic aspirations of the Georgian and Ukrainian peoples, in the process downplaying Moscow's concerns that they were anti-Russian demagogues who would undermine Russian influence and damage Russian interests. The United States contributed to these fears by affirming its support for Georgian and Ukrainian NATO membership (as well as stepping up bilateral assistance to both countries).

Given its geopolitically tinged view of international politics, the Kremlin saw the Rose and Orange Revolutions less as exercises in democracy promotion than as the most dangerous steps yet in a U.S.-led campaign to surround, contain, and weaken Russia—notwithstanding the end of the Cold War and the still-prevailing rhetoric of partnership. This view reflected a persistent critique of U.S. foreign policy, whether in the Balkans, Iraq, or now, in the former Soviet Union—that Washington selectively employed the rhetoric of democracy as a cover for overthrowing governments that challenged its interests. That this promotion of "democracy" was now occurring right on Russia's borders made it still more dangerous from the Kremlin's point of view. Russia could reluctantly accept U.S.-led efforts to oust Saddam Hussein because it did not have any truly vital interests at stake in Iraq. In Georgia and—still more—Ukraine, vital Russian interests were very much at stake, particularly if U.S.-backed regime change resulted in Georgia and Ukraine joining NATO.

If Russia's calculation in the aftermath of 9/11 was that signing up to be a privileged partner of the United States was the surest path to enhanced international influence and deference to its interests in the post-Soviet space, by the time of the colored revolutions a few years later, it seemed that deferring to U.S. leadership had led Washington to take Moscow for granted at the global level and to encourage the rise of hostile governments around Russia's periphery. Washington did so largely in the mistaken belief that Russia and the United States now shared a similar worldview, and that the traditional geopolitical concerns underpinning Russian foreign policy were no longer relevant in an era of U.S.-Russian comity, any more than they were in relations between, say, the United States and Germany or the UK.

The war in Georgia, which broke out in the summer of 2008 was in many ways a direct consequence of the colored revolutions, as well as a reaction to Washington's reliance on the unilateral use of force and proclivity for confronting Russia (and others) with a series of faits accomplis dating back to the conflicts in the Balkans in the 1990s. It also came at the end of a period of mounting U.S.-Russian confrontation that spilled over into a variety of issues. In the first half of 2007 alone, serious disputes broke out between Moscow and Washington over U.S. plans for missile defense systems in Eastern Europe, Russia's decision to suspend its participation in the Conventional Forces in Europe (CFE) Treaty in response, agreements by the United States to provide military training to Bulgaria and Romania, negotiations over Kosovo's status, and Russian support for separatist regimes in Transnistria (Moldova), South Ossetia, and Abkhazia (Georgia), not to mention the ongoing crackdown on prodemocracy protesters in Russia itself. As he continued to centralize power and crack down on civil society at home, Putin was becoming increasingly vocal in cautioning that the Bush administration's refusal to take Russian interests into consideration was jeopardizing U.S.-Russian cooperation. At the 2007 Munich Security Conference, he warned starkly that:

> More and more we are witness to the flouting of the basic principles of international law. Above all the rights of one state are overtaking separate norms, indeed the entire system of [international] law. The United States is overstepping its national borders in every field: in economics, in politics, even in the humanitarian sphere. . . . And this, of course, is very dangerous.[65]

While Putin's Munich speech was read as marking a return to the kind of standoff with the United States not seen since the Cold War, it was in fact of a piece with Russia's strategy vis-à-vis the United States ever since the 9/11 attacks. Rather than an ideologically charged global confrontation, U.S.-Russian hostility during the second half of the 2000s grew out of a Russian belief that its decision to bandwagon with the United States after 9/11 had not led to reciprocal deference to Russian interests on the part of Washington, and that a more assertive stance (enabled by Russia's ongoing economic boom) was needed.

Recognizing that their partnership was foundering, both sides sought to arrest the slide into confrontation, but neither was willing to make the difficult decision to prioritize fixing the bilateral relationship over other, seemingly more pressing strategic concerns. Eventually, a new, albeit more restrained attempt at defining the exact nature of the U.S.-Russian partnership emerged during the final Bush-Putin summit in Sochi in April 2008, when Washington and Moscow signed a new Strategic Framework Declaration. The document defined areas of strategic cooperation between Moscow and Washington with an eye toward the presidential transitions in both countries. It aimed at filtering out the disagreements that had long complicated the bilateral relationship and focusing on the numerous areas where U.S.-Russian cooperation was both possible and desirable.

At the top of the list was arms control, with Moscow and Washington pledging to seek a legally binding successor to the START I agreement, continue cooperating on nonproliferation, and continue seeking agreement on missile defense. The declaration also focused on economic cooperation, the other area where common interests continued to prevail. Most notably, it committed both sides in concrete terms to overcome the barriers to Russia's WTO accession.[66] While laudatory, all of these aims had been part of the U.S.-Russia agenda for many years; their inclusion merely served to emphasize lack of a positive conception for moving beyond the transactional relationship that continued to prevail. The Strategic Framework Declaration also did not address the two most pressing challenges to U.S.-Russian cooperation: Washington's refusal to accept restraints on its ability to project power abroad, and Moscow's belief that U.S. policy in the post-Soviet space was a direct threat to both its regional influence and its security.

At Camp David in 2003, Bush and Putin downplayed the significance of a series of other U.S.-Russian disagreements: over the war in Iraq, over oil supplies, and over U.S. missile defense plans. All of these issues remained unresolved, and made the attainment of the kind of close U.S.-Russian cooperation many Russian elites still envisioned nearly impossible. This accumulation of disputes is evidence that the strategic partnership between Moscow and Washington was always based more on hope than on a realistic assessment of the two sides' interests. It grew out of the need to make common cause in Afghanistan, but did not account for the facts that their long-term strategic priorities in other parts of the world often diverged and that Moscow often believed the United States was unwilling to offer it any quid pro quo for making the difficult choices it was demanding.

These problems remained unresolved even while Russia viewed the situation in the post-Soviet space as spiraling increasingly out of control. Kyrgyzstan had its own colored revolution in 2005 (albeit one that did not end up with a more pro-American government in power), while the abortive rising in the Uzbek city of Andijon was crushed by government security forces. Meanwhile, Russia's worst fears seemed confirmed when Saakashvili's Georgia and Yushchenko's Ukraine petitioned for NATO membership and the alliance—ignoring Russian protests—proved receptive, agreeing at its April 2008 summit in Bucharest that both Ukraine and Georgia would eventually become members.

In response, Moscow stepped up its campaign to weaken both Saakashvili and Yushchenko through economic pressure, including energy cutoffs to Ukraine and an embargo on Georgian exports, and increasingly stark warnings about the dangers of continuing to pursue NATO membership. Russia's strongest lever for influencing Tbilisi and Kyiv was the potential for separatism, with the breakaway provinces of South Ossetia and Abkhazia in Georgia and the large Russian community in Ukraine's Crimean Peninsula potentially threatening the integrity of the Georgian and Ukrainian states. Russia had used these levers warily since the Soviet collapse, recognizing the potential for separatism to open Pandora's box across the post-Soviet space (including in Russia itself, where Chechnya continued to fester).

As both countries careened toward NATO membership with U.S. backing, Moscow began playing the separatist card more openly. Putin had warned Bush in early 2008 that "Ukraine is not even a state," a comment many in the West read to imply that if pushed too far, Moscow would seek to undermine Ukraine's territorial integrity.[67] In Georgia, Russia boosted its assistance to the separatists in South Ossetia and Abkhazia, quietly stepped up its military preparations, and staged a series of provocations apparently designed to goad the mercurial Saakashvili into overreacting, thereby providing a pretext for Moscow to use force in support of the separatists. The United States was well informed of these Russian actions, and warned the Kremlin that it was risking its relationship with the West. Washington largely failed to understand, however, that Russia regarded its influence and security in the post-Soviet space as a more crucial interest than cooperation with the United States, and resented that the Bush administration was apparently forcing it to choose between the two. Washington's failure to grasp the utter centrality of the former Soviet Union to Russian foreign policy left it off guard when Russian troops poured across the border into Georgia on August 8, 2008, a step that precipitated the greatest crisis in U.S.-Russian relations since the end of the Cold War, and one that many Western observers believed spelled permanent doom for the idea of a U.S.-Russian partnership.

THE RESET, 2009– ?

Yet paradoxically, the war laid the foundation for the third U.S. effort since 1991 to fashion a truly cooperative relationship with Moscow. Coming in the midst of a U.S. presidential campaign, the war initially created an imperative within much of the U.S. political establishment to get tough with Russia. Senator John McCain, the Republican presidential candidate, was unambiguous in his support for Georgia and unstinting in his criticism of Russia. Declaring "we are all Georgians," McCain reiterated his calls for Russia to be expelled from the G8, suggested introducing a UN Security Council resolution condemning Russian actions, and urged consultations with both European allies and other states in the former Soviet Union (including Ukraine and Azerbaijan) that might feel threatened by the Russian invasion.[68] Commentators supporting McCain called for still more active measures, including the dispatch of military assistance to Georgia, a step that, in a mirror image of the 1999 Priština airport debacle, might well have put U.S. personnel in the line of fire.[69]

The war put the Democratic nominee, Illinois senator Barack Obama, in an awkward position, insofar as his campaign had already developed a critique of the Bush administration's Russia policy as too needlessly confrontational. Obama condemned the Russian invasion and called for Russian troops to withdraw from Georgian territory, but avoided threatening Moscow or claiming that the war would inevitably affect long-term relations. Rather, Obama expressed his hope for "a future of cooperative engagement" with Russia, while reminding Moscow that its newfound power conferred the responsibility to be a constructive member of the international community rather than indulge in "regression to the conflicts of the past."[70]

The damage caused by the war to U.S.-Russian relations was less enduring than many observers initially feared. In its last months in office, the Bush administration seemingly recognized the extent to which the war had backed the United States into a corner. Washington's rhetorical and material support for Georgia (as well as Ukraine) had emboldened Tbilisi into antagonizing Russia, even though the United States was not in a position to provide much in the way of material support. Despite the condemnation it endured from Washington and its European allies, Moscow had demonstrated to Georgia and the other CIS states that it was not averse to using force to bring them into line, and that Washington would not be able to save them. The war also put discussion of Georgian and Ukrainian NATO aspirations on ice, precisely as the Russians had hoped; when NATO foreign ministers gathered in Brussels in December 2008, they did not discuss membership action plans for Georgia and Ukraine even though the alliance remained committed on paper to eventual membership for both countries as agreed in Bucharest that April.

Moscow recognized that the impact of the war on its relations with the West—especially the United States—was serious, but could have been much worse. Having made its point with Georgia and feeling the economic consequences as foreign investors increasingly pulled out of the country, the Kremlin was already hinting by the autumn of 2008 that it was eager to renew cooperation with the U.S. Even before the November 2008 U.S. election, Medvedev had tasked a group headed by the former diplomat and Kremlin adviser Aleksei Gromov with designing a packet of measures to advance relations with the West, above all the United States.[71] While appreciating that Washington had not overreacted to the war, the Kremlin was also guided by a recognition that the unfolding economic crisis was going to have serious consequences for Russia, and that it would need Western help both to alleviate the short-term pain and to fix the structural weaknesses the crisis had exposed.

Obama came into office at the start of 2009 determined to get relations out of the morass into which they had fallen. Unlike Bush, Obama also saw Russia as a top priority for U.S. foreign policy from his first days in office, and was willing to spend political and diplomatic capital to repair a relationship that had increasingly gone offtrack. What further distinguished Obama's approach from that of either Bush or Clinton was the deliberate emphasis on severing the link between Russia's domestic development and relations with the U.S. Whereas the Clinton and Bush administrations had, for different reasons, operated on the assumption that Russia's ultimate trajectory would lead it to become a full member of the liberal democratic West, Obama's ambitions were more restrained. Whether or not Russia sought full integration with the West, the new president argued that Moscow and Washington had a range of common interests that they should pursue free from the baggage of past disappointments or future expectations—even as the United States continued to support the full sovereignty of Russia's neighbors as well as democratic development inside Russia itself.

In congressional testimony given shortly after the war in Georgia, Obama's principal Russia adviser Michael McFaul (who would go on to become director of Russian affairs on Obama's National Security Council) argued that U.S. policy toward Russia had to move beyond the stale dichotomy of seeking integration on Western terms or containing Russia in the event that it refused. Instead, the United States should actively support its allies and partners against Russian pressure, even as it engaged with Moscow directly on areas of mutual interest. McFaul argued that the Bush administration's attempt to distance itself from Russia before 2008 had left Washington with little leverage to prevent or counter the invasion of Georgia. While the United States should still encourage Russia to pursue full integration with the West over the long term, McFaul argued that in the meantime the United States needed the ability to work with Russia where the two had common interests, regardless of Russia's failings.[72] Under Obama, engagement would be a tool both to promote U.S. interests and to encourage Russia's eventual transformation, rather than a carrot to be dangled in front of the Kremlin should its behavior improve.

The dominant metaphor for Obama's Russia strategy was the reset button, an image invoked by Vice President Joseph Biden at the February 2009 Munich Security Conference, where he argued that "the U.S. and Russia can disagree but still work together where [their] interests coincide" (the Munich conference, of course, was the same venue where two years previously Putin had condemned the United States for overstepping its bounds and seeking to impose itself around the world).[73] The premise of the reset was that Washington and Moscow should acknowledge their past missteps—and their lingering differences, for instance over Georgia—without allowing them to impede progress on other areas of common interest. By working together over a gradually expanding range of issues, the two sides would build up trust and the habit of cooperation, which would over time broaden the range of common interests and change the two sides' expectations.

The United States would start by focusing on areas where agreement seemed easier (again, particularly arms control), in order to both ingrain the habit of cooperation among the respective bureaucracies, and to test the sincerity of Moscow's interest in better relations. Washington would simultaneously work to deepen economic ties between the two countries, in part because the low level of U.S.-Russian trade and investment ties left both countries with few stakeholders in improved relations. Boosting economic ties was also, like arms control, an area where Moscow had a clear incentive to play a constructive role. If the initial reset succeeded, the two countries could move on to dealing with more intractable problems such as missile defense, Russia's relationship with NATO, and energy security.

Russia's response to Obama was contradictory at first, but became more welcoming as time went on and the reset increasingly appeared to be a serious strategic choice on the part of the United States. Initially, Russia appeared eager to test the youthful new president's mettle. Breaking with tradition (and protocol), Medvedev gave his annual address to the Federal Assembly the day after Obama's historic election victory, which was deliberately overshadowed in the state-controlled Russian media. In his speech, Medvedev announced that Russia would deploy Iskander ballistic missiles in the Kaliningrad enclave to counter the alleged threat posed by U.S. plans to deploy a missile defense system in Poland and the Czech Republic.[74]

Despite the hints of menace in Medvedev's threat to deploy missiles on the borders of NATO allies Poland and Lithuania, Moscow simultaneously held out a wary olive branch to the new U.S. administration. Lavrov suggested that:

> Russian-U.S. relations would benefit greatly from the establishment of an atmosphere of mutual trust and mutual respect, which characterized the relationship between the presidents of the two countries over the last eight years but which not always showed itself at the lower levels. Paradoxically, there was

more mutual trust and respect between the two states during the Cold War. Perhaps, it was because there was less lecturing then about what a state should be and how it should behave.[75]

As Obama was settling into the White House, it seemed that both Moscow and Washington were searching for ways to get the relationship back on track. Moreover, the two sides shared a common critique of the recent past, arguing that the United States had focused too heavily on Russian domestic politics (which had become increasingly authoritarian during Putin's second term) and had ignored clear Russian signals that certain actions—especially further NATO expansion inside the former Soviet Union and construction of the East European missile defense system—were unacceptable and would be resisted even if the cost to Russia's reputation and relations with the West were high.

The Obama administration sought to draw a line beneath the disputes of the recent past and focus on areas where U.S.-Russian cooperation could be advanced. While the United States would welcome and offer incentives to encourage the development of such pragmatic cooperation into a broader rapprochement, it would avoid the temptation of seeing Russia as only either a potential strategic partner or a menace to peace and stability. If he could reduce tensions by addressing Moscow's major criticisms of U.S. policy, Obama hoped to gain Russian cooperation in addressing the worsening situation in Afghanistan and Washington's mounting confrontation with Iran over Tehran's nuclear program. The goal was not to renew the attempt at integrating Russia into the West, but to establish a mutually beneficial, albeit largely still transactional relationship.

Obama and Medvedev met for the first time on the sidelines of the G20 summit in London at the beginning of April 2009. They emerged with a shared commitment to a new arms control agreement to replace START I (scheduled to expire at the end of 2009), to collaborate in seeking curbs on the Iranian and North Korean nuclear programs, and appeared to reach agreement on steps toward Russia's WTO entry. While the two leaders were unable to resolve the standoff over Washington's plans for missile defense in Eastern Europe, Medvedev renewed Russia's offer to study alternatives, including construction of a joint missile defense system.[76] The substance of these agreements was limited, but the very fact that the two sides seemed committed at the highest levels to enhancing their cooperation (only eight months after the invasion of Georgia) was an important signal.

When Obama traveled to Moscow for his first bilateral summit with Medvedev in July 2009, the two leaders sought to provide more substance to the abstract notion of the reset. They agreed to establish a new Bilateral Presidential Commission—essentially a restored and upgraded version of the Clinton-era Gore-Chernomyrdin commission—with working groups on issues ranging from nuclear security to business development and economic relations to health care.[77] While the commission would rarely grab headlines, it was designed to provide a forum for regular working-level interactions, and to focus on pragmatic cooperation (including between business and civil society) rather than grandiose questions of Russia's relationship to the West.

Medvedev and Obama also signed an agreement allowing the U.S. military to use Russian airspace to move forces and equipment en route to Afghanistan (Russia agreed to a parallel ground transit arrangement with NATO that the U.S. military also exploited as part of the so-called Northern Distribution Network, or NDN). In part, Moscow's agreement to step up its assistance to the war effort was driven by concern that the situation in Afghanistan was getting out of hand and beginning to threaten Russian interests directly.

Beside its continued worry that a resurgent Taliban could spread radicalism and instability into Central Asia, Russia believed that Afghanistan's opium trade was creating both a security and a public health problem at home. Facing a rising tide of addiction inside Russia, Moscow was eager for the allied forces to undertake a more comprehensive campaign to eradicate Afghanistan's poppy crop—while the United States worried that eradication would deprive poor Afghan farmers of their livelihood and drive them into the arms of the Taliban. By taking on a more active role, Moscow hoped to enhance its ability to press for a more active counternarcotics strategy on the part of coalition forces. This approach was similar to the one pursued after the 9/11 attacks, when Moscow calculated that cooperating closely would be the best opportunity for gaining influence over the United States' Afghanistan strategy. Some observers also saw the offer of transit rights as a means to gain leverage with the United States over the question of missile defense, or as the first step in Moscow's plans to reassert its interests in a postconflict Afghanistan.[78] Whatever the motivation, the United States welcomed a decision that would allow it to reduce its dependence on an increasingly dangerous and unreliable Pakistan to move equipment into Afghanistan.

The Obama administration was eager to build on this promising beginning, focusing initially on the familiar challenge of arms control. Obama announced in September 2009 that the United States would reconfigure its plans for missile defense in Eastern Europe, plans that had become a major rallying cry for Russian hard-liners and were even cited by Medvedev and Putin as representing a significant obstacle to deeper U.S.-Russian cooperation. Obama abandoned the Bush administration's commitment to placing interceptors in Poland and a radar station in the Czech Republic, choosing instead to initially deploy interceptors on ships and at land sites closer to the Iranian border in southeastern Europe; these initial deployments could be supplemented with others later as Washington's analysis of the Iranian threat evolved (the bureaucratic name for this concept was European Phased Adaptive Approach, or EPAA). The Obama administration announced that the reconfiguration was based on new assessments of Iran's capabilities, which focused more on short-range missiles capable of hitting Europe rather than long-range missiles that could hit the United States. Obama's critics at home—as well as some Russian commentators—argued he had given in to Russian pressure, including Medvedev's threat to place missiles in Kaliningrad.

Both Medvedev and Putin welcomed the U.S. president's "brave" decision, though the Russian military soon questioned whether the new configuration was any less threatening to Russia's deterrence capability.[79] Officially, Moscow termed Obama's decision merely the rectification of a mistake, rather than a concession that Russia would have to reciprocate.[80] Still, having focused its earlier opposition on the placement of the U.S. system in Poland and the Czech Republic rather than the concept of missile defense as such, the Kremlin was not in a position to take a hard line against Washington's new plan and still claim it hoped to improve the overall relationship. Eventually (at the November 2010 NATO-Russia summit in Lisbon), it would agree to cooperate with the United States and NATO to build a combined missile defense system covering all of Europe—a step with potentially far-reaching consequences for Russia's relationship with both the United States and Europe. Both Medvedev and Lavrov subsequently warned that missile defense would be a critical litmus test for the future of the reset: either the United States and Russia would succeed in designing a new architecture that met both of their needs, or a new arms race would soon break out.[81]

With the impediments of missile defense in Eastern Europe and NATO expansion moving into the background, it became possible for Moscow and Washington to advance onto the next phase of the reset, namely identifying areas where United States and Russian interests were largely aligned already and working to secure positive agreements. At the top of the agenda was replacing the START I agreement, which was set to expire in December 2009. Not only did START I impose hard caps on the numbers of warheads and delivery vehicles the United States and Russia were allowed to keep in their arsenals, it also provided for a stringent verification regime that allowed each country to ensure the other was not cheating. The SORT agreement, signed by Bush and Putin in 2002, had imposed lower ceilings for weapons, but relied on the verification provisions of START I. If START I were allowed to lapse, the two sides would be unable to be confident the other was abiding by its SORT commitments.

Given START I's impending expiry, replacing it was a natural priority for Moscow, which feared it would be unable to keep up should the United States decide to expand and modernize its nuclear arsenal. Russia wanted an agreement that codified its claim to strategic parity with the United States, and that reinforced its broader argument that effective security in the twenty-first century had to be equal and indivisible.[82] For Washington, arms control was attractive because of Obama's stated commitment to eventually eliminating nuclear weapons and his desire to convince other states to abjure developing them. Since both Moscow and Washington clearly wanted a treaty, focusing initially on arms control also made sense in the context of the reset by building trust and showing that the two sides could work together on problems of common interest.

Yet it soon became clear that while Moscow and Washington might share a general interest in cutting their arsenals, their specific concerns differed enough that reaching an agreement before START I expired might be impossible. Washington and Moscow were at odds over rules for counting warheads and delivery vehicles (e.g., how to count a heavy bomber capable of holding multiple bombs), how much access to give inspectors from the other country, and how to share telemetry data without compromising state secrets. More importantly, they disagreed over whether and how to address Moscow's concern about the missile defense system that Obama was still committed to building in some form and which the Russians wanted covered by the new treaty.

These disagreements forced the negotiations to drag on well past the December 2009 expiration of START I (since both sides were satisfied with the direction of the negotiations, they agreed to continue abiding by START I's provisions until a new treaty was signed). It was not until April 2010 when the two sides ultimately agreed on the text of the so-called New START agreement, which capped warheads at 1,550 apiece (with each side free to determine the allocation of those warheads within the triad of ICBMs, SLBMs, and heavy bombers), along with separate limits for launch vehicles.[83] On missile defense, the two sides compromised by including a reference in the treaty's preamble to the "interrelationship" between offensive and defensive arms but acknowledging that currently existing technologies did not "undermine the viability and effectiveness" of either side's offensive capabilities.[84]

Even after the agreement was signed, it became clear that ratification by the U.S. Senate would not be automatic, since many senators had come to view the agreement as a unilateral concession to a weaker adversary that would only hamstring the United States' ability to maintain its status as the world's leading nuclear power, or because they feared its preamble effectively prevented Washington from developing missile defense capabilities. The Senate approved the treaty in a lame-duck session at the end of 2010, but not before tacking on a resolution laying out its concerns over missile defense, nuclear modernization, sharing of telemetry data, and other miscellanea. Meanwhile, the Russian side maintained it would withdraw from the new treaty if it determined that U.S. plans for an antiballistic missile system posed a threat to Russia's deterrent capability, regardless of their geographic parameters—much as Moscow had used the Bush administration's withdrawal from the ABM Treaty as a justification for its conditional ratification of START II.[85]

These disputes highlighted one of the major challenges to the Obama administration's reset policy, namely, that it relied to a certain degree on getting "deliverables" as a means of gradually shifting both sides' strategic calculations. Yet for the moment at least, the notion of reaching limited agreements as a means of building trust and pursuing deeper cooperation in the future appeared borne out. Russia's continuing economic difficulties bolstered Medvedev's argument that Russia had to lower the temperature of its disputes with the developed West if it was to lay the foundation for a durable recovery that would give substance to Moscow's Great Power aspirations. Meanwhile, Moscow increasingly accepted Obama's logic that clearing away deep-seated disputes would enable the United States and Russia to "elevate [their] cooperation to a higher level."[86]

Both sides saw the lack of economic ties as a critical weakness in the bilateral relationship and made the boosting of trade and investment a major aim of the reset policy. In 2009, only about 4 percent of Russia's inward foreign direct investment originated in the United States, while bilateral trade turnover was only $25.3 billion, or barely one-twentieth of U.S.-China bilateral trade and approximately 1 percent of total U.S. trade.[87] Moreover, such U.S. investment as did make its way to Russia was heavily concentrated in the volatile energy sector, despite Medvedev's push for economic modernization and diversification. (See figure 3.1.)

The lack of U.S.-Russian economic integration meant that the business communities in the two countries, often the loudest voice in favor of close

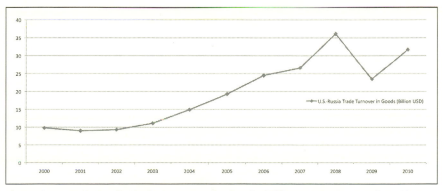

Figure 3.1.   U.S.-Russia Trade Turnover in Goods (billion USD). *Source:* http://www.census.gov/foreign-trade/balance/c4621.html

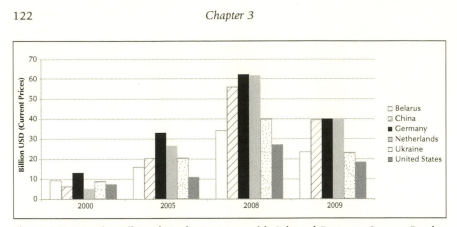

Figure 3.2.   Russian Bilateral Trade Turnover with Selected Partners. *Source:* **Russian State Statistics Committee (Goskomstat). http://www.gks.ru/bgd/regl/b10_13/IssWWW .exe/Stg/d6/25-06.htm. http://www.gks.ru/bgd/regl/b10_13/IssWWW.exe/Stg/d6/ 25-07.htm**

political relations, did not carry much weight in discussions about U.S.-Russian relations. Nor could mutual economic interest provide an incentive for the two countries to settle their differences. Promoting trade and investment would not in itself suffice to transform the U.S.-Russian relationship, but both sides recognized that deeper economic ties could help align their interests more effectively and create common interests where none had previously existed.

The draft foreign policy document leaked by the Russian Foreign Ministry in May 2010, which gave substance to Medvedev's vision of foreign relations as a tool for development, argued that Russia needed to deepen its cooperation with the United States precisely in order to harness U.S. economic might on behalf of Russian modernization. It called for boosting U.S. investment into Russia, lowering barriers to bilateral trade, and learning from U.S. experience how to nurture innovation and regulate business. It also called on Washington to revive the so-called 123 Agreement on civilian nuclear cooperation that Bush had withdrawn during the Russo-Georgian war, eliminate sanctions on Russian companies engaged in business with Syria and Iran, and urged the United States to curb its use of antidumping provisions to limit the import of Russian raw materials.[88]

The Bilateral Presidential Commission also focused much of its efforts on the economic relationship. Its various working groups discussed ways to promote bilateral trade and investment, both at the level of government (encouraging further reform of Russia's judiciary and fighting corruption) and individual firms (coordinating visits by representatives of U.S. technology and social media companies to Russia). Meanwhile, business groups such as the Russian Union of Industrialists and Entrepreneurs and the U.S. Chamber of Commerce collaborated to develop business partnerships, with the blessing of officials in both Washington and Moscow. Medvedev's visit to the United States in June 2010 was marked by a series of deals involving U.S. companies, notably the software giant Cisco Systems, which agreed to invest $1 billion in Medvedev's planned high-tech center at Skolkovo.

The U.S.-Russia reset increasingly appeared to be one of the Obama administration's signal foreign policy successes. Not only had Washington and Moscow made headway on major issues such as Afghan transit and missile defense, but the Bilateral Presidential Commission and the growing volume of business deals were beginning to lay the foundation for a more mature relationship, one full of day-to-day interactions and less dependent on achieving "deliverables" in the field of hard security. Nonetheless, powerful constituencies in both countries argued that the U.S.-Russian rapprochement constituted a sell-out of important national interests. Given the emphasis the Obama administration placed on the reset as a foreign policy success, it was perhaps inevitable that its Russia policy would become entangled in the hyperpartisan atmosphere of Washington, creating a risk that political change in the United States could set back much of the post-2008 rapprochement. That danger is more acute because U.S.-Russian cooperation did not bring in its train a convergence of values or a common threat perception, apart from continued aversion to Islamist radicalism and wariness about China. The relationship's dynamic, in other words, had become increasingly positive, but it remained transactional—and dependent on continuing recognition of Russia's Great Power aspirations (a recognition not all American politicians were willing to grant).[89]

REMAINING CHALLENGES

Russia, along with China, is one of the few large powers whose worldview and interests are frequently incongruous with those of the United States. The divergence of interests (and values) between Moscow and Washington on issues such as containing Iran and maintaining the post-Soviet status quo in the former USSR limits the prospects that the U.S.-Russian rapprochement of recent years can solidify into a strategic alliance. This divergence is most evident in the post-Soviet space, which remains the central concern in Russian foreign policy, but is reflected as well in areas of high priority for Washington, above all the greater Middle East.

From the wars in Iraq and Afghanistan to the standoff over Iran's nuclear program and the search for a solution to the Israeli-Palestinian conflict, the Middle East has remained the central focus of U.S. foreign policy for more than a decade. Meanwhile, restoring its economic competitiveness, tackling its debt, not to mention coping with the rise of China and the emergence of transnational threats ranging from terrorism to climate change are the key long-run challenges facing the United States. At best, Russia figures heavily in only a few of those priorities (addressing the rise of China and transnational threats). Russia's situation is somewhat different. Compared with the United States, Russia is something of a bit player in the Middle East (its leaders have often expressed an interest in a larger role in the Israeli-Palestinian peace process or the campaign to dissuade Iran from producing nuclear weapons, but continue to face the reality that Russia enjoys little strategic leverage in the region). Given its traditional geopolitical approach to foreign policy, Russia has also mostly been on the sidelines for discussions of emerging transnational threats—though Medvedev has made an effort to have Russia play a larger role in these discussions. Instead, Russia's foreign policy priorities lie largely around its borders, inside the former Soviet Union, where it has struggled to accommodate growing Western engagement.

Iran has always been a particularly difficult challenge for U.S.-Russian relations, given the salience of Iran to the United States, which has sought to isolate the Islamic Republic ever since the 1979 revolution, and the vastly different views of Iran that prevail in Washington and Moscow. Russia has often seen Iran as a helpful, if troublesome, partner and an important regional actor. At moments of particular U.S.-Russian tension, moreover, Moscow has deliberately sought to develop closer ties with Tehran as a way of putting pressure on the U.S. Yet since Iran has been a higher priority for the United States (and its allies) than for Russia, Moscow's relations with Tehran have often appeared instrumental, blowing hot and cold depending on the state of Russia's relations with the U.S. From Washington's perspective, one of the major accomplishments of the reset has therefore been Russia's increased cooperation in sanctioning and isolating Iran over its nuclear program.

Iran remains one of Moscow's major customers for industrial goods as well as conventional weaponry. Iran's diplomacy in the region has also largely coincided with Russia's. The two countries worked together to end the civil war in Tajikistan in the 1990s, and Moscow has appreciated Iranian restraint in Central Asia.[90] Such restraint extends as well to Iran's dealings with the Muslim populations around Russia's border. In contrast to its behavior during the first Chechen war (1994–1996), Tehran largely refrained from supporting the Chechen rebels during the war that began in 1999 or during the more recent round of instability in the North Caucasus.[91] At the same time, as one of the major nuclear powers itself, Russia has been consistently opposed to the proliferation of nuclear weapons. Despite its potentially lucrative participation in the overt, civilian side of Iran's nuclear program, Moscow has been clear under both Putin and

Medvedev that it will act to keep Tehran from developing a nuclear weapons capability.

At times, Russia has tried to act as a bridge to the Iranians, urging Tehran privately to come clean to international inspectors, and offering in late 2005 to provide uranium for Iranian civilian reactors on the condition that Russian engineers carry out the enrichment (on Iranian territory) and take possession of the used fuel afterward so that it could not be reprocessed for weapons use.[92] Though backed by the United States and Europeans as a way to prevent Iran from developing an indigenous enrichment capability, this scheme was rejected by Tehran, which claimed—perhaps not unreasonably—that it did not trust the Russians. Once the existence of a secret Iranian enrichment facility at Qom was revealed in September 2009, Russia offered to take possession of the enriched uranium and transform it into fuel to produce medical isotopes, which Tehran claimed to be the eventual goal of the Qom facility.[93]

Of course, since a nuclear-armed Iran would pose more of a danger to the United States and its allies than to Russia, Moscow has generally been more flexible with the Iranians and more indulgent of their nuclear program's ambiguity. Russia has resisted American pressure to cease its involvement in the civilian side of Iran's nuclear program, above all construction of a nuclear reactor at Bushehr, which could bring in over $1 billion (mainly to the state-owned firm Atomstroieksport) and serve as an effective advertisement for the Russian nuclear industry in other countries. Yet in part out of nonproliferation concerns and in part out of a desire to maintain leverage with the United States, Moscow dragged out the work at Bushehr for years before finally agreeing to provide fuel to allow the plant to begin operations in mid-2010 (a step the United States grudgingly accepted since Russia would maintain custody of the uranium fuel throughout the entire power cycle).

Meanwhile, Russia has generally supported U.S. efforts to impose multilateral sanctions on Iran over its nuclear program through the UN Security Council—while opposing unilateral U.S./European sanctions as an example of Washington overstepping its bounds and seeking to impose its will on others. At the UN, Russia voted in favor of all four rounds of sanctions proposed by Washington, including the June 2010 package targeting financial transactions involving the Iranian Revolutionary Guard Corps, but it continued to criticize additional unilateral sanctions pursued by the United States and European Union.[94] Once again, Russia's main concern was preserving the centrality of the multilateral UN process, and with it, Russia's continued status as a player in the region.

Similarly, Moscow signed a contract with Tehran in December 2005 for the delivery of advanced S-300 surface-to-air missiles that would make a U.S. or Israeli airstrike on Iranian nuclear sites extremely difficult. Under pressure from Washington and Tel Aviv, Russia repeatedly put off delivery of the missiles. When it agreed to support toughened UN sanctions against Tehran in June 2010, Moscow made a point of insisting that the sanctions did not cover its contract for the S-300s. A few months later, however, Medvedev signed a decree officially cancelling delivery of the missiles. In a comment widely presumed to reflect the Kremlin's thinking on the matter, Duma Foreign Affairs Committee chairman Konstantin Kosachev remarked that Iran's "flawed foreign policies" had left Russia no choice but to void the contract—even though the decision would cost Russia at least $800 million.[95] Put differently, Moscow cancelled the S-300 contract as part of its contribution to the improvement in U.S.-Russian relations sparked by the Obama reset, recognizing that it had more to gain from cooperation with the United States than by trying to remain in Iran's good graces at the expense of mounting hostility from Washington.

While Russia largely remained on the sidelines as a wave of revolutions broke out across the Middle East in the first months of 2011, its response to NATO intervention in Libya was a litmus test for the evolution of both U.S. and Russian thinking. In contrast to the 2003 Iraq war, the U.S. role in Libya was relatively modest. France and Britain were the loudest voices in favor of using military force to protect Libyan civilians and rebels from longtime Libyan dictator Moammar Qaddafi—and once the initial aerial barrage to implement a no-fly zone was completed, Washington was eager to hand over the initiative to its partners. And when the coalition launched airstrikes against Qaddafi's forces, it did so with wide-ranging international support, including from the Arab League. It also obtained a resolution in the UN Security Council authorizing "all necessary steps" to protect Libyan civilians. As a permanent member of the Security Council, Russia had an opportunity to block to resolution, which it elected not to do (Russia abstained, as did China).

Nevertheless, Russian officials quickly and repeatedly criticized the coalition, both for exceeding the mandate given to it by the Security Council, and for allegedly killing civilians through indiscriminate use of air power. Prime Minister Putin went even further, telling a group of defense workers that the calls for intervention were reminiscent of a medieval crusade—though he was quickly rebuked my Medvedev.[96] Russia's limited response to the Libyan campaign reflected a belief that, in contrast to Iraq in 2003, the United States was not out to upend established international rules. While Moscow remained uncomfortable about what it viewed as intervention in Libya's internal affairs, it recognized that the coalition's aims were more limited—not the installation of a client regime in the guise of democracy promotion, but the protection of civilians. It also helped that France was the prime mover behind the decision to intervene while the United States was extremely reluctant, and that Russia's own financial and political interests in Libya were more limited than they had been in Iraq.

If Russian and U.S. interests have sometimes aligned in the Middle East, they have more frequently diverged across the former Soviet Union—though the Obama administration's more restrained approach to Ukraine and Georgia in particular has tempered what has long been the most divisive issue in U.S.-Russian relations. Russia views the former Soviet Union as the locus of its most important security challenges, and has shown it is willing to pay a higher price than the United States to secure its interests in the region. For that reason, U.S. attempts to engage in a tug-of-war with Moscow for influence in the former Soviet Union largely failed. Without enhancing U.S. influence in the region, they merely complicated U.S.-Russian relations. Even respectable political circles in Moscow continue to attribute the Rose and Orange Revolutions to U.S.-led machinations, while more extremist politicians have voiced concern that events in Tbilisi and Kyiv were merely a rehearsal for U.S. plans to implant a pro-American regime in Moscow itself.[97]

The invasion of Georgia, which was loudly condemned in the United States, was Russia's most overt attempt at undermining Western (especially U.S.) influence in the region. Even without ousting Saakashvili, the Kremlin demonstrated the limits of Washington's reach and placed other wayward CIS members on notice about the costs of ignoring Russian interests. The Kremlin gambled that the United States would judge its relationship with Russia too important to jeopardize over a small country in the South Caucasus. With uncharacteristic bluntness, Lavrov informed Washington that it had to "choose between defending its prestige over a virtual project [i.e., Saakashvili] or a real partnership [with Russia] which requires joint action."[98] To a great degree, the Kremlin's gamble appeared to pay off; despite tough words, the U.S. response was effectively limited to withdrawing the 123 civilian nuclear cooperation agreement from congressional consideration (though the Obama administration later resubmitted it, and it came into effect at the end of 2010).

The fact that the postrevolutionary governments in Kyiv and Tbilisi sought NATO membership fed into Russian fears that the United States was intent on containing or even rolling back Russian influence in its own neighborhood, especially since the Bush administration expressed qualified support for these ambitions.[99] In Moscow, the assumption was that postrevolutionary states would adopt an anti-Russian political orientation, as the Baltic countries did in the 1990s and as Ukraine (under Yushchenko) and Georgia did more recently.[100]

Washington had largely supported Saakashvili and Yushchenko as a step in the "right" (i.e., liberal and democratic) direction. At the same time, however, the new regimes were welcomed for their presumed foreign policy priorities as well, since both Saakashvili and Yushchenko portrayed their movements in anti-Russian, pro-Western terms—unsurprisingly, given Moscow's determination to maintain the old regime in power in the face of massive street demonstrations. Whatever the initial foreign policy orientation of their movements, in other words, Saakashvili and Yushchenko were forced by the revolutionary dynamic that brought them to power to look to the West for support, primarily as a result of Russia's clumsy attempts to keep them out of office in the first place (which, in Yushchenko's case, involved an assassination attempt in which the Russian security services may have been complicit).

As the democratic promise of the Orange and Rose Revolutions was undermined by corruption and paralysis in both countries, U.S. support came to depend almost entirely on Georgia and Ukraine's foreign policy orientation, a fact not lost on the Ukrainian and Georgian leadership— or on Moscow.[101] Russia increasingly condemned U.S. support for the Saakashvili and Yushchenko regimes (not to mention authoritarian governments in key countries such as Azerbaijan and Kazakhstan) in the name of democratic legitimacy as embodying a double standard, especially as U.S. criticism of Russia's own antidemocratic behavior increased. Moscow was particularly enraged when U.S. vice president Dick Cheney made a highly provocative speech in Vilnius about Russia's imperial attitude toward its neighbors and retreat from democracy, and then flew to Astana where he praised the democratic credentials of Kazakhstan's authoritarian president, Nursultan Nazarbayev.[102]

Though Washington had already grown thoroughly disillusioned with both Saakashvili and Yushchenko by 2008, it was the Russo-Georgian war that truly forced the United States to reconsider its support for both leaders, given the damage U.S. support was doing to relations with Moscow. The Bush administration tried to distance itself from Saakashvili's decision to use force against South Ossetia and Abkhazia, the step that precipitated Russia's intervention in the first place. The Obama administration backed away still further, as part of a strategy that effectively prioritized relations with Russia. While maintaining its calls for Russia to abide by the terms of the cease-fire and withdraw its troops to their prewar positions, Obama's secretary of state Hillary Clinton made clear during a visit to Tbilisi in July 2010 that the Georgians should avoid provoking Moscow, emphasizing that their only hope of regaining control of the breakaway provinces was through domestic reform that would entice the South Ossetians and Abkhazians back into the fold.[103]

In contrast to 2004, when Ukraine held a new presidential election in the spring of 2010, the United States assiduously avoided taking sides, merely calling for the election to be free and fair. When Viktor Yanukovych, whose fraudulent "win" in 2004 precipitated the Orange Revolution, was elected in a vote that foreign observers certified as meeting international standards, Obama joined Medvedev in congratulating the new Ukrainian president. Though Yanukovych had the reputation of favoring closer integration between Ukraine and Russia, his acceptance by the United States was an important signal to Moscow that the Obama administration was not seeking to roll back Russian influence from the post-Soviet space as it believed previous U.S. administrations had done.

While Obama's warier approach to Ukraine and Georgia helped reduce tension with Moscow, the presence of U.S. forces in Central Asia as part of the war in Afghanistan remained an irritant. Although Putin himself authorized the deployment of U.S. forces in Uzbekistan and Kyrgyzstan in late 2001, Moscow clashed repeatedly with Washington over the duration of their presence. Even in 2001, the Kremlin was keen to insist that while the United States had legitimate reasons for stationing troops in Uzbekistan and Kyrgyzstan, they could only stay for a fixed amount of time. When Tashkent ordered the U.S. troops to leave following calls for an investigation into the massacre of demonstrators in Andijon, the Russians stood solidly behind the Uzbeks, as did the Shanghai Cooperation Organization. Moscow also repeatedly pressured Bishkek over the presence of U.S. forces at Manas.

Yet the renewal of U.S.-Russian cooperation in Afghanistan during the early years of Obama's presidency was facilitated by a determined campaign on the part of the United States to persuade Moscow that Washington lacked any long-term military ambitions in Central Asia, a campaign that led Moscow to stop pressing Kyrgyzstan to expel U.S. forces from Manas and facilitated increased U.S.-Russian coordination. Medvedev and Obama even issued a joint statement condemning the interethnic violence that roiled Kyrgyzstan in the spring of 2010, and later agreed to pursue joint humanitarian projects in the country.[104] Once Moscow stopped believing that the United States saw the post-Soviet space as a "grand chessboard," it proved increasingly accepting of a U.S. role in the region—especially in Central Asia with its importance for checking the spread of instability from Afghanistan.

Of course, Russia has not stopped viewing maintaining its influence in the post-Soviet space as a top foreign policy priority, any more than it did when it assented to the deployment of U.S. forces in Uzbekistan and Kyrgyzstan in the first place. With the reset, the Obama administration has sought to effectively end the post–Cold War period in which the geopolitical alignments of Russia and its neighbors are a prize to be won in favor of seeing these countries as fully mature, sovereign entities that will make foreign policy decisions on the basis of their own national interests—even if their leaders define those interests to include remaining in Russia's orbit, as Yanukovych has seemingly done. At the same time, by assiduously cultivating Moscow and giving genuine consideration to Russian interests, the Obama administration has reduced the scope for confrontation even within the post-Soviet space.

The Obama administration's restraint has however encountered significant opposition within elements of the U.S. political establishment (especially among partisans of George W. Bush who saw support for the Rose and Orange Revolutions as a matter of faith), some of whom have charged Obama with sacrificing Washington's democratic allies to a quixotic desire for partnership with the Kremlin.[105] The potential for further political instability in the post-Soviet space, coupled with the ongoing debate about the wisdom of Obama's approach hold the potential for the region to again become a flashpoint in relations between Moscow and Washington.

CONCLUSION

In the early 1990s and again in the early 2000s, U.S.-Russian relations entered periods of great hope for the future. Those hopes, however, were founded on a series of misplaced assumptions: that Russia was on path to become a full member of the democratic and capitalist West, that like Germany and Japan after 1945 it would agree to join a common security community led by the United States, and that with the end of the bipolar standoff of the Cold War the struggle for influence around Russia's borders had come to an end. When those illusions were punctured, U.S.-Russian relations increasingly turned into a pale, de-ideologized shadow of the Cold War. The arrival in power of Dmitry Medvedev and Barack Obama in 2008–2009 set off a new round of optimism, tempered however by the bitter experience of the past two decades. In Medvedev's call to liberalize and modernize, and Obama's invocation of a "humble" foreign policy, Moscow and Washington appeared set to launch a new phase in their relations, one where cooperation was increasingly a habit, rather than an aspiration. Arriving with limited ambitions, Medvedev and Obama offered their countries a chance to avoid the mistakes of the past, where their relationship became too burdened with expectations to develop meaningful foundations.

In his speech on the basic principles of Russian foreign policy in the aftermath of the Georgian war, Medvedev sounded a very Putinist tone, condemning U.S. unipolarity but emphasizing Russia's interest in friendly relations with all countries—including the United States—as long as they recognize Russia's place as a major power and its special role in the CIS.[106] Yet the transition from Putin to a Putin-Medvedev diarchy and the dramatic events of summer 2008—war and the Russian stock market's collapse—helped reexpose the fissure in the Russian elite between Eurasianists and others about how to deal with a United States suffering from its own period of uncertainty. Elements within the Russian bureaucracy used the transition period to question the importance of relations with Washington.[107] The military, busy formulating a new statement of doctrine that identified

NATO expansion as a major threat to Russian security, stepped up its air- and seaborne patrols even while cozying up to American bête noire Hugo Chávez and threatening to sell advanced hardware to Syria and Iran. Yet a financial crisis that Russian observers increasingly argued had punctured holes in the country's claims to global might and a new U.S. president who appeared willing to give Moscow the engagement and respect it desired combined to increasingly sideline those calling for renewed confrontation.

Russian opposition to U.S. foreign policy over the past two decades—in Iraq as in the former Soviet Union and elsewhere—has for the most part been connected to Russia's larger goal of restoring its status as a Great Power and autonomous player on the international stage, rather than ideologically driven a priori opposition to U.S. policy in the manner of the USSR. Much of the seemingly perpetual concern in the United States about the outbreak of a new Cold War, especially in the aftermath of the war between Russia and Georgia, thus misses the point. The first Cold War was a disaster for Russia, and no sane Russian would want to repeat the experience.

Thanks to the original Cold War, however, the United States is still central to Russian thinking, and hence Russian policy toward the United States remains the prism through which foreign policy more generally is filtered. When Russian statesmen talk about multipolarity and a multivector foreign policy, they really are making an argument about Moscow's position with regard to Washington. Consequently, those Russian actions that have fed worries about a new Cold War (Putin's 2007 Munich speech, gas cutoffs affecting Western Europe, the invasion of Georgia) seem above all predicated on a desire to remind the United States that Russia still matters. The point is not confrontation for the sake of confrontation, or even challenging U.S. hegemony, but not allowing Washington to get away with ignoring Russia.

Putin, of course, spurned his closest advisers on multiple occasions to ensure that tensions with the United States did not spiral out of control, whether over the issue of American troops in Central Asia or over the Baltic states' inclusion in NATO. That rejection of the zero-sum mentality that has so long dominated U.S.-Russian relations meant that when Putin lashed out at the United States (for instance, in his Munich speech), his words got Washington's attention.[108] The more cooperative tone in evidence since Obama became president is likely to have a similar effect. If Russia's default position is not to criticize, it will get more of a hearing in Washington on those moments when it does choose criticism.

Moscow has typically portrayed actions with anti-U.S. overtones as a reaction to Washington's own policy choices, making clear that it was willing to seek close ties with Washington as long as the United States did not actively undermine what Moscow saw as its own vital interests—above all in the post-Soviet space. Moscow even depicted the invasion of Georgia and recognition of South Ossetia and Abkhazia as a response to the West's recognition of Kosovo (a decision that Moscow insisted set a precedent for separatist conflicts elsewhere) and support for Georgian and Ukrainian NATO membership. This focus on reciprocity and equal treatment is one major legacy of the Cold War and the centrality of U.S.-Soviet bilateral relations, not only to Soviet foreign policy but to international security generally.

Russia's overall strategy has long been to seek cooperation with the United States to the extent that doing so does not conflict with its Great Power ambitions. Its ability to do both has depended to a great extent on how Washington reciprocated; whether or not it was willing to work together with a Russia that did not fit the pattern established by Germany and Japan after 1945—or the East European states after 1989. As long as the United States believed at least implicitly that the end of the Cold War had brought about the "end of history" and that the post–Cold War world would operate largely according to the rules devised by and for the Western powers themselves at the end of World War II, it would struggle to work with any major power which rejected that paradigm.

By the second decade of the twenty-first century, Americans themselves were increasingly aware that history, even European history, had not ended with the Soviet collapse. Whether the emerging post–post–Cold War world will be multipolar, nonpolar, or merely post-American, the rise of new states and nonstate actors capable of influencing global order has forced the United States to give others a larger say in designing the rules and institutions that will govern international life in the twenty-first century, from the G20 to an overhauled International Monetary Fund. Russia is not necessarily a "rising" state in the same way as its BRICS partners, but like them it is an increasingly confident, competent power whose interests are not entirely congruent with those of the United States. Only if the United States can accept Russia as it is and create space for it to play a responsible role in new and reformed international institutions will it be able to break free from the damaging cycle of expectation and disappointment that has characterized U.S.-Russian relations since the end of the Cold War. The challenge lies not merely in pressing the reset button, but in laying the foundation for a relationship based on mutual respect and common interests that is durable enough to survive the inevitable disagreements, and in appreciating the limits of U.S. power to actually shape Russia or its interactions with the rest of the world.

4

Europe

Between Integration and Confrontation

Europe continues to hold an anomalous position in Russia's foreign policy strategy. Like the United States, Europe is part of the broad coalition of democracies making up the West. Yet despite this shared identity and a shared commitment to democratic values, the Kremlin has often approached the U.S. and Europe on the basis of quite different calculations. For Russia, the U.S. remains important principally as the strongest political and military force in the post–Cold War world, one that often conducts diplomacy on the basis of the same geopolitical considerations underlying Russian foreign policy itself.

Besides being a geographic expression, Europe of course also implies the web of institutions and shared values that sprang up in the aftermath of World War II. Since the end of the Cold War, these institutions—above all the European Union (EU) and North Atlantic Treaty Organization (NATO)— have expanded eastward, taking in countries that had long been in the Russian/Soviet sphere of influence. Europe's dense web of institutions, with their effects on the sovereignty of their members, has no analogue elsewhere in the world. For this reason, Russia's relationship to Europe operates simultaneously on two levels: that of Moscow's bilateral ties with countries like Germany, France, and Poland, as well as that of its ties with the institutional structures of the EU, NATO, the Organization for Security and Cooperation in Europe (OSCE), and other multilateral organizations.

During Putin's presidency, Russia often tried to play off individual European countries—especially larger West European powers—against the institutional center, even while at times also using Europe collectively as a counterweight against the United States. Under Medvedev, Moscow has increasingly focused on improving relations with its onetime satellites in Eastern Europe—above all Poland—in order to depoliticize its relationship with Europe and tap European capital markets in the service of Medvedev's campaign for economic modernization.

Despite extensive economic ties, the relationship between Russia and Europe has endured a series of crises since the end of the Cold War, in part due to the evolving political identities of both Russia and Europe. During the 1980s, the Soviet Union began a strategic retreat from Eastern Europe. Into the resulting vacuum stepped the modern European institutional web. Within two decades, both the EU and NATO had expanded to include most of the former Warsaw Pact states (apart from Russia itself and the non-Baltic former Soviet republics).[1] While Europe does not possess a military potential comparable to that of the United States, the expansion of both NATO and the EU has nonetheless substantially changed Russia's security landscape and fed into Russia's postimperial anxieties. Expansion has deprived Russia of the strategic glacis it acquired at the end of World War II and made Russia and Europe close, if somewhat uncomfortable, neighbors. Insofar as Russia views itself as less than a full participant in institutional Europe, Europe's expanding reach represents a challenge to Russia's attempt to develop a distinct model of development and an autonomous foreign policy.

The halting steps that Brussels has taken toward the creation of an integrated Common Foreign and Security Policy (CFSP) including a Common Security and Defense Policy (CSDP), and the signing of the Lisbon Treaty with its centralization of EU foreign policy under a new High Representative have also affected Russian calculations. The gradual consolidation of EU foreign policy has forced Moscow to confront the sudden appearance of a new, potentially significant security actor right on its border—even if a common European foreign policy remains more an aspiration that a reality for the time being.[2] Besides aspiring to play a greater international role, the new, larger EU has been more assertive toward Russia than the old European Community or the original fifteen-member EU of the 1990s ever were. European states that traditionally maintained close relations with Russia— such as (West) Germany, with its tradition of *Ostpolitik*—looked on uncomfortably as states in the new Europe such as Poland and the Baltic states pushed the EU in a more confrontational direction, often at the expense of the EU's own cohesiveness. Yet Moscow's more recent push to change the terms of its relationship with Warsaw and the Baltic states appears driven by a recognition that if forced to choose, even its closest allies in Europe will prioritize EU solidarity over their relationship with Moscow.

Like the EU, NATO's expansion to the East altered Russia's security calculations, buttressing Cold War–era anxieties about Russia's strategic isolation and encirclement. Given that NATO was created precisely to counter

Soviet geopolitical ambitions in Europe, many Russians continue to view the alliance with substantial mistrust. With the Cold War over and the Warsaw Pact relegated to Trotsky's proverbial dustbin of history, NATO often seems equally outmoded from Russia's perspective. During the 1990s, Primakov and others called for the alliance to be disbanded altogether, or at least subordinated to some kind of pan-European security structure like the OSCE.[3] Medvedev's call to establish a new Euro-Atlantic security architecture is likewise motivated by a desire to sideline NATO and create a more inclusive framework for European security in which Russia is a full participant. As for NATO itself, Russian officials have been careful to emphasize that they do not view the alliance as such as a threat, but are adamantly opposed to it offering membership to Russia's post-Soviet neighbors, to the transfer of NATO military assets closer to Russia's frontiers, and to NATO's use of force without the sanction of the UN Security Council, where Moscow maintains a veto.

While NATO's continued existence was a source of frustration in Moscow in the immediate post-Soviet years, the alliance's decision to take in the former Warsaw Pact states was particularly unwelcome, especially as the Kremlin believed former U.S. president George H. W. Bush and his European counterparts had given their word that, in exchange for Russia tolerating the presence of a united Germany in NATO, the alliance would not expand any further.[4] Instead, NATO moved to include Russia's former satellites in Eastern Europe (including the Baltic states), openly discussed the possibility of bringing in Georgia and Ukraine, and greatly expanded its capacity for out-of-area operations near Russia's borders.[5] While Moscow had many reasons for sending troops into Georgia, concern about Tbilisi's NATO ambitions was among the most critical. Indeed, the post-2008 rapprochement between Russia and the West was made possible in large part because the war forced the United States to accept its European allies' arguments against extending offers of membership to Georgia and Ukraine.

Despite its fears about the consequences of NATO expansion in its own security, the Kremlin leadership has often emphasized the necessity of good relations with Europe, given Russia's proximity and the two sides' interdependence. The imperative for good relations is particularly evident in the economic sphere, since Europe—especially Eastern Europe—remains a major market for Russian exports. Russia's dependence on Europe as a customer is matched by Europe's dependence on Russia as a supplier, especially of oil and gas. Europe is also Russia's main source of foreign investment (accounting for approximately a third of Russia's precrisis stock of FDI).[6] Lowering the barriers to economic cooperation with the Europeans is therefore among the most important foreign policy components of Medvedev's plans for modernizing the economy.

While long desirous of good relations with the EU, Russia has remained firmly opposed to joining the Union, much less NATO—though Russian membership in both organizations has been mooted at various times since 1991, including by Putin on a few occasions and in late 2010 by the director of the Foreign Ministry's policy planning staff.[7] Even though Putin and Medvedev have repeatedly stressed that Russia is "an integral part of European civilization," Russia's insistence on remaining outside the institutional framework of Europe means that Russia has approached the normative foundations of Europe cautiously.[8] As Europe's identity increasingly comes to be based on a consensus about values and institutions, the Great Power ambitions that have motivated Russian foreign policy for most of the country's post-Soviet history, not to mention Russia's authoritarian politics, have often put it at odds with the postmodern and postimperial Europe taking shape on its borders.

Insofar as Moscow's more recent emphasis on modernization and modernization alliances implies a redefinition of Russian *derzhavnost'* to give economic considerations greater weight, the Russian and European worldviews are liable to increasingly converge, while Moscow portrays its ambition to create a social market economy like the ones that emerged in Western Europe after World War II as part of an embrace of its European heritage.[9] Most West European leaders in any case stress the economic side of their relationship with Russia, at the expense of the traditional security relations that have dominated the U.S.-Russian agenda—even after the war in Georgia.[10] The post-2008 economic crisis, which called into question Russia's entire political-economic model and provided the greatest test of European solidarity since the foundation of the EU, only increased the importance of economic ties for both sides.

Nor, given the centrality of the United States to Russian foreign policy thinking, is it possible to ignore the impact of the U.S. on relations between Russia and Europe. Ever since the early years of the Cold War, Moscow has attempted to take advantage of the differences between Europe and the United States for its own ends. The end of the Cold War has done little to change this pattern, and the cooling of U.S.-European ties over the war in Iraq promoted Russian attempts to maneuver between Washington and Brussels. Similarly, the Georgian conflict exposed a continuing rift between the U.S. and at least the West Europeans over the nature of the Russian challenge and the appropriate response to it. Medvedev's call for a new European security architecture likewise was interpreted by many as a ploy to pry Europe from its strategic alignment with the United States. The Obama reset and Moscow's attempt to improve relations with Eastern Europe, however, helped close the gap between U.S. and European approaches to Russia, creating a shared emphasis on engagement and integration with Russia on both sides of the Atlantic.

Shortly after the September 11 attacks, Moscow pursued rapprochement with the U.S. on the basis of a shared commitment to fight terrorism, enlisting U.S. support for its campaign in Chechnya in the face of European opposition. During the run-up to the war in Iraq, Russia pursued a mirror image of this strategy, banding together with France and Germany to oppose a U.S.-led attack on Saddam Hussein. Russia's maneuvering between Washington and Brussels has been more sophisticated in recent years, as Moscow has largely realized that at the end of the day, the EU will not jeopardize its relationship with the United States for the uncertain prospect of Russia's friendship. Instead of openly playing the U.S. and EU against each other, Russian diplomacy increasingly promoted the emergence of a strategic triangle of the U.S., EU, and Russia. In part, the idea of a strategic triangle with the U.S. and the EU was part of Russia's broader strategy of, in the words of Foreign Minister Lavrov, "restoring manageability to world affairs in accord with other centers of power."[11] In other words, a trilateral U.S.-EU-Russian partnership could take the place of the abortive special relationship with the U.S. as a means of returning Russia to a position as a key pillar of the new international order.

Given Russia's proximity to Europe and the importance of Europe's markets for Russian goods (especially energy), economic integration continued even when political relations between the two sides deteriorated. Yet the economic benefits Russia derives from Europe have appeared imperiled at times by Moscow's geopolitical maneuverings, above all its attempts to use energy supplies as a means of obtaining political leverage over both post-Soviet Ukraine and Belarus and the countries of the EU themselves. A fundamental tension has long existed in Russia's policy toward Europe, between the desire for economic cooperation, even integration, and the power-political imperatives that became a more visible element in Russian foreign policy during the Putin years. The economic crisis that began in 2008 pushed Moscow to seek deeper economic engagement with Europe in order to aid its own recovery—and as a mechanism for the long-term transformation of the economy that would give substance to Russia's aspiration to play a greater role in both European and global security. So too did Medvedev's modernization agenda, with its emphasis on reducing political tensions and seeking access to foreign technology and foreign capital, of which Europe is a critical source.

For the future, much will depend on the fate of the European experiment, namely, the durability of and extent of European solidarity, which has already been much tested by an economic crisis that called into doubt the viability of the common currency and a growing backlash among European publics at the encroachment of Brussels-based institutions. It will also depend on whether Europe can develop an effective framework for managing its partnership with Russia—and whether Russia will learn to accept greater European involvement with its post-Soviet neighbors.

RUSSIA AND THE EUROPEAN UNION

The most salient factor in the evolution of Russia's foreign policy in Europe has been the transformation of the European Union itself. From 1992, when the Maastricht Treaty brought the EU into being and laid the foundation for ever closer union among its members, the EU has become an increasingly important international actor in its own right, despite continuing institutional flux and the disunity among the bloc's now twenty-seven members. The EU's emergence from the American shadow has also forced Moscow to increasingly differentiate its approaches to Europe and the U.S.

Putin's Russia initially sought to cooperate with the EU while emphasizing that Russia "does not set itself the task of becoming a member of the EU."[12] This cooperation, however, remained troubled by European distrust of Russia's overall direction and an ongoing tug-of-war over the borderlands between Russia and Europe. At the same time, because the EU must reflect the position of the states it comprises, Brussels had had difficulty articulating a coherent approach to dealing with Russia. Significant disputes long existed within Europe—between old and new members of the EU and between large and small countries—leaving the EU unable to agree on any sort of comprehensive strategy for relations with Russia. Russia's attempts to play on these differences have, paradoxically, been one of the main factors driving the various European countries together.

For much of the past two decades, EU members resorted to bilateral arrangements with Moscow when it served their interests to do so (especially on the question of energy supplies).[13] The growth of bilateral arrangements increased Russian bargaining leverage, allowing the Kremlin to play different European states off one another and limiting the range of issues where Russia found itself confronting a solid European bloc. Meanwhile, countries like Poland and the Baltic states that have little leverage with Russia on their own have at times sought to push the EU as a whole into a more confrontational posture, to the discomfort of states like Germany that long had cozier arrangements with the Kremlin. Yet when pressed, Germany and other West European powers have largely stood behind their East European partners, making clear to the Russians that they had little to gain from encouraging splits within the EU and prompting Moscow to pursue rapprochement with its onetime satellites, above all Poland.

As a result of the EU's various internal cleavages, its goals for policy toward Russia have long been fairly modest. In 2007 the European Commission described its priorities toward Russia as:

Fostering the political and economic stability of the [Russian] Federation; in maintaining a stable supply of energy; in further co-operation in the fields of justice and home affairs, the environment and nuclear safety in order to combat "soft" security threats; and in stepping up cooperation with Russia in the Southern Caucasus and the Western NIS for the geopolitical stability of the CIS region, including for the resolution of frozen conflicts.[14]

The legacy of repeated energy disputes with Moscow, the war in Georgia, and the post-2008 financial crisis convinced many European officials of the need to develop a more ambitious agenda for relations with Russia, one that would deepen economic and institutional connections and make Moscow more of a stakeholder in European stability and prosperity. Europe's most important tool in advancing the relationship is its economic influence: taken as a whole, the EU is Russia's largest trading partner by far and an important source of investment and technology. Indeed, the idea of modernization alliances championed by Medvedev initially took fruit with Europe, with the two sides formalizing a "partnership for modernization" at their summit meeting in Rostov-on-Don in May–June 2010. Such engagement in pursuit of what Angela Stent and Eugene Rumer term a "broad based strategic partnership" (rather that the more limited U.S.-Russian rapprochement heralded by the Obama administration's reset) was more of an imperative for the EU than the U.S. given Europe's proximity to Russia and inability to insulate itself from the consequences of poor relations.[15] The political subtext of the modernization partnership and other agreements is precisely to make it harder for either side to disentangle itself from the other's economic embrace, creating both a community of interests among business and the political leverage that economic dependence brings.

The EU, of course, began its life as an economic organization, growing out of Franco-German heavy industrial cooperation in the early 1950s. Given the economic focus of the resulting European Economic Community (EEC), even during the height of the Cold War Moscow was willing to forge economic links with Western Europe, though without necessarily accepting the legitimacy of the EEC as a political actor.[16] With the end of the Cold War and the consolidation of the EEC into the more integrated, more explicitly political EU, Russia continued to value the West Europeans as trading partners while also forging direct links to the EU as an institution. In the 1990s, even as Moscow consistently opposed the expansion of NATO into Eastern Europe, it supported the growth of the EU as a means of satisfying the East Europeans' desire to anchor themselves in the West while not threatening Russia's own security.

Yet, as with the United States, relations between the EU and Russia suffered from unfulfilled expectations on both sides. At the end of the Cold

War, Moscow expected to be greeted, like West Germany in the 1950s, with an influx of foreign aid and investment as well as rapid integration into the institutional web of the new Europe. Brussels, meanwhile, assumed that Russia would rapidly adopt Western (or, more precisely, European) values regarding human rights, democracy, and free markets.[17]

Both were to be disappointed. Even as Russia and the EU signed a Partnership and Cooperation Agreement (PCA) in 1994, they regarded each other warily. Primakov, as foreign minister, revived the Soviet-era practice of trying to split Europe from the United States, particularly during the conflicts in the Balkans at the end of the 1990s.[18] Beginning in 1994, Russia was also engaged in a vicious civil war in Chechnya, where its troops' employment of brute force against the civilian population brought stiff objections from the EU, including calls that Russia be expelled from the Council of Europe for its brazen violation of the council's human rights norms.[19]

Russia's authoritarianism has also been a major source of contention with Europe, even more so than in Moscow's relationship with the United States. Since the start of the war on terror, Washington has been willing to overlook to a significant extent the antidemocratic trends under way in Russia, a tendency that the reset has perhaps unwittingly reinforced by shifting Washington's focus to areas where the U.S. and Russia agree (in comparison with its predecessor, the Obama administration also downplayed democracy promotion as an explicit goal of U.S. foreign policy). The degree of Russia's acceptance into the European family will largely depend on the extent to which Moscow is willing and able to adopt European norms in fields like rule of law, freedom of the press, electoral transparency, and the like—all of which deteriorated during Putin's presidency, and where Medvedev's reformist rhetoric has outstripped his accomplishments. Since the U.S. is more interested in Russian cooperation on a geopolitical level, the question of values, while not irrelevant, remains by comparison a secondary concern.

If democracy and all its attributes remain an area of deep disagreement between Russians and Europeans, a certain wariness about American hegemony has at times served to bring Moscow and Brussels closer. In 1999, Moscow elaborated its approach to relations with the EU in a document known as the "Medium-Term Strategy for the Development of Relations between the Russian Federation and the European Union (2000–2010) [*Strategiya razvitii otnoshenii Rossiiskoi federatsii s Evropeiskim soyuzom na srednesrochnuyu perspektivu (2000–2010 gody)*]," which Putin, in his first stint as prime minister, helped to draft.[20] This strategy document, presented by the Russians to their EU counterparts at the Helsinki summit in October 1999, was designed to govern Russian policy toward the EU until 2010. Like the roughly contemporaneous Russian Foreign Policy Concept, the Medium-Term Strategy emphasized Russia's interest in the creation of a multipolar world order, where international law constrained the ability of any single state to impose its will through force—precisely as Moscow argued the United States had just done in Kosovo. It praised Europe as Russia's strategic partner in this endeavor to establish a multipolar order and a system of collective security in Europe. The document did make clear that Russia's leadership viewed the country as a Euro-Asian state that by virtue of its size and history was not interested in any kind of formal association with—much less eventual membership in—the EU. At the same time, it held out the possibility of Russia playing a greater role in pan-European security, perhaps by way of the OSCE, which Moscow held out as a way to check what the Medium-Term Strategy termed "NATO-centrism in Europe."[21]

While the Medium-Term Strategy was designed to shape Russian relations with the EU for a full decade, Russia gradually became less sanguine about the EU. One major factor in this estrangement was the rapprochement with the United States in the first years of Putin's presidency, which altered how the Kremlin approached its goal of promoting multipolarity. By 2001, bandwagoning with Washington, rather than balancing against it, appeared the most effective way to promote Russia's status as a major actor in world affairs. The September 11 attacks only reinforced Putin's strategy of promoting better ties with the U.S. while approaching the moralizing EU warily. The attacks brought the U.S. and Russia together in advocating a muscular approach to Islamic terrorism. Both meanwhile frequently found themselves in opposition to Brussels (not to mention Berlin and Paris), which remained skeptical of the forceful methods advocated by the Bush and Putin governments.[22] Unlike the United States, following September 11 the EU and its members did not moderate their criticism of Russian behavior in Chechnya or of the Kremlin's conduct during the 2003 parliamentary and 2004 presidential elections. More generally, the EU largely rejected the kind of power-driven geopolitical thinking common to both Russia and the U.S., focusing on the need for better policing and improved international cooperation rather than military force as the keys to defeating the terrorist menace in Afghanistan, Chechnya, and elsewhere.[23]

While the U.S.-Russian rapprochement of 2001–2003 had the effect of sidelining Europe, the EU's own development as an actor in international affairs limited the Union's ability to cooperate with Russia. Somewhat paradoxically, while the EU's emphasis on the "soft" aspects of security in response to the September 11 attacks put it at odds with a Kremlin still employing massive force in its own antiterrorist campaign in Chechnya, the potential development of the EU as a more effective wielder of "hard" power had a similar effect.

In the wake of the terrorist attacks on the United States and conscious of the EU's tepid response to mass killing in Bosnia and Rwanda in the 1990s, the Council of Europe adopted the first comprehensive EU security strategy in December 2003.[24] The following year, the EU established an integrated European Defense Agency to coordinate the strategic planning of member states, while the EU also took over policing and peacekeeping responsibilities in Macedonia and Bosnia, respectively, and launched its first major out-of-area operation in the Democratic Republic of Congo (DRC).[25] By 2004, the EU, NATO, and several European national governments all had authority over troops in the field, in theaters ranging from Kosovo to Iraq to the DRC, even if Brussels continually fell behind on its plans to upgrade (and fund) the EU's security capabilities.

The increased willingness of both the EU collectively and its member states individually to deploy troops outside the long-established framework of NATO had important implications for the way the Kremlin approached its relationship with the EU. The sharp distinction Russian leaders in the 1990s made between the "good" EU and "bad" NATO became less clear-cut, as Moscow no longer saw the two organizations' roles as fully distinct.[26]

Of course, the EU's emergence as a distinct foreign policy actor has not always been smooth. The backlash in many EU countries toward the deployment of troops in Afghanistan, increasing questions about the EU's legitimacy growing out of the debates over the Lisbon Treaty, not to mention the consequences of the economic crisis that roiled the Continent starting in 2008 have all contributed to a retrenchment of the EU's foreign policy ambitions—and even contributed to uncertainty about the long-term viability of the EU itself. As the EU has focused more on getting its own fiscal house in order (including bailing out heavily indebted members such as Portugal, Ireland, and Greece), it was less able to conduct an ambitious collective foreign policy, and individual member states' approaches to Moscow again took center stage. The mutual restraint imposed on Russia and the EU by the crisis is one of the factors facilitating the attempts of both sides to deepen the relationship in the years since 2008.

In addition to fears about the growing securitization of the EU, Moscow worried about the effects of EU expansion and the potential impact on EU foreign policy of the East European countries, which have long been more skeptical of Russia. Thanks to the simultaneous processes of expansion and defense integration within the EU, Russia now finds Europe right on its borders and on the borders of unstable states like Moldova and Ukraine that Russia continues to consider part of its own security zone.[27] In contrast to its opposition to further NATO expansion, Russia has not raised any overt objections to the prospect of Ukraine's membership in the EU (and for economic reasons, might even prove supportive), though increased momentum toward strengthening EU defense capacity might risk replaying the debate over NATO membership for the former Soviet republics. Nevertheless, proposals to deepen Brussels' relationship with Kyiv have often been a point of contention with Moscow, whether over EU attempts to modernize Ukraine's energy transit system or to sign a free-trade agreement that would reorient Ukraine's economy increasingly toward the West.[28]

The cooling of relations between Moscow and Brussels that took place in the first years of Putin's presidency coincided with the first major wave of EU expansion to the East and the host of complications—technical as well as political—that ensued for Moscow.[29] Russian observers identified a trend toward Brussels devaluing the supposedly objective criteria for EU membership in favor of political criteria linked to the EU's international security role. In the Russian view, only the predominance of geopolitical criteria over the EU's historic emphasis on economic development, shared values, and democracy could explain the interest in admitting the countries of the Western Balkans or Turkey—much less the South Caucasus—into the EU.[30] Given the Russian proclivity to view the world in traditional balance-of-power terms, it is hardly surprising that many Russians see the EU's continued expansion, like NATO's, as part of a process of reestablishing containment of Russia.

As a result of its mounting skepticism of the EU as an organization, Russia increasingly emphasized bilateral relations with states in Europe as an alternative to working through Brussels. This approach fit more neatly with Moscow's belief in the supremacy of states and distrust of international organizations and norms. States, so the reasoning goes, can at least be expected to act in their national interest and to be less moralistic about democracy, human rights, and the like than the EU as a whole.[31]

Moreover, the member states of the EU have long had diverging views of Russia as an actor in the international system. Germany under Gerhard Schröder (1998–2005) and Italy under Silvio Berlusconi (2001–2006 and 2008–present) were on particularly good terms with Putin's Kremlin, and thus it made sense for the Kremlin to seek a privileged partnership with these states parallel to its relationship with the EU as a whole.[32] Schröder especially was perceived to be close to the Russian president and at times even under his influence—an impression that Schröder's decision at the end of his term as chancellor to take a position with the joint concern building a gas pipeline from Russia to Germany did nothing to alleviate.[33] Even since Schröder's departure from office and replacement by the Christian Democrat (and onetime citizen of the German Democratic Republic) Angela Merkel, Berlin's fundamental interest in close relations with Russia has not changed, regardless of attitudes in Brussels or Warsaw. Even Merkel, much warier of Putin than her predecessor, maintained a high level of Russo-German engagement, embodied in the slogan "*Wandel durch Verpflechtung*," or "change through engagement."[34] Germany, with France, was at the forefront of the campaign to relaunch relations with Russia in the messy aftermath of the war in Georgia and was a leading advocate for Moscow's campaign to improve relations with Poland, which has been central to the launching of deeper EU-Russian engagement during Medvedev's presidency.

Under Putin, all of the EU member states with which Russia sought improved bilateral relations were in Western Europe. Russia's 2007 Foreign Policy Review listed improved bilateral relations with Germany, France, Spain, and Italy as priorities for Russian diplomacy. It also advocated the creation of a special French-German-Russian "trilateral political dialogue" as part of its strategy for enhancing Russia's role as a "stabilizing factor in the Eurasian space."[35] Outreach to Russia's onetime satellites in Eastern Europe has however only become a priority since Medvedev came to power. Poor relations with Poland facilitated the emergence of a Warsaw-Washington axis during the Putin/Bush years, encouraging the U.S. to step up its presence in Eastern Europe in ways that Moscow found threatening. The proposed ballistic missile shield the Bush administration sought to base in Poland and the Czech Republic was the most significant example of how Russia's estrangement from Eastern Europe drove its closest European neighbors ever further into the arms of the United States. The U.S.-Russia reset has thus helped lay the foundation for Moscow's rapprochement with Eastern Europe by alleviating Russian fears that states such as Poland and Lithuania would become launching pads for a U.S.-led containment effort.

Another area where the consequences of tension between Russia and Eastern Europe have been particularly stark is the debate over Europe's dependence on Russian energy. Russian plans to build two new undersea bypass pipelines, Nord Stream and South Stream, would be especially beneficial to the two EU countries with which Russia enjoys the closest political ties, Germany and Italy, respectively. Nord Stream, which is already being built by a consortium including Gazprom and the German firms Wintershall and E.ON as well as the Dutch company Gasunie, would run under the Baltic Sea to Greifswald in the German state of Mecklenburg-Vorpommern. By cutting out current transit countries Poland, Belarus, and Ukraine, Nord Stream would turn Germany into a hub for Russian gas sales to Europe and a recipient of transit fees. Similarly, the still-speculative South Stream project, which would run under the Black Sea and up the Balkan Peninsula to Italy and Austria, would benefit those countries (as well as the Italian gas company Eni and Electricité de France, which are building the pipeline together with Gazprom) financially and tie them closer to Moscow, while reducing their dependence on gas transited across Ukraine.

The political importance of the two bypass pipelines is reflected in the fact that former German chancellor Schröder accepted a position as head of the shareholders' committee of Nord Stream AG, while former Italian prime minister Romano Prodi was offered, but declined, a similar position with South Stream AG. Yet Russia's often fraught relations with Eastern Europe have significantly complicated the debate over sales of Russian energy, especially given Russia's practice of specially cultivating Berlin, Paris, and Rome. This development became particularly significant in the aftermath of the 2006 and 2007 energy crises, when Germany rushed to approve the construction of Nord Stream, which Radosław Sikorski, then Poland's defense minister, likened to the notorious 1939 Molotov-Ribbentrop Pact in its consequences for Poland.[36]

In similar fashion, the crisis in Georgia exposed a deep East-West fault line within Europe over dealing with Moscow. The West Europeans—France and Germany—blocked U.S. president Bush's proposal to extend NATO membership action plans to Georgia and Ukraine during the February 2008 NATO summit in Bucharest. After fighting broke out six months later during France's EU presidency, French president Nicolas Sarkozy was instrumental in negotiating a cease-fire, and without assigning blame, called for both Russia and Georgia to resume negotiations for a political solution to the conflict.[37] France later even agreed to sell Russia advanced amphibious assault ships that Georgia protested could be used to mount another invasion. As the Russian occupation of the disputed provinces continued, Sarkozy and German chancellor Merkel attempted to increase the pressure on Moscow to comply without simultaneously jeopardizing broader EU-Russian cooperation, while Silvio Berlusconi's Italy remained firmly in Moscow's camp.[38]

With Poland in the forefront, the East Europeans called on the EU to take a much firmer line from the beginning, demanding sanctions in response to the Russian invasion. Other European countries with neither strong economic ties to Russia nor a history of confrontation with Moscow (such as Spain) were less interested in any action at all.[39] Such divisions in Europe made it easier for Moscow to ignore pressure to complete its withdrawal from Georgia, firm in the belief that the EU would prove unable to adopt a common position with any teeth.

Yet if the EU could not unite behind Georgia, it could rally together when one of its own members felt intimidated by Moscow, as several East European states did by the planned bypass pipelines, or by a Russian embargo on Polish meat imports. The reality of EU solidarity, especially when communicated to Moscow by someone close to the Russians such as Merkel, gave the Kremlin an incentive to reconsider its attempts to benefit from East-West dissension in the EU. Addressing the concerns of many Europeans that its plans for new bypass pipelines would expose them to politically motivated energy disruptions, Moscow began signing up East European states to participate in South Stream. Serbia, Bulgaria, Croatia,

Slovenia, and—most importantly—Hungary signed agreements allowing the pipeline to cross their territory, making it all but impossible for Russia to stop deliveries to them without affecting the EU as a whole.

The impact of Europe's East-West divide has also been felt on the issue of getting the EU's newer members to abide by existing EU-Russia agreements, especially the Partnership and Cooperation Agreement (PCA). The PCA, which was signed in 1994 but only came into effect in December 1997, was designed to regulate the evolution of relations between Russia and the EU. It emphasized political dialogue leading to the "gradual integration between Russia and a wider area of cooperation in Europe," as well as promoting Russia's transition to democracy and laying the foundation for deepening economic cooperation.[40] The PCA created a series of interlocking arenas for the Russians and Europeans to discuss their concerns, including semiannual summits at the head of state/government level, a permanent partnership council at the ministerial level, the so-called foreign ministers' troika, and regular consultations between working groups covering a series of common concerns. This series of consultative bodies and the regular schedule of meetings occurring under their auspices make the EU-Russian relationship unique in its level of institutionalization.[41] The inability of Moscow and Brussels to complete talks on a new PCA has made it difficult to translate the political rapprochement that has taken place since the Russo-Georgian war into a more durable set of interlocking institutions cementing Russia's partnership with Europe.

As with negotiations for the initial PCA in the mid-1990s, a new agreement has been held up by uncertainty on the Russian side over how to simultaneously deepen engagement with the EU while guaranteeing Russian security and preserving Russia's freedom of action. Moscow is pressing for a document that affirms the importance of the EU-Russia strategic partnership, essentially confirming Russia's status as a Great Power on an equal plane with the EU as a whole while limiting the ability of the EU to pressure Moscow over issues of democracy and human rights. Energy, specifically Moscow's reluctance to sign off on the Energy Charter Treaty, which would require Russian companies operating in Europe to unbundle their production and transit operations in line with the EU's so-called Third Energy Directive, and allow European companies unrestrained access to Russia's pipeline network, has long been a significant point of contention. More broadly, the EU's focus on complex, often low-level projects (for instance on environmental protection) is at odds with Russia's preference for less substantive, but more visible statements on global security.[42]

Putin and then-European Commission president José Manuel Barroso first discussed the possibility of replacing the PCA with a broader, legally binding treaty in April 2005. On the Russian side, both liberal Westernizers and many in Putin's inner circle supported signing a new treaty. For

Westernizers, of course, a treaty relationship with the EU is attractive because of the influence it would have on Russia's domestic development and foreign policy orientation. For *derzhavniki* and *siloviki*, conversely, such a formalized relationship would confirm Russia's position as a major power, giving it a special status in terms of its relationship to Europe and confirming its special responsibility for upholding order in its backyard.[43] A new PCA would also aid Russia's deeper integration with Europe, for instance, by laying the foundation for an agreement on visa-free travel and facilitating joint investment projects, including in countries of the former Soviet Union. Consequently, a new PCA would be an important mechanism for anchoring the political rapprochement that has developed since 2008 into a more durable partnership with practical benefits to both sides.

Nonetheless, negotiations on extending or replacing the PCA have been held up by objections in both the EU and Russia. One of the major disputes centers on energy supplies, which both Moscow and Brussels acknowledge have become an increasingly important piece of the relationship since the signing of the original agreement in 1994. Moscow's decision to cut off gas supplies to Ukraine in January 2006 and January 2009, and to Belarus in January 2007, shocked European leaders into recognizing the degree to which they themselves depend on Russia for energy supplies.[44] The gas cutoffs, especially those in 2006, were generally interpreted in the West as part of Russia's allegedly neoimperial foreign policy, rather than as a dispute over pricing and back payment. As a result, European leaders whose own economies depended on Russian gas (and who were affected directly when Kyiv and Minsk decided to siphon off EU-bound gas to make up for the shortfall caused by the Kremlin's actions) became acutely aware of their own vulnerability to the whims of Gazprom and its patrons in the Kremlin—and to the sometimes unpredictable governments in Minsk and Kyiv with their stack of unpaid debts to Gazprom.

This sense of vulnerability was reinforced by a series of Russian attempts to acquire "downstream" (i.e., distribution) assets inside the European Union, even while taking a hard line against foreign acquisitions of energy sector assets inside Russia itself. In order to secure Europe against the consequences of any future attempts to blackmail neighboring states with the prospect of oil and gas cutoffs, Brussels for a time insisted that a new PCA with Russia include Russia's adherence to the so-called Energy Charter Treaty, which came into effect in 1997 and which lays out a series of principles governing the trade, investment in, and transit of energy resources. In essence, the charter would ensure that WTO rules on nondiscrimination apply to the trade in energy between Russia and the EU while also laying out a set of rules for cross-border investment in the energy sector.[45]

Negotiations on extending or renegotiating the PCA have also at times been held up by disputes between Russia and its neighbors in Eastern

Europe, though the post-2008 Russo-Polish rapprochement has at least mitigated this challenge to a new agreement. Warsaw held up negotiations on a new PCA for over two years over Russia's decision to ban the import of Polish meat, while Vilnius also objected to a new agreement as long as Russia blocked oil deliveries through the Druzhba pipeline (a dispute arising out of Lithuania's decision to sell a refinery to a Polish rather than a Russian company).[46] The seemingly minor issues of veterinary inspections and meat quality turned into a major stumbling block largely because they served as a proxy for the larger series of disagreements between Russia and its neighbors in Eastern Europe—disagreements that Moscow has in recent years sought to quietly resolve.

Because the EU negotiates on the basis of consensus, Warsaw's insistence on a resolution of the meat dispute effectively prevented the rest of the EU from moving forward with negotiations on replacing the PCA. While EU officials publicly backed the Poles (and Lithuanians) and expressed frustration with what they considered Russia's use of the meat issue for political ends, in private, many officials in Brussels condemned Polish intransigence.[47] Yet by standing firm in the face of Russian pressure, the West European leaders and the EU as a whole demonstrated to Moscow that they would prioritize the EU's commitment to collective action, in turn convincing Russia of the need to reconcile with Poland and other East European countries as a down payment on better relations with the EU as a whole.

Beyond the challenge of gaining new members' adherence to the PCA, the EU has adopted a series of programs for dealing with countries around its borders that, collectively, reflect the EU's uncertainty about Russia. First came the European Neighborhood Policy (ENP) in 2003. Designed to bring coherence to the series of PCAs existing between Brussels and neighboring countries, the ENP aimed at creating between the EU and nearby states "privileged relationship[s], building upon a mutual commitment to common values" (mainly through bringing partner states' legislation in line with the EU *acquis communautaire*).[48] Russia rejected inclusion in the ENP because it saw the demand to coordinate its legislation with the principles contained in the *acquis communautaire* as interference in its internal affairs and because it objected to being given the same status as the smaller states covered by the ENP. While continuing to seek cooperation with Brussels on a range of issues, the Kremlin remained unwilling to surrender any of its sovereignty to the multinational EU. EU Enlargement Commissioner Romano Prodi expressed the nature of EU-Russian cooperation as "anything but institutions," a formula Putin also came to endorse.[49]

Instead of participating in the ENP, Russia agreed to the creation of the so-called Four Common Spaces at the May 2003 St. Petersburg summit. The Common Spaces—economics; freedom, security, and justice; external security; and research, education, and culture—provided a framework for bringing Russia and the EU closer without the formalities of integration, allowing Russia to maintain its position that it merited a special status on account of its size and importance.[50] Russia's insistence on this special status was particularly important given the normative aspect of the ENP. By urging its neighbors to adhere to the provisions of the *acquis communautaire*, Brussels was, in the Russian view, essentially attempting to export its own value system and laws that had been made without Russian participation.

Russia was similarly wary about the EU's so-called Eastern Partnership (EaP), which Poland and Sweden first announced in May 2008, but was only formalized by Brussels seven months later, with the shock of the war in Georgia still fresh. Essentially an attempt to deepen the EU's interactions with several post-Soviet states around its frontiers (Belarus, Moldova, Ukraine, Georgia, Armenia, and Azerbaijan) in order to prepare them for eventual membership through increased aid and preparation for eventually establishing a free trade area, the EaP looked to Moscow more like an example of the old-fashioned zero-sum thinking that saw the former Soviet Union as a chessboard for East-West struggles. At the very least, the Kremlin worried that the EaP was a platform for Brussels to meddle in the domestic affairs of the post-Soviet states in ways that would incline their governments against Russia. The fact that Russia itself was not included in the partnership only heightened this impression in Moscow. Lavrov charged that the EU, which had loudly condemned Moscow's commitment to maintaining a sphere of influence around its borders during the war with Georgia, was busy creating its own sphere of influence at Russia's expense. EU diplomats also made clear any state recognizing South Ossetia or Abkhazia would be ineligible for the EaP, a step the Russian foreign minister likened to blackmail.[51] Nor was it lost on Moscow that the principal backers of the EaP, apart from Sweden, were former Warsaw Pact countries who saw the EU's continued eastward expansion as a kind of insurance policy against Russian revanchism.

The salience of Europe's East-West divide for the EU's relations with Russia may nonetheless finally be waning, thanks to a rapid and unexpected improvement in ties between Russia and the largest East European EU member, Poland. Having endured a history of Russian invasions and occupations dating to the eighteenth century, Poland long remained skeptical that post-Soviet Russia had shed its atavistic imperial instincts, often playing the role of Cassandra to Europeans eager for deeper engagement with Russia. Poland's relations with Russia became particularly fraught under the right-wing, pro-U.S. government of the Law and Justice Party led by the Kaczyński twins (Lech Kaczyński was president from 2005 until his death in April 2010, while his twin brother Jarosław served as prime minister in 2006–2007). Even as Russo-Polish trade increased rapidly under the Kaczyńskis, Warsaw looked on skeptically at the warming of ties between Berlin and Moscow (including their collaboration to build the Nord Stream gas pipeline), at the growth of authoritarianism in Putin's Russia, and at Russian attempts to obfuscate the historical record—particularly the legacy of World War II and the 1941 massacre of the Polish elite at Katyń Forest.[52] In response to its concerns about Russia, the Polish government sought enhanced security cooperation with the U.S. (culminating in an agreement to station U.S. antiballistic missile interceptors on Polish territory), a strategy that Moscow in turn viewed as threatening.

The nadir came with the war in Georgia. Even before the war, Lech Kaczyński had been among the strongest supporters of extending NATO membership to Georgia and Ukraine. After the fighting started, he led a delegation of East European leaders that flew to Tbilisi to express solidarity with the embattled Saakashvili. Just days later, Kaczyński signed an agreement with U.S. secretary of state Condoleezza Rice authorizing the deployment of the planned U.S. missile defense system on Polish territory. Moscow responded by announcing that the agreement made Poland a legitimate target for nuclear retaliation.[53]

The estrangement benefited neither Moscow nor Warsaw. Russian attempts at deeper integration with the EU as a whole were frustrated by Polish opposition. Even Germany, Russia's closest European partner, made clear that if it wanted to lower the barriers to the movement of Russian goods (including energy) and people into Europe, Moscow would first have to make up its quarrels with Warsaw. Moreover, Russian intransigence was bringing about the very development it was designed to prevent, namely, the extension of U.S. military power in Russia's neighborhood. It was also sharpening European and U.S. resistance to the idea of overhauling the Euro-Atlantic security architecture to give Russia a more pronounced role.[54] For Poland, the prospect that it would be cut out of the trade in Russian energy when Nord Stream was completed and the (admittedly remote) possibility of a military confrontation with Russia were contingencies to be avoided at all cost. Both sides, moreover, recognized that reducing political tensions would bring about economic benefits in the form of increased cross-border trade and investment.

The first steps in the rapprochement came shortly after the war in Georgia, an event that sparked a reconsideration of European security imperatives on both sides of the old Iron Curtain. Putin met with Donald Tusk, Jarosław Kaczyński's more pragmatic successor as prime minister, on the sidelines of the Davos forum in February 2009 (unlike the Kaczyńskis, Tusk saw reconciliation with Russia as one of Poland's critical foreign policy objectives). A special intergovernmental committee headed by the foreign ministers of Russia and Poland to promote bilateral strategic cooperation that had not met since 2004 was revived in early 2009, with a focus on deepening cross-border ties at the local level and easing the movement into and out of Russia's Kaliningrad exclave. Lavrov and his Polish counterpart also agreed to expand the work of a commission dealing with questions of historical memory, while declaring that "historical problems must not intrude on our present and future relations—much less overwhelm them."[55]

In fact it was to be history that laid the foundation for the broader Russo-Polish reconciliation. Putin traveled to Gdańsk to commemorate the seventieth anniversary of the outbreak of World War II in September 2009, where he energetically denounced the Molotov-Ribbentrop Pact and said, in a speech that caught observers completely off guard, that he wanted a "relationship between Russia and Poland free from the ghosts of the past."[56] In early April 2010, Putin invited Tusk to a ceremony at Katyń marking the seventieth anniversary of the massacre, the first time a Polish leader had been invited to the site. President Lech Kaczyński did not attend the joint ceremony, but arranged to make a separate visit a few days later. He was en route to Katyń when his plane crashed outside of Smolensk in heavy fog on April 10, killing him and ninety-five others.

The sudden death of Lech Kaczyński and many other members of the Polish elite recalled the horrors of the Katyń massacre seventy years earlier, but rather than poisoning Russo-Polish relations, accelerated the rapprochement already under way. Putin and Medvedev moved quickly to express their sympathy to the Polish nation; Medvedev attended Kaczyński's funeral in Kraków, where he expressed hope that the tragedy would bring the two countries closer together, and declared a day of mourning in Russia for the late Polish president. Putin was visibly moved when he visited the crash site. Poles from the new interim president Bronisław Komarowski to the Archbishop of Kraków Stanisław Dziwisz (long regarded in Moscow as an intransigent Russophobe) acknowledged the sincerity of Russian grief and the hope that the tragedy would help the two countries overcome the burdens of the past, paving the way for the renewal of Russia's partnership not only with Poland, but with Europe as a whole. Polish foreign minister Sikorski was not alone in believing that with Moscow's response to the death of Lech Kaczyński, "a psychological breakthrough has occurred."[57]

RUSSIA AND NATO

If expansion has been a major stumbling block in relations between Russia and the EU, the inclusion of new members has come close to completely derailing relations between Russia and NATO on a number of occasions.

NATO, after all, remains a military alliance devoted above all to issues of "hard" security, and for many Russians still carries the associations of the Cold War, when its very raison d'être was to check Russian power. Given the built-in hostility between NATO and the Soviet Union, statesmen on both sides recognized in the early 1990s that achieving some kind of reconciliation between the alliance and post-Soviet Russia was going to be a critical, if quite difficult task.

Yeltsin and Kozyrev believed reconciliation was a realistic goal, one they could sell to the Russian establishment on the basis of the conviction that with the end of the Cold War, NATO no longer posed a threat to Russian interests despite the crumbling of the Warsaw Pact and the implosion of the Soviet military machine. In particular, Yeltsin and Kozyrev were able to take solace in a seeming promise they had extracted from the major Western powers (above all, the U.S.), that NATO would not seek to expand to fill the power vacuum resulting from the dissolution of the Warsaw Pact and the collapse of the Soviet Union. Yet as the Russian crisis deepened during the latter part of the 1990s, this understanding unraveled, and the North Atlantic Alliance embarked on the largest campaign of expansion in its history, while simultaneously modernizing and upgrading its military capacity.

As president, Putin initially sought to manage tensions with NATO while taking advantage of the repercussions from expansion to assert Russia's own agenda with the alliance. Putin gave some hints that he did not regard NATO, even in its expanded form, as a major problem. Indeed, as president he pursued more wide-ranging and durable cooperation with NATO—in Afghanistan and elsewhere—than Yeltsin ever did. In the early part of Putin's presidency, he also tried vocally to downplay the impact of NATO expansion on Russian security as part of his larger strategy of making Russia an indispensable partner for the West. As relations between Russia and its erstwhile partners in the West frayed, NATO's geographical and technical growth revived old Russian fears about the purpose and scope of the alliance and led Moscow to take steps to limit the impact of the new NATO on its own security. The prospect of NATO taking in Ukraine and Georgia, which the 2008 Bucharest summit affirmed would happen at some unspecified future date, coupled with Russia's own political-military revival was instrumental in precipitating the conflict between Russia and Georgia. With its invasion, Moscow sought both to force the alliance to reconsider its interest in expanding up to Russia's borders and to instruct the leaders in Kyiv, Tbilisi, and elsewhere in the former Soviet Union about the limitations of Western power in the region.

The Russo-Georgian war, though, paved the way for both Russia and NATO to rethink their approaches and to put forward new ideas to address the problem of European security. Although the West continued to insist that Georgia and Ukraine would eventually be admitted to NATO, the war forced the alliance, as well as leaders in Kyiv and Tbilisi, to recognize that NATO membership was at best a long-term aspiration (in any case, the victory of Viktor Yanukovych in Ukraine's 2010 presidential elections made the question of Ukrainian membership largely moot, since one of Yanukovych's first substantive foreign policy steps was to formally withdraw Kyiv's application for membership). At the same time, the Obama administration chose to consciously downplay discussion of future NATO expansion as part of its campaign to reset relations with Moscow (most European NATO members had been lukewarm about further expansion in the first place).

While expansion has provided the backdrop for the most serious quarrels between Russia and NATO, tensions stretched back to the first years of the 1990s, when the end of the Cold War called into question the purpose, and indeed the very existence, of the North Atlantic Alliance. The leaders of Central and East European states who had been members of the defunct Warsaw Pact pressed to be admitted into NATO both as a way to anchor their own societies to the secure democracies of the West and to provide a level of insurance against the possibility of renewed Russian aggression. NATO leaders' own desire to assure the East Europeans that their Cold War–era estrangement from the mainstream of European development was not permanent often clashed with their ambition to promote the consolidation of democracy in Russia itself—since talk of NATO expansion empowered revanchist, anti-Western forces in Moscow and undermined those like Kozyrev arguing for a close partnership with the West.

Western leaders sought to mollify the Russians by assuring them that NATO expansion was not designed to confront or isolate them and by suggesting that a new European collective security mechanism could not function without Russia. Moscow argued that in continuing to nonetheless rely on NATO as the main provider of collective security, Europe (and the U.S.) consigned Russia to a secondary role. This critique received little serious attention outside of Russia, at least until the Russo-Georgian war gave concrete form to Moscow's long-standing argument that its exclusion from the European security architecture posed a threat to Europe's security and stability. One major consequence of the war has been, perhaps surprisingly, increased efforts from both sides to promote Russia's deeper integration into European security institutions, whether by changing the terms of Moscow's relationship with NATO, considering Russia's admission into NATO as a full member, or fundamentally overhauling the nature of Europe's security architecture by creating new institutions that include Russia as a full partner.[58]

The very fact that the security rules for post–Cold War Europe were being written without Russian participation necessarily created resentment in Moscow and reinforced the tendency toward zero-sum thinking on the part of Russian politicians, generals, and diplomats.[59] Since NATO moreover appeared to be extending its geographical reach into an area Moscow had long regarded as an area of special concern, Russian leaders claimed they had a justification for trying to wall off other such areas—especially the territory of the former Soviet Union—from Western interference. In this way, the bipolar logic of the Cold War reasserted itself in a new form even as the lines dividing Europe were being redrawn farther to the east.

Yeltsin's Kremlin consequently opposed any expansion of NATO that did not include a path to membership for Russia itself (as Yeltsin suggested to Bill Clinton in September 1992)—though soon realizing it had little leverage to prevent such an eventuality.[60] With some trepidation, the Yeltsin administration approved Russian membership in the NATO Partnership for Peace (PfP) program in 1994, as did most of the former Soviet republics. Partnership for Peace, the result of a bureaucratic compromise between supporters and opponents of NATO expansion in the United States, functioned both as a halfway house on the road to full NATO membership and an alternative form of partnership for countries that would not or could not aspire to full membership. While calling on members to uphold NATO's commitment to democracy and transparency in their own governance, the framework agreement establishing PfP provided for a loose form of association, with individual members free to choose the level of cooperation with NATO with which they felt comfortable (with an emphasis on defense reform).[61] In terms of NATO's relationship with Russia, the role of PfP was mostly about reducing tensions and building cooperative intermilitary relationships rather than preparing a path for political integration. On this limited basis, the Duma approved Russian participation in PfP in June 1994.

Before the year was out, however, the thaw in relations that PfP was supposed to have produced had been overtaken by NATO's decision to take in new members in Central and Eastern Europe (Poland, the Czech Republic, and Hungary in the first round). The Russian elite was stunned by this reversal, which had occurred as a result of strong pressure from the United States. Yeltsin and foreign minister Kozyrev warned that expansion could derail the wary rapprochement between Russia and the West that had taken place since the end of the Cold War. NATO's commitment to expand, which it undertook at a ministerial meeting in December 1994, undermined hopes among Russian liberals that PfP could serve as a kind of bridge to more general agreement between Russia and NATO. Yeltsin himself cautioned that NATO expansion would bring in its wake a new era of "cold peace."[62]

While the alliance's leadership justified expansion on the basis of new security threats originating in the chaos of the Balkans and the spread of

Islamist extremism, to Moscow NATO remained the NATO of the Cold War and its expansion a sign that the West still sought to contain Russia. When the final decision to expand was made in July 1997, then-foreign minister Primakov characterized it as "a big mistake, possibly the biggest mistake since the end of the Second World War."[63] Even liberal Russians like Anatoly Chubais argued against NATO expansion, fearing it would lead to Russia's isolation and the empowerment of hard-line, anti-Western forces and the marginalization of those, like Kozyrev, who had sought Russia's integration with Western institutions.[64] This assessment was shared by many in the U.S. establishment as well, including such major figures as former defense secretary Robert McNamara, former senators Gary Hart, Sam Nunn, and Bill Bradley, former national security adviser Adm. Stansfield Turner, and Paul Nitze, architect of President Truman's containment strategy, who argued in a joint open letter to President Clinton that U.S.-led efforts to expand NATO not only jeopardized the future of the arms control regime but would also "bring Russians to question the entire post–Cold War settlement."[65]

Despite his firm opposition to NATO expansion, Yeltsin sought both to ameliorate domestic hostility and seek compensation from the Western powers for doing so. With its nuclear arsenal still intact, Russia's own security was not directly endangered by the expansion of NATO, a fact Yeltsin understood quite well. Yet the alliance's expansion in the face of what Moscow believed were promises to the contrary from George H. W. Bush, secretary of state James Baker, German foreign minister Hans-Dietrich Genscher, and others deepened the gulf between Russia and its neighbors in Europe as well as the United States.[66] NATO realized the nature of the dilemma created by expansion and spent much of the time between the announcement that Poland, the Czech Republic, and Hungary would be admitted (in 1994) until the actual induction ceremony (in 1999) trying to come up with a way to proceed without causing a rupture with Moscow.[67]

At least until Putin's ascension to power, this circle could not be squared. The firestorm of criticism that broke out in Moscow when NATO announced its plans for expansion played a major role in discrediting Kozyrev's strategy of partnership with the West. If the West was not going to accept Russia into its clubs but would take advantage of Russian weakness to advance its own military frontiers at Russia's expense, then Kozyrev's quest for partnership seemed to have been a fool's errand, as the hapless foreign minister himself well understood.[68]

The appointment of Primakov as foreign minister was in large part an attempt by Yeltsin to co-opt the nationalist opposition that had grown up around the issue of NATO's expansion. Primakov portrayed himself as an implacable foe of NATO, particularly in its expanded form. Yet, like Yeltsin, he was realistic enough to understand that expansion was going to proceed regardless of Russia's actions and that the best Moscow could do under the circumstances was to accommodate itself to the new reality and attempt to extract some kind of quid pro quo for not making unnecessary trouble. Despite his belief that NATO expansion was a mistake of historic proportions, Primakov admitted that "the expansion of NATO is not a military problem; it is a psychological one," and sought to adjust Russian perceptions of the alliance to the extent possible, a task for which the ex-spymaster had much more credibility with hard-liners in the Duma than did the liberal intellectual Kozyrev.[69]

It was under Primakov's stewardship that Russia participated in the creation of the first organization designed to integrate Russia into NATO's decision-making structure, the so-called Permanent Joint Council (PJC), which was established under the NATO-Russia Founding Act signed in Paris in May 1997.[70] The Founding Act was a kind of declaration of principles governing the interactions between Russia and the expanded alliance, though in large part it served merely as a concession to Moscow for having to accept NATO's decision to expand. It declared unambiguously that "NATO and Russia do not consider each other as adversaries" and have a "shared commitment to build a stable, peaceful and undivided Europe, whole and free, to the benefit of all its peoples."[71] The PJC provided for the presence of a Russian representative at NATO headquarters and for regular meetings at the ministerial level to discuss issues of common concern. At the time, the PJC was heralded as marking a real watershed in relations between a Russia no longer committed to expanding its territorial reach and a West that had abandoned containment as a principle of its foreign policy (Polish, Czech, and Hungarian membership in the alliance notwithstanding).

By signing the Founding Act and agreeing to participation in the PJC, Primakov recognized at least tacitly that the NATO of the late 1990s was a fundamentally different organization from the NATO of the Cold War and that the alliance's newer incarnation did not pose a direct threat to Russia. This recognition, however, continued to come up against the ingrained hostility of the Russian political and military elite to NATO as such and to NATO's expansion into Eastern Europe in particular. NATO's bombing campaign against Yugoslavia in 1999 deepened Russian hostility toward the alliance, and Moscow responded in part by suspending its participation in the Permanent Joint Council and withdrawing its representative from NATO headquarters in Brussels. The PJC's ineffectiveness was glaring.[72]

Primakov, of course, gave vent to the sentiments of many Russians who were disenchanted with the way NATO had pushed them aside. The Russian foreign minister responded by breaking off relations with the alliance and even threatening to aid Belgrade directly. The Yugoslav campaign also coincided with the renewal of hostilities in Chechnya. With NATO expressing support for Kosovo's independence from Serbia, many in the Russian elite saw worrying parallels with Chechnya and blamed NATO for supplying, or at least inspiring, Chechen separatism as part of a larger strategy of encircling and weakening Russia. Fear of NATO involvement with the rebels played at least some role in the Kremlin's decision to embark on a full-scale military campaign in response to the rebels' incursion across the Chechen border into Dagestan in August 1999.[73]

One major consequence of the second Chechen war, of course, was the emergence of then-prime minister Vladimir Putin as the most popular figure in Russia, the only man seen as capable of finishing off the Chechens and standing up to NATO's alleged anti-Russian intrigues. Putin's approach to NATO was on the whole similar to Primakov's, though with an even greater emphasis on ameliorating the consequences of expansion. Putin sought to limit Russian opposition to the alliance and its activities, realizing that Moscow had a weak hand when it came to influencing NATO strategy. Putin acknowledged in October 2001 that Russia could live with even an expanded NATO, as long as NATO itself became more of a political organization and less of a traditional military alliance. He moreover emphasized that Russia would not repeat its at times hysterical denunciations if NATO should decide to expand again in the future.[74] The new Russian president soon gave a more concrete demonstration of his determination to improve NATO-Russia relations. The NATO secretary-general, Lord George Robertson, was among the first foreign dignitaries scheduled to come to Moscow after Putin's inauguration. Over the objections of his generals, Putin refused to cancel Robertson's visit in response to the crisis in Kosovo. Instead, Putin met personally with Robertson, and their talks led to the restoration of full relations between NATO and Russia.[75]

Robertson's visit was particularly important in that it laid the foundation for the establishment in 2002 of the NATO-Russia Council (NRC), which was designed to supplant the PJC and address Russian worries that the existing institutions for cooperation failed to give enough weight to Russian concerns. The establishment of the NATO-Russia Council gave Moscow a greater degree of influence with the alliance but was also more generally one component of Putin's policy of cooperation with the West adopted in the aftermath of September 11.[76]

Under the previous arrangement, NATO members would negotiate an agreed position among themselves before bringing the matter to Russian attention in the context of the PJC. Moscow complained that this procedure forced it to accept a series of faits accomplis and left it little opportunity to influence actual decision making. Instead of this "16 + 1" format, the NRC was designed to operate on the basis of consensus, with Russian representatives involved in all phases of the negotiating process (though without the ability to veto decisions that had been accepted by all the NATO member states).[77] Under the NRC, Russia created the post of ambassador to NATO to participate in monthly meetings of the council.

The presence of a permanent Russian representative at NATO headquarters did much to alter the dynamic of the relationship, encouraging cooperation and collaboration on a day-to-day basis and building trust between the two sides.[78] Observers noted a qualitative change in the way representatives from Russia and NATO dealt with each other in the framework of the NRC, compared with the old PJC. Most fundamentally, it appeared for much of the 2000s that "the parties not only want to limit damages, but to achieve something in common."[79] Still, the war in Iraq and NATO's continuing commitment to expansion exposed the limits of even this more formalized arrangement. Putin's appointment of the outspoken nationalist and former head of the *Rodina* Party Dmitry Rogozin as ambassador to NATO (where he once hung a portrait of Stalin on his office wall in Brussels) in January 2008 signaled a move away from accommodation on the part of Moscow, which was increasingly frustrated with its inability to shape NATO decision making.[80]

Rogozin's theatrics aside, NATO-Russia cooperation within the NRC remained pronounced, especially in the area of counterterrorism—at least until the council was suspended by the Western powers in September 2008 to punish Moscow for its invasion of Georgia. Given that like Russia, NATO members including the United States, the United Kingdom, and Spain have all suffered major terrorist attacks since 2001 and that NATO has made counterterrorism one of its key missions, cooperation with Moscow on this issue has been relatively straightforward. Russia and NATO have conducted joint naval patrols in the Mediterranean Sea to prevent the smuggling of unconventional weapons (Operation Active Endeavor, the only time a non-NATO member has participated in alliance activities under the auspices of Article 5 of the North Atlantic Treaty on self-defense), have staged joint training drills (especially in order to prepare civil defense personnel for dealing with a terrorist attack), and have even conducted joint exercises on theater missile defense.[81] The NRC has also been instrumental in bringing together Russian and Western intelligence analysts to assess the development of al Qaeda and the emerging terrorist threat to Central Asia.[82] More recently, Moscow stepped up its cooperation with NATO's International Security Assistance Force (ISAF) in Afghanistan, signing a transit agreement permitting NATO to make use of Russia's road and rail network to move supplies to Afghanistan, while trying to influence the alliance to take a stronger stand against the Afghan drug trade that is having serious public health consequences inside Russia.

Despite their shared interest in combating terrorism, the second round of NATO expansion set off a firestorm among the Russian elite comparable to that of the mid-1990s. This time, Russia's objections centered not just on the fact of continued NATO expansion but also on the fact that it was the Baltic states specifically—formerly constituent parts of the Soviet Union and strategically located across from St. Petersburg—that were being invited into the alliance. Among the conditions Moscow had seemingly extracted from the Western powers in exchange for putting up with the initial round of NATO expansion in the 1990s was a promise that no further expansion would take place, especially with regard to the Baltic states, with even Yeltsin declaring in May 1998 that the inclusion of the Baltics in NATO was a redline for Moscow.[83] As in the days of Primakov, though, once NATO indicated it would invite the Balts into the alliance regardless of Russian opposition, Putin's Kremlin scrambled to salvage what it could from the relationship and secured approval of the NRC as a kind of compensation for swallowing the inclusion of Lithuania, Latvia, and Estonia in NATO.

Beside the problems resulting from the presence of NATO assets close to Russia's borders, the second round of NATO expansion has also posed a dilemma for the Kremlin because the Baltic states and Slovenia (unlike the other NATO member states) had not signed the Conventional Forces in Europe (CFE) Treaty. This agreement, initially signed in 1990, aimed at limiting the number and type of military units stationed on the territory of the signatories ("from the Atlantic to the Urals") in order to head off the possibility of a blitzkrieg-type conventional offensive by either NATO or the old Warsaw Pact.

An updated version of the CFE Treaty was signed in Istanbul in 1999, replacing the original treaty's outdated emphasis on arms limitation by bloc (NATO and Warsaw Pact) with new national limits. However, NATO expansion complicated the implementation of this Adapted CFE Treaty. The Western signatories refused to ratify the treaty until Russia withdrew its forces from Georgia (which Russia had done—excepting one base in Ajaria—before the August 2008 war) and Moldova/Transnistria.[84] Russia refused the demand to withdraw from Transnistria in large part because of the perception of increased vulnerability resulting from the expansion of NATO up to the border of what Russia perceives as an exclusive security zone, and because its interference in the CIS's "frozen conflicts" gives it an important mechanism for exerting influence over its neighbors, while the financial benefits from smuggling across Transnistria's porous borders provided another inducement for Russian units to stay.[85] Meanwhile, the presence of Russian forces in the breakaway republics of Abkhazia and South Ossetia (which Moscow no longer regards as Georgian territory) has exacerbated the dispute over these so-called Istanbul commitments— since the Western powers argue that Russian forces have once again occupied Georgian territory without the consent of the government in Tbilisi. The presence of Russian troops in Moldova and Georgia gave the

Kremlin the ability to sow chaos in these countries if necessary, and hence a kind of insurance against any "aggressive actions" on the part of NATO.[86] The alliance's decision in principle to offer Tbilisi and Kyiv a path to membership was perceived in Moscow as just such an action, and justified to Russian strategists the decision to maintain a military presence in the frozen conflict zones.

While Western leaders were initially hopeful that the uproar over NATO's expansion would eventually pass, Moscow's response became more neuralgic during Putin's second term (even before NATO agreed to the eventual membership of Georgia and Ukraine), once NATO members began discussing the possibility of placing significant military assets on the territory of new member states. Lavrov warned NATO in September 2007 that the presence of antimissile facilities in the former Warsaw Pact states (as well as the independence of Kosovo) was a critical issue where Moscow would not engage in "horse trading."[87] When, in response to the invasion of Georgia, Warsaw announced it had at least reached agreement with Washington to station parts of a planned antiballistic missile interceptor system (as well as an advanced air defense battery to defend the interceptors) on Polish territory, a leading Russian general responded by claiming Poland had opened itself up to the possibility of nuclear retaliation.[88]

Russia also protested against agreements signed in 2005 allowing the U.S. to establish military bases in Romania and Bulgaria (in part to replace the Karshi-Khanabad facility in Uzbekistan from which it was recently evicted) as violating the terms of the CFE Treaty—and justifying its own military presence in Transnistria.[89] Russian fears for the future of the CFE regime became even more evident once the United States announced it would station antimissile batteries on the territory of the new members. After a series of sharp exchanges on the subject in the spring of 2007, the Kremlin announced it was suspending its participation in the CFE Treaty altogether. While the Obama administration's announcement that it was suspending plans to deploy missile defense systems in Poland and the Czech Republic was greeted with relief in Moscow, the decision to consider alternative sites in the Balkans set off a new round (albeit more muted) of hand-wringing by the Russian military about the encroachment of U.S. military assets up to Russia's borders and threats to the NATO-Russian balance of power.[90]

Putin's own reaction to the potential inclusion of the Baltic states in NATO was initially rather muted—or in the words of the Foreign Ministry, "calmly negative [*spokoino negativnoe*]."[91] Yet while Putin worked to ameliorate Russian hostility to NATO's second round of expansion, the response among the Russian elite as a whole has been, and remains, more hostile. Perhaps unsurprisingly, it is the Russian military that has led the bureaucratic opposition in Moscow to working more closely with NATO. To be sure, Putin initially removed some of the most vocal opponents of NATO per se and NATO-Russian cooperation in particular from their positions in order to facilitate greater cooperation; the two most notable victims of this purge were former defense minister Igor Sergeev and head of the Defense Ministry's international department Col.-Gen. Leonid Ivashov.[92]

Despite its general subservience to the Kremlin, the Duma in 2004 saw fit to formally condemn the Baltic states' inclusion in NATO and adopted a resolution suggesting Moscow might reconsider its strategic approach toward the alliance as a result.[93] This warning was echoed initially by the Foreign Ministry as well. Even while Putin authorized renewal of contacts with NATO following the September 11 attacks, Russian diplomats cautioned that the alliance's further expansion, to include the Baltic states, could derail the whole framework of cooperation. Deputy foreign minister Yevgeny Gusarov warned that Russia would take "adequate measures of a military and political nature" should NATO decide to bring Lithuania, Latvia, and Estonia into the alliance.[94]

The Baltic states' inclusion in a way thus helped pave the way for the conflict between Russia and Georgia, insofar as NATO had ignored increasingly strident Russian warnings about the consequences of further expansion. While the war seemed to put an end to discussion of Georgian or Ukrainian NATO membership for the foreseeable future, it did not change the beliefs of many in the Russian elite that further NATO expansion continued to represent a grave danger. The new Russian Military Doctrine, released after numerous delays in February 2010, emphasized that among the leading threats to Russia's security remained:

> Attempts to endow . . . the North Atlantic Treaty Alliance (NATO) with global functions realized through violation of the norms of international law, [and] to bring military infrastructure of NATO member states up to the borders of the Russian Federation, including through the bloc's expansion. . . .
>
> [and] the expansion (escalation) of military forces of foreign states (or groups of states) on territories bordering the Russian Federation and states allied to it.[95]

If expansion has been the largest stumbling block between Russia and NATO, then the question of NATO's role in the post–Cold War world has surely been second. In 2001, Putin had suggested that Russia would be open to deepening cooperation with a NATO that saw its mission more as promoting stability and democracy among its new members rather than functioning as a traditional military bloc.[96] Continued expansion, however, undermined Russian faith that the organization had adapted itself to a new mission that no longer required seeing Russia as a threat, as did the robust out-of-area operations undertaken by NATO in the Balkans, Afghanistan, Libya, and elsewhere, and the alliance's commitment to continue expanding.[97] Yet by 2007, the Russian Foreign Ministry lamented that the transformation of NATO had "frozen." It cautioned:

> NATO's real adaptation to the new conditions of [international] security can only succeed if it is willing to engage in equal partnership with other countries and regional organizations. . . . Our relationship to the transformation of NATO will depend . . . on the degree to which it observes international law, including the prerogatives of the UN Security Council, and takes account in deed rather than in word Russia's security interests.[98]

NATO's new Strategic Concept, released at the December 2010 Lisbon summit, sought to address some of these concerns, though it maintained NATO's commitment to conduct "out of area" operations such as its interventions in Afghanistan and Libya in the future. While Moscow welcomed the new Strategic Concept, which clearly emphasized that NATO saw Russia as a partner rather than a rival, Moscow will no doubt in practice continue to chafe at the alliance's increasingly global, expeditionary role. The Lisbon summit also set the stage for a "reset" in relations between Russia and the Atlantic Alliance. Instead of fighting over expansion as they had done in 2008, Russia and the NATO countries identified areas of common interest where they could work in tandem. These included stabilizing Afghanistan; combating piracy, terrorism, and drug trafficking; and—potentially most significant—developing a shared missile defense architecture.[99] While translating this agreement into practice proved challenging, the very idea that Russia and NATO could agree to work together against shared challenges originating outside Europe was a sign that both sides recognized the threats they will face in the future will be radically different from those of the past.

One aspect of Moscow's strategy for dealing with NATO that is often overlooked in the West is Russia's somewhat sporadic attempts to re-create at least the façade of a bipolar relationship through the promotion of its own security alliances paralleling and counterbalancing NATO. The Shanghai Cooperation Organization, or SCO, was for a time seen as a possible replacement for the old Warsaw Pact, a counterhegemonic bloc of large states dedicated to checking the expansion of American influence around the world.[100] While the role and geographic scope of the SCO remains somewhat in flux (see chapter 5), Moscow has been more successful in organizing at least a small-scale analogue to NATO under the auspices of the Collective Security Treaty Organization (CSTO, in Russian *Organizatsiya Dogovora o Kollektivnoi Bezopasnosti*, or ODKB). Established on the basis of the 1992 Tashkent Treaty, the CSTO is essentially the international security arm of the CIS (comprising Russia, Belarus, Armenia, Kazakhstan, Uzbekistan, Kyrgyzstan, and Tajikistan). Part of the CSTO's importance to

Russia lies in the fact that the agreement establishing the organization prohibits members from joining any other international security bloc (i.e., NATO). In this way, the existence of the CSTO helps ameliorate Russia's fear of encirclement, insofar as the organization remains intact.

Russian leaders have sought to establish the CSTO as a kind of Eurasian counterpart to NATO and have advocated the creation of security arrangements based on the cooperation and integration of NATO and the CSTO. Lavrov has on multiple occasions raised the possibility of NATO-CSTO cooperation to bring stability to postconflict Afghanistan.[101] Several Russian analysts also suggested cooperation between the CSTO and NATO to deal with the fallout of the ethnic violence that struck CSTO member Kyrgyzstan in June 2010. The Kyrgyz unrest, however, highlighted many of the CSTO's shortcomings: given the military weakness and mutual distrust of many CSTO member states, any deployment would have to comprise principally Russian troops, while the non-Russian members of the bloc did not want to create a precedent or provide diplomatic cover for new deployments of Russian "peacekeepers" outside Russia's borders. Given such shortcomings, NATO is reluctant to be drawn into an institutional relationship with the CSTO.

Russian officials complain that while they are forced to deal with NATO collectively, NATO and its members refuse to approach the CSTO in the same light. Instead, they see Western attempts to negotiate with Russia and the other CSTO members on a bilateral basis as an attempt to undermine the organization's solidarity and weaken Russia's influence over its neighbors in the CIS, particularly since NATO continues to moot plans for expansion further into Eurasia.[102]

While Moscow would like for the CSTO to take on a more active international security role, it is not wedded to the organization as a vehicle for promoting its multilateral/multipolar ambitions. Medvedev's suggestion for a new Euro-Atlantic security architecture including Russia would render NATO in its current form obsolete, or at the very least dramatically reduce its importance. Unsurprisingly, the West's response has been tepid, even though the underlying logic for integrating Russia more deeply into Europe's security architecture is compelling.[103] While Russia and Europe continue to regard each other as a potential threat, security cooperation remains difficult, both sides remain distracted from dealing with more immediate and more dangerous challenges, and countries between them remain targets for competing influence.

The essential bargain Putin offered NATO at the beginning of his term in office—a reasonably phlegmatic response to then-current plans for expansion in exchange for the alliance's transformation into a more political organization—has not been realized, at least not yet. The mismatch between NATO's structure and its continually evolving functions has created difficulties not only in the alliance's relationship with Russia, but also with regard to the war in Afghanistan, the success or failure of which will play a major role in determining whether NATO remains relevant in the twenty-first century. As in its relations with Russia, the alliance's success in Afghanistan—not to mention Libya, where NATO took control of a UN-authorized mission to protect civilians from the forces of Moammar Qaddafi in early 2011—will depend on its ability to adapt to dealing with contingencies far removed from those it was designed to confront when it was formed in the 1940s.

As NATO works to recast its relationship with Russia away from the Cold War–era model of confrontation, one possible avenue for building cooperation from the ground up is missile defense. While the U.S. plan to construct a missile defense architecture in Europe has long rankled a Kremlin fearful that its own deterrent capacity would be undermined, the idea of building a collaborative system involving the U.S., the European NATO allies, and Russia has long appeared one way of squaring the circle. Putin offered the U.S. use of Russian radar facilities in the Caucasus when plans for a U.S.-led missile defense system in Europe were mooted during the Bush administration. The Obama administration's modification of its predecessor's missile defense plans into the so-called European Phased Adaptive Approach (EPAA) addressed some Russian concerns, but Washington also pushed to bring Russia on board as a partner in the system's construction and operation. Since the Obama administration sought to embed the EPAA in NATO as a way of securing allied consent, the NATO-Russia Council became the vehicle for selling the project to Moscow. The two sides agreed at the December 2010 Lisbon summit to cooperate in building a new missile defense system covering all of Europe, directed in principle against the threat of a missile attack from the Middle East. While the details remain to be worked out, the underlying concept is for the two sides to build independent systems capable of communicating and sharing data.

While the prospects for a fully operational system to come on line within a decade as the EPAA scheme calls for appear dubious on both financial and technological grounds, the political effect on relations between the West and Russia could nonetheless be significant. Collaborating on missile defense would mark the first time NATO and Russia worked together to build something new in such a sensitive area. The hope on both sides appears to be that missile defense can serve as a test case and a prototype for further security cooperation in the future. In this regard, NATO's proposal to collaborate on missile defense appears designed in part to address the same problem Medvedev raised with his proposal for a new treaty on European security—namely, Russia's continued exclusion from the institutions and agreements that define the security landscape in

Europe, which remains bifurcated more than two decades since the end of the Cold War. As Lavrov noted in his annual overview of Russia's foreign policy accomplishments at the start of 2011, the success or failure of missile defense cooperation with NATO will prove critical as a "test of the sincerity of [the West's] declarations that security is indivisible."[104]

EUROPE AND RUSSIAN ENERGY DIPLOMACY

While global energy prices remained at historically high levels in the years leading up to 2008, the implications of oil and gas for the relationship between Russia and Europe became increasingly problematic. Much more than the United States, which gets the bulk of its imported energy from North America and the Middle East, the EU is heavily dependent on Russia for deliveries of both oil and gas, with more than a third of Europe's oil imports and 42 percent of its gas imports originating in Russia (together oil and gas accounted for more than 70 percent of EU imports from Russia before the economic crisis).[105] Russia's role as an energy supplier to Europe encompasses not only direct production for the European market but also its role as a transit corridor, particularly for gas originating in the Caspian basin and Central Asia.

The EU's reliance on Russia for its energy has, not surprisingly, raised alarms in much of Europe about potential vulnerability to Russian pressure. These fears were stoked by Gazprom's decision to cut off supplies to Ukraine and Belarus, disputes over Russian purchases of transit infrastructure inside the EU, concerns over declining output inside Russia, and the war in Georgia, which threatened Europe's principal non-Russian pipeline corridor. Despite Europe's fears, the Russian leadership argues that dependence is a two-way street and that while Europe may have little choice but to import oil and gas from Russia, Russia itself has equally little choice of customers, given the paucity of pipelines capable of delivering energy to Russia's neighbors in Asia and the expense of liquefying gas to be carried by tanker to the United States and the rest of the world (Russia's position on this issue is slightly ingenuous, insofar as the Kremlin has been actively courting alternative customers for its energy riches, particularly in East Asia). In the long run, the dramatic collapse in European demand following the economic crisis, coupled with a growing global market for liquefied natural gas (LNG) and the discovery of significant unconventional (shale) gas in Central Europe may help make energy less significant as a point of contention between Europe and Russia.

Pipeline diplomacy has been an important component of Russian foreign policy for much of the past decade as the Kremlin has sought to maneuver between the demands of Europe, Asia, and the former Soviet states in a way that maximizes both profit and influence. The consolidation of state control over the energy sector that took place under Putin has for this reason been a key element in the projection of Russian power abroad. The displacement of Khodorkovsky, state-owned oil company Rosneft's (heavily discounted) purchase of Yukos, and the state's increased stake in national champions Gazprom and Rosneft all made it easier for the Kremlin to take advantage of the country's mineral riches as a way of promoting its foreign policy goals, as Putin and his allies have advocated since the 1990s.[106] The Kremlin's ability to make decisions about the distribution of Russia's energy riches coupled with the dominant position enjoyed by Russian gas (and, to a lesser extent, oil) in the European market has been critical to Russia's quest for expanded international influence. On the other hand, by creating perverse incentives and raising obstacles to international energy companies' operations inside Russia, the Kremlin has arguably blunted what is sometimes referred to as its "energy weapon," by encouraging its European customers to look to other regions and new technologies to meet their energy needs.

Europe's dependence on Russian energy dates back to the Cold War, when, despite ideological differences and the standoff between NATO and the Warsaw Pact, the Kremlin built pipelines to Europe as a way of earning hard currency and creating a wedge between Europe and the United States (which opposed increased Soviet energy sales to its European allies). Of course, for Russian energy to reach Western Europe, it had to cross the territory of Moscow's East European allies, who received oil and gas from Russia at subsidized prices to ensure their loyalty. With the end of the Cold War, this pipeline infrastructure has largely remained in place.

The very state of dependence in which Europe finds itself has limited the EU's options in dealing with Russia—whether muting its objections on antimonopoly grounds to Gazprom's swallowing up of competitors or opposing serious sanctions in response to the invasion of Georgia.[107] Of course, the Kremlin has gone beyond threats in dealing with former Soviet republics, including the three Baltic states that are now members of the EU and NATO; state-owned oil pipeline operator Transneft cut deliveries to Lithuania and Latvia when those states sold a major refinery and an oil terminal, respectively, to non-Russian companies.

Most notorious, though, were the decisions to stop sending gas to Ukraine in both January 2006 and 2009 in a seemingly perpetual dispute over pricing and back payments colored by tension over the legacy of the Orange Revolution. The Ukrainian gas crises, along with a 2007 analogue in Belarus awoke downstream countries (whose own deliveries suffered when Kyiv and Minsk began siphoning off Europe-bound gas to counteract the effects of the Russian cutoff) to the vulnerabilities their own dependence on Moscow created.

Seeking sources of oil and gas not subject to Russian control has been central to European energy diplomacy since the early 1990s. The most well known example of this approach is the Baku-Tbilisi-Ceyhan (BTC) oil pipeline from the Caspian Sea to Turkey's Mediterranean coast (a roughly parallel gas pipeline from Baku to Erzurum also opened in late 2006). BTC is hardly the only example of this new pipeline diplomacy, with Europe and the United States actively engaged in negotiations for the establishment of a new pipeline route dubbed the Southern Corridor running from the Caspian and Central Asia through the Caucasus on to Turkey and the EU. Several consortia are competing to build pipelines through the Southern Corridor, the largest of which (planned to run from Erzurum through the Balkans to Austria) is known as Nabucco.

The Kremlin has strongly opposed the establishment of a new pipeline corridor that skirts Russian territory, and has been promoting its own pipelines (Nord and South Stream) to undermine support for Nabucco. Russia has also been attempting to lock up large amounts of oil and gas production outside its borders (especially in Turkmenistan, Kazakhstan, Azerbaijan, and Uzbekistan, but also in non-CIS states such as Nigeria) as well as the infrastructure for transporting it to the outside world. One consequence of the post-2008 fall in energy prices and the indebtedness of Russia's state-owned energy companies is the need for Russia to sign up foreign partners to help pay for new pipelines. China, for instance, provided $25 billion in financing for the construction of a spur on the Eastern Siberia–Pacific Ocean (ESPO) oil pipeline running from Siberia to the Chinese city of Daqing. In exchange, Beijing locked up a twenty-year supply of oil at concessionary prices (see chapter 5).

For the time being, the bulk of Russia's existing pipeline infrastructure leads to Europe, which has had the somewhat paradoxical effect of making Moscow dependent on the Europeans as consumers of their energy as much as it has left Europe little choice but to turn to Russia as a supplier. The discovery of significant reserves of shale gas in Eastern Europe could, however, dramatically alter the economic geography of energy sales, sharply reducing the need for Central and East European states to import large quantities of Russian gas and undermining the mutually dependent relationship between Russian suppliers and East European consumers. So too could Europe's construction of infrastructure to accommodate significantly larger LNG imports from countries such as Qatar and Algeria. Of course, Europe's increasingly insistent push to find alternatives to Russian gas also provides a foundation for Medvedev's push to wean the Russian economy off its dependence on hydrocarbon sales.[108]

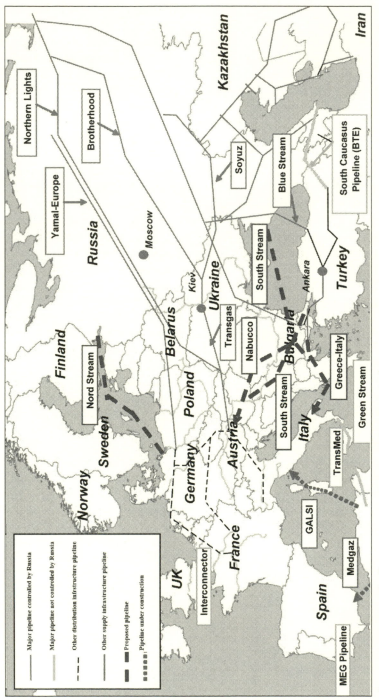

Figure 4.1.   Energy Pipelines to Europe. *Source:* JBC Energy GmbH

Despite the decline in European demand and the prospect that the EU will increasingly get its gas from non-Russian sources, Moscow continues to press for its own pipeline projects, in part out of a conviction that European demand will eventually increase once the effects of the economic crisis have blown over. Not only will new pipelines increase the sheer quantity of oil and gas Russia can export, they will also change the economic geography of the relationship by differentiating between European states' access and ability to profit from Russian energy—unless the EU succeeds in creating an integrated gas market among its members.

This element of the Russian strategy has been most notable in the quest to build Nord Stream, which, when built, will tie Germany directly to Russia, bypassing Poland and the Baltic states, and South Stream, which if built would supply southern and central Europe while bypassing Ukraine (across which 80 percent of the gas currently sold by Russia to the EU passes). For the time being, it remains unclear whether Nord Stream will lead to reductions in the amount of gas Russia sends to Europe through the existing pipelines. Nord Stream's planned annual capacity is 55 billion cubic meters (bcm), about 20 percent of the total amount of gas currently shipped by Russia to the EU. Given Moscow's lack of investment in boosting production and lack of clarity regarding its ultimate intentions, many Europeans worry that Nord Stream (and South Stream, designed to carry an additional 63 bcm) will not increase Russia's overall deliveries but will merely reroute existing volumes in ways that benefit some EU members (Germany and Italy) at the expense of others (Poland and the Baltic states) as well as the EU as a whole. Until Nord Stream comes online, Russia cannot cut off energy supplies to the Poles and Balts without imperiling deliveries to countries farther downstream, since Poland and the Baltic countries could still siphon off gas as Ukraine did during its gas disputes with Russia.

Moscow's calculation appears similar with regard to South Stream, which appears designed in large part to undermine support for the U.S.-sponsored Southern Corridor between the Caspian gas fields and southeastern Europe.[109] Thanks to Gazprom's close links with the Kremlin and ability to make decisions without the complicated attempts at coordination that often bedevil the Europeans, it has been able to move rapidly to secure bilateral deals with the states along the route of South Stream. [110] Gazprom's financial difficulties and questions about the future of European demand have however made South Stream appear increasingly illusory, especially since the Central Asian states slated to provide its gas are increasingly turning to China instead.

Moscow argues that the bypass pipelines are both justified on purely economic grounds and will prove beneficial to Europe as well as to Russia. Gazprom's largest operating expense is the transit fees it pays to the countries its pipelines cross. With so many states taking a cut, the price consumers in (for instance) Germany pay for Russian gas is substantially higher than the price they would pay for gas that transited only the Baltic Sea.[111] Moreover, several of the transit countries—especially Ukraine—are unstable politically and chronically behind on their payments to Gazprom. Ukraine suffered an extremely severe recession in the context of the global economic crisis that broke out in the autumn of 2008, with GDP contracting by more than 15 percent in 2009 and the IMF stepping in with $25 billion in loans to keep Ukraine from defaulting (in part conditioned on Kyiv's willingness to raise the price its consumers pay for gas).[112] Under the circumstances, the prospect of further billing disputes with Gazprom remains real, even with the ouster of Viktor Yushchenko in favor of a more pro-Russian government in Kyiv.

Unsurprisingly, the reaction to Nord Stream and South Stream has been sharply different in countries that stand to benefit directly, such as Germany, and those, such as Poland, that would potentially find themselves vulnerable to supply cuts. Backed by Germany, Italy, and others, the European Commission has officially termed Nord Stream a priority EU project, thanks to its potential to dramatically expand the amount of pipeline gas available to Europe. Yet in August 2009, the EU's energy commissioner was forced to publicly rebuke the president of Lithuania and the chairman of the European Parliament (a Pole) for casting doubt on the EU's commitment to Nord Stream.[113] The EU's ability to reconcile its desire for the increased capacity that Nord Stream promises and the concerns of states that would be bypassed will continue to pose a major challenge to forging a common strategy for engaging Russia. The most effective policy response, liberalizing Europe's markets and building new interconnector pipelines to enable gas to flow freely between EU member states, has long been championed in Brussels in the face of opposition from major national utilities in Germany and elsewhere. If the push for liberalization succeeds, the EU will be in a much better position to reciprocate Moscow's interest in deeper economic integration without provoking concern that integration will only increase Moscow's leverage over its customers.

Apart from pipelines, the EU has another energy-related concern, namely, the Kremlin's and Gazprom's attempts to extend their reach in Europe through the acquisition of downstream assets (pipelines, refineries, and other infrastructure) inside EU member countries. Thanks to the legacy of Soviet infrastructure, the distribution networks in the Baltic states have long been in Russian hands. More recently, Gazprom has signed deals with major corporations in Italy, Germany, the Netherlands, and France to acquire a stake in their infrastructure for energy distribution to Europe, and has pushed insistently to take control of Ukraine's distribution network as the price of forgiving Kyiv's massive debts. Coupled with its already dominant control over the transit routes bringing gas to Europe, Russia's acquisition of downstream assets has increased European fears about Moscow's ability to shape Europe's foreign policy. From the European perspective, this danger is especially acute because of what Brussels sees as Russia's lack of reciprocity—while Gazprom is in theory at least free to buy up assets in downstream EU countries, Russia for the most part refused to allow European companies to buy Russian upstream assets. The reluctance to allow foreign companies to purchase a stake in Russian infrastructure has been one of the major reasons that Moscow refuses to sign the Energy Charter Treaty.

Without the charter or a similar arrangement, the Russia-EU energy trade remains poorly regulated and unpredictable, as Russia's gas supply disputes with Ukraine have made clear. The gas cutoffs of 2006 and 2009—like the war in Georgia—also served as a wakeup call for many European leaders about the dangers of European institutions' lack of engagement with Russia. While the 2006 gas crisis was driven by an explosive mixture of Russian pique at Yushchenko and frustration at Ukraine's mounting debts to Gazprom, the political side of the dispute dominated news coverage in both Europe and the U.S. The general lack of familiarity with the commercial details led foreign observers to cast the worst possible light on Russian motives.[114] The EU and its members were caught almost entirely off guard by the dispute, and by Gazprom's decision to reduce the flow of gas to Ukraine (as well as by Ukraine's decision to siphon gas bound for Europe for its own needs). One important outcome was the formation of an early warning mechanism designed to give Brussels advance warning of future threats to supply and laying out practical steps to limit the impact of future supply disruptions.

These mechanisms did not prevent the outbreak of another, more serious Russo-Ukrainian gas dispute in January 2009 that left much of Southern and Eastern Europe without gas for more than two weeks. Yet this time, the EU seemed to have a better grasp of the issues at stake, and the European reaction was more subdued. The EU received warnings in December 2008 about potential difficulties when the existing Russo-Ukrainian supply contract expired at the end of the year, and began convening meetings of energy security experts to plan for future contingencies. Though caught off guard once again by Gazprom's decision to cut deliveries, Brussels acknowledged that the cutoffs resulted from a commercial dispute between Gazprom and Ukrainian energy monopoly Naftohaz, and sought to avoid assigning blame to one side or the other. It also worked to broker agreements between the two companies and between Moscow and Kyiv, while providing monitoring teams to oversee implementation. In a retrospective analysis of the crisis, the European Commission acknowledged that the severity of the crisis for European consumers resulted in large part from the weakness of internal EU monitoring mechanisms and the reliance on national governments to collect and distribute information about gas flows. The result was a greater focus on strengthening the EU's internal energy market, and a renewed emphasis on diversification.[115] At the same time, Brussels recognized that its lines of communication with Moscow needed strengthening, and that the EU itself should play a larger role in addressing Ukraine's weaknesses (financial and infrastructural) that facilitated the crisis in the first place.

By 2009, Russian ambitions vis-à-vis the EU had changed as well, in large part because of the serious recession Russia's economy had been enduring since the autumn of 2008, which demonstrated all too clearly the importance of European trade and investment for Russia's economic health. In addition to energy, the EU had long been the most important source of trade and foreign direct investment (FDI) into Russia. Before the crisis, Germany was Russia's largest trading partner, while Cyprus, the Netherlands, Luxembourg, and the UK were the top four sources of Russian inward FDI (in the case of Cyprus, much of the money was held by Russian businessmen in Cypriot banks). Already spooked by the political uncertainty stemming from the Russo-Georgian war and Putin's implied threats of nationalizations, foreign investors pulled out of Russia in droves when the economic crisis hit in the autumn of 2008. Total FDI fell by 41 percent in 2009, and large declines continued into the first half of 2010.[116] Meanwhile, the drop in demand resulting from the crisis also caused trade to plunge. German exports to Russia fell by 36 percent in 2009, while Russian exports to Germany fell by 30 percent.[117]

The decline in foreign trade directly imperiled Russians' standard of living; it also potentially undermined the close political bond Moscow had forged with Berlin (and other major European trading partners) in previous years and threatened Russia's integration with Europe. Meanwhile, since Russia's economy relied heavily on foreign investment to fund research and development outside the natural resource sector, the outflow of foreign investment that began in late 2008 threatened Medvedev's plans for modernizing the Russian economy and sustaining the rise in living standards that most Russians had enjoyed over the previous decade. Of course, the crisis affected Europe too, helping to convince European leaders to moderate their opposition to investment from Russia, including in the energy sector.

Medvedev's modernization alliances strategy consequently paid particular attention to Europe, which already had close economic linkages with Russia as well as the technology and know-how that Russia needed to develop a modern, knowledge-based economy. The Foreign Ministry strategy document leaked in the spring of 2010 focused especially on Germany as a modernization alliance partner, and Medvedev reiterated his support for the idea during a summit with Merkel in June 2010. The Foreign Ministry paper even discussed specific joint ventures where German and Russian companies could cooperate to improve Russian infrastructure and develop Russian industry.[118] In a speech to Russian diplomats in July 2010, Medvedev likewise argued that Russia needed modernization alliances with not only Germany, but other major developed economies (principally in Europe) as well: France, Italy, the UK, as well as the United States.[119] At an EU-Russia summit meeting in Rostov-na-Donu in the spring of 2010, the EU embraced Medvedev's notion of an economically focused alliance that would promote Russian modernization and, many Europeans hoped, pave the way for Russia's political transformation as well. Both sides portrayed the modernization alliance concept as growing out of gains that had been achieved in the context of the Four Common Spaces, as well as a bridge to reaching agreement on a new PCA.[120]

From the EU's perspective, the idea of a modernization alliance with Russia is consistent with the long-standing objective of enhancing the institutional links between Russia and Europe. The emphasis on the private sector is one important way in which the concept of modernization alliances moves beyond the state-level interactions at the heart of the Four Common Spaces. At the same time, by using the private sector as an anchor for further integration, the EU runs the risk that economic disputes will interfere with the process of politically driven reconciliation. Given Russia's inconsistent record on issues connected to the rule of law, corporate governance, and investor protection, more European investors mean more opportunities for commercial disputes—especially those with political overtones driven by factions within the Russian elite. EU governments do not want to find themselves in the middle if European companies again fall victim to Russia's sometimes predatory investment climate.[121]

Some EU governments though are wary of Medvedev's modernization alliance concept. They worry that Russia's economic modernization is not possible without a parallel political liberalization that so far at least has not been forthcoming—and that if Medvedev's modernization strategy fails because of a lack of political reform, Russian integration with Europe will be a casualty. On the other hand, some Europeans fear that Russia will in fact succeed in modernizing its economy without liberalizing its politics. In that case, the EU could well find itself living next door to a more powerful but still authoritarian and irascible Russia.

CONCLUSION

Russia's approach to dealing with Europe remains caught between mutual dependence and mutual fear. Moscow and Brussels need each other economically, yet Russia's energy policy, authoritarianism, and involvement in the affairs of its neighbors have all limited its ability to seek fuller integration with the evolving institutional web of Europe. Plenty of institutional ties exist, ranging from the PCA to the Four Common Spaces to the NRC, yet old-fashioned geopolitics remain quite relevant, much more so than in relations among the EU states themselves. The economic crisis that began in 2008 strengthened the imperative on both sides to pursue deeper integration, but it did not entirely do away with long-standing fears about, respectively, Russia's ambition to dominate the Continent or the EU's insistence on intervening in Russia's internal affairs by focusing on issues such as democratization and the rule of law.

Of course, in comparison with Russo-U.S. relations, which remain dominated by yardsticks of traditional security, the relationship between Russia and Europe operates simultaneously on a range of levels. The very complexity of ties between Moscow and Brussels (not to mention Berlin, Rome, and Warsaw) has on the whole meant that the relationship has not been subjected to the drastic swings that have at times characterized interactions between Russia and the United States. Geographical proximity and the resulting economic interdependence have to a significant degree insulated Russia and Europe from such shocks. At the same time, of course, Europe has never posed a security threat to Russia on par with that of the United States. Even NATO, whose expansion Russia has consistently opposed, is seen as dangerous mostly on account of its U.S. component. Europe's own halting securitization has only partially changed this calculus on the part of the Kremlin.

Even though Europe itself is not generally seen as a first-order threat to the security of the Russian Federation, the relationship between Moscow and Brussels has at times suffered on account of the very different approaches to international affairs adopted by the two sides. The pattern is most evident when it comes to discussions about the expansion of both the EU and NATO. For most European countries, especially West European countries, the value of these institutions lies above all in their ability to reconcile former enemies and expand the realm of democracy and open societies into new regions. To Russia, though, both the EU and NATO sometimes appear merely tools of an expanded, aggressive West that has not fully broken with the Cold War–era logic of containment and continues to see Russia as a potential danger that must be hedged against. Both Moscow and Brussels seek further integration—whether through formal modernization alliances or merely the lowering of barriers to trade, investment, and travel—as a tool for reducing the salience of security issues in the relationship, even as they confront the mistrust that results from their divergent approaches to security.

The war in Georgia was, if nothing else, a signal from the Kremlin that it had had enough of the West's encroachment and that it would begin pushing back, at least around the fringes of Europe. Yet by helping to solidify the boundaries between the European and Russian (or Eurasian) spheres, the war paradoxically laid the foundation for Brussels and Moscow to start afresh. Freed (at least for a time) from the need to actively compete for influence in Ukraine, Georgia, and elsewhere in the former Soviet Union, the EU and Russia had an opportunity to pursue the economic cooperation and integration both sought.

Europe though remains a sometimes baffling partner for Moscow. Unlike the U.S., which is at least an old, familiar rival, for Russia the new Europe remains something of an unknown quantity, and it is precisely on account of the resulting uncertainty that Russia's policy toward Europe in all its institutional embodiments has been so complex and contradictory. Europe, as much as Russia itself, remains in search of a stable identity for the long term. Until those identities can fully coalesce, the nature of relations between Russia and Europe will remain at once interdependent and confrontational. The question for the future is whether economic interdependence, which looks set to increase apace, will alter the tenor of the relationship sufficiently that lingering disputes about basic political values, not to mention the role of the U.S. in European security, will no longer be capable of sparking crises. The challenge remains to solidify the economic and political links between Russia and Europe before a new commodity-fueled economic boom leads factions of the Russian elite to question Medvedev's modernization alliances, and the close ties with Europe that they require.

5

Rising China and Russia's Asian Vector

The emergence of China represents a different kind of challenge for Russian foreign policy. Russia's post-Soviet decline coincided with China's rapid emergence as an economic and geopolitical power that, unlike the United States or the major European powers, shares a long land border with Russia and is not necessarily a satiated, status quo power—notwithstanding its oft-professed commitment to a "peaceful rise." Despite the uncertainty surrounding Chinese intentions and the inherent difficulty for a relatively diminished power like Russia to reconcile itself to the rise of another, Russo-Chinese relations over the past two decades have mostly continued a warming trend that began in the late 1980s. Nonetheless, many Russian analysts see China as the biggest long-term threat to Russia's security, even if they are reluctant to openly discuss the possibility of a Russo-Chinese confrontation.

While managing relations with the West and preserving Russian influence within the post-Soviet space have been the main priorities for Russian foreign policy, relations with China have developed rapidly over the past two decades, driven in part by a desire to overcome past difficulties and in part by a shared aversion to the Western-dominated world order that appeared imminent with the end of the Cold War. Following the Sino-Soviet split that broke out in the early 1960s, Moscow and Beijing endured a series of war scares that culminated in armed clashes along their border in the spring and summer of 1969. The rapprochement between Washington and Beijing brokered by the Nixon administration further exacerbated tensions between China and the USSR. With the Soviet collapse and China's decision to jettison Marxist-Leninist orthodoxy, the rivalry for leadership of the global Communist movement was replaced by a common fear of exclusion from the centers of power in the post–Cold War world.

As in relations with the United States, Russia's approach to China has been characterized by a geopolitical understanding of the world, a preference for bilateral interaction between Great Powers, and a willingness to make short-run compromises in order to avoid being dragged into fruitless quarrels.[1] Sino-Russian cooperation has become significantly more visible and substantive in recent years, despite the growing disparity between Russian and Chinese power. Trade and investment have increased rapidly. Moscow and Beijing have joined together to oppose the U.S. invasion of Iraq, and to call for the withdrawal of NATO forces from Central Asia. They have institutionalized their relationship through regular summit and working-level meetings and through security cooperation in the Shanghai Cooperation Organization (SCO). They have promoted economic cooperation, particularly in the energy sphere, through projects such as the Eastern Siberia–Pacific Ocean (ESPO) pipeline, financed by Beijing in exchange for guaranteed access to Russian oil.

China is a key regional partner but also a country whose support is necessary in order for Russia to play the geopolitical role to which its elites aspire. Russia's ability to promote a multipolar world order is heavily dependent on the cooperation of China, since Russia by itself is no longer rich, powerful, or influential enough to shape the international order on its own. Cooperation with China provides Moscow with a kind of diplomatic force multiplier and an alternative to pursuing integration with the West, particularly since the Chinese model of authoritarian capitalist development holds great appeal for members of the Russian elite reluctant to embrace democratization.

China is also critical to Russia's economic development. The value of trade between the two countries quintupled in the decade between 1996 and 2006, and continued expanding rapidly until the onset of the economic crisis in Russia in 2008.[2] China remains a crucial source of labor for Russia's underdeveloped Far East, where the mass exodus of Russian workers after the fall of the Soviet Union led to the collapse of the local economy. In recent years, migrants from China have been central to both retail trade and agriculture in Siberia and the Far East, despite hostility from much of the local population and the Kremlin's own ambiguous attitude toward migrants. China's importance for the Russian economy also extends to the energy sector. Construction of pipelines to Asia is one strategy Russian energy producers have adopted as a means of reducing their own dependence on Europe (with its troublesome eastern fringe) as a purchaser of Russian oil and gas. Beijing also was long an important customer for the Russian military-industrial complex, which relied on Chinese purchases to remain viable while Russia's own military was in a period of retrenchment.

Finally, China remains for many Russians an attractive model of a country that has achieved rapid economic growth without sacrificing extensive state control over society.[3] It is precisely this success in achieving development without liberalization that has made China an attractive partner for those Russian elites uncomfortable with the West's conditions (especially relating to democratization) for achieving a real strategic partnership. For that reason, Medvedev's quest to tie Russia more closely to Europe while reducing tensions with the United States raises important questions for Russia's future relationship with China, especially if the two countries' political systems diverge and support inside Russia weakens for the idea of seeing China as a counterweight to the West.

Of course, China's own closed political system has not kept it from playing an active role in a largely Western-dominated political and economic order (though Beijing, like Moscow, has pressed to reshape that order to give rising powers a greater stake in global security and prosperity). Though politically less open than Russia, China has rushed into the global economy while pursuing wholesale deregulation and opening its doors to foreign investment to a much greater extent than Russia. While Beijing has been one of the biggest winners in the post–Cold War realignment, and therefore wary of Russian attempts to upset the balance, the post-2008 global economic crisis accelerated a push by both Moscow and Beijing to reform international institutions such as the IMF, the (increasingly irrelevant) G8, and even the dollar-denominated system of global monetary reserves to give newly "rising" non-Western powers a greater stake in the system. Yet if the crisis aided China's geopolitical ascent by accelerating the shift of economic dynamism from the West to Asia, its effects on Russia were more mixed; in some ways the crisis actually exacerbated the differences between Russian and Chinese priorities despite the two countries' shared commitment to multipolarity.

Medvedev's first trip abroad as president took him to China (and Kazakhstan), where he praised Russia's relationship with China for its "dynamism, mutual trust, and progress toward a stronger strategic partnership."[4] Russo-Chinese economic links have indeed expanded since Medvedev took office, and the relationship has become increasingly formalized in a series of regular meetings. These developments are part of a broader rapprochement under way since the last days of the Soviet Union, which took on added momentum during Putin's presidency. Putin told a Chinese newspaper in 2004 of his satisfaction that "we have overcome all the tensions and disagreements [between Russia and China] that existed in the past. Today there is not a single problem we cannot openly and in an absolutely friendly manner discuss and find a mutually acceptable solution."[5]

All the same, China remains something of an uncomfortable neighbor. Many Russian officials continue to believe that China will be among

Russia's most dangerous future rivals. China's attractiveness as an ally is offset in the minds of many officials by the fear that Russia itself is not safe from the growing power and influence of its giant neighbor; as one Russian analyst described it, the Russo-Chinese partnership is really an "alliance of a rabbit and a boa constrictor."[6] The rapidity of China's economic and military growth, during an era when Russia itself was going through a series of convulsions and crises following the demise of the Soviet Union, has greatly increased the power disparity between the two countries, as indeed has the post-2008 economic crisis (while Russia's economy shrank by nearly 8 percent in 2009, China's grew by almost 9 percent).

Though the volume of trade between Russia and China continues to rise, Russian analysts worry their country is becoming locked in a kind of neocolonial economic relationship, exporting primary commodities (energy, timber, minerals) and importing Chinese finished goods. Many Russians likewise question the construction of oil and gas pipelines to China because of the danger of increasing Moscow's dependence on Beijing, even if China represents a vast, and rapidly growing, market for Russian hydrocarbons. Such fears help animate Medvedev's modernization agenda, with its focus on moving Russia beyond being merely a raw materials appendage to its more dynamic neighbor and establishing better political relations with the West as the source of a political and social modernization that China cannot provide.

Likewise, China's military modernization has been a double-edged sword for Russia. While Chinese weapons purchases and tactical innovations are focused primarily on the possibility of a conflict across the Taiwan Straits rather than on land combat with its northern neighbor, the long history of Russo-Chinese border disputes has given Russian strategists pause, despite the signing of a series of border treaties between the two countries since the end of the Cold War. The Russian Defense Ministry quietly considers China a potential adversary (fear of China is an unspoken subtext to much of the military's declaratory fixation on conventional, state-based threats such as NATO), even though China was long the Russian military-industrial complex's best customer. Russia's own military modernization started comparatively late, has been heavily focused on overcoming years of neglect and decay rather than on enhancing the country's conventional strength, and remains controversial within the high command. While Russia's stockpile of nuclear weapons shrinks in line with various arms control agreements between Moscow and Washington, China—which is not a signatory to START I, SORT, or the 2010 U.S.-Russian New START agreement—continues to expand its own nuclear arsenal.[7]

Official statements of policy such as the Russian Military Doctrine openly discuss the dangers of a conventional war with NATO and are cited by the brass as a justification for opposing military downsizing. An important, if unstated subtext, however, is growing concern about China's own military rise. Though Russian military leaders have long refused to mention China as a potential foe (largely out of a desire not to provoke their more powerful neighbor), the military has begun hinting in recent years that it does not consider a conflict with China as lying outside the realm of possibility.[8] It has even conducted war games against an unnamed enemy that happens to share numerous similarities with the Middle Kingdom.[9]

The mounting disparity in economic and military weight between China and Russia continues to have important strategic consequences. Most notably, China has taken advantage of its newfound economic and political power to expand its sway in Russia's traditional sphere of influence in Central Asia. The result has been an intensified struggle for influence and resources in the Central Asian states, with both Moscow and Beijing seeking to lock up energy and pipelines for economic as well as geopolitical reasons.[10] Rapidly growing Chinese trade and investment in the region have reduced Russian power, reorienting Central Asia's economies to the East and giving Central Asian leaders the opportunity to balance between Russia, China, and the West.

Russia has sponsored the creation of regional organizations to provide an institutional framework for its influence and to contain the rivalry between Moscow and Beijing. Such regional groupings, above all the Shanghai Cooperation Organization (SCO), have gone some way toward ameliorating the Russo-Chinese rivalry in Central Asia. The SCO has benefited China by institutionalizing its presence in Central Asia both economically and in security terms.[11] For Russia, the SCO provides an additional means of maintaining Russian influence in the former Soviet Union (along with groups like the CIS, the CSTO, EurAsEC, and a series of bilateral agreements) and for keeping an eye on Beijing's activities in the region.

The SCO itself, however, has also become the subject of its two leading members' ambitions, not to mention a lack of clarity regarding its ultimate role. Russia and China have articulated contrasting strategies for the future development of the SCO and the limits of its eventual membership. Especially under Putin, some Russian thinkers advocated using the SCO as a kind of replacement for the old Warsaw Pact, that is, as a kind of geopolitical counterweight against the U.S. and a NATO that has increasingly committed itself to conducting out-of-area operations and drawing Russia's neighbors into its orbit.[12] China prefers using the SCO to combat militant Islamist organizations threatening the Central Asian republics as well as Chinese Xinjiang, and to confront the "three evils" of terrorism, separatism, and extremism.[13] The continuing tug-of-war between Beijing and Moscow over the future of the SCO is one of the principal reasons the organization has failed to become a major security player, and why Moscow has increasingly shifted its gaze to the Collective Security Treaty

Organization as an alternative vehicle for maintaining its influence in Central Asian security.

For much of the recent past, Moscow's approach to the bilateral relationship with China has emphasized security concerns—balancing against the U.S. and NATO, extending the Russian sphere of influence in Central Asia, and maintaining a rough military balance—while Beijing has focused more on the economic components of the relationship, especially gaining access to Russia's raw materials reserves. These competing perspectives and the competing goals underpinning them have contributed to the wariness with which the two powers regard each other, despite their cooperation. Russian wariness has only increased as China has grown more powerful and assertive. Precisely for that reason, one of the motivations behind Medvedev's modernization agenda and pursuit of rapprochement with the West is the desire to avoid falling too far into the Chinese embrace.

To a great extent, Russia's China policy is a function of its larger strategic vision of carving out an independent role for itself on the world stage. In this capacity, China is a useful ally, one whose economy (with its massive demand for energy) nicely complements Russia's own, and which shares Moscow's commitment to a multipolar world order based on the principle of sovereign Great Powers. Of course, Moscow also continues to cultivate the Western powers (as well as other major Asian countries such as Japan and India), and given its closer proximity and history of participation in European security, few Russians are willing to embrace China at the expense of ties with the West, especially as the power disparity between Moscow and Beijing widens and China becomes a more prominent player on the global stage in its own right. China is without doubt an important partner for Russia. The Sino-Russian relationship, though, is heavily instrumental, based on overlapping interests and subject to future swings as Russia continues to define its overall position between Europe and Asia.

RUSSIA AND CHINA IN A MULTIPOLAR WORLD

Much of China's attractiveness as a strategic partner for Russia stems from the fact that Moscow and Beijing have parallel understandings of international order in the twenty-first century. Both are profoundly uncomfortable in a world dominated by the United States where Western norms regarding democracy and human rights reign supreme. According to the Russian Foreign Ministry, Russo-Chinese cooperation is a result of "Russia's long-term national interests and the similarity of [our] approaches to the fundamental questions" of international politics.[14] The central Russian concept of *mnogopolyarnost'*, or multipolarity, has a Chinese equivalent—*duojihua*— which is frequently employed in official documents describing the nature of the emerging world order.[15] Russo-Chinese cooperation at the United Nations, on arms control, and elsewhere is to a significant degree predicated on the fact that Beijing and Moscow both believe that a world dominated by a handful of Great Powers in which sovereignty and national interest provide the framework for conducting international relations is most conducive to their own well-being. Such a world has to accommodate a variety of political systems, without conferring any special rights on Western-style liberal democracies, or assuming that all states will eventually become liberal democracies themselves.

Russian interest in a closer partnership with China is consequently a partial reflection of the state of Russia's relationship to the West, especially the United States. If Moscow perceives its interests are being ignored by Washington, a partnership with China, itself a powerful outsider, enhances Moscow's ability to challenge the legitimacy of an international order based on Western norms and where leading institutions give disproportionate weight to the Western liberal democracies. Russia's embrace of non-Western-dominated international organizations such as the G20 and the BRICS (Brazil, Russia, India, China, South Africa) forum stems precisely from this wariness about the hegemony of Western norms in many other international institutions. Like Russia, China's Communist government rejects the idea of universal standards for democracy and human rights and believes state sovereignty is absolute (even for post-Soviet republics like Georgia). China thus strongly opposed the bombing of Yugoslavia and Iraq, has defended the right of Iran to establish its own nuclear program, and attacked U.S. democracy promotion efforts as unwonted interference in other countries' internal affairs. On all these issues, Beijing made common cause with Moscow, and the partnership between the two grew closer each time.[16]

Despite the very real gains made in Russo-Chinese relations since the mid-1990s, China is at best a part-time ally of the Kremlin, one whose rush toward economic modernization at times threatens to leave Russia in the dust. China's lukewarm reaction to the war in Georgia was one example of the limits of Beijing's interest in closer ties with Russia. Moreover, China long sought to maintain good relations with the U.S. as part of its "peaceful rise" strategy, even at the depths of the U.S.-Russian standoff in the Bush-Putin years. Beijing was reluctant to go as far as Putin's Russia did in criticizing U.S. unilateralism, even if it shared Russian concerns that the Bush administration was destabilizing the global order. The post-2008 economic crisis, meanwhile, has further cemented the links between the U.S. and its largest creditor, giving them both a stake in the status quo (even if talk of a so-called G2 world is misplaced and political tensions are rising) that Russia lacks. For all of Medvedev's support for the Obama administration's reset policy, Russia remains less important to

Washington than China. Particularly in economic terms, "China's indispensable partner is the United States; Russia's is Europe or, more specifically, Germany."[17]

Chinese and Russian perspectives also diverge on several important global issues. In particular, Beijing is much more of a player than Moscow in addressing transnational issues such as setting rules for global trade and financial flows and coping with climate change. In part, these diverging perspectives are the result of China's larger economy and more extensive integration into the world economy. Yet they are also the consequence of Russia's general fixation on traditional geopolitics and measures of power. Despite the efforts of Medvedev and others to shift Russians' understanding of what it means to be a Great Power in the twenty-first century, compared to China, Russia remains underequipped to tackle many of the transnational challenges that shape international security in the modern world. One manifestation of this problem is Russia's proclivity for trying to balance the U.S. and China, even when it might be beneficial for Russia to act as a bridge between Washington and Beijing.

China, of course, is not a passive object of Russian policy, and has its own reasons for seeking cooperation with Moscow. The benefits to Beijing in seeking a closer partnership with Moscow are numerous: guaranteed supplies of oil and gas, diplomatic support in the UN Security Council and against the expansion of U.S. power in the Asia-Pacific region, transfers of military technology, and decreased tension along the Russo-Chinese frontier that allows Beijing to focus its attention on Taiwan and global challenges.

Many Russian observers, especially those with liberal, pro-Western tendencies, are therefore skeptical about what Russia stands to gain from closer association with China. Former foreign minister Kozyrev argued against embracing Beijing because, as the stronger power, China would be more able to bend Russia to its ends than vice versa. Russian liberals continue to fear that Beijing is using the budding Russo-Chinese partnership to estrange Russia from its Western partners and force it into dependence on China for diplomatic support as well as economic development.[18] For Kozyrev, China and Russia were rivals for foreign investment, and the prospect of a Russo-Chinese rapprochement provided Beijing with a means of pressing the West to admit it to the World Trade Organization and back down over Taiwan.[19]

Kozyrev's perspective is still shared by many pro-Western Russians. To the extent that the West and China are competing poles in the struggle for Russian allegiance, seeking closer cooperation with Beijing implies a comparable distancing from the West. In this way, the Russian Westernizers and their opponents share a common outlook on the importance of China for Russian foreign policy as a possible counterweight (whether for good or ill) to the West. Yet given the level of interdependence between Washington and Beijing—ranging from Chinese manufacturers' reliance on U.S. consumers to the Chinese government's vast holdings of U.S. debt to the role of U.S. security guarantees in checking the emergence of Japan and South Korea as military rivals to China—the Russian paradigm in some ways limits Moscow's options in relations with both the U.S. and China.

This dichotomous approach of seeing the West and China as competing poles of attraction for Russian foreign policy was a somewhat recent development. Despite their emphasis on better relations with the Western world, Russian leaders in the early 1990s sought to simultaneously promote improved ties with China. Moscow's ability to seek improved relations with both Beijing and Washington stemmed largely from the Kozyrev-era belief that traditional notions of power and interest were no longer relevant in the same way they had been during the Cold War. By the middle of the 1990s, when NATO expansion and Western intervention in the Balkans had become a reality, the notion of a strategic partnership between Moscow and Beijing based on the idea of promoting a multipolar world and resisting the expansion of Western (i.e., American) power became more prominent in the rhetoric of both sides. The establishment of the Russo-Chinese strategic partnership in 1996 coincided with the downfall of Kozyrev and the emergence of a new, more assertive approach to diplomacy on the part of Yevgeny Primakov and his associates.

This partnership not only allowed Russia to more successfully resist the expansion of Western power and influence in its neighborhood but also provided an alternative concept of Russia's identity as a state and a civilization, one lying in Eurasia rather than Europe. If the faith of Kozyrev and his backers that Russia's historical destiny lay in the West was misplaced, then perhaps China would prove a more welcoming partner. Beijing was perfectly happy to stay silent about Russia's actions in Chechnya (indeed, the Chinese government consistently backed Russia's right to act as it sees fit in Chechnya, in return for Moscow's firm commitment to a "one China" policy) and made no demands for political or economic reform as a condition for better relations.[20]

More generally, because China is a nation-state (in international relations terms) rather than a value-driven multilateral agglomeration like the West, the very nature of its relationship with Russia has been different. Unlike the West, China cannot offer Moscow the prospect of integration into multilateral institutions such as the G8, NATO, or the WTO. Instead of a relationship based on rules and values, Russia's relationship with Beijing is much more a traditional geopolitical partnership, where each side is out to maximize its national interest (however it chooses to define that amorphous concept). For a Russia that remains deeply protective of its own sovereignty, such a partnership is in many ways a more natural and comfortable fit, regardless of its greater cultural and historical affinity with the West. Such was the case even in the 1990s when Russia was more or less considered to be an emerging democracy. Under Putin, as Russia moved increasingly to emulate the Chinese model of authoritarian capitalism, the mutual affinity between Beijing and Moscow only increased, much to the discomfort of those who conceived of Russia as a fundamentally Western country.[21]

During Medvedev's presidency, a degree of rebalancing has occurred, as Moscow has sought to make up many of its quarrels with the West in the interest of economic development. While Moscow has emphasized that its rapprochement with the U.S. and Europe is not directed against any other state or group of states, ties with Beijing have cooled as China has grown rapidly and expanded its influence in areas Russia considers its geopolitical hinterland, above all Central Asia.[22] The draft foreign policy strategy leaked in May 2010 was quite restrained in its discussion of China. While touting the advantages of modernization alliances with major Western countries, the document merely noted that:

> We must pay special attention to monitoring China's growing role in international affairs, including the consequences of Beijing's activity for our global and regional interests . . . with particular attention to the evolving situation in the Group of 20, the BRIC, and the SCO, as well as the UN Security Council (*where under current conditions our support is becoming more important for the Chinese than their support is for us* [emphasis added]).[23]

In the early 1990s, the belief that China could balance the growing influence of the United States had to overcome not only the skepticism of those like Kozyrev, who saw a long-term partnership with the U.S. as a more promising route for Russia's development, but also the outright hostility of many nationalists and members of the military. After all, China had been a serious rival to the Soviet Union for leadership of the international Communist movement and even contemplated the possibility of war with Moscow during the height of the Cultural Revolution. The fact that large swaths of the Russian military and nationalist right remain anti-American has not necessarily made them pro-Chinese (racial factors play a role, as does fear). Primakov, the most influential supporter of multipolarity as a Russian strategic goal—and hence of a rapprochement with Beijing—fought a bitter, though ultimately successful battle with parts of the defense establishment that continued to view China as a military rival and source of a "yellow peril" menacing the Russian Far East.[24]

More than a decade later, the Russian military was more open about China's ability to directly threaten Russia than it ever had been in the 1990s. In September 2009, Lt. General Sergey Skokov, chief of staff to the

Russian ground forces, publicly discussed what a war between Russia and China would look like, while in March 2010, the Russian army deployed two additional brigades along the frontier with China near the Far Eastern city of Chita. That summer, with Medvedev in attendance, the Russian armed forces for the first time conducted large-scale military exercises (dubbed Vostok-2010, or East-2010) in the Far East, emphasizing combined arms operations, the use of advanced command and control techniques, and ultimately the launch of tactical nuclear weapons. The only foe against whom such a major operation would be necessary is the Chinese People's Liberation Army, which Moscow made a point of inviting to watch the demonstration of Russian military might.[25]

BETWEEN RAPPROCHEMENT AND RIVALRY

The first hints of warming in the Sino-Soviet relationship came during the late 1980s. Mikhail Gorbachev visited Beijing in June 1989 and announced the normalization of relations between the USSR and China, effectively putting an end to the three-decade-old Sino-Soviet split. Momentum toward rapprochement continued under Yeltsin, who issued a December 1992 declaration terming China a "friendly" state and announced the creation of a Russo-Chinese "strategic partnership" during a visit to Beijing in April 1996.[26] In the unsettled 1990s, Russia's nascent rapprochement with China represented a major achievement for the country's foreign policy.[27] Nonetheless, as with other strategic partnerships undertaken by the Yeltsin administration (including that with the United States), the overall aim of the Russo-Chinese partnership remained somewhat vague, despite some real successes such as demarcating and demilitarizing the Russo-Chinese border, expanding trade, adopting a common perspective on the challenges facing the post–Cold War world, and institutionalizing ties through regular diplomatic contacts.[28]

In part, the impetus for better Russo-Chinese relations in the 1990s came from the United States, whose unilateral activities in the Balkans, commitment to NATO expansion, and questioning of established arms control regimes created unease in both countries. On the Russian side, this unease contributed to the elevation of Primakov to the Foreign Ministry and the proclamation of Russia's commitment to creating a multipolar world order. In April 1997, Yeltsin and Chinese leader Jiang Zemin signed the "Joint Declaration on a Multipolar World and the Establishment of a New World Order" during Yeltsin's state visit to Beijing. The declaration affirmed Moscow and Beijing's commitment to "respect for sovereignty and territorial integrity, mutual non-aggression, non-interference in each other's internal affairs, equality and mutual advantage, peaceful coexistence and other universally recognized principles of international law."[29] In essence, the declaration grew out of the desire of both sides to register their disapproval with the way the post–Cold War international security architecture was evolving, though it contained little in the way of a positive program for reversing developments that had taken place since the fall of the Soviet Union.

Primakov sought to give the budding geopolitical rapprochement with Beijing greater heft by using it as the foundation for a multilateral dialogue on the preservation of an international order based on state sovereignty and the leading role of the Great Powers. In 1999, Primakov put forward the idea of a strategic triangle comprising Russia, China, and India as a kind of counterhegemonic bloc comprising nearly half the world's inhabitants. Neither Beijing nor Delhi was particularly enthusiastic about the idea at the time (both were more subtle in expressing their discomfiture at U.S. foreign policy), but the logic underpinning such an approach has been evident in some Russian thinking about the future of the Shanghai Cooperation Organization.[30]

In May 1997, Primakov gave a major address to the Association of Southeast Asian Nations (ASEAN) Regional Forum, where Russia has observer status, suggesting that the Russo-Chinese agreement on forming a multipolar world could serve as a model for partnership agreements with other ASEAN states. He also cited the Shanghai Agreement (the document that would lay the foundation for the SCO) as another example of Russia's commitment to building a multipolar and, in his view, more stable and equitable world.[31] As Primakov took pains to point out, though, his support for closer relations with China was not based on the kind of visceral anti-Americanism associated with some in the Eurasianist camp of Russian politics. Rather, as Primakov explained in 2005, Russia cannot afford to be dependent on any one country or group of countries for its stability and security. Instead, "only . . . diversification, rather than concentration on one foreign policy vector or another creates the possibility for building optimal conditions for securing Russia's external security."[32] As former Russian diplomat Alexander Lukin noted, Communists welcomed the rapprochement between Moscow and Beijing for constraining U.S. power, while even some liberals welcomed the new climate of reduced Sino-Russian tensions, which could free Moscow to focus on getting its own house in order.[33]

While the initial impetus for increased Russo-Chinese cooperation in the 1990s came from a desire to resolve old problems as well as a shared concern about a U.S. threat to international stability, once the process was under way, it took on a momentum of its own. This rapprochement came to encompass a wide variety of issues, from military cooperation to energy to intelligence sharing.[34] Much of the 1990s-era warming between Moscow and Beijing was based on energy, beginning with a 1996 agreement between the two governments on energy cooperation and continuing with the signing of a protocol in 1999 approving the construction of an oil pipeline (what would eventually become ESPO) from Siberia to China.[35] A much-discussed 2001 Treaty on Friendship and Cooperation also had an economic underpinning; the agreement opened the way for Moscow to begin negotiations with Beijing on the construction of this pipeline.[36]

The initial period of warming Russo-Chinese relations in the 1990s also encompassed defense cooperation, with a series of agreements on troop limitations and the promotion of high-level dialogue between the Russian and Chinese militaries. The improved climate in military relations between the two sides was the more significant because it laid the foundation for greater economic cooperation in the defense sector. China soon emerged as the largest customer for Russian weaponry and technology, which came for a time to account for a substantial percentage of Russian export revenue.[37]

The improved relationship between Russia and China was likewise embodied in a number of more concrete agreements. One of the first benefits of the new climate in relations was a resolution of literally thousands of outstanding border disputes between the two countries. Given the vast population disparity between Northern China and the Russian Far East, the series of border agreements signed in the 1990s (the first such agreement was actually signed by a dying Soviet government in 1991) especially benefited Russia. It drastically reduced the likelihood of Chinese intervention in areas of the Russian Federation with substantial ethnic Chinese populations and secured Beijing's acceptance of changes to the frontier imposed in the nineteenth century on a weakened China. Negotiations on delimiting the entire 2,700-mile frontier continued piecemeal for over a decade. The two sides signed a treaty fully resolving their territorial disputes in October 2004, and the last pieces of disputed territory (two small islands in the Amur River) were finally disposed of during Lavrov's July 2008 visit to Beijing.[38]

In addition to establishing demarcation commissions to draw an agreed-upon frontier, Russo-Chinese border agreements attempted to finesse outstanding disputes, for example, by agreeing to the joint development of the once-disputed islands in the Amur and Ussuri rivers between the two countries.[39] While much of this work was of a technical nature, the continued momentum toward a full territorial settlement had a fundamentally political purpose (particularly given the long history of border skirmishes between China and the USSR) and benefited from the direct involvement of the political leadership in both countries—in sharp contrast to the still-festering territorial disputes between Russia and Japan. In Russia, the border agreements often set off sharp protests from regional officials and nationalists concerned about the precedent of giving away Russian territory, while public opinion was also generally hostile.[40] Nonetheless, the Kremlin's insistence on following through with the agreements (and pushing them through a sometimes skeptical Duma) while not seeking similar accords with Japan is indicative of the importance Putin and his allies placed on Beijing as a geopolitical partner.

Meanwhile, more active cooperation between Russia and China was developing in the context of opposing the spread of Islamic radicalism, separatism, and terrorism in Central Asia. The explosion of Islamic radicalism in the wake of the Afghan civil war posed a direct threat to both Russian and Chinese interests in the region, even before September 11, 2001, and the subsequent deployment of American forces to Afghanistan. Moscow had been confronting the specter of Islamic radicalism since the outbreak of hostilities in Chechnya in the mid-1990s; though the Chechen rebels were motivated largely by secular nationalist goals, foreign jihadist ideology became more prominent as Chechnya spiraled further into chaos.[41] Violent Islamic radicalism was an even greater problem in large swaths of Central Asia, where it posed a threat not only to local secular strongmen (generally Russophone ex–Communist Party first secretaries) but also to Russian and Chinese influence in the region.

China meanwhile had to worry about its Xinjiang province, where the restive Turkic-speaking, Muslim Uyghur majority continues to chafe under Beijing's rule and has the potential to become a fertile breeding ground for jihadist groups. For Moscow, Beijing, and the Central Asian leaders, the Islamist threat provided another rationale for seeking deeper regional integration and multilateral cooperation. The consolidation of the SCO into a full-fledged regional security organization (including Uzbekistan, which does not even share a border with China) owed much to its participants' interest in sharing information, resources, and experience in combating the perceived Islamist threat.[42]

In July 2001, Moscow and Beijing signed a Treaty of Friendship and Cooperation, the first comprehensive agreement between the two countries since before the outbreak of the Korean War in 1950. This accord was significant as well in that it encapsulated Russia and China's shared aversion to a unipolar world dominated by the United States. It grew out of the initiatives of leaders, especially in China, to ground the improved climate in relations in a concrete agreement.[43] With demarcation of the Russo-Chinese border nearly completed, the potential for military confrontation apparently reduced on account of the Russian military's decline, and the emergence of unilateral action by the United States as a major irritant for leaders in both Beijing and Moscow, the treaty both reflected how Russian and Chinese interests had undergone a fundamental realignment in the decade since the collapse of the Soviet Union and laid the foundation for more intensive Sino-Russian cooperation in the future.

The treaty called for Russia and China to stop aiming nuclear weapons at each other and to commit to the "no first strike" principle. It also affirmed the two sides' acceptance of each other's territorial integrity (i.e., Beijing agreed to give Moscow a free hand in Chechnya in exchange for a reaffirmation of Russia's commitment to the "one China" policy). On the level of geopolitics, the treaty enshrined Moscow and Beijing's commitment to eschew interference in the internal affairs of other countries and to strengthen the United Nations as the key forum for resolving international disputes.[44] Such language was far from meaningless, given both countries' worries about the role being played by the United States, particularly in the Balkans (the treaty was signed two months before the September 11 attacks), and about U.S. President Bush's declared interest in withdrawing from the ABM Treaty.[45] In this way the Russo-Chinese agreement was as much an effort at coordinating against the perceived excesses of U.S. unilateralism as it was about overcoming the legacies of the past in Sino-Russian relations.

At the same time, of course, the treaty was vague enough to be open to multiple interpretations. Given the continued interest of both Russia and China in good relations with the United States, the agreement had to be couched in terms that, while indicating displeasure with Washington's actions, did not threaten either signatory's ability to cooperate with the U.S. (particularly the ability to trade). The actual agreement was largely free from specific commitments to act, and Moscow was at pains to deny that the treaty was directed against any outside power, especially the United States.[46] Russian deputy foreign minister Aleksandr Losyukov declared after the signing, "To say that our partnership with China is directed against anyone in the West is entirely inaccurate. I think it must be understood in the West that there are boundaries beyond which neither Russia nor China is prepared to go."[47] Top U.S. officials also sought to downplay the importance of the treaty, arguing that given the volume of shared interests, it was perfectly logical for Moscow and Beijing to sign such an agreement.[48]

Under Putin, Russian diplomacy toward China continued to strike a balance between promoting better relations with Beijing and not overly complicating ties with the U.S. in the process. Despite the rise of China and despite the greater attention being paid to improved Russo-Chinese relations, it still remained the case that Russian foreign policy under Putin was Western-centric. Putin's approach was somewhat more subtle than that of Primakov and his associates, who were more overt about using China as a counterweight to the United States. Putin's repeated assertions that Russia's destiny is European appeared in part designed to mollify Western critics who would see a Sino-Russian rapprochement as evidence that Russia was turning its back on the West.

At the same time, the Kremlin, especially under Putin, rarely hesitated to hold up a deeper Russo-Chinese partnership as a bogeyman to fend off Western hectoring about Russia's dubious commitment to upholding Western norms of democracy or human rights, giving China an opportunity to use Russia as a cat's-paw in its own periodic quarrels with the West. In the aftermath of Russia's invasion of Georgia, Beijing (like Russia's other putative allies in the SCO) gave only reluctant backing to the invasion without accepting the independence of South Ossetia and Abkhazia. China was perfectly willing to see Russia deal a blow to the notion of colored revolutions—and to contrast Moscow's heavy-handed intervention with its own preference for soft power, a contrast not lost on the Central Asian states being courted by both Moscow and Beijing.[49]

To be sure, China shares Russia's discomfort at the idea of uncontrolled political change, as well as the expansion of Western influence in Eurasia. With the U.S. bogged down in Iraq, Russia and China began cooperating in opposing the U.S. drive to spread democracy. In both Beijing and Moscow, the Bush administration's democracy promotion efforts appeared a fig leaf for a campaign to expand U.S. influence abroad through the installation of friendly regimes. In the face of this perceived threat, Russia and China united around a worldview that emphasized each state's right to choose its own political system as well as, domestically, a preference for authoritarian politics and capitalist economics with a heavy dose of state intervention.[50]

This so-called Beijing Consensus was a notable development of the Putin years, thanks to Russia's own increased skepticism regarding the virtues of democratic government and a perception that U.S. interest in democracy promotion under Bush was selective and driven by the needs of U.S. foreign policy rather than a moral commitment to democracy and human rights. The notion of sovereign democracy—Kremlin ideologist Vladislav Surkov's postulate that each country has a right to take its own path to democracy without foreign interference—was essentially the Russian contribution to the Beijing Consensus, which helped frustrate U.S. efforts to promote democracy in the CIS, the Middle East, and elsewhere.[51] This shared understanding was most directly embodied in the so-called Joint Declaration on the International Order of the Twenty-First Century, signed in July 2005 during Chinese president Hu Jintao's visit to Moscow. This declaration affirmed the two sides' shared commitment to "a just and rational world order" based on international law, multilateralism, state sovereignty, and the leading role of the UN in resolving global problems.[52]

While Russo-Chinese relations may lack the formal institutional apparatus of Russia's interactions with the West, the regular series of meetings between Putin and his Chinese counterparts (Jiang Zemin until 2003, then Hu Jintao) imparted a sense of predictability to the relationship it had hitherto lacked. The 2005 treaty was supplemented by an action plan on implementation that laid out a framework for deepening Sino-Russian cooperation in the years ahead, paying special attention not only to economics but also to increasing cooperation in the spheres of security and defense.[53] Medvedev, who visited Hu in Beijing shortly after being inaugurated during the summer of 2008, has continued this effort to foster regular high-level dialogue, with summits between the Russian and Chinese presidents becoming an annual occurrence, in addition to regular meetings on the sidelines of multilateral events such as summits of the BRICS forum and the G20.

Such interest in an enhanced Russo-Chinese dialogue was partly the result of the long-term trend toward closer cooperation between the two states, but interest was also boosted by the atmosphere of crisis surrounding the decision by the United States to attack Iraq in 2003 despite the UN Security Council's refusal to authorize the use of force. The U.S. decision for war revived Russian and Chinese fears about the dangers stemming from unipolarity and unilateralism on the part of the United States. Beijing and Moscow both opposed Security Council resolutions laying the groundwork for a U.S.-led invasion of Iraq and called for Washington to allow UN weapons inspectors to continue their work.[54] The standoff over Iraq, along with Washington's broader diplomatic assault on the states termed by President Bush the "axis of evil" (Iraq, Iran, and North Korea) reinforced both Russian and Chinese fears about the dangers of untrammeled American power and provided an impetus for greater coordination between Moscow and Beijing.[55]

At the same time, the tensions created by September 11 in some ways complicated Putin's task of trying to balance between the West and China. Since Washington's response to the attacks created substantial discomfort in Beijing, the Russian decision to support the U.S. invasion of Afghanistan was poorly received by the Chinese.[56] Moscow's decision to share intelligence with the United States and to authorize the deployment of U.S. troops in Central Asia as part of the campaign in Afghanistan was made over Chinese objections.[57] Yet after suggesting to Washington that he might be open to constructing a joint U.S.-EU-Russian theater missile defense system, Putin went out of his way to reassure Beijing that Russia, like China, remained fully committed to the ABM Treaty.[58] Of course, with the lapsing of the ABM Treaty following Washington's withdrawal, the U.S. and Russia again began discussing missile defense cooperation, culminating in their agreement at the 2010 NATO–Russia Council summit in Lisbon to build a combined ABM architecture. China's response to the prospect of U.S.-Russia (and NATO-Russia) missile defense cooperation has unsurprisingly been skeptical.

RUSSO-CHINESE ECONOMIC TIES

Economic congruence has long been central to Russo-Chinese relations. China's rapidly growing demand for energy to feed its booming economy has coincided with the emergence of Russia as one of the world's leading producers of both natural gas and oil. Meanwhile, Beijing's modernization of the People's Liberation Army and Navy was initially accomplished to a great extent through the purchase of Russian weapons and the licenses to produce them domestically—in the process saving the Russian military-industrial complex from complete collapse during the lean years of the 1990s. This cooperation in the energy and military-industrial spheres has also benefited from and contributed to the political rapprochement between Russia and China, which has removed barriers to economic activity. As Russia's economy again went into a tailspin during the autumn of 2008, Beijing's deep pockets became an important lifeline, with significant Chinese investments being made in Russian commodities and infrastructure even as Western investors were pulling out of Russia. With trade between Russia and Europe still depressed by the economic crisis, China edged in front of Germany to become Russia's largest trading partner in 2010.[59] The strong economic ties between the two countries provide an important anchor for their political relations, reducing the likelihood of a serious deterioration at least in the short-medium term.

With the reduction in political tension between Moscow and Beijing, bilateral trade boomed before the financial crisis, especially in the border region, where a huge population disparity and the resolution of border disputes created an opportunity for expanded cross-border trade and migration. Trade with China is critical for the Russian Far East in particular. Given the vast distances involved and the lack of communications infrastructure between the Far East and European Russia, the economies of many Far Eastern regions are more closely tied to China than to the rest of Russia. This cross-border integration, which is most visible in the retail trade conducted by Chinese entrepreneurs in towns and cities along the border, is largely the result of market forces unleashed by the collapse of the Soviet Union. For the economically deprived Far East, the opportunity to build economic links to China offers the chance to participate in globalization without having to go through Moscow and represents the most promising opportunity for the region's economic recovery.[60]

The growth in trade between Russia and China is also a reflection of political developments, especially efforts on both sides to boost bilateral trade and economic cooperation, as well as economic liberalization in both China and (to a lesser extent) Russia. Indeed, the rapprochement between Moscow and Beijing in the 1990s was most clearly visible in the deepening integration of the two economies. While the bulk of Russian exports to China consisted for most of the 1990s of natural resources (energy as well as minerals and timber), followed by military technology, over the past decade both the volume and range of goods being traded have expanded significantly, with aircraft and other vehicles, electronics, and machinery all contributing a significantly higher percentage of Russian exports to China than they had in the 1990s.[61] In aggregate terms, in 1999 the total value of Russo-Chinese trade was $5.5 billion.[62] It reached more than $58 billion in 2008, the last year before the economic crisis, falling to $38.8 billion in 2009 (much of the decline was due to Russian firms' reduced demand for Chinese machinery) before rebounding rapidly in 2010.[63]

In comparison, Chinese investment in Russia has lagged. Compared with the EU, China has contributed a fairly small share of Russia's inward FDI. Since (unlike most investment from the West) Chinese investment is usually made by state-controlled entities, Moscow worries that increased Chinese FDI will give Beijing greater control over the Russian economy. Nonetheless, Moscow has made boosting Chinese investment a priority. In the summer of 2010, the Russian Ministry of Economic Development and Trade announced that it was seeking to boost Chinese inward investment from $2 billion to $12 billion in ten years' time, and would actively recruit Chinese companies to buy stakes in Russian industries.[64]

Bilateral negotiations between Russia and China during Medvedev's presidency have increasingly focused on economic issues—especially Russian oil and gas exports, but also on gaining Chinese support for Russian membership in the WTO, arms sales, Chinese participation in the privatization of Russian companies, and the economic impact of Chinese immigration on the Russian Far East. Major impediments to improved economic relations include high Russian tariffs on Chinese consumer goods as well as pervasive corruption in the Russian customs service. Chinese support for Russian membership in the WTO is in part based on the calculation that, when admitted, Russia will have to bring its tariff regime in line with WTO standards and make a real effort to crack down on corruption.[65] Still, fear of China's economic might and concern about Moscow's ability to maintain its hold over the Far East continue to impose obstacles to deeper regional economic integration.

Economics has been a bone of contention between Moscow and Beijing in other ways as well. As an energy supplier, Russia's desire for high prices and security of demand clash with China's interest in low prices and a diversity of supply. Moscow, not to mention Russian regional leaders, worries openly about the effects of Chinese investment in the Russian economy. Such worries are particularly acute in sectors the Russians consider strategically important (such as energy and defense), to the extent that the Kremlin has openly blocked Chinese firms from participating in auctions for Russian energy firms.[66] Despite the growing variety of goods exported from Russia and Putin's own efforts at boosting Russian exports to China, bilateral trade continues to be dominated by Russian energy and Chinese finished consumer goods—largely because of the low quality of most Russian manufactures.

Both the cooperative and competitive aspects of Russo-Chinese economic interaction are most clearly visible in the energy sector, which under Putin came to play a central role in Russian foreign policy generally and Russo-Chinese relations in particular. Since the bulk of Russian oil and gas is pumped from fields in Siberia and the Far East, Russian energy should theoretically enjoy a comparative advantage in Asian markets as a result of proximity and lower transportation costs relative to energy extracted from the Middle East or elsewhere. Russian oil and gas are also attractive to China for a series of geopolitical reasons. Thanks to its rapid industrialization and economic growth exceeding 8 percent per year even in the context of the global financial crisis, China has rapidly become the world's third-largest oil consumer (after the United States and Japan). Its own reserves are inadequate to meet the needs of its economy. Meanwhile, China's growth and modernization have positioned it as a potential rival and strategic competitor to the U.S., and Washington has consequently sought ways of gaining influence and leverage over China.[67] Given U.S. naval supremacy, China's ability to import oil by tanker from the Middle East could be cut off relatively easily. Under the circumstances, Russian oil and gas appear increasingly attractive: pipelines from the Russian Far East to China could not be disrupted by the U.S. Navy, and Moscow is less likely than its neighbors in Central Asia to accept U.S. diktat in the event of a clash between the U.S. and China. Of course, Russian oil companies, with strong backing from the Kremlin, are also busy trying to establish as much control as possible over the production and supply infrastructure in Central Asia, even as China attempts to peel off individual states by signing bilateral deals.[68]

On the Russian side, the construction of oil and gas pipelines to China is attractive as a way of achieving the security of demand that is central to Russian ideas of energy security (and which have been a major stumbling block in Moscow's negotiations with the EU). At the same time, boosting energy exports to China would fit into the larger Russian foreign policy strategy of achieving maximum influence through balancing. In 2009, Russia exported over 183 billion cubic meters (bcm) of natural gas, of which barely one-quarter bcm went to China, while the former Soviet states collectively exported 447.1 million tons of oil, of which only 26.6 million tons went to China.[69] Not only does China represent a vast untapped market for the Russian energy industry, it also provides the Kremlin with an alternative to excessive reliance on Europe as a customer.

The potential of the Chinese market, along with the geopolitical advantages of balancing between East and West, was responsible for Russian interest in the construction of the ESPO oil pipeline running from Angarsk in Western Siberia to the Chinese industrial center of Daqing, a proposal long fraught with complications for Russia's Asian strategy. A major reason for the paucity of Russian energy sales to China has been the lack of pipeline infrastructure. Russian oil is transported to China primarily by rail, which is more expensive and less efficient than pipelines, while Russian gas can only be sold to China in the form of LNG sent by ship to ports on China's eastern coast. Russian pipeline monopoly Transneft began mooting the idea of a pipeline to Daqing in the mid-1990s, but lack of capital and political uncertainty prevented construction from beginning for more than a decade.

Moscow and Beijing at last reached a basic agreement on the scope of the project in July 2001. The project was to cost around $3 billion and be completed by 2005. In May 2003 the Chinese National Petroleum Company (CNPC) and Russia's Yukos signed an accord on the actual construction and operation of the pipeline. The agreement called for Russia to provide for the bulk of the cost, with China covering expenses for the section from the Chinese frontier to the terminus at Daqing.[70] The deal had broad support within the Kremlin, including from then-prime minister Mikhail Kasyanov. The Daqing pipeline promised Russia a major stimulus for developing new energy production sites in Siberia as well as a guaranteed market for Russian energy and the prospect of greater economic integration between China and Russia's struggling Far East.[71]

Yet the agreement soon fell through, becoming both a catalyst for and a casualty of the Kremlin's assault on Yukos and its founder Mikhail Khodorkovsky as Putin and his *silovik* allies stepped in to prevent the consummation of the deal. For them, the proposed agreement with Beijing appeared to threaten Russia's national security and ability to make use of its most valuable resource. Above all, the construction of the proposed pipeline (especially by a privately held oil company like Yukos) seemed to imperil Moscow's aspiration to carve out a substantial international role by tying the Russian economy too tightly to China and reducing the country's ability to function as an independent actor in the international system. For similar reasons, the Kremlin blocked Chinese attempts to purchase Slavneft when it went on the block in December 2002, sought to establish control over energy transport routes from Central Asia at Chinese expense, and stepped up pressure on foreign energy firms working to develop new fields on Sakhalin Island near the Chinese coast, with Gazprom eventually seizing control of the most important projects.[72]

Russia insisted on maintaining control over the firms supplying energy through its pipelines, effectively giving the Kremlin a free hand to manipulate prices and supplies (much as it did to Ukraine and Belarus). Beijing, along with Yukos, unsurprisingly resisted Russian demands for full ownership of the pipeline, and the Kremlin decided that it could not accept such a strategically valuable piece of infrastructure in the hands of either the Chinese or the unreliable Khodorkovsky without sacrificing too much of its foreign policy autonomy.[73] Despite lobbying from Chinese premier Wen Jiabao and a loan of $6 billion from Chinese banks to finance the Kremlin's purchase of Yukos, Putin's intervention effectively killed the deal.[74]

With the idea of a pipeline to Daqing seemingly off the table, the Kremlin returned to an alternative proposal for a pipeline to East Asia that would remain entirely on Russian territory, with its terminus at Kozmino Bay, near the port of Nakhodka on the Sea of Japan. The cabinet of Prime Minister Mikhail Fradkov formally approved the building of a pipeline to Kozmino in December 2004. This route was substantially more expensive than the Chinese variant, since the pipeline would have to snake its way for thousands of kilometers along the Russo-Chinese frontier (plans called for the pipeline's total length to reach 4,130 kilometers, versus 2,400 kilometers for the Daqing route) through remote wilderness where construction would be difficult and expensive. Transneft, which would be responsible for operating the pipeline, initially put the cost of the Kozmino route at around $11.5 billion (the price went even higher when the route was altered in 2004 to avoid ecologically sensitive regions near Lake Baikal), or nearly quadruple the cost of building to Daqing.[75]

Despite the increased cost, Putin and his allies backed the Kozmino route both because of financial incentives offered by Japan (which would be the most likely customer) and because of the increased strategic flexibility a pipeline wholly on Russian territory would provide. Desperate to reduce its dependence on oil from the Middle East (currently 90 percent of Japanese oil imports originate in the Persian Gulf states), Tokyo offered to provide as much as $14 billion for the construction of the Kozmino route, while allowing Transneft to maintain ownership of the completed pipeline. China, meanwhile, had offered only to pay for construction of a pipeline from Daqing to the Russian frontier, and in exchange demanded ownership of the pipeline infrastructure on Chinese territory.[76]

The Kozmino route also provided Russia greater strategic flexibility, allowing it to avoid becoming overly reliant on any one country as a customer for its oil in the Far East (as had happened with Turkey following construction of the Blue Stream gas pipeline, when Ankara unilaterally reduced the price it was willing to pay for Russian gas, secure in the knowledge that Gazprom could not sell the gas to anyone else). Since the terminus at Kozmino would be on Russian territory, the Kremlin would retain control over the ultimate destination of oil passing through the pipeline. Transporting oil from Kozmino to Japan by ship would be relatively inexpensive, but unlike a pipeline that terminated on foreign territory, Moscow would still have the option of shipping oil from Kozmino to China, Southeast Asia, or even North America. In this way, Russia would reduce its dependence on any one state (i.e., China), a consideration that fit well with Putin's emphasis on promoting Russia's foreign policy independence. Construction on the first segment, from Taishet (where the pipeline's upstream terminus was moved after protests over the environmental impact of building at Angarsk, which is located close to the shore of Lake Baikal) to Skovorodino, was completed October 2009, with the onward segment to Kozmino Bay scheduled to open by 2014.

Of course, the decision to build the pipeline to Kozmino was bound to ruffle feathers in Beijing, and soon after the announcement that the Kremlin favored the Kozmino route, it sought to address Chinese concerns. Even if Beijing's hoped-for oil pipeline did not materialize, the Russian government promised it would build a separate pipeline bringing natural gas to China (thereby also reducing Moscow's dependence on an increasingly wary EU to buy its gas).[77] With Yukos out of the way and the Kremlin again in a position to balance between China and Japan, Moscow also began openly suggesting in mid-2004 that it might be open to building a spur from the Taishet-Kozmino pipeline to Daqing. During Putin's visit to China in October 2004, economics and trade minister German Gref explicitly promised to begin construction on the spur route to Daqing by the end of the year.[78] Despite such promises, nothing happened on the ground for several years, even though Beijing had agreed to finance construction of the spur from Skovorodino.

It took the financial crisis that hit Russia in 2008 to finally clear the way for the deal to build the Daqing spur to be consummated. Russia's state-owned energy companies were among the most significant victims of the crisis, which left them heavily indebted as global energy prices plunged. Their debts, along with the credit crunch that afflicted Russian banks further imperiled plans to increase oil production in Eastern Siberia and the Far East, which will likely be necessary as demand for Russian energy, especially in Asia, continues to rise. With its economy continuing to grow rapidly despite the crisis elsewhere in the world, Beijing had accumulated vast currency reserves, allowing it to drive a hard bargain with the cash-strapped Russian energy companies, which finally struck a deal in February 2009. In exchange for a loan of $15 billion to Rosneft to refinance its debts and $10 billion to Transneft to pay for construction of the spur, China secured a twenty-year supply of oil (estimated to be fifteen million tons per year) from the pipeline at a concessionary price; the Daqing spur was completed by September 2010.[79] The unusual long-term contract allowed China to lock in supplies of non–Persian Gulf oil at a bargain price, while for Russia the deal both aided the Kremlin's strategy of diversifying its customer base and helped address the problem of the energy industry's inability to pay for infrastructure investments. On the other hand, the financial arrangement highlighted China's growing ascendancy in Asia. Moscow got the pipeline it wanted, but only by sacrificing its ability to control how the oil flowing through it would be sold and by giving Beijing a significant discount relative to prices on the global spot market.

What was long Russia's second-largest export to China—weapons and military technology—reflects a similar contradiction between financial advantage and strategic dependence. On the one hand, the Kremlin was long eager to sell Beijing everything from AK-47 assault rifles to advanced antiship missiles as a way of earning export revenue and promoting the Chinese military's dependence on Russian suppliers. On the other hand, the Russian brass continues to have profound misgivings about the nature of Chinese ambitions (present and future) and has expressed its opposition to selling Beijing top-of-the-line military technology out of fear that one day Russia could find itself attacked with its own weapons. This ongoing debate pitting the Kremlin and much of the military-industrial complex against the uniformed leadership speaks to the generally anomalous position China holds in Russian strategic calculations, at once a valued ally in the quest to promote a more balanced world alignment and perhaps the most dangerous potential foe.

The debate is particularly important because military technology is one of the few fields where Russia can compete on an equal basis with Western firms and because unlike U.S. or European defense contractors, the Russian military-industrial complex is willing to sell its wares indiscriminately, including to regimes Western firms and governments try to shun (e.g., Sudan, Syria, Venezuela, and Iran).[80] China, which the U.S. views as a strategic competitor, and which was cut off from U.S. and EU weapons deliveries following the 1989 Tiananmen Square massacre, is the supreme example of Moscow's mercantile (some might say mercenary) approach to weapons sales.

The list of Russian military technology that has found its way into Chinese hands is lengthy. It includes advanced Russian aircraft (Su-27 Flanker interceptors and Su-30 MKK fighter-bombers), S-300 surface-to-air missiles (SAMs), up to ten *Varshavyanka* class (Kilo class in NATO nomenclature) diesel submarines, and four top-of-the-line *Sovremenny* class destroyers.[81] In addition to such advanced hardware, Beijing has acquired the licenses to produce many Russian platforms (including the Su-27) domestically and has employed thousands of Russian engineers and designers in its own military-industrial complex.[82] In recent years, Russia has become increasingly reluctant to sell top-of-the-line systems (such as the Su-33 combat aircraft and the S-400 air defense system) to the Chinese, both for fear of strengthening a potential rival and to prevent further reverse engineering.

Particularly during the 1990s, when Moscow's own spending on the military fell to historic lows, the ability to sell weapons abroad (particularly to China, whose army and navy were already using primarily Soviet-model weaponry) was a major factor in keeping the Russian defense industry afloat.[83] Chinese purchases of Russian arms reached $2 billion per year by 1999 (jumping significantly following NATO's intervention in Kosovo) and roughly $2.2 billion by 2003.[84] Meanwhile, even as the Russian Ministry of Defense allocated larger sums for arms purchases as well as research and development following Putin's ascension to power, Russian industrialists still generally preferred selling to the Chinese (and Indians, and anyone else who paid on time and in cash), since much of the money Moscow allocated for military procurement disappeared through corruption or wastage.[85]

During Putin's second term, though, arms sales to Beijing declined rapidly. By 2010, they were close to nil (see figure 5.1). The decline stemmed from a variety of sources, including the Russian military's increasing fear of China, Russia's own economic recovery (which made arms sales to China less critical and spurred new weapons purchases by the Russian military), and resentment at Beijing's proclivity for reengineering and reselling Russian technology to third countries in direct competition with the Russian defense industry. In response to the drying up of sales to China, Russia increasingly turned to other customers for its weapons, notably (to China's intense dismay) India and Vietnam.[86] While it remained upset at Chinese reverse engineering, the Russian defense industry continued seeking business in China, realizing that if it stayed out entirely, it would have little leverage to press its complaints. Moscow also feared being permanently shut out of the lucrative Chinese market.[87]

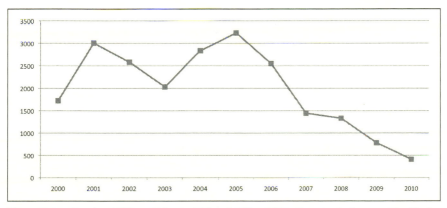

Figure 5.1.   Russian Military Sales to China (Million USD, Constant). *Source:* Stockholm International Peace Research Institute

The issue of arms sales to China in many ways continues to pit two powerful elements in Russian foreign policy thinking against each other—a mercantile policy of enriching the state and seizing export markets versus expansion of Moscow's geopolitical influence, which China threatens. China was long a good customer, with a near limitless appetite for Russian weapons technology. At the same time, China remains a potential strategic competitor to Russia, one that the defense establishment views with increasing concern. Given the influence of powerful economic interests that make up the so-called Kremlin, Inc., some in Moscow worry that the state may not be able to ensure that Russia's national interests are paramount in decisions regarding the sale of advanced weapons to the Chinese.

THE SHANGHAI COOPERATION ORGANIZATION

From the early 1990s, the deepening of bilateral ties between Russia and China has been predicated to a considerable extent on the desire to balance against the dominant power of the United States. With its ability to project power and influence anywhere in the world, Washington provided an important impetus for many of the milestones in Sino-Russian relations. The 1997 declaration on the formation of a multipolar world was above all a warning to the U.S. that China and Russia would not accept an international order dominated by Washington. China's interest in buying advanced weaponry from Russia, and Russia's willingness to sell such weaponry despite its own concerns about Chinese intentions, was also linked to how Beijing and Moscow have viewed U.S. power.

One element of the Russo-Chinese rapprochement that caused significant consternation in the West was the consolidation of the Shanghai Cooperation Organization (*Shankhaiskaya Organizatsiya Sotrudnichestva*, or ShOS) into a reasonably cohesive multilateral bloc founded on the principles of multipolarity and national sovereignty—precisely those values that U.S. intervention in the Balkans and Iraq challenged. While the SCO may have failed to live up to the more ambitious vision of some of its founders, its principal members, Russia and China (other members are Kazakhstan, Kyrgyzstan, Uzbekistan, and Tajikistan, while Iran, Mongolia, India, and Pakistan are observers, and Turkmenistan and Afghanistan are often invited to participate in SCO activities), view the organization as something more than just a forum for resolving mutual difficulties. Particularly during the era of heightened U.S.-Russian tension during the second terms of George W. Bush and Vladimir Putin, U.S. analysts looked on with great trepidation at an organization that united Moscow and Beijing, opposed a U.S. military presence in Central Asia, overtly rejected the U.S. democratization agenda as unwarranted interference in countries' internal affairs, aspired to a larger regional security role, and actively reached out to Iran—the country Washington considered the single greatest menace to peace in the world.[88] Despite Washington's fears, the SCO has remained less than the sum of its parts, because its ringing declarations of solidarity mask significant tensions between Moscow and Beijing, especially over their respective influence in Central Asia.

The SCO was created in 2001, on the basis of a treaty signed in 1996 by Russia, China, Kazakhstan, Kyrgyzstan, and Tajikistan. The original 1996 Shanghai Treaty (as well as a supplementary agreement signed in 1997) merely committed the signatory nations to undertake force reductions and confidence-building measures along their mutual borders. The driving force behind the initial agreement was the signatories' concerns about Islamic extremism (Kabul had just fallen to the Taliban, and Taliban-inspired movements were active throughout Central Asia and the Caucasus). These so-called Shanghai Five, along with Uzbekistan, signed the Declaration of the Shanghai Cooperation Organization in June 2001. According to the declaration, the SCO aimed at:

> Strengthening mutual trust, friendship and good-neighborliness among member states; broadening effective cooperation among them in the political, economic/trade, scientific-technical, cultural, educational, energy, transportation, ecological, and other spheres; mutual striving to support and strengthen peace, security and stability in the region; and constructing a new democratic, just, and rational international order.[89]

The declaration, as well as subsequent documents adopted by the organization's members, was broad enough that it could be interpreted in a number of ways. On the one hand, the SCO's emphasis on resolving economic disputes and promoting mutual cooperation seemed fairly benign. Then again, the focus on "constructing a new democratic, just and rational international order" seemed to indicate that the SCO was really designed to act as a check on U.S. power in the region. Subsequent SCO statements, including those opposing U.S. missile defense plans and calling for U.S. troops to depart from Central Asia, indicate the extent of its members' discomfort with the United States' post–Cold War geopolitical role in Central Asia and elsewhere. A number of observers in the West also saw the SCO as a deliberate attempt on the part of China and Russia to weaken U.S. influence in the region and secure monopolistic control over energy resources, perhaps even as a nascent authoritarian rival to NATO.[90] To some extent, Washington's problem with the SCO is merely that the U.S. itself is not a member and has not been invited to participate.[91]

To be sure, much U.S. concern about the SCO is overblown. For all its talk of military cooperation and integration, the SCO has no standing force of its own, much less a general staff or any of the other attributes of a unified command structure. SCO members remain free to make their own decisions on security matters, including the right to join other blocs and alliances without consulting other member states.

Besides, the Central Asian members of the SCO also belong to NATO's Partnership for Peace program, and most have strong bilateral ties with the United States (which provides large amounts of military assistance to Kazakhstan, Kyrgyzstan, and Tajikistan).[92] The aftermath of the September 11 attacks, when SCO members Kyrgyzstan and Uzbekistan signed bilateral agreements with Washington to permit the stationing of U.S. forces on their soil over the qualms of both Moscow and Beijing, was a clear example of the organization's limits as a tool for coordinating foreign policy.[93] So, too, was the 2008 war in Georgia, when an SCO summit refused to give Moscow more than equivocal support for its military intervention. Its members agreed merely to "express their deep concern in connection with the recent tension around the issue of South Ossetia, and call on the relevant parties to resolve existing problems in a peaceful way through dialogue, to make efforts for reconciliation and facilitation of negotiations."[94] Pointedly, the summit refused to endorse Russia's position that South Ossetia and Abkhazia had become independent states as a result of the conflict.

Moreover, the SCO member states face diverse regional security threats, of which Islamic extremism and terrorism (whether in the guise of the Islamic Movement of Uzbekistan and its offshoots, Hizb-ut-Tahrir, or China's East Turkestan Islamic Movement) are among the most prominent. Much of the SCO's security focus has in fact been directed at promoting cooperation among member states in intelligence sharing and joint law enforcement activities against such Islamic radicals. These include the 2001 Shanghai Convention on Terrorism, Extremism, and Separatism and the establishment in 2004 of the SCO's Regional Anti-Terrorist Structure (RATS).[95]

As the situation in Afghanistan worsened during the mid-2000s, Moscow saw the SCO as a possible means of institutionalizing a foreign presence outside the scope of NATO's International Security Assistance Force, but was rebuffed by skepticism from Beijing—not to mention NATO itself—about the organization's ability to materially improve security and stability in Afghanistan. Attempting to counter the image that its main function was to limit the reach of outside powers, the SCO hosted a major conference in Moscow in March 2009 where its members pledged, alongside delegates from the CSTO and major Western powers, to coordinate their activities toward security in Afghanistan as a means of reducing the threat of terrorism and drug trafficking.[96] Indeed, in dealing with the conflict in Afghanistan, the SCO's main role has been to limit the impact of the cross-border drug trade and terrorism, rather than direct involvement in the conflict between the Taliban and the internationally backed government of Hamid Karzai. The organization has also worked directly with Kabul to coordinate efforts against terrorism, drug trafficking, and organized crime.[97]

While jointly combating the shared challenge of Islamic extremism, China and Russia continue to disagree about the proper role for the SCO and about how it should affect relations with the United States. As fairly traditional Great Powers, both China and Russia have emphasized bilateral ties rather than participation in overarching organizations (especially in the field of security). Besides, Russian and Chinese interests in a number of key areas diverge sharply. Most starkly, Russia is trying to hold onto the vestiges of its empire, while China is rapidly expanding its sphere of influence through investment and other forms of soft power in Russia's backyard. Beijing would like to use the SCO as a vehicle for promoting economic ties among member states, leading to the eventual formation of an SCO customs union that would mainly benefit Chinese exporters. Russia meanwhile has actively blocked attempts at deepening intra-SCO economic integration in favor of bilateral accords and agreements under the auspices of organizations it alone dominates, principally the Eurasian Economic Community (EurAsEC).[98]

On balance, the SCO is more of a forum for Beijing and Moscow to keep an eye on each other than a tool for mounting a joint challenge to the status quo. The SCO benefits China by allowing Beijing to boost its exports and providing a mechanism for the participation of the Chinese military in regional security issues.[99] While Beijing generally treats the SCO as a bridge for expanding its own role in Central Asia, Russia benefits from the institutionalization of its partnership with China and from coordination of member states' policies on dealing with terrorism, drug trafficking, and other regional security problems. The greatest benefit to Russia from the SCO, however, may be precisely that the organization gives Moscow some leverage over the expansion of Chinese power into Central Asia.

Some Russian strategists (like Dugin) would like to see the SCO transformed into a kind of latter-day Warsaw Pact, using it to build a bloc of revisionist states to actively challenge post–Cold War U.S. hegemony.[100] Even Putin though denied that Beijing and Moscow had any such ulterior motives for setting up the SCO. He argued in 2006 that the SCO emerged because "after the bipolar world collapsed there was a demand for other centres of power. We understand this great principle but we are not planning anything like that. The SCO has a good future. We are not going to turn this organization into [a] military-political bloc."[101] To the extent that the SCO has found itself in opposition to the United States on issues ranging from the presence of American troops in Central Asia to the supremacy of the UN

Security Council in authorizing the use of force, it has generally been the result of incompatible visions about the nature of the international order and opposition to specific U.S. actions, rather than any kind of deep-seated anti-Americanism on the part of the SCO collectively or its members individually.[102] Medvedev has portrayed the SCO as a mechanism for coordinating a response to common challenges, particularly the global financial crisis, and a forum for strengthening the voices of member states on the international stage, rather than a bloc with a geopolitical mission.[103]

To be sure, the most visible aspect of SCO activity has been in the security sphere, though the organization plays an increasingly prominent role in building economic (as well as cultural) links between its member states. In the field of economics, the 2003 Framework Agreement as well as a series of technical implementation accords signed in 2004 laid the foundation for expanded trade links within the SCO space. Russia would like to use the SCO as a vehicle for promoting jointly funded pilot projects in fields ranging from energy to transportation—in other words to channel more Chinese money into regionally significant projects.[104] The increased attention being paid to economic as well as cultural issues by the leadership of the SCO is an indication that the group, despite its shared commitment to multipolarity, is in fact an organization without a clearly defined mission. Beijing, Moscow, and the Central Asian states all have their reasons for wanting better mutual relations, though there is much less consensus on the long-range goals for their partnership.

Agreement on the SCO's role in hard security issues is even more elusive. In political-military terms, the SCO is a fairly loose partnership. Unlike NATO, it does not require members to spend a fixed percentage of their budget on its operations. In contrast to NATO—or even the CSTO—it does not have a mutual defense clause (something akin to NATO's Article 5) or any standing forces of its own. The degree of attention paid by the SCO to geopolitics has in any case varied over time. SCO members gave particular attention to this component of their relationship in the aftermath of the 2003–2005 colored revolutions in Georgia, Ukraine, and SCO member Kyrgyzstan, which appeared to provide a template for overturning the status quo throughout the post-Soviet space. Largely as a result, the SCO increasingly set itself up in opposition to the U.S.-led campaign for democratization. As Lavrov remarked following the 2007 SCO ministers' meeting in Kyrgyzstan:

> It is clear to everyone that one-sided approaches to solving regional and international problems, [those] not relying on international law, are out of place, and that ideological approaches to international affairs, including any kind of "democratization" schemes are ineffective because they do not account for the historical, cultural, and civilization peculiarities of the countries involved.[105]

Given the widespread belief among ruling elites in the CIS that the colored revolutions benefited from Western assistance, the SCO's growing focus on security in subsequent years at times took on, at least implicitly, an anti-Western tint. The SCO's 2005 Astana summit (in which Iran participated for the first time as an observer) adopted a declaration demanding the departure of U.S. troops from their bases in Uzbekistan and Kyrgyzstan, perhaps the high-water mark for the SCO's collective distrust of the West.

Shortly thereafter, the SCO held its first large-scale joint exercises (dubbed "Peace Mission 2005") involving both the Russian and Chinese militaries. Despite the alarming (in the West) image of Russian and Chinese soldiers jointly conducting maneuvers euphemistically referred to as "antiterrorist operations," in fact the Peace Mission operation and its sporadic sequels reflect all the ambiguities of Russo-Chinese relations and uncertainty over the precise role of the SCO.[106] Peace Mission 2005 appeared designed primarily as a way for Russia to showcase new weapons systems it was eager to sell to China as well as to send a political signal to the United States, Taiwan, and perhaps the Koreas about China's and Russia's shared commitment to reducing U.S. influence in Eurasia.[107] Notably, though, Beijing had requested that the exercises take place in southeastern China, directly across the straits from Taiwan, as a way of intimidating the independence-minded Taiwanese government. Despite its firm support for the one China principle, Russia had little interest in being dragged into a conflict over the status of Taiwan and demanded a different venue for the maneuvers, ultimately settling on the Shandong Peninsula on the Yellow Sea. The 2007 Peace Mission exercises, held in Russia's Chelyabinsk *oblast* and paid for exclusively by Moscow, were a significantly smaller affair. Only sixty-five hundred personnel took part (versus ten thousand in Peace Mission 2005), while tanks and naval forces were entirely lacking.[108] Subsequent Peace Mission exercises in 2009 and 2010 were smaller still (around three thousand soldiers in each), while Moscow was emphatic in arguing that the maneuvers were solely designed to deal with the danger posed by international terrorism, rather than conventional military threats.

The first SCO summit of Medvedev's presidency came shortly after the invasion of Georgia, in late August 2008 in the Tajik capital of Dushanbe. Besides seeking, with quite limited success, the organization's backing for the Russian invasion, Medvedev described the SCO's founding as resulting in particular from the "recognition of the necessity for coordinating efforts to promote regional security and stability," which, in his view, the organization had done following the recent war.[109] In spite of the other members' hesitance to accept the Russian position on Georgia, Medvedev laid out an ambitious agenda in other areas where Moscow hoped the SCO would be able to generate coordination, including combating terrorism and drug trafficking, policy toward the war in Afghanistan, and economic cooperation. He was also keen to give the SCO observer states a more substantive role in an effort to enhance the organization's influence. And while the Dushanbe summit echoed past Russian language on the importance of international law and the need to resolve disputes without resorting to force, Moscow's tortured effort to carve out an exception for its intervention in Georgia was a clear indication that the SCO remains less than the sum of its parts.

FAR EASTERN CHALLENGES

While the main Western narrative about Russo-Chinese relations focuses on military cooperation via the SCO, along with shared opposition to the West's influence in Central Asia and the spread of democracy, less attention is typically paid to what may be the most intractable threat to the Russo-Chinese strategic partnership—the fate of Siberia and the Russian Far East. Eastern Siberia and the Far East are the most sparsely populated and economically deprived regions of the Russian Federation. Despite the Kremlin's centralization of power from regional barons, its ability to control these regions remains limited by long distances, poor communications, and a lack of funding. As Medvedev noted at a development conference in Kamchatka, "If we do not work more actively [to develop the region], in the final analysis we could lose everything."[110]

Meanwhile, economic pressures and a porous border have led to significant Chinese migration to Siberia and the Far East (much of it temporary labor migration). Chinese immigrants—initially small-scale traders, followed by farmers, laborers, and entrepreneurs—have begun transforming the landscape of the region. While critical to the area's economic recovery, their presence has inflamed nationalist passions inside Russia, fueling talk of a creeping Chinese takeover, or at least the gradual sinicizing of Siberia and the Far East. Such nationalist discourse has become widespread in Russia and is at times even exploited by the Kremlin for its own ends. While Russian fears of losing Siberia and the Far East to China are excessive, the growth of nationalist, anti-Chinese sentiment among a broad segment of the population (including in the military) could pose a significant challenge to continued Russo-Chinese cooperation, while a reorientation of the region's economy to Asia could further sap Moscow's influence over its distant hinterlands.

Despite the strategic challenges China poses to Russia, Russian public attitudes are generally positive. A 2009 poll by the All-Russian Center for the Study of Public Opinion (VTsIOM) found that 47 percent of Russians believe Russia and China will be partners or allies in the twenty-first century, while 29 percent thought they would be rivals and only 5 percent thought they would be enemies. (See also table 5.1.)

Table 5.1   On the whole, how would you characterize current relations between the people of Russia and China?

	2005	*2007*	*2009*
Friendly	15%	19%	17%
Good, neighborly	19	17	17
Normal, calm	40	40	39
Cool	11	10	10
Tense	3	3	5
Hostile	2	1	1
Difficult to say	10	10	11

Source: VTsIOM, 16 Jun 2009, http://wciom.ru/index.php?id=268&uid=12005.
Note: Asked of 1,600 respondents in 140 population centers in June 2009. Margin of error 3.4 percent.

Russia's problems and perceived vulnerability in the Far East are both economic and demographic. Although Siberia and the Far East contain the vast majority of Russian oil and gas reserves, they are among the poorest, most sparsely populated, and most remote parts of the Russian Federation. Moreover, their importance is bound to increase as existing sources of oil and gas in Western Siberia and the Urals run out, even as Moscow commits itself to exporting ever larger quantities of oil and gas. Eastern Siberia alone is estimated to possess at least as much oil as the entire U.S. (around twenty billion barrels), along with vast quantities of natural gas. Developing the region and bringing its resources to market will cost up to $100 billion by 2020.[111] Given its physical proximity and seemingly insatiable demand for natural resources, China will play a critical role in the Russian Far East's economic future. Medvedev has made cross-border cooperation one of the pillars of regional development for the Far East. The "Program for Cooperation Between Regions of the Far East and Eastern Siberia of the Russian Federation and the Northeast of the PRC (2009–2018)," which Medvedev and Hu signed in September 2009, lays out an ambitious program for Chinese investment in resource extraction and infrastructure development—though the agreement was widely criticized in Russia for cementing the country's allegedly neocolonial economic relationship with China.[112]

Improving the parlous economic state of the Russian East will require more than injections of cash, however. It will need trade and economic integration, which in turn demand openness to outside goods and people. It will also need workers, since Russia's demographic collapse is particularly severe in Siberia and the Far East, which have experienced a massive population outflow since the end of the USSR. Because of the great distances and poor communications between the Far East and Western Russia, since the 1990s the regional economy has increasingly become integrated into an Asian exchange network, closer to Beijing than to Moscow, despite the Kremlin's attempts to limit the expansion of Chinese businesses. The Russian authorities have raised tariffs, lowered the threshold for importing Chinese goods tax-free, and nixed several Chinese proposals for building infrastructure linking the two countries (including a railway from northeastern China to the coast north of Vladivostok and cross-border special economic zones), while the impact in the Far East of Moscow's general crackdown on foreigners in the retail trade has most affected Chinese migrants.[113]

Much of the reason for Russia's reticence about the Far East's economic links with China has to do with fears that the region is moving inexorably into China's sphere of influence. The collapse of the Soviet border regime and the subsequent series of agreements with Beijing to demarcate the frontier have facilitated cross-border trade between the Russian Far East and China, leading to substantial Chinese immigration into Russia.[114] The Amur River divides the roughly seven million people of the Russian Far East from the thirty-eight million of China's Heilongjiang province. Many Russians fear that the population disparity, coupled with a porous border, will inevitably lead to massive Chinese migration into the Russian Far East, changing the region's ethnic makeup and perhaps laying the foundation for a political takeover by Beijing.

As Clifford Gaddy and Fiona Hill have argued, given its extreme climate and distance from major population centers, the Russian Far East is actually *overpopulated* relative to areas of the world with comparable climates, such as Alaska and northern Canada.[115] Still, given the Russian economy's reliance on resource extraction and the fact that most natural resource deposits are located in Siberia and the Far East, in the short run at least, maintaining a reasonably stable population is an economic necessity for Russia. Due to high mortality rates as well as massive out-migration by native-born inhabitants, the region's population is falling even more rapidly than that of Russia as a whole.

The imbalance between the Russian and Chinese sides of the border, along with the opportunities for trade, farming, and the provision of services have already contributed to the migration (legal as well as illegal) of hundreds of thousands of Chinese into Russia. Officially, thirty-five thousand Chinese nationals live in the Russian Federation. Unofficial estimates vary widely, with nationalist figures—including some government officials—citing inflated numbers to pressure the Kremlin into taking action. Estimates by respected observers generally range from two hundred thousand to five hundred thousand at any one time, though such figures include both settlers and the much higher number of labor migrants who ultimately return to China. [116] In any case, the post-2008 economic crisis, which hit Russia much harder than China, and the gradual aging of China's population seem to have slowed the influx in recent years, though without quelling widespread fears of a Chinese takeover among swathes of the Russian population.[117]

While this Chinese immigration has succored the regional economy and offset to some degree the out-migration of the native population, it has also stoked nationalist passions on the part of many, even highly placed Russians. It is certainly not uncommon to hear Russians in both Moscow and the Far East express unease at what is often portrayed as the creeping sinicization of the border region. Rhetoric about the Chinese demographic threat has been a staple of Far Eastern politics since the 1990s; political leaders and journalists have done much to fan the flames.

Russian fears about the future of the Far East take a number of forms: fear that Moscow's neglect will feed regional separatist movements, fear that the center's weakening hold will leave the region vulnerable to Chinese aggression, or the fear of a more invidious invasion by Chinese migrants who will irrevocably transform the character of Siberia and the Far East, even if Beijing never exercises formal control. Russian alarmists point out that Beijing has never completely accepted the 1858 and 1860 unequal treaties by which Russia acquired vast areas of the Far East from a Qing Dynasty in terminal decline—despite the plethora of border agreements Moscow and Beijing have signed in recent years—and that modern Chinese textbooks do not acknowledge Russian sovereignty over the region.[118] Of course, many also see China's military buildup as creating a direct threat to Russia's possession of Siberia.

Even Putin contributed to the popular concern about Russia's ability to hold onto the Far East, calling for increased migration controls lest "the local population [of the Russian Far East] will in the future be speaking Japanese, Chinese and Korean."[119] Putin's government made it more difficult for Chinese entrepreneurs to import goods into Russia, banned foreigners (which, in the Far East, primarily meant Chinese) from working in the retail trade, and even imposed restrictions on the ability of Russian citizens to work or reside close to the frontier. Such steps represent one of the ways the Kremlin fell in behind the nationalist rabble-rousing of groups like the DPNI, even at the cost of exacerbating tensions with China.

As China's economic importance for Russia has grown, top officials have made a greater push to keep nationalist passions in check toward the Chinese. Reversing his position on the need for migration controls, Prime Minister Putin noted in a televised August 2010 interview that the influx of Chinese citizens to regions on the Russian border such as Heilongjiang was being carefully managed by Beijing to promote economic growth and ethnic rebalancing, not to set the stage for large-scale migration into the

Russian Far East—and that in the long run Russia too would benefit from economic growth on the Chinese side of the border.[120]

RUSSIA AS AN ASIAN POWER

China, of course, is hardly Russia's only major concern along the Asian vector of its foreign policy. Russian engagement with Asia more generally has expanded since the end of the Cold War and since the economic boom that transformed the "Asian Tigers" into economic powerhouses. The financial crisis of 2008 encouraged Russian firms to increasingly reach out to Asia in search of new markets and new investment. The crisis provided the impetus for transforming the BRIC group, originally conceived by an analyst at the investment bank Goldman Sachs, into a full-fledged international organization (BRIC became BRICS when South Africa joined in late 2010). Moscow used the now-annual BRICS summits (and the related RIC—Russia, India, China—trilateral ministerials) as a tribune for demanding the redesign of global institutions such as the IMF to give rising powers a greater say, and for promoting economic links among the BRICS/ RIC powers.

Russia has also played at least a supporting role in regional security, for example, as a (fairly passive) participant in the six-party talks on North Korea's nuclear program and through its participation in regional organizations such as APEC, ASEAN, and the East Asia Summit. Yet the general prioritization of relations with the West, the absence of strong regional institutions analogous to the EU or NATO in Asia, and the fact that Russia's own center of gravity lies in the Western part of the country have all kept Moscow from playing a particularly active role in Asian affairs outside of a few important bilateral relationships and its postimperial role in Central Asia.

Putin actively sought for Russia to play a larger role in Asian security and economic cooperation as part of his campaign to make Russian into a truly global power, while Medvedev has pushed for greater regional economic integration as a means of harnessing Asia's rapid growth and promoting development in the Russian Far East.[121] Putin stepped up Russian participation in summits of ASEAN, while Russia joined ASEAN's regional forum (ARF) as an observer, in large part to ensure Russian access to the rapidly growing markets of Southeast Asia.[122] Under the auspices of the 2003 Bali Concord, Moscow proposed establishing formal institutional links between ASEAN and the SCO, a step that would greatly enhance Russia's influence as a pivot between the two organizations; more recently it has sought to establish a similar connection between the SCO and APEC, which is becoming increasingly important as a source of investment for developing Russia's Far East, and which Russia will chair for the first time in 2012.[123]

As part of his drive to modernize the Russian economy, Medvedev has paid particular attention to the challenges facing the Far East, where he estimated that less than 1 percent of the region's GDP is tied to modern, innovation-driven industries. To remedy this situation, Medvedev has pushed for deeper economic integration between the Russian Far East and the powerful, modernizing economies of East and Southeast Asia, arguing that "integration with the countries of the [Asia-Pacific Region], I think everyone understands this, are a very serious resource for growing the economy of the Far East and all of Russia."[124] In particular, Medvedev has called for free trade agreements between Asian countries and Russia's Far Eastern provinces and official support for joint ventures with Asian firms. At the same time, Medvedev recognizes that a larger Russian economic presence in the region will bring with it greater political commitments. Consequently he is also seeking a more active role for Moscow in regional security arrangements.

Nonetheless, Asia remains more fragmented politically than Europe, and the bulk of Russia's diplomatic activity in the region is focused on bilateral relations with major powers, especially (in addition to China) Japan and India. As a close ally of the United States, a wary rival of China, and a potentially vast market for Russian energy, Japan is a key economic and security actor in the region, and one that Moscow must continue to balance cautiously against China. Lingering hostility between Japan and Russia dating from the end of World War II continues to complicate the relationship. Ownership of four small and sparsely populated islands remains a major thorn in bilateral relations, largely because of domestic considerations in both countries. Russian nationalists have insisted the Kremlin take a hard line over these so-called Southern Kuril Islands (called the Northern Territories by Japan), while pragmatists eager to reach an accord with Tokyo see little point in dragging out a dispute over four sparsely populated rocks in the Pacific.

Putin and then-Japanese premier Junichiro Koizumi signed an action plan to advance bilateral relations in 2003, calling for increased contacts at both the official level and between business and citizen groups. Nonetheless, the inability to resolve the impasse over the Kurils has remained a major impediment to deepening ties.[125] It is also a sharp contrast to the alacrity with which Moscow and Beijing moved over the past decade-plus to resolve their territorial disputes. While Medvedev evinced an initial desire to resolve the dispute, nationalist posturing by Japan's new Democratic Party government led Medvedev to make the first ever visit by a Russian president to the islands in October 2010, significantly ratcheting up tensions.

Despite the failure to resolve the territorial dispute, the Kremlin continues to view Japan as a useful counterweight against China and as another source of potential investment for reviving the Far East. Indeed, fear of becoming too closely intertwined with Beijing has been a major factor driving Russian officials to seek better relations with Tokyo (for instance in the debate over routing the ESPO pipeline). Of course, Japan is also a close ally of the United States, and relations with the U.S. are never far from Russian calculations on Japan. Moscow's decision to accommodate China as a counterweight to the U.S. has at least indirectly prevented a closer rapprochement with Japan. Conversely, concern about Chinese influence has at times led Russia to seek closer relations with Japan as a means of retaining a free hand.

The construction of the ESPO pipeline, whose first stage came online in December 2009, represents a major step forward in Russo-Japanese economic relations, and when completed will give Moscow greater flexibility in its relations with China, knowing that Beijing is not the sole East Asian customer for its energy. For Japan, which is entirely reliant on imported energy to power its economy, the selection of Kozmino as the terminus for Russia's Pacific pipeline is a matter of vital economic and political importance. Despite the depth of public hostility in Japan to any compromise over the Kurils, the need to secure non–Middle Eastern sources of energy as well as a desire to prevent the emergence of a real partnership between Russia and China has at times encouraged greater flexibility on the territorial issue.[126]

Though the search for an eventual territorial settlement and official end to World War II have dominated the diplomatic agenda between Moscow and Tokyo, the changing dynamics of Asian politics have forced both sides to consider a much broader range of issues, particularly in the security realm. With Japan showing signs of loosening the post-1945 strictures on the deployment of its military, Russian strategists must also increasingly take into account Japan's role as a hard security actor with regard to China, the Korean Peninsula, and elsewhere. Moscow has been eager to prevent the outbreak of hostilities on the Korean Peninsula and has consequently worked, both through the six-party talks on North Korea's nuclear program and bilaterally with Pyongyang, to reduce tensions and head off the threat of outside intervention. In this regard, Japan and Russia have, for the most part, found themselves on the same page.[127]

Moreover, since Japan and Russia do not share a land border and since Japan's population is declining almost as precipitously as Russia's, the immigration issue has not roiled Russo-Japanese relations as it has done with ties between Moscow and Beijing. If Russia's relationship to China is in large part a function of its relationship to the United States, then it is equally true that relations with Japan are largely a function of relations with China. Moscow's ability and willingness to overcome its fraught history with Japan will thus depend to a great degree on how its strategic partnership with China develops in the twenty-first century.

The other Asian giant, India, presents a challenge of a different sort for Moscow. As a traditional partner of the Soviet Union and one of Russia's BRICS and RIC associates, India continues to be a major purchaser of Russian weapons as well as various types of consumer goods—though the overall value of trade has fallen precipitously since the collapse of the Soviet Union. Then again, in the post–Cold War world, democratic India has found itself moving closer to the United States as it pursues its own calculations about resisting China's inexorable rise and pursuing its long-standing feud with Pakistan. India's close ties to the USSR were in large part the result of the Washington-Islamabad partnership. With the fall of the Soviet Union, Delhi lost its superpower patron, while India's own economic growth since the 1990s has significantly lessened the need for such a partnership. Still, Moscow and Delhi signed a friendship and cooperation treaty in 1993 and a joint declaration on creating a strategic partnership in 2003. Within the BRICS forum, India has been less assertive than Russia or China in calling for the overhaul of existing international institutions, a stance highlighting the general lack of common interests that continues to limit the BRICS grouping's influence.

Rhetoric aside, the relationship between India and Russia has suffered as China has become the major pole for Russia's Asian policy while India and the United States have moved to overcome their own legacy of mistrust. Instead of aligning itself with a seemingly unreliable Russia, India has generally found itself competing with Pakistan for the affections of the United States. By moving closer to Washington (a process symbolized above all by the U.S. decision to provide India with nuclear fuel for its civilian reactors despite Delhi's nuclear weapons tests and refusal to sign the Nonproliferation Treaty), India signaled its own desire for strategic independence.[128] Both Russia and India, in other words, have found reason to focus their attention elsewhere for much of the past decade.

Yet as a major emerging economy, India represents another potential customer for Russian energy and another potential lever to use as a means of limiting Chinese power in the region. India also remains valuable as a buyer of Russian weapons (fully 70 percent of India's military equipment is Russian made) and has provided firm support on Chechnya while keeping quiet about developments in Russian domestic politics that other democracies have criticized.[129] Trade turnover has risen rapidly too (albeit from a low initial base), to an annual value of $8 billion in 2009, which Moscow and Delhi are seeking to boost to $20 billion by 2015.[130] India's rapidly growing economy, coupled with a foreign policy generally perceived in Moscow as unthreatening have also laid the groundwork for a deeper economic cooperation between the two countries. India joined the SCO as an observer in 2005 (Russia has endorsed India becoming a full member of the SCO, though China remains opposed) and has subsequently participated in a variety of the organization's more substantive activities, including those connected to counterterrorism and counternarcotics, as well as the building of a transportation network linking Central and South Asia. India and Russia both worry about the potential for militant Islam spilling out of Afghanistan to threaten their interests in the region. Along with the U.S., Russia also supports India's bid for permanent membership on the UN Security Council.[131]

On the whole, Russian policy toward India appears designed to compensate for a long period of neglect, beginning in the 1990s, when the emphasis on East Asia allowed the old Soviet-Indian partnership to shrivel and opened the way for the United States to successfully court Delhi. Russia's renewed attention to this relationship, however, cannot but complicate the task of deepening the strategic partnership with China, which itself has increasingly come to see in India a (democratic and increasingly pro-Western) rival for leadership in Asia.

CONCLUSION

Russia's rapprochement with China over the past two decades has in many ways reflected the larger evolution of Russian foreign policy since the end of the Cold War. Although Gorbachev began the process in the late 1980s, the real warming came in the decade and a half following the installation of Primakov as foreign minister. For Primakov as well as his successors, China was useful as an alternative to the emphasis on Russia's European/ Western identity during the first post-Soviet years. In a larger sense, the Russo-Chinese rapprochement fit in with Moscow's interest in returning to the world stage as an independent Great Power. Given that in many ways Russia is too weak and divided to represent a pole unto itself in a multipolar world, a true partnership with China would allow Russia to pursue this goal more persistently. That calculation, indeed, seems to underlie Primakov's and Putin's quest for better relations with Beijing. For pro-Western liberals, it is precisely because China represents an alternative model for Russia that it is so dangerous a partner. Under Medvedev, the nuance has shifted slightly, with Moscow's increasingly seeking to leverage its partnership with Beijing for economic development and support for refashioning the global economic and political architecture to the benefit of rising powers, but with Russian diplomacy's center of gravity oriented more decisively toward the West.

To be sure, there is a range of more mundane reasons why Russian leaders should seek good relations with a rapidly growing and developing China. Expanded trade offers the best chance to resurrect the economy of the Russian Far East. Reduced friction over border questions diminishes the likelihood of future clashes. Post-Soviet Russia has had similar incentives to pursue closer relations with many of its neighbors, including the EU and Japan. Yet relations with China have in many ways been better and more consistent than Russo-European or Russo-Japanese ties, despite mounting concerns about the impact of China's rise on Russia itself. The West may still be the top priority for Russian policy makers, but relations with China are in a sense the true touchstone for understanding where Russian foreign policy is heading. As China enters the twenty-first century apparently poised to become a new superpower, the onetime superpower to its north will have little choice but to make China a priority in its own right, independent of Moscow's relationship with the West. In such a world, Russia will have little choice but to pursue a multivector foreign policy that simultaneously emphasizes both its Asian and Western aspirations. Moscow has become proficient at this task in the context of balancing against Western influence. The challenge will be to find ways of deepening its engagement with both simultaneously, even as Washington and Beijing seek to prevent their own relations from degenerating into a Cold War–style standoff. If Russia can successfully integrate its approaches to the two strongest powers of the early twenty-first century, it will vindicate the long-held aspiration of many in its elite to act as a bridge between East and West.

6

Playing with Home Field Advantage?

Russia and Its Post-Soviet Neighbors

The states of the former Soviet Union, most of which belong to the Commonwealth of Independent States (CIS, in Russian *Sodruzhestvo nezavisimykh gosudarstv*, or SNG), play a unique role in Russian foreign policy thinking. The post-Soviet space is at once a postimperial periphery with extensive economic links to and a shared cultural heritage with Russia, but also has since the Soviet collapse increasingly become a contested zone between Russia and other major powers.[1] Though Moscow now officially abjures the term, the press and public often still describe the post-Soviet space as the "Near Abroad (*blizhnoe zarubezh'e*)," implying that Russia's post-Soviet neighbors are less foreign and less fully sovereign than states in the "Far Abroad," and that relations with them do not precisely constitute *foreign* policy. This paternalistic tendency has become increasingly problematic for Russia as its post-Soviet neighbors have gradually developed the capacity to act autonomously on the international stage, and forged links with outside powers including the United States, Europe, and China.

The outside world's encroachment has forced Moscow to reconcile its at times incompatible desires for cooperative relations with other major powers and for a dominant position inside the borders of the former Soviet Union. Moscow remains particularly sensitive about its influence in the post-Soviet space and its most serious quarrels with outside powers since 1991 have centered on the region. Yet clichés about renewed Russian imperialism or a modern-day version of the nineteenth-century "Great Game" miss the point. Leaving aside Dugin and his followers, no Russian in any position of authority or influence seriously contemplates seeking to restore the Soviet Union. This includes Putin, who remarked in his 2005 address

219

to parliament that the Soviet collapse was "the greatest geopolitical catastrophe of the century" (a statement quoted more frequently than his related observation that anyone who wants to bring the USSR back "has no brain").[2] Two decades of independence have moreover greatly strengthened the institutions and identity of Russia's post-Soviet neighbors, giving them a capacity to engage the outside world on their own terms in a way that, for instance, the Central Asian khanates of the nineteenth century lacked. Nor has Russia sought to reflexively exclude outside powers from its post-Soviet backyard; Moscow explicitly blessed an American military presence in Central Asia after 9/11 and has more recently cooperated with the U.S. to bring supplies and weapons to Afghanistan across Central Asia. Here as elsewhere, the emphasis is on maintaining generally cooperative relations with the other major powers, promoting Russia's geopolitical resurgence, and taking advantage of economic opportunities to benefit both Russia as a state and the oligarchic-bureaucratic elite that runs it.

What is different about the post-Soviet space, from the perspective of Russian foreign policy, is the extent of Russian interests in the region and the levers of influence available to the Kremlin that it lacks in other parts of the world. Given Russia's long history of foreign invasions and the belief (widespread among Eurasianists but also part of much mainstream thinking) that it remains surrounded by hostile states and movements on all sides, Russia's post-Soviet neighbors provide a kind of strategic depth, whether against NATO in the west or the Taliban in the south (or, sotto voce, China in the east). Russia remains particularly sensitive about its influence in the post-Soviet space, and major crises have broken out at moments when the Kremlin believed outside powers were seeking to displace it in the region, most notably in the context of the so-called colored revolutions that broke out in several post-Soviet countries between 2003 and 2005.

This interest in maintaining influence across the post-Soviet space is intimately linked to the Kremlin's ambition to restore Russia's status as a major power. Russia's international power and influence have historically been closely linked to outward expansion, while periods of weakness have coincided with territorial contraction, few more severe than that of the period between 1989 and 1991 which saw the collapse first of the Warsaw Pact and then the USSR itself. For many elites, the reassertion of Russia's influence beyond the borders of the now-shrunken Russian state is a natural outgrowth of the country's political and diplomatic revival since the 1990s, as well as a mechanism for ensuring Russia's global standing alongside the other major powers.

Much of Russia's interest in the former Soviet Union is also economic. The post-Soviet region is at once an important source of raw materials for Russian industry and a crucial market for Russian goods. Given patterns of development dating to the Soviet era (or earlier), many Russian businesses have a competitive advantage inside the former USSR in the form of personal ties among businessmen; common technical and administrative standards reinforced by the establishment of the Eurasian Economic Community (EurAsEC), the Russia-Belarus-Kazakhstan Customs Union, and the planned Russia-Belarus-Kazakhstan Single Economic Space (scheduled to debut in 2012); as well as mutual familiarity among elites with a common Soviet past. For some Russian analysts (Eurasianists in particular), regional economic integration additionally provides an alternative to globalization, particularly since much of the infrastructure for regional integration such as railroads, pipelines, and supply chains has existed since Soviet days. One of the principal tensions in the Russian debate about foreign policy therefore is over whether to prioritize regional or global ties, a choice that has had profound consequences for Russia's interactions with the West and international institutions.

Russia retains many additional tools of influence across the CIS that it lacks elsewhere, including the presence of Russian troops in some neighboring countries (Moldova, Kyrgyzstan, Tajikistan, Georgia, Azerbaijan, Belarus, Ukraine, and Armenia), support for regional separatists in the context of the so-called frozen conflicts, and control of oil and gas across much of the CIS.[3] Russia also possesses a degree of soft power unmatched by any outside state. Most elites across the CIS continue to do business in Russian, even if they increasingly speak local languages at home with their non-Russian-speaking children. Some post-Soviet countries, including the non-CIS members Estonia and Latvia, as well as Ukraine and Kazakhstan, have significant ethnic Russian minorities, often concentrated in cities and in strategically significant areas such as the Crimean Peninsula.

In the early 1990s, the non-Russian parts of the former Soviet Union (especially its Caucasian and Central Asian peripheries) were perceived as little better than dead weight, to be left behind as rapidly as possible as Russia raced forward to apparently join the developed West.[4] It was only during the Primakov interlude that Moscow began paying more attention to the republics of the CIS, eventually coming to view the maintenance of a zone of "privileged interests" in the region as one of the principal pillars of Russia's standing as a Great Power. Competition with other Great Powers remained an important element. Even under Putin, this competition could be downplayed at moments when cooperation with the other major powers took priority, most notably in the context of the U.S.-led war in Afghanistan. Medvedev has placed greater emphasis on reducing the element of competition with outside powers, at times hinting that cooperation with the U.S. and Europe is a greater long-term strategic interest than preservation of an exclusive sphere of influence in the former Soviet Union.[5]

Of course, the "post-Soviet space" encompasses a wide variety of states, ranging from Moldova in the west to Tajikistan in the east, and Moscow's approach to them is hardly monolithic. The European republics (Belarus, Ukraine, and Moldova, plus the three non-CIS Baltic states) have served as a buffer zone between Russia and the expanding Europe of the EU and NATO. The Caucasus and Central Asia, on the other hand, have been important to Moscow initially as a zone of instability and insecurity along Russia's vulnerable southern frontier, and as critical pieces of Russia's attempts to leverage its control of energy distribution to boost its international influence. Starting with the pipeline diplomacy of the 1990s (and expanding in the aftermath of the 9/11 attacks), these states have become the locus of a complex diplomatic and economic dance between Russia, its onetime superpower rival to the west, and increasingly, its new challenger in the east.

The ability of the South Caucasus states (Armenia, Azerbaijan, and Georgia) to resist Russian influence has been directly proportional to their ability to attract non-Russian energy infrastructure and diversify their export routes. Georgia, of course, has been something of a special case, thanks to the legacy of perhaps the most intractable of the many so-called frozen conflicts dotting the post-Soviet periphery. Moreover, Mikheil Saakashvili, elevated to the Georgian presidency on the heels of the 2003 Rose Revolution, was in a sense the first truly post-Soviet leader in the CIS (i.e., his formative experiences came after the Soviet collapse). Both his decidedly pro-Western foreign policy leanings and his challenge to the oligarchic capitalist economic model prevalent throughout the former Soviet Union continues to represent the most sustained challenge to Russian influence in the region, even after Georgia's disastrous 2008 war with Moscow.

Central Asia, meanwhile, has been a zone of instability where Moscow has found itself forced, especially since September 11, 2001, to choose between the evils of Islamist extremism and an American military presence on its periphery. Early in the campaign against the Taliban, U.S. troops were deployed to Uzbekistan and Kyrgyzstan, initially with Russian approval. Russian troops, meanwhile, remained in Tajikistan as a result of their role in ending that country's civil war, while Moscow deployed forces in Kyrgyzstan in 2003 to match the American presence. Yet when Kyrgyzstan's interim government begged for peacekeepers to contain a wave of pogroms against the country's Uzbek minority in the spring of 2010, the Kremlin demurred, as though, having been accorded the status of regional broker it long desired, it could not figure out what to do with it. Confronting political instability, a rising tide of Islamism in some areas, the ongoing presence of American troops, and steadily increasing Chinese economic penetration, Central Asia remains one of Russia's most vexing foreign policy challenges.

Unsurprisingly, Moscow's approach to the CIS has been central to its Great Power ambitions. Its leading role in the CIS (along with its nuclear arsenal and seat on the UN Security Council) is what allows Russia to portray itself as a major power, while its relations with other major powers have been determined to a significant degree by the willingness of those powers to accommodate Russian interests within the post-Soviet space. As Russia gradually sheds its Soviet/imperial past, its approach to its former dependencies continues to evolve in line with the growing recognition that while the CIS may be a zone of "privileged interests," maintaining an exclusive sphere of influence in the region is no longer realistic.

THE EUROPEAN CIS: SHADOWBOXING OVER UKRAINE

With their proximity to and potential for integration with Europe, Belarus, Ukraine, and Moldova have especially tested Moscow's ability to reconcile its desire for cooperative relations and deeper economic integration with Europe on the one hand, and a leading role within the boundaries of the former USSR on the other. Russian influence in all three European CIS member states remained strong after the fall of the Soviet Union. In Moldova, Russian sponsorship of the Transnistrian separatist regime and the presence of Russian peacekeepers have served throughout the post-Soviet period to check Chişinău's foreign policy autonomy. Meanwhile Belarus's dictatorial ruler Aleksandr Lukashenko has long been forced to rely on Russia for diplomatic and economic support as a result of the West's hostility to his regime, even after Russia began ratcheting up energy prices in 2007.

The situation in Ukraine has always been more complicated. With its large population (including significant numbers of ethnic Russians and ethnic Ukrainians whose native tongue is Russian), relatively developed economy, strategic location between the Black Sea and Europe, as well as its significance as the cradle of East Slavic culture, Ukraine is in many ways the most important non-Russian state in the CIS.[6] As either a bridge between Russia and Europe or a wall dividing them, Ukraine's geopolitical orientation will always have a profound effect on Russia's relations with its Western neighbors.

Following the 2004 Orange Revolution, Ukraine's complex identity as a state on the border (the word *Ukraina* means "borderland") between Russia and Europe exacerbated the split between Putin's Russia and the West, while the downfall of the Orange coalition in 2010 facilitated a limited rapprochement. Russia and the U.S./Europe backed different sides in the Orange Revolution, largely on the basis of the foreign policy visions articulated by the competing camps. The Orange Revolution revealed a deep divide within

Ukrainian society, but also between Russia and its putative partners in the West over the status of the post-Soviet space in the post–Cold War international order more broadly. The new era in Russian-Western relations heralded by Putin's decision to back the U.S. in Afghanistan appeared to end in the flurry of charges and countercharges hurled by Moscow and Washington during the standoff over the Orange Revolution. Likewise, the 2010 election of the Kremlin-backed Viktor Yanukovych, in a vote that Washington recognized as being largely free and fair, helped facilitate the rapprochement between Russia and the West pursued by Dmitry Medvedev.

On one level, the struggle for Ukraine touched off by the Orange Revolution highlighted just how much circumstances had changed since the end of the Cold War. The very idea that a Ukrainian government could turn its back on Russia, seeking integration with the European Union—and more importantly, NATO—reflected the degree to which Russian power had waned since 1991. By 2004, that collapse was ending, and Russia's active participation in the struggle over Ukraine's future was a sign of things to come. Yet as the election of Yanukovych—who made a point of taking his first foreign trip to the EU rather than Russia—demonstrated, Ukraine itself has developed as a state in the past two decades, and has a strong interest in remaining free of Russian domination, a fact that some Russian Eurasianists still struggle to accept. In the long run, this consolidation of Ukrainian statehood may be the most significant barrier to the reemergence of an imperial tendency in Russian foreign policy and the most important factor facilitating Russia's integration with Europe, with Ukraine as a bridge for European ideas and standards to spread into the former Soviet Union.

Before the Orange Revolution, Ukraine was for the most part content to perch between East and West. Participation in NATO's Partnership for Peace and the GU(U)AM (i.e., Georgia, Ukraine, Azerbaijan, and Moldova, joined for a time by Uzbekistan) organization of ex-Soviet republics seeking distance from Moscow were balanced against membership in the CIS and a friendship and cooperation treaty with Russia ratified by the Verkhovna Rada (the Ukrainian parliament) in 1998.[7] For the westward vector of Ukraine's foreign policy, GU(U)AM was particularly important in that it united members of the CIS who were both seeking energy independence from Russia and (apart from Ukraine itself) confronted Russian-backed separatists on their territory. The formation of GU(U)AM was intimately linked to the construction of the Baku-Tbilisi-Ceyhan (BTC) oil pipeline, the construction of which allowed Ukraine to import oil by ship directly across the Black Sea from the Turkish port of Ceyhan. In this way, Ukraine significantly reduced its dependence on Russian energy supplies and moved into closer political alignment with Azerbaijan, Georgia, and Moldova, all of which have sought to limit the reassertion of Russian influence in the

CIS.[8] Participation in GU(U)AM, however, could easily be interpreted in Moscow as an unfriendly act, and former Ukrainian president Leonid Kuchma's government was careful not to alienate Moscow entirely, especially as support for Kuchma within Ukraine dwindled as his government became bogged down in a series of scandals.

Still, Kyiv's stated interest in deeper integration with the West continued for most of Kuchma's term in office (1994–2004).[9] By the eve of the Orange Revolution, however, the Kuchma government's corruption, involvement in arms smuggling to Saddam Hussein's Iraq, and possible complicity in the murder of an investigative journalist had made it increasingly toxic to the West, deepening its reliance on Russia.[10] The semi-rapprochement between Kyiv and Moscow in Putin's first term was reflected in increasingly frequent attempts to coordinate the two countries' integration into and participation in European structures such as the OSCE and the Council of Europe.[11] This approach, termed in Ukraine as "returning to Europe with Russia," was elaborated with the help of the Moscow-based Foundation for Effective Politics (*Fond effektivnoi politiki*), headed by the Kremlin spin doctor Gleb Pavlovsky.[12]

Beset by scandal and increasingly unpopular, Kuchma sought Russian help to engineer a transition to a reliable successor in 2004. This controlled transition got out of hand when manipulation by Kuchma and his allies in Moscow became too blatant to ignore. The fall of Kuchma and the contested succession that brought to power the pro-Western Viktor Yushchenko revealed deep underlying tensions within the Ukrainian political elite and exposed Ukraine to the competing geopolitical ambitions of Russia and the Western powers at a moment when both were already reassessing their post-9/11 cooperation. For Moscow, a Yushchenko presidency was a specter to be avoided at all cost. Russia's leaders had an opportunity to familiarize themselves with Yushchenko during his term as prime minister from 1999 to 2001, when he concentrated on reforming the Ukrainian economy, at the expense of oligarchs with close connections to Russia.[13] In addition, Yushchenko—whose wife held American citizenship—promoted Ukrainian membership in NATO and was supported by various groups of Ukrainian nationalists (mostly from the Ukrainian-speaking western part of the country) whose activities Moscow viewed as anti-Russian.

A series of underhanded maneuvers was undertaken to prevent Yushchenko from winning the 2004 elections. These included at least two assassination attempts—including one that left Yushchenko disfigured from severe dioxin poisoning, the employment of agents provocateurs who attempted to tar the Yushchenko campaign by associating it with neo-Nazi organizations (a maneuver not as bizarre as it might seem, given the existence of a vocal neo-Nazi fringe within the Ukrainian nationalist movement), and massive violations of campaign finance regulations. While much about the lead-up to the 2004 election remains murky, it is certain that Moscow was at least cognizant of many of the dirty tricks being employed, some at the behest of Pavlovsky and other Russian strategists with Kremlin connections.[14]

Apart from attempts to sabotage the Yushchenko campaign before the election, the Kremlin pushed hard in the November 21, 2004, runoff vote for its favored candidate, the former transportation manager (whose past also included jail time for robbery and assault) Viktor Yanukovych, to assume office despite widespread allegations of fraud in the conduct of the election.[15] Exit polls showed Yushchenko ahead by a comfortable margin (52 percent versus 43 percent for Yanukovych), but the official results gave Yanukovych a narrow victory, thanks to suspiciously high voter turnout levels in the Russian-speaking eastern part of Ukraine.

Moscow and Putin himself had openly supported Yanukovych during the campaign, making joint public appearances with the Ukrainian premier, while Moscow also helped Russian businesses channel money to the Yanukovych camp.[16] The Kremlin, along with the Kuchma government, which was hoping for an orderly transition of power and protection against potential prosecution after leaving office, was also complicit in the activities of figures like Pavlovsky, who were responsible for devising and implementing various techniques to ensure a Yanukovych victory. Once the votes were in, moreover, the Kremlin urged international acceptance of Yanukovych's supposed victory, ignoring outside observers' conclusion that the results had been falsified.

Putin immediately declared the vote fair and strongly criticized both the Ukrainian opposition (led by Yushchenko) for its failure to accept the "results" of the election and—seemingly unaware of the irony—outside powers for their willingness to intervene in Ukraine's internal affairs.[17] U.S. secretary of state Colin Powell meanwhile declared unambiguously that because of widespread fraud and manipulation, the U.S. could not accept the official results.[18] Many Ukrainians also rejected the results, and major protests soon broke out in Kyiv and cities in western Ukraine with heavy concentrations of Yushchenko voters. Even as the protests by orange-clad Yushchenko backers mounted, Russian leaders refused to back down from their support of Yanukovych until the Ukrainian Supreme Court stepped in and ordered the runoff between Yushchenko and Yanukovych to be held again. The whole process resulted in Yushchenko's eventual victory—and a Russian realization that continued resistance was jeopardizing both its influence in Kyiv and its relationship with the West.[19] Yushchenko was sworn in as post-Soviet Ukraine's third president on January 23, 2005.

The Kremlin had clearly botched its handling of the crisis and contributed directly to the outbreak of the Orange Revolution shortly thereafter.

Moscow's overt support for Yanukovych during the campaign offended many Ukrainians, who saw it as a display of Russian paternalism (or worse). Repeated attempts to gain recognition for Yanukovych as president also damaged Russia's standing with the Western powers, which saw Russian intervention in Ukraine's politics as a form of renewed Russian imperialism, particularly as the Orange Revolution took place in the shadow of Putin's creeping authoritarian restoration inside Russia. Russian leaders also perceived the events in Ukraine through the lens of geopolitics, and interpreted the West's condemnation of the election as part of a broader campaign to undermine Russian influence across the former Soviet Union. The Bush administration's commitment to democracy promotion and invasion of Iraq helped feed this perception.

Western officials, of course, denied trying to pull Ukraine out of Russia's sphere of influence through their support of Yushchenko. Instead, they generally portrayed their rejection of Yanukovych's victory as a consequence of insisting that democratic procedures be respected.[20] The United States in particular did have something of a stake in the Ukrainian elections, since a wide range of official and semiofficial organizations (from USAID to the National Democratic Institute and International Republican Institute to George Soros's Open Society Foundation) provided money and expertise to the Yushchenko-led democratic opposition. Although this aid was designed to ensure a fair electoral process and was not given directly to any Ukrainian party or candidate, supporters of the Kuchma-Yanukovych camp objected, not without some justification, that U.S. policies favored Yushchenko in practice.[21]

As with Georgia's Rose Revolution the previous year, overt Russian support for the status quo candidate meant that the opposition of necessity turned to the West for support, even if the initial impetus for both colored revolutions had more to do with domestic challenges than hostility to Moscow. In this way the Kremlin's determination to prevent Ukraine and Georgia from drifting toward the West had become self-defeating. By refusing to do business with Yushchenko, Moscow ensured that he would turn to the West, unlike others in the Orange camp who were interested in merely a more representative government—or a redistribution of assets—and sought to steer clear of geopolitical quarrels.

The Kremlin's actions in Ukraine also poisoned its relations with the U.S. and Europe, feeding the perception that Putin was bent on imperial renewal. In fact though, Moscow was not seeking a serious quarrel with the West, but came to conclude that Yushchenko had crossed its redlines (particularly when he announced Ukraine's intention to seek NATO membership). As long as Yushchenko remained in power (until 2010), Moscow kept up the pressure on him, even while Medvedev was actively campaigning for better relations with the U.S. and Europe.

Moscow used a number of tools to undermine Yushchenko, manipulating disputes over payment arrears for oil and gas deliveries, threatening military retaliation should Ukraine secure NATO membership or expel Russian warships from their base at Sevastopol, denouncing Yushchenko in the Russian and Ukrainian press, and maintaining support for the president's rivals—including Yanukovych and Yushchenko's former prime minister, Yulia Tymoshenko (herself a onetime leader of the Orange movement).

Even Medvedev got in on the act once he became president: in a video posted to his blog in August 2009 and an open letter to the Ukrainian president, Medvedev accused Yushchenko of sins ranging from endangering European energy supplies, to supporting a branch of the Orthodox Church independent of the Moscow Patriarchy, to aiding Georgia during its war with Russia the previous year. He declared that Russia would not send a new ambassador until Kyiv reversed its "anti-Russian" policy, and expressed hope that a "new Ukrainian leadership" would be open to restoring Ukraine's historical partnership with Russia.[22] This continuing pressure on Yushchenko did not however interfere with Medvedev's pursuit of rapprochement with the West—since the struggle over Ukraine was always less about the broader relationship between Russia and the West than about ensuring that the U.S. and its European allies respected Russian interests in the post-Soviet space.

By the end of his first term, Yushchenko's popularity had evaporated, largely because of the global economic crisis, which saw Ukrainian GDP shrink by more than 15 percent in 2009—among the worst outcomes in the industrialized world—but also because of the perpetual sniping between Yushchenko and other leaders, many of whom consulted with Moscow.[23] Yet when Yanukovych defeated Yushchenko's reelection bid in April 2010, Moscow had occasion to learn to be careful for what it wished. Yanukovych did quickly retract Ukraine's application for NATO membership, in line with a public that generally opposed joining the alliance, and agreed to a new lease for the Russian Black Sea Fleet's Sevastopol base. Yet he also emphasized his desire for deeper economic and political integration with the EU (including eventual visa-free travel and establishment of a free-trade area) while pushing back against Moscow's attempts to reinforce its dominance of the Ukrainian economy. Yanukovych resisted Putin's proposal to merge the Russian and Ukrainian energy transit monopolies, and his refusal of NATO membership was coupled with an equally forceful rejection of membership in the Russian-dominated CSTO or the Russia-Belarus-Kazakhstan Customs Union.

Yanukovych's presidential campaign was heavily bankrolled by oligarchs from eastern Ukraine who, while largely Russian-speaking, understood that integration with Europe offered greater commercial opportunities relative to continued reliance on Russia.[24] And since Yanukovych was about as pro-Russian a leader as the Kremlin could reasonably expect to get in Kyiv, it had less scope for manipulating or undermining him than it did with Yushchenko—a reality the Ukrainian leader fully grasped. Yanukovych's simultaneous courting of Russia and Europe was a good example of how Russia's post-Soviet neighbors have increasingly developed the capacity to act autonomously on the international stage, sharply limiting Russia's ability to maintain an exclusive sphere of influence in the region.

Even with a generally pro-Russian leader in Kyiv, the most intractable source of Russo-Ukrainian discord—energy—continues to bedevil the relationship between the two countries. Besides importing large quantities of Russian hydrocarbons for its own consumption, Ukraine also happens to be the principal transit route by which oil and gas originating in Russia or Central Asia make their way to European markets. Energy disputes between Moscow and Kyiv consequently cannot be isolated from both countries' relations with Europe, and hence the United States.

Though disputes between Moscow and Kyiv over debts and prices for energy were a common source of tension during the presidencies of Kuchma and even his predecessor Leonid Kravchuk, the Orange Revolution changed the broader context within which these disputes played out. What had previously seemed like arcane commercial disputes took on a harder edge as Russia sought to use its control of energy supplies to turn up the pressure on Yushchenko and the West pushed back against what it increasingly viewed as a form of imperial revanchism.

Gazprom's decision to raise the price of gas supplied to Ukraine, first broached in March 2005, ended up badly shaking Russia's relations with both the EU and the U.S., while subsequent disputes cast both Russia and Ukraine in a bad light and encouraged the Europeans to accelerate their quest to find energy from alternative sources. Apart from Western interest in Ukraine for its own sake, the broader consequences of the gas disputes resulted from the fact that Western Europe itself is heavily dependent on Russian gas supplies, 80 percent of which reach Europe after transiting Ukrainian territory. Even during the Kuchma years, Kyiv sought to take advantage of Russia's dependence on Ukraine as a supply corridor to demand high tariffs for the use of pipelines on its territory. It also (like Belarus) fiercely resisted Russian attempts to secure an ownership stake in its pipeline infrastructure in exchange for debt forgiveness—a stance Yanukovych has also pursued as president. In 2000, Gazprom sought to undercut Ukraine's transport monopoly by mooting the prospect of a new undersea pipeline (which eventually became Nord Stream) bypassing Ukraine entirely. Kuchma as well as his then-prime minister—Viktor Yushchenko—strongly opposed this attempt to limit Ukraine's leverage and its transit revenue.[25]

Throughout Putin's presidency, the question of payments for Russian

gas festered as a major impediment to improved Russo-Ukrainian relations, especially once the Orange Revolution opened up a significant gap
between Russian and Ukrainian priorities more broadly. The dispute became a crisis when Gazprom cut off deliveries on January 1, 2006, over
the unresolved price dispute and Kyiv's unpaid bills. Gazprom had begun
by demanding an increase in the price paid by Kyiv from $50 per thousand
cubic meters (tcm) to $160, starting in January 2006 (even though the
existing contract setting prices at $50 was set to run through 2009). Al-
though Gazprom's initial demand for increased payments was made in
the summer of 2005, Kyiv did not respond until Gazprom threatened in
mid-December to cut off supplies at the start of the new year unless the
Ukrainian government and its state-owned energy company Naftohaz
Ukrayiny accepted the increased price. Ukraine refused the higher rate and
charged Russia with violating existing agreements, whereupon Gazprom
executives told Kyiv it now would have to pay $230/tcm instead of the
originally proposed $160.[26] When the government of prime minister Yury
Yekhanurov refused to sign an agreement on Gazprom's terms, the Russian gas monopoly stopped deliveries on January 1.[27]

Kyiv responded to the resulting shortages by announcing it would siphon off Europe-bound gas from pipelines crossing its territory. While the
Ukrainian authorities represented their actions as a response to blatant
imperialism on the part of Russia, Moscow claimed the entire affair was a
simple commercial dispute. The Russian Foreign Ministry, in a press re-
lease on the first day of the crisis, termed Ukraine's actions "an attempt to
blackmail the countries of Europe with the threat of the illegal confisca-
tion" of gas for which the Europeans had already paid, as well as a desperate maneuver to enhance the ruling coalition's popularity in the run-up to
parliamentary elections that the Orange parties were predicted to lose.[28]
After much acrimonious rhetoric on both sides, the dispute was (temporarily, at least) settled on January 4, when Gazprom and Naftohaz Ukrayiny signed an agreement setting the price for Ukraine's gas purchases at
$95 per tcm—payable in cash only rather than the mix of cash and barter
theretofore prevailing.[29]

For many observers in the West, the dispute fit the narrative constructed
by Ukraine's Orange camp since the revolution of early 2004, in which
Ukraine's transition to democracy and a pro-Western foreign policy ran
headlong into the restored Russian imperialism of Vladimir Putin's Kremlin.[30] The Ukrainian authorities consciously sought to encourage this
perception. Yekhanurov told Western ambassadors that Russia was not
only in violation of a commercial agreement but was actively threatening Ukrainian sovereignty, a statement made the more significant by the
fact that Britain and the United States had signed a commitment to defend
Ukraine's political and economic sovereignty in 1994 in exchange for

Kyiv's surrendering the nuclear weapons that had been left on its territory by the Soviet military.[31] The bulk of Western opinion, both public and official, indeed appeared to assign blame for the crisis and the resulting gas shortages in Europe to Russia's neoimperialist policies in the CIS rather than to either a commercial dispute or manipulation by the Ukrainian authorities.[32] Similar disputes and cutoffs had happened before, but Russia's turn toward authoritarianism under Putin and the rise of the pro-Western Yushchenko in Ukraine meant that the 2006 dispute was playing out at a moment when it appeared the entire post-Soviet status quo that had existed since 1991 was in flux.

Ukraine (like Russia) has heavily subsidized domestic gas sales, providing a disincentive for conservation. Consequently, Ukraine's gas consumption is profligate. Moreover, because Ukraine itself produces little gas, much of the cost of Ukrainian inefficiency has been borne by Gazprom, which, as a state-run company, is not subject to the full measure of market discipline affecting private companies.[33] Rather, since Gazprom is for all intents and purposes an arm of the Kremlin (or, more cynically, vice versa), Moscow believed it had good reasons for subsidizing gas exports to Ukraine as long as it could gain noneconomic benefits from doing so.

In other words, Russia's decision to reduce its subsidies by demanding a higher price was more than anything a recognition that its attempts to keep Ukraine in its sphere of influence through economic incentives had failed. If Moscow was not gaining foreign policy benefits from its (expensive) subsidization of the Ukrainian economy, there remained little reason for state-controlled Gazprom to keep throwing money at Kyiv. The Russian demand for higher prices reflected in a general way many of the demands that European governments had long been making: to reduce the role of barter in economic exchange among the post-Soviet states, to increase Gazprom's overall transparency, and, most importantly, to internalize the notion that the former Soviet republics had become fully sovereign states. Indeed, Moscow justified its demand that Kyiv pay more for its gas by pointing out the (much higher) price paid for Russian gas by consumers in Europe and suggesting that if Ukraine wanted to be a European state, it should pay its bills like one.[34] While Moscow was more than happy to have an excuse to cause mischief for Ukraine's pro-Western leadership, the pro-Russian shift in Ukrainian politics under Yanukovych did not resolve the underlying gas dispute.

Around the same time, Gazprom started charging other CIS states higher rates for their gas too. Of course, the transition to market prices was compromised by politics: subsidies for countries that Moscow counted as reliable allies (or which allowed Gazprom a stake in their distribution systems) such as Belarus and Armenia were reduced more gradually than for Yushchenko's Ukraine. The inconsistent transition to market prices reflected the ongoing tension in Russia's foreign policy between the pursuit of state power and the pursuit of personal wealth on the part of Kremlin, Inc.

Moscow and Kyiv conducted another round of negotiations on gas prices in October 2006, more than two months after Yanukovych had become prime minister and after it had become clear that Ukraine's prospects for joining the EU or NATO in the immediate future were slim.[35] Yanukovych's return did not prevent Gazprom from demanding another price increase for 2007. The Russian media reported that Moscow was offering Kyiv gas for $130/tcm (in line with the prices outlined in the Yanukovych government's budget, rather than the $230 Gazprom had been demanding) in exchange for Ukraine holding a referendum on NATO membership and affirming its agreement to allow the Black Sea Fleet to keep its base at Sevastopol until 2017.[36] While the deal that was finally signed confirmed that Ukraine would pay only $130/tcm, the only conditionality discussed in the aftermath touched on coordinating Moscow and Kyiv's entry into the World Trade Organization.[37]

The agreement however did nothing to resolve the underlying problems of Ukraine's payment arrears and Russia's hostility to Yushchenko, who remained president. The impact of these structural problems on relations was exacerbated by the fact that Gazprom had insisted on signing only one-year contracts with Kyiv. Each subsequent winter, negotiations to renew the agreement raised the same issues and tensions that had burst forth in 2006. For two years, Moscow and Kyiv managed to paper over their differences in time to avert a new showdown, but at the start of 2009, these problems once again flared into a full-fledged crisis whose impact on Europe was even greater.

In October 2008, Putin and Ukrainian prime minister Yulia Tymoshenko (who had made her own fortune in the gas business) reached an agreement envisioning a three-year transition to European market prices, but left it to the energy companies to sign a contract and finalize a price for the coming year. Meanwhile, Gazprom announced in December that Naftohaz had racked up more than $2.1 billion in unpaid bills and penalties. Though it eventually agreed to pay around $1.52 billion, Naftohaz argued with Gazprom's figure and announced it would not make any more payments for 2008. Gazprom responded by declaring that if Naftohaz had not settled its debts and agreed on a pricing formula for 2009 by the end of the year, it would demand $400/tcm, while Putin himself threatened to shut off Ukraine's gas supplies entirely if Kyiv responded as in 2006 by interfering with transit to Europe.[38] Despite this saber-rattling, Kyiv still refused Moscow's terms.

Still with no contract in place, Gazprom began shutting off the taps on January 1, arguing that it was merely responding to Ukraine's stack of unpaid bills. As before, Gazprom continued supplying gas for onward sale to Europe, which Ukraine then started siphoning for its own needs. On January 7, Gazprom made good on the threat to cease all deliveries through Ukrainian pipelines to punish Kyiv for its "theft" of gas destined for Europe. For twelve days, no gas at all transited Ukraine; downstream countries that relied heavily or entirely on Russia (and its pipelines across Ukraine) such as Bulgaria and Serbia were left quite literally out in the cold. It was not until January 19 that an agreement was finally signed, and an additional day until the gas started flowing again.

The new agreement called for prices to adjust quarterly on the basis of oil prices on the global spot market, starting at 80 percent of the European level for 2009 and rising to the full European level starting in 2010 (on a "netback" basis, i.e., taking into account the lower cost of transit to Ukraine). For the first quarter of 2009, that meant a price of $450/tcm— though with global oil prices falling rapidly as the financial crisis took hold, that figure would drop sharply over the course of the year.[39] Given the severity of the crisis in Ukraine, Kyiv remained chronically behind on its payments for gas, even after the International Monetary Fund (IMF) stepped in. Unable to rapidly raise domestic prices (particularly in the midst of a recession), Ukraine remained trapped by its dependence on Russian subsidies, and vulnerable to a repetition of its gas crises, while Russia saw the renewed dispute as validating its case for building the Nord and South Stream bypass pipelines.

If the 2009 gas crisis was for Ukraine largely a repeat of 2006, the European reaction proved rather different. Having been through this situation before, European governments and publics seemed more familiar with the issues at stake. Rather than reflexively blaming Russian imperialism, they generally apportioned blame to both sides for their shady dealings, insensitivity to European concerns, and downright incompetence. In part, Russia did a more effective job of image management during the 2009 crisis, with Gazprom officials (including deputy CEO Aleksandr Medvedev) making public appearances in Russia and in Europe to argue their side of the case, while Putin himself met with European energy executives to discuss possible solutions. The European Commission declined to take sides, though in the early stages of the crisis it did remind Ukraine of its obligations under the Energy Charter Treaty (which, unlike Russia, Ukraine has ratified) to maintain uninterrupted supplies. The crisis did force the EU to take energy security more seriously, with greater attention being paid to alternate pipelines, market liberalization, and alternative sources of energy (including nuclear power and unconventional gas), but did little to dampen enthusiasm for accessing more Russian gas through Nord Stream and South Stream.

Not only were the Europeans better prepared in 2009, but as the democratic promise of the Orange Revolution faded, the Europeans had gradually become more jaded about the ineffectual Yushchenko, the *"gazovaya printsessa* (gas princess)" Tymoshenko, and Ukraine's other supposed reformists, who continued to fight among themselves for power and control of the lucrative Russian gas trade. This more cold-eyed assessment of Ukrainian politics made it easier for the Europeans (and Americans) to patch up their differences with Moscow and Gazprom, which now looked less like imperial revanchists than just another group of shady *biznesmeny,* no better or worse than their Ukrainian counterparts—but more important in the long run to Europe's energy security given Russia's vast reserves.

Even after Yanukovych became president following his February 2010 electoral victory, Moscow continued seeking to leverage its subsidies of Ukrainian energy purchases for its own political ends. An agreement signed by Medvedev and Yanukovych in April 2010 granted Russia a new lease on the Sevastopol naval base through 2042, in exchange for the removal of a 30 percent export duty on purchases of Russian gas, which Kyiv projected would save around $40 billion.[40] Nonetheless, Kyiv ended up paying $230/tcm at the time the deal was signed (down from $300 on the eve of the deal, but still well above the $130 it was paying in 2007), with prices readjusted on a quarterly basis.[41] With Ukraine's economy still in deep recession and the country's budget bleeding red ink, Yanukovych was forced to turn to the IMF to head off a potential default on Ukrainian debt. In exchange for a commitment of nearly $15 billion, the IMF demanded Yanukovych stop subsidizing domestic gas prices, a step that would help solidify Ukraine's public finances while promoting greater energy efficiency.

Despite all their recriminations over the previous few years, by 2010, Moscow and the West had thus both found themselves demanding that Kyiv start paying more for gas. Yanukovych's return to power and withdrawal of Ukraine's application for NATO membership had meanwhile pushed aside the other major impediment to Russo-Western reconciliation. For the time being at least, the most dangerous potential flashpoint between Russia and the West appeared largely under control. With a government in Kyiv that respected Russian redlines, Moscow was more willing to pursue rapprochement with the West, both within Ukraine and more generally.

THE CAUCASUS: GEORGIA'S CHALLENGE

The Caucasus remains the most troubled of Russia's peripheries. Both the North Caucasus (constituent republics of the Russian Federation including Chechnya, Dagestan, Ingushetia, North Ossetia-Alania, Adygea, Karachevo-Cherkessia, and Kabardino-Balkaria) and the South Caucasus (the independent states of Armenia, Azerbaijan, and Georgia plus the disputed provinces of South Ossetia and Abkhazia that Russia seized from Georgia in the August 2008 war) are beset by a plethora of tribal, religious, and ethnic conflicts. Because of the close links between peoples on both sides of the Russian border, instability in the independent South Caucasus states has a direct impact on the security of the Russian Federation, and vice versa. For Moscow, the region has had a dual importance: on the one hand, as a source of instability, connected above all to the simmering conflict that began in Chechnya and has now spread to other Muslim regions of the North Caucasus, and on the other, as a result of the competing ambitions of the South Caucasus states.

Azerbaijan and even more Georgia have sought since the end of the Soviet Union to go their own way, linking directly to international markets in order to hedge against excessive reliance on Russia. Their strategic location and—in the Azeri case—possession of significant oil and gas resources prompted outside powers to take an interest in the region, too. Russia has meanwhile sought, with mixed success, to keep the Caucasian states within its own sphere of influence. Its invasion of Georgia was a signal to Tbilisi and others that there is a large price for directly challenging Russian interests, but also the consequence of Moscow's waning ability to rely on other means of limiting outsiders' influence in the region.

Georgia was long a flashpoint in relations between Russia and the West, the more so since the rise of President Mikheil Saakashvili, a U.S.-educated lawyer who came to power as result of the so-called Rose Revolution of 2003, the first colored revolution directed against a post-Soviet autocrat (in this case, the former Soviet foreign minister Eduard Shevardnadze, who had ruled Georgia for a decade). While Shevardnadze's Georgia had little affinity for Russia and was at times less than helpful in Moscow's campaign to restore its control over Chechnya, Russo-Georgian relations worsened dramatically under Saakashvili as Tbilisi pursued fast-track integration into Western structures, especially NATO.

The deterioration of relations since the Rose Revolution was evidence of Moscow's view that foreign influence—and especially a foreign military presence—around its borders constituted a direct threat to Russian security. Moscow's problem with Saakashvili was in part that he came to power without Kremlin support, in part that he attempted to end the frozen conflicts on Georgia's territory that Moscow had done much to inflame, but above all that he and his supporters saw Georgia as an aspiring outpost of the West. This worldview underpinned Georgia's open interest in NATO membership (along with the Baltic states, it remains the only USSR successor state to unambiguously court the alliance), its decision to send troops to Iraq and Afghanistan, as well as the extensive financial and military assistance it received from Western sources. The prospect of Georgian NATO membership fed into Russian fears of encirclement by a hostile military alliance and provided Moscow's justification for seizing the breakaway provinces and attempting to oust Saakashvili.

For Russia's leaders, the Georgian rush into the West's embrace was both an embarrassment and a threat. Like the subsequent Orange Revolution in Ukraine and despite the Kremlin's near-total control of the political process inside Russia, the toppling of Shevardnadze fed Russian fears of the West's encroachment and the potential for similar disorder to break out in Russia itself—though Russia's elite had little love for Shevardnadze, Gorbachev's onetime foreign minister and the man whom many Russians regarded as the principal gravedigger of the USSR.[42] Of course, Shevardnadze himself blamed U.S. financier and political activist George Soros for underwriting the Rose Revolution.[43]

More importantly, the Rose Revolution was also seen in Moscow as an example of how the Bush administration used democracy promotion as a cynical cover for efforts to spread U.S. influence around Russia's borders. Moscow viewed Western support for routing the Baku-Tbilisi-Ceyhan pipeline through Georgia and receptiveness to the idea of Georgia joining NATO as inducements for Tbilisi to turn its back on Moscow, and the West's support for Saakashvili appeared to fit this narrative as well.[44] Moreover, while the Rose Revolution represented the first time public discontent had upset the orderly transfer of power from one oligarchic collective to another in the CIS, similar bouts of unrest soon broke out in Ukraine (the Orange Revolution), Kyrgyzstan (Tulip Revolution), and Uzbekistan (the bloody and abortive uprising in Andijon). Saakashvili seemed to represent the crest of a wave threatening the cozy and profitable status quo that benefited many powerful people in Moscow.

With the situation in Chechnya approaching a crisis point in early 2004, Saakashvili also had a potentially dangerous weapon in his hands in the Chechen rebels who moved back and forth across the Georgian frontier. In February 2004, Russian defense minister Sergey Ivanov accused Tbilisi of providing sanctuary to the rebels, even issuing them passports. He then suggested Russia might withdraw from its commitments under the CFE Treaty (which limited Russia's ability to deploy forces along its European and Caucasian borders) and halt the withdrawal of Russian forces from Georgia if Tbilisi did not adopt a more cooperative approach on Chechnya.[45]

Saakashvili also appeared to be actively promoting anti-Russian unrest elsewhere in the CIS. In August 2005, he signed an agreement with then-Ukrainian prime minister Yulia Tymoshenko establishing the Community of Democratic Choice (CDC) as a possible democratic, pro-Western alternative to the CIS. According to Saakashvili, "The CDC will support other democratic aspirants in the region by encouraging countries at various stages of integration with Euro-Atlantic institutions to advise and support states outside the Euro-Atlantic sphere."[46] This expansive vision of its mission, along with the CDC's stated interest in bringing civil society into the foreign policy process, made it look to Moscow like a kind of democratic Holy Alliance aiming to spread colored revolutions throughout the post-Soviet space.

If the West's influence in Georgia was underpinned by pipelines—principally BTC and the roughly parallel Baku-Tbilisi-Erzurum (BTE), or South Caucasus, gas pipeline—and ideological affinity with Saakashvili, Russia's influence flowed largely from its involvement in the frozen conflicts in South Ossetia and Abkhazia. The Kremlin posed as protector of the two regions and their independence-minded populations, which had attempted to break away from Georgia in the first chaotic years after 1991 (as well as of Ajaria, which sought to transform itself into an autonomous part of the Georgian state). Both the Ossetians and the Abkhaz have large numbers of coethnics living on the Russian side of the Russo-Georgian frontier, mainly in the regions of North Ossetia-Alania and Adygea, respectively. Destabilization and irredentism on the Georgian side of the border thus have potentially serious implications for Russian security in the North Caucasus, a fact supporters of Russia's intervention in the frozen conflicts often tout.[47]

At the same time, the Kremlin used the existence of the frozen conflicts (in Georgia as well as in Moldova and Azerbaijan) to keep a leash on post-Soviet states' ambitions of joining the EU or NATO, which are pledged to not admit member states with unresolved territorial disputes.[48] The existence of the breakaway provinces and the Kremlin's willingness to prop them up even while attempting to play the role of peacekeeper (under the fig leaf of the CIS) and mediator had poisoned Georgian attitudes toward Russia since the early 1990s. Saakashvili and his political opponents (including Shevardnadze) were equally hostile to the continued Russian presence in the breakaway regions and to Moscow's interference in what they considered Georgia's internal affairs—a fact that continues to complicate Russian attempts to meddle directly in Georgian politics.

Both South Ossetia and Abkhazia established their de facto separation from Georgia in the course of bloody conflicts in the early 1990s. These wars created hundreds of thousands of refugees (largely ethnic Georgians driven out by Abkhaz and Ossetia militias, few of whom ever returned home) and led to the fragmenting of the Georgian state.[49] The massive numbers of refugees, most of whom have been living away from their homes for two decades, bedeviled any attempt to impose a solution on the South Ossetian and Abkhaz conflicts even before the 2008 Russo-Georgian war, and became a still more intractable barrier to reconciliation afterward as the number of displaced persons swelled further.

Yeltsin's Kremlin eventually sent peacekeepers to South Ossetia and Abkhazia under the auspices of the CIS to keep the warring sides apart and, in Tbilisi's view, to impose a check on Georgia's sovereignty and territorial integrity.[50] Under the protection of these peacekeepers, South Ossetia and Abkhazia became increasingly tied to Russia politically and economically during the subsequent years. During the Putin years, residents of the breakaway regions received Russian passports, effectively turning them into citizens of the Russian Federation and de facto internationalizing their quarrel with Tbilisi. It was on the basis of protecting these Russian "citizens" from Georgian aggression (along with allegations of Georgian attacks on Russia's peacekeepers) that the Kremlin justified its invasion of Georgia and seizure of the breakaway provinces in 2008.

More than on almost any other issue, the frozen conflicts highlighted the contradictions inherent in Russia's approach to its role in the former Soviet Union. The Kremlin long struggled to square its backing for Abkhaz and South Ossetian separatists with its own broader interest in drawing the states of the former Soviet Union into its orbit, not to mention its support for the principles of state sovereignty and international law. Indeed, the consolidation of the GU(U)AM group was in many ways a reaction to Russia's manipulation of these frozen conflicts. Likewise, Russia's pious concern for the fate of civilian populations in the breakaway regions of Georgia appeared hollow alongside the devastation Russian forces inflicted on Chechen civilians, while Moscow's rhetorical support for the principle of sovereignty and territorial inviolability (e.g., with regard to Serbia) have been hard to reconcile with its backing for the Abkhaz and South Ossetian separatists.

As long as South Ossetia and Abkhazia were discontented bits of Georgia with a Russian peacekeeping presence, they were useful bargaining chips and sources of leverage for Moscow, keeping the pressure on Tbilisi and discouraging Western backing for Kosovo's independence (Russian diplomats frequently drew parallels between Kosovo and South Ossetia/Abkhazia, warning that any move to secure Kosovo's independence from Serbia would serve as a precedent in Georgia). By keeping the conflicts in Abkhazia and South Ossetia frozen, Russia was able to keep Tbilisi's pro-Western leanings in check and sharply limit the possibility that Georgia would be accepted as a member of either the EU or (more crucially) NATO. The West's decision to recognize Kosovo's independence and Saakashvili's misguided attempt to seize South Ossetia by force in the summer of 2008 reduced Russia's incentives to keep the conflicts frozen and provided a pretext for military intervention.[51]

Saakashvili's ascension to power in January 2004 highlighted the fragility of this status quo in the breakaway regions, insofar as the new Georgian president refused to accept what most Georgians saw as Russia's ongoing violation of Georgian sovereignty and international law. Saakashvili had staked his political credibility on restoring Georgian territorial integrity, though during his first meeting with Putin in February 2004, the new Georgian president expressed a willingness to look for joint solutions to a problem for which he argued neither Putin nor he himself bore personal responsibility. While Saakashvili spoke of the need for dialogue with Russia, he also left no doubt about his commitment to restoring Georgian sovereignty over all of the republic's territory, or about his willingness to court Western assistance to do so.[52]

The English-speaking, Columbia-educated Georgian president was confident that his close relationship with Western powers (above all the U.S.) would insulate him against Russian intervention. His confidence in Western backing at times led Saakashvili to act rashly. In a joint press conference with Putin in June 2006, he declared of the frozen conflicts that "the reality is that the annexation of our territory is underway."[53] After his first bridge-building visit to Moscow, moreover, Saakashvili went to Washington, where he pressed the Bush administration for additional security and economic assistance in order to lessen Georgia's dependence on Moscow.[54] During and immediately after the Rose Revolution, Saakashvili's government did receive substantial aid from the U.S., including $3 million to pay the salaries of Georgian military personnel and an agreement, signed in January 2004, to provide upward of $10 million in general financial assistance. Moscow perceived this aid, along with the completion of the BTC pipeline across Georgian territory soon after the installation of Saakashvili's overtly pro-Western government, as proof of the connection between the Rose Revolution and Western geopolitical designs in the Caucasus.[55]

Having successfully restored Tbilisi's control over the rebellious Ajaria region through a combination of intimidation and force, Saakashvili moved during the summer of 2006 to retake the upper portion of the Kodori Gorge, an area Moscow had long alleged to be a refuge and staging ground for Chechen rebels, and which cut across the boundary between Abkhazia and Georgia proper. The gorge had been demilitarized as a result of the 1994 Moscow Accords ending the first Georgian-Abkhaz war, and it remained a major flashpoint until the next war.[56]

In July 2006, Saakashvili sent troops from the Georgian Interior Ministry into the gorge to depose a local strongman. With this police operation completed, Tbilisi installed a loyalist Abkhaz government-in-exile in the area newly renamed "Upper Abkhazia." Tbilisi's intent was clearly to provide an alternative to the Abkhaz separatist leadership in hope of reconciling Abkhazia as a whole to living under Georgian rule. Saakashvili's efforts in "Upper Abkhazia" disturbed the Abkhaz separatist regime in Tskhinvali as well as Moscow, which saw its influence in the region threatened by a government in Tbilisi it had already come to despise.[57]

In South Ossetia, the Georgian authorities similarly tried to create a competing center of power in the fall of 2007. Tbilisi sponsored a presidential vote in those parts of South Ossetia inhabited principally by ethnic Georgians, which resulted in a victory for the pro-integrationist parties headed by Dmitry Sanakoev (a onetime Ossetian separatist). Russia, as well as the international community in the form of the OSCE, condemned the election for disrupting ongoing negotiations to ameliorate tensions on the ground.[58] For Tbilisi, of course, the point was not to reduce tensions in the breakaway regions, but to "unfreeze" the frozen conflicts altogether in Georgia's favor. In practice, Sanakoev had little authority, and South Ossetia as a whole remained outside Tbilisi's writ, setting the stage for Saakashvili's desperate gamble in August 2008 to retake the region by force.

Saakashvili's push to unfreeze the South Ossetian and Abkhaz conflicts ensured that relations with Moscow remained overtly hostile. Russia did its part to stir up tensions as well, engaging in provocative military actions (including overflights of Georgian territory by Russian air force planes and a string of suspicious bombings that Tbilisi blamed on Russian intelligence agencies). The prewar nadir came in late 2006, after Georgian security services arrested four Russian officers and accused them of espionage and sabotage. In a television broadcast discussing the arrests, Georgian defense minister Irakly Okruashvili blamed Russia for fomenting the South Ossetian and Abkhaz conflicts and demanded the withdrawal of Russian peacekeepers from Georgian territory.[59] The Russians responded by alleging that Tbilisi was trying to provoke Russia to overreact in order to build Western sympathy and accelerate the process of NATO integration.[60] Putin termed the arrest of the alleged spies "an act of state terrorism" and "a legacy of [Stalin's secret police chief and Georgian native] Lavrenty Pavlovich Beria."[61] Insofar as both sides were seeking to overturn the status quo, both probably had a point.

Moscow responded to the arrests, and Tbilisi's decision to parade the arrested Russian agents before the television cameras, by recalling its ambassador and suspending the withdrawal of Russian troops from Georgia proper, even after Tbilisi agreed to deport the agents to Russia. The Kremlin also suspended transportation links between the two countries, banned Georgia's major exports (wine and mineral water), stopped issuing visas to Georgian citizens, and announced a crackdown on the large ethnic Georgian diaspora inside Russia, whose remittances were critical for the Georgian economy. The crackdown culminated in the deportation of around seven hundred ethnic Georgians from Russian territory, which Moscow claimed was an anticrime measure (though members of other nationalities, criminals or otherwise, were not rounded up in the same way).[62]

The Kremlin had essentially upped the ante in an attempt to make the cost of achieving Saakashvili's goals too high. In the event, Russian policy largely backfired. The disproportionate assault on a small, pro-Western country being considered for NATO membership merely fed U.S. and European perceptions that Putin's Russia had become a danger to the post-Soviet status quo, which in turn further emboldened the Georgians. Domestically, these actions helped legitimate an ugly streak of xenophobia in Russian society to the benefit of rabid nationalist groups such as the DPNI, some of whom remained opposed to the Putin government anyway.[63] If Moscow was going to teach Tbilisi a lesson, it would have to use other means.

For the subsequent two years, little was done to restore trust in Russo-Georgian relations. Even as Moscow withdrew the last of its troops from Georgia proper in the latter part of 2007 (where they had been based since the fall of the USSR), it ramped up its presence in the breakaway regions, especially Abkhazia. Tbilisi interpreted this move as preparation for war, though the Kremlin argued that it was Saakashvili who was bringing arms into the region.[64] With the conflicts still frozen, Saakashvili's decision to disperse antigovernment protesters with force in November 2007 damaged his democratic credentials in a West that was already reconsidering Georgia's suitability for NATO membership. Saakashvili, however, continued to believe that the U.S. and (to a lesser degree) Europe would protect him from overt Russian retaliation. It was to be a costly mistake.

The dam finally broke in the summer of 2008 when, with the world's attention focused on the opening of the Olympics in Beijing, Saakashvili responded to a new round of Russian provocations by ordering his forces to retake South Ossetia. Starting on August 7, Georgian troops launched an artillery barrage against the South Ossetian capital of Tskhinvali and moved to seize control of the region's infrastructure from the separatist regime. The attempt to seize South Ossetia provided the Kremlin with the excuse it had been seeking to go after Saakashvili. The day after the Georgian incursion against Tskhinvali, massed Russian forces began crossing into South Ossetia through the Roki Tunnel, while the Russian air force carried out strikes on targets in both South Ossetia and Georgia proper.

Moscow quickly ramped up its propaganda war against Saakashvili as well. It charged the Georgian government with ethnic cleansing against the Ossetian population in Tskhinvali and other population centers and justified its decision to send troops on the basis of defending the civilian population (many of whom had been granted Russian passports) and the Russian peacekeepers that Georgia charged were now part of a hostile occupying army.[65] New Russian president Medvedev gave a terse announcement of the Russian invasion, arguing that the Georgian peacekeeping contingent in South Ossetia had opened fire on its Russian counterpart and claiming Tbilisi's "act of aggression" had resulted in the deaths of "civilians, women, children, the elderly, and the majority of them citizens of the Russian Federation."[66]

After driving the overmanned Georgians out of South Ossetia, Russian forces continued into Georgia proper, seizing the key city of Gori and Georgia's main east–west highway, blockading the Black Sea port of Poti, and systematically destroying Georgian military assets and other infrastructure. Russian troops also moved into Abkhazia, retaking the Kodori Gorge from the Georgians, who had redeployed all available troops (including their forces serving in Iraq) to defend Tbilisi. In South Ossetia, local militias rampaged behind Russian lines, looting, pillaging, and driving out the remaining ethnic Georgian population, which fled en masse into Georgia proper.[67]

Despite agreeing to a cease-fire negotiated by French president Nicolas Sarkozy five days after the start of Russo-Georgian hostilities (i.e., on August 13), Russian troops remained in Georgia for several weeks thereafter, systematically destroying military hardware in an attempt to weaken Georgia and prevent it from undertaking any further attempts at seizing the disputed regions.[68] After the tame Duma had voted to recognize South Ossetia and Abkhazia as independent states, Medvedev agreed, and Russia became the first state to extend diplomatic recognition to the two breakaway regions (it would be followed by Nicaragua, and eventually Venezuela and the Pacific archipelago of Nauru, each of which extracted significant financial assistance from Moscow in exchange).[69]

For the first time since the collapse of the Soviet Union, Moscow had undertaken a major cross-border military operation—in the face of the outside world's almost unified condemnation. The United States and Europe strongly protested Russian behavior and threatened Moscow with a range of punishments, some symbolic (expulsion from the G8), others real (the cancellation of a lucrative civilian nuclear cooperation accord with Washington). None of it mattered. The invasion of Georgia and recognition of the breakaway regions reflected a calculation in Moscow that the strategic pause—Gorchakov's *sosredotochenie* or Stolypin's *peredyshka*—following the collapse of the Soviet Union was over. It was a signal to the rest of the world that Russia continued to regard the CIS as its own sphere of influence, where it would not tolerate having its interests ignored. It also signaled the limits of the West's influence—and capacity to project power—in the former Soviet Union. Many Western leaders came to recognize that their strategy of seeking to limit Russian influence in the region came with large associated costs, particularly since the confident Russia of 2008 was not the crumbling Russia of 1994.

While the legacy of Russia's invasion of Georgia remains an irritant in relations with the West, in a somewhat paradoxical way, it also served as a starting point for the rapprochement pursued under Medvedev. Some of the most intractable issues raised by the August 2008 war remained unresolved years later, including the status of the breakaway republics. Despite an energetic campaign by Moscow to win diplomatic recognition for South Ossetia and Abkhazia, even close Russian allies in the CIS—not to mention China—refused, wary of setting a precedent for either separatism or legitimizing Russian military intervention in the affairs of its neighbors. The two statelets remained in a kind of limbo, not unlike what Northern Cyprus has endured for decades following its unilateral proclamation of independence (recognized only by Turkey) in 1976.

Since the U.S. and Europeans never recognized the independence of South Ossetia and Abkhazia, they continued to regard the presence of Russian forces as violating the cease-fire agreement negotiated by Sarkozy in August 2008 (not to mention the Conventional Forces in Europe Treaty), which called for Russian troops to evacuate Georgian territory. Moscow of course argued that South Ossetia and Abkhazia no longer constituted Georgian territory, and moved to strengthen its military presence (which provided the breakaway governments' only defense against attempts by Tbilisi to recover them), especially in the strategically important Black Sea littoral of Abkhazia.[70] The issue of Russian deployments also deepened the divide over the status and future of the CFE Treaty, since the U.S. and other Western powers claimed that the Russian troops' presence constituted a renewed violation of the so-called Istanbul Commitments (a Russian promise to withdraw troops from Georgia and Moldova in exchange for NATO's agreeing to modernize the treaty to Russia's benefit)—though Germany in particular argued that the commitments must be modified in light of the new reality on the ground in the South Caucasus.[71]

Yet in terms of relations between the West and Russia, the war had something of a silver lining. For the West, the war served as a wakeup call to the consequences of ignoring and isolating Russia. Suddenly, Moscow's warnings about the dangers of NATO expansion drawing new lines in Europe and the recognition of Kosovo setting a dangerous precedent received concrete expression. The war provided a glimpse into an abyss where NATO expansion actually diminished security for both old and new members, where the value of NATO's Article 5 commitments themselves were called into question, and where a return to a Cold War–style standoff with Moscow did not appear out of the question. While officially remaining committed to Georgian membership at some point in the future, ever since the war NATO actively downplayed the possibility.

After a suitable period where they duly threatened Moscow with a variety of less-than-convincing consequences, Washington and Brussels also accepted the need for active engagement with Russia, including on issues related to security in the post-Soviet space. The challenge, especially for the Obama administration became learning to square the reconciliation with Moscow they agreed was necessary with the desire not to abandon Georgia, which remained after the war the most liberal and pro-Western (non-Baltic) state in the former Soviet Union, despite Saakashvili's many faults.[72]

For Russia, the war and its consequences showcased the limits of the Putin-era economic, military, and geopolitical revival. While Russia achieved its military objectives, it faced greater resistance and suffered higher casualties than anticipated—including the loss of several aircraft to Georgian ground fire. The war induced foreign investors to pull out of Russia, touching off a serious downturn that the global crisis of late 2008 only exacerbated, and giving the lie to many officials' claims that Russia had decoupled itself from the global economy. The Russia that emerged from the five-day war was shorn of much of the hubris that had characterized its international behavior leading up to the conflict, and became less interested in resisting Western hegemony than in getting its own house in order.

Meanwhile, the war stoked extreme skepticism of Russian motives across the CIS, where countries from Belarus to Uzbekistan sought to rapidly diversify their foreign policy options, as well as in Eastern Europe, which increasingly pushed NATO to reaffirm its Article 5 commitments and back them up with concrete military planning and exercises. In strategic terms, the war was a pyrrhic victory for Moscow, one that Medvedev and other supporters of modernization knew could not be repeated without burying their vision of a respected, globally competitive Russia. The dose of realism that the war thrust upon both Russia and the West forced both to rethink some of their basic assumptions in ways that highlighted the importance of finding a new modus vivendi with regard to both Georgia and the post-Soviet space more broadly.

CENTRAL ASIA

While the Western CIS and the Caucasus have often found themselves caught between the competing poles represented by Russia and the West, the situation in Central Asia is further complicated by the region's proximity to both China and the unstable maelstrom of Afghanistan and Pakistan. For much of the Soviet period, Central Asia was an imperial backwater, important mainly as a producer of primary goods such as cotton and as a dumping ground for political opponents. The early post-Soviet period did not see much change; it was only under Primakov and then Putin that Russian diplomacy again began paying sustained attention to the region. Central Asia turned into a region of strategic interest for Russia, as well as outside powers like the United States and China, primarily for two reasons: Islamist extremism and economic opportunities connected largely (though not entirely) to energy.

The Central Asian leaders were not even consulted about the eventual dissolution of the USSR and were notified that they had become rulers of independent states only after the fact. The five primarily Muslim republics of Central Asia (Kazakhstan, Uzbekistan, Turkmenistan, Kyrgyzstan, and Tajikistan) came into the world in 1991 as inchoate entities, with a weak sense of national identity and underdeveloped institutions, and where loyalty to the newly created states and their Russian-speaking strongmen was tenuous at best. For Kozyrev and other pro-Western figures around Yeltsin in the early 1990s, Central Asia was a millstone holding Russia back from integration with the West. In consequence, they drastically scaled back Russia's military cooperation with the Central Asian states, while Gaidar's economic reform led to their expulsion from the ruble zone. It was Russia's apparent indifference to the region that led all five Central Asian states to join NATO's Partnership for Peace in 1994.[73]

Only under Primakov did Moscow begin seeing its lingering influence in Central Asia as an asset. Here was an area where Russia continued to have important advantages and where its ability to play the role of regional broker could enhance its influence with outside powers. This more active Russian approach was embodied in President Yeltsin's September 1995 decree proclaiming the CIS a top foreign policy priority for Russia. With this decree, Moscow essentially gave itself an exclusive right to manage the security of its neighbors throughout the CIS, though in practical terms, Russia's enhanced influence was at the time felt most in Central Asia. Local rulers increasingly came to see the Kremlin as the ultimate guarantor of their security against the perceived Islamist threat—and against each other.[74] Yet for Primakov, renewed Russian attention to Central Asia was designed to compensate for Russia's lack of influence in the rest of the world. It was only under Putin that the Kremlin began to view enhanced influence in the region as a means to a larger global role rather than an alternative to it.

Another factor driving Russia's return to the region was trepidation at the rise of radical Islamism in Afghanistan as well as neighboring Central Asia. The power vacuum that emerged following the Soviet withdrawal from Afghanistan and the subsequent collapse of Soviet rule in Central Asia provided fertile ground for the development of a new politics based on somewhat fictive tribal loyalties, while veterans of the Afghan war introduced a new, puritanical strain of Islamic thought to a region that had traditionally worn its religion lightly.[75] This nexus of tribalism and religion erupted into war in Tajikistan in 1992, followed shortly thereafter by the redeployment of Russian troops outside the border of the Russian Federation to deal with the consequences.

The Tajik experience, itself following soon after the end of the Soviet Union's Afghan apotheosis, did much to color subsequent Russian perceptions of developments in Central Asia. Alongside other foreign ideological imports, radical Islam, at times manifesting itself in acts of terrorism, spread throughout parts of Central Asia in the 1990s. This strain of Islam posed a direct threat to the secular, Russian-speaking apparatchiks who inherited power after the Soviet collapse and who were, however mercurial, vastly preferable from the Kremlin's perspective to either Taliban-style fundamentalism or the chronic warlordism it had replaced in Afghanistan.[76]

When he first came to power in 2000, Putin emphasized on several occasions that the principal threat to Russian security came from the south, that is, from Islamic radicalism in the Caucasus and Central Asia (of course, Putin's rise was intimately connected with the worsening security situation in Chechnya in the late 1990s and the growth of demands inside Russia for taking a much harder line against Islamist radicalism).[77] As that threat seemingly diminished following the Taliban's fall from power and the winding down of hostilities in Chechnya, Moscow's fundamental threat calculus shifted. The pro-Taliban Islamic Movement of Uzbekistan (IMU), which was blamed for a series of bombings targeting the repressive Uzbek government as well as armed incursions into Kyrgyzstan in 1999 and 2000, was decimated by U.S. bombing attacks in Afghanistan shortly after 9/11, suffering hundreds of casualties and the death of its leader, Juma Namangani. Meanwhile, the peace treaty signed in 1997 by the government and (partially Islamist) opposition forces in Tajikistan, contrary to the expectations of many, largely held firm. The spate of bombings inside Russia conducted by Chechen and allied Islamist forces, which was responsible for much of Moscow's interest in stamping out Islamist groups throughout the CIS, also abated. Russia's killing of Chechen rebel leaders Aslan Maskhadov, Ibn al-Khattab, and Shamil Basaev, coupled with pro-Moscow strongman Ramzan Kadyrov's brutal efficiency in restoring order to Chechnya, made the internal Islamist threat to Russia seem less immediate—even though the situation in Dagestan, Ingushetia, and other Muslim regions in the North Caucasus continued to deteriorate.[78]

With the strategic challenge posed by Islamist extremism seemingly under control, Moscow was able to pursue a broader strategic agenda toward its Muslim neighbors. Putin began focusing on the longer-term project of reestablishing Russia's leading role in the post-Soviet space, which required limiting the role played by outside powers such as the United States and China.

Putin's first foreign trip as prime minister was to Tajikistan, in November 1999, when he sought to promote the electoral fortunes of the secularist, pro-Russian incumbent then named Emomali Rakhmonov (the Tajik leader subsequently de-Russified his surname, becoming Emomali Rakhmon). The following month Putin traveled to Uzbekistan, signing a series of bilateral deals aimed at bringing Tashkent more directly into the Russian orbit.

In practice though, the Uzbeks continued to hedge their bets, joining the independence-minded GU(U)AM forum in April 1999.[79]

The invasion of Kyrgyzstan by IMU militants in August 1999 provided Putin with an opportunity to step up Russian involvement throughout Central Asia. The militants' threat to regional stability, coupled with the Kyrgyz government's clear inability to repulse them on its own suggested that only outside intervention could defend the secular status quo.[80] In response to the IMU's cross-border invasion, Putin immediately began seeking a rapprochement with Uzbekistan, the country most seriously threatened by the IMU and in many ways the key to regional stability (though also the most wary of Russian influence). Though Tashkent refused for the time being to back out of GU(U)AM or to join Russian-sponsored multilateral groups like the Collective Security Treaty, it agreed to limited participation in training exercises with Russia and signed a series of bilateral security cooperation agreements with Moscow.[81]

This strategy received a boost in the changed regional security landscape that emerged from the September 11, 2001, terrorist attacks on the U.S., which originated in Afghanistan and led a previously disinterested United States to prepare a massive influx of resources into Afghanistan and the surrounding region—including the establishment of major air bases at Karshi-Khanabad, Uzbekistan and Manas International Airport on the outskirts of the Kyrgyz capital Bishkek. Instead of seeking to keep the U.S. out of Central Asia entirely, the Putin administration changed tack in Central Asia in line with its new strategy of posing as Washington's indispensable ally in the unfolding "war on terror." Putin acquiesced to the U.S. deployments in the face of serious opposition from his generals, since, in the words of Gleb Pavlovsky, "it is better to have Americans in Uzbekistan than to have the Taliban in Tatarstan."[82] Russian leaders recognized that given the scale of the carnage unleashed on 9/11 and their own vulnerability to Islamic terrorism (Russia has over twenty million Muslim citizens and abuts some of the least stable of Islam's "bloody borders"), gaining the cooperation of the United States in the ongoing struggle against jihadism was enough of a strategic imperative to overcome worries about the effects of American power inside the boundaries of the former USSR, at least temporarily.[83]

At the same time, cooperation with the Americans seemed to offer the best opportunity for Russia to reassert its Great Power ambitions, since it was essentially offering to play a key role in a campaign that (if successful) would have major implications for the future shape of much of the world. In any case, leaders in Uzbekistan, Tajikistan, and Kyrgyzstan made clear in the weeks immediately following the attacks that they wanted U.S. troops deployed in the region to protect their own governments against Taliban-inspired Islamists like the IMU.[84] Putin was thus in some sense reacting to events beyond his control—categorically refusing to allow U.S. troops into Central Asia risked sacrificing whatever influence Moscow retained in the region, and under the circumstances it appeared better to make a virtue of necessity, as Pavlovsky suggested.

The initial U.S. military intervention drove the Taliban from power and inflicted a crushing blow on the strongest of the Central Asian Islamist groups, the IMU, which had contributed to regional instability through its cross-border raids, kidnappings, and bomb attacks (allegedly including one that narrowly missed killing Uzbek president Islam Karimov in 1999).[85] However, the U.S. invasion of Iraq in early 2003, which Russia strenuously opposed, drew attention and resources away from the Afghan campaign, while the overall deterioration in U.S.-Russian relations in subsequent years (the result in part of Russian opposition to the war in Iraq) complicated the Kremlin's plans for using an alliance with the U.S. as a springboard for achieving greater international influence. The result was an increasing drive by the Kremlin to secure its own position in Central Asia while sidelining the U.S. (as well as China).

Moscow's acceptance of a large U.S. military presence in Central Asia was very much the choice of a lesser evil, one that the Russian leadership was keen to end as soon as circumstances in Afghanistan allowed. With the initial U.S. success against the Taliban (and the IMU), the Kremlin soon began to argue that the U.S. presence had run its course and should be wound down. Otherwise, Moscow feared that the stationing of U.S. forces in Central Asia would become permanent, and would act as a constraint on Russian influence, much like the colored revolutions elsewhere in the CIS. When Washington criticized the Karimov regime in Uzbekistan for its May 2005 massacre of demonstrators in the city of Andijon, Russia backed Karimov's demand for U.S. forces to vacate Karshi-Khanabad. Russia was also instrumental in pressing the Shanghai Cooperation Organization to issue its so-called Astana Declaration in July 2005, which argued that with the military campaign against the Taliban seemingly on the verge of success, the U.S.-led coalition should set a deadline for the withdrawal of all its troops from Central Asia.

Of course, with the U.S. focusing its efforts on Iraq after 2003, the situation in Afghanistan quickly deteriorated, and Moscow once again found itself caught between the twin evils of tolerating a protracted U.S. military presence in Central Asia and a resurgent Taliban spreading instability throughout the region. Moscow's strategy consequently became one of hedging. On the one hand, it offered to play a much more active role in the campaign against the Taliban. While not offering to send its own troops to Afghanistan (given the experience of the Red Army in the 1980s, deploying Russian troops to Afghanistan was politically impossible), Moscow agreed to provide extensive logistical support.

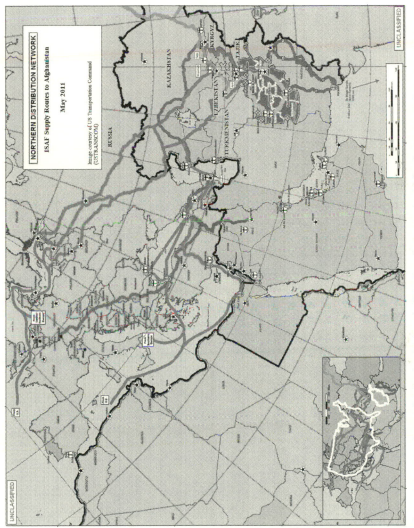

Figure 6.1. Northern Distribution Network, ISAF Supply Routes to Afghanistan, May 2011. *Source:* Image courtesy of US Transportation Command (USTRANSCOM)

In January 2009, Russia, Uzbekistan, and Kazakhstan signed transit agreements permitting the U.S. and NATO to ship supplies across their territory, reducing the coalition's reliance on the increasingly vulnerable supply corridor through Pakistan. Eventually, this Northern Distribution Network (NDN) also came to encompass Tajikistan, Kyrgyzstan, Azerbaijan, Georgia, Latvia, and Turkmenistan.[86] As U.S.-Russian relations warmed under the Obama administration's reset policy, Russia became an increasingly important partner in the anti-Taliban campaign, permitting as many as forty-five hundred U.S.-troop flights per year to cross its airspace and allowing the transit of supplies and equipment on its railways (ironically given Russian concern about U.S. bases in Central Asia, the men and materiel shipped through Russia on the NDN had to be collected at Manas before deployment to Afghanistan).

For Russia, participation in the NDN was driven by a similar calculation to that lying behind the initial decision to acquiesce to the presence of U.S. troops in Central Asia in 2001–2002: by positioning itself as an indispensible partner in what President Obama called a "war of necessity," Moscow would be able to strengthen its own hand in dealings with Washington—particularly if it could convince Washington that Russian logistical cooperation made a long-term U.S. presence in Central Asia unnecessary.

Moscow also sought to match the U.S. presence in Kyrgyzstan by setting up military bases of its own. The Russian air base at Kant, which opened in early 2003, was the first new long-term deployment of Russian troops outside the borders of the Russian Federation since the end of the Cold War. It was designed to counter the expansion of American influence in Central Asia that occurred in the wake of the Afghan invasion, and to take advantage of the Central Asians' disappointment that the U.S. presence in the region had not brought them greater economic benefit.[87] Russia continued to maintain a troop presence in Tajikistan as well, in part to help maintain internal security following the civil war of the 1990s, but also as a tool of Russian influence in the region.

Moscow eventually upgraded and expanded the facilities at Kant, under the aegis of the Collective Security Treaty. Moscow also signed an agreement with former Kyrgyz president Kurmanbek Bakiyev in August 2009 authorizing the establishment of a second Russian military base at Osh, in the volatile Ferghana Valley. The Osh base was designed both to serve as a hub for the CSTO's Rapid Reaction Force, and to give Moscow greater influence should the situation in Afghanistan continue deteriorating. Yet the planned deployment of Russian troops in Osh was strongly opposed by Uzbekistan, which along with Belarus refused to participate in the Rapid Reaction Force. Tashkent worried that the presence of additional Russian forces in the region would upset the balance of power (Osh is located less than thirty kilometers from the Uzbek-Kyrgyz border), and could stir up extremist forces in the region. Not lost on Tashkent or the other Central Asian governments were the lessons of the recent Russo-Georgian war, which fed worries that the presence of Russian forces could provide a pretext for Moscow's intervention into the Central Asian states' affairs.[88] This distrust of Russian intentions, as well as the mutual suspicion between the various Central Asian governments consequently remains a significant barrier to the expansion of Russian influence in the region.

Moscow has nonetheless employed a variety of techniques to convince the Central Asian leaders to follow its lead on the base issue—though as U.S.-Russian relations improved and Moscow became increasingly concerned about the consequences of a precipitous U.S. withdrawal from Afghanistan, it gradually reconciled itself to U.S. forces staying at Manas until the conflict ended. Since Bakiyev had been heavily dependent on Russian support for his rise to power in the aftermath of the 2005 Tulip Revolution, Moscow long believed it could pressure him into demanding the U.S. leave Manas (Bakiyev was publicly skeptical of the U.S. military presence in the first place). In the spring of 2009, with the global economic crisis raging, Medvedev offered Kyrgyzstan a $2 billion loan plus a $150 million grant to complete work on a major hydroelectric station; the next day, Bishkek announced that the U.S. would have to vacate Manas in six months' time.

However, Kyrgyz politicians and diplomats very quickly let it be known that they would be willing to extend the lease on the base if the U.S. increased its rent payments. These hints became increasingly insistent as Bishkek realized that the crisis-hit Russian government was having difficulty coming up with the promised funds—and as it came under increasing pressure not only from the U.S., but also from the Afghan government itself, to continue allowing the coalition to use Manas as a supply and transit hub. In June 2009, Washington and Bishkek announced that the lease on Manas was being renewed. U.S. rent payments tripled to $60 million per year, while Washington also agreed to provide more than $100 million in aid for development and counternarcotics efforts (the base was relabeled a "transit center" to allow Bishkek to claim it had followed through on its promise to keep U.S. "bases" out of its territory). While Moscow admitted that this reversal was an internal matter for Kyrgyzstan, it was clearly unhappy, publicly pointing out that Bishkek had gone back on repeated promises to close the facility entirely.[89]

Having bucked Moscow to renew the lease on Manas, Bakiyev continued alienating both his own people and the Russians. The new lease for Manas was accompanied by a series of contracts for servicing the base that, on investigation, appeared to benefit companies owned by relatives and associates of the Kyrgyz president. At the same time, several opposition figures and independent journalists were attacked, including some who were allegedly assaulted and killed by Kyrgyz security forces in neighboring countries. Repeating one of the principal mistakes of his predecessor Askar Akayev (ousted by the Tulip Revolution), Bakiyev appointed family members to important posts, including his son Maksim to head the country's development agency and his brother Zhanysh as head of internal security. Meanwhile, Bakiyev conducted talks with the U.S. on establishing a military training center in the southern Kyrgyz city of Batken, which would greatly complicate Russian plans for a new CSTO base close by at Osh.

Relations between Bishkek and Moscow grew increasingly testy even as the Kyrgyz public became exasperated with Bakiyev's oppression and nepotism. In early March 2010, Russia's state-dominated media outlets suddenly stepped up their criticism of Bakiyev (many Kyrgyz rely on Russian press and television for news), while Moscow decided to raise tariffs on Russian energy imports. Shortly thereafter, protests against Bakiyev broke out in Bishkek and other cities. Security forces loyal to the president fired indiscriminately, killing scores but—in contrast to events in Uzbekistan's Andijon five years earlier—failing to disperse the crowds. Bakiyev ultimately fled the country, turning power over to a weak provisional government.

Russia's role in the ouster of Bakiyev was murky but significant. Though it was intolerance of dissent, widespread corruption, poverty, and nepotism that turned the Kyrgyz public against him, the Russian press' demonization of the Kyrgyz leader and the decision to ratchet up energy tariffs—leading to a tripling of utility rates—stoked public discontent at a moment when he was particularly vulnerable. To some observers, the events of March and April 2010 looked like a colored revolution in reverse, as if Moscow had mastered the techniques it accused Washington of employing to install Saakashvili and Yushchenko.[90]

In any event, the continued sparring over military bases and Russia's involvement in pushing Bakiyev from power emphasized the contradiction between Russia maintaining its role as chief arbiter in the region while pursuing reconciliation with the West. Yet the Taliban's growing resurgence, coupled with Obama's promise to begin drawing down the U.S. presence in Afghanistan in mid-2011 forced Moscow to rebalance these competing imperatives. Belatedly recognizing that Afghanistan's growing instability represented a direct threat to its own interests, Moscow began downplaying its opposition to the U.S. presence at Manas. It also coordinated closely with Washington on restoring stability in Kyrgyzstan after Bakiyev's ouster and the outbreak of pogroms against the country's Uzbek minority in the summer of 2010. As with Russian participation in NDN, the more flexible attitude toward Manas was an example of how Moscow has remained open to foreign involvement in the region, and indeed encouraged it when doing so is perceived as furthering Russian national interests, rather than attempting to seal off the post-Soviet space entirely from outside influence.

Alongside its desire to check the spread of Islamist radicalism, Russia's involvement in Central Asia has also been driven by economic interest, connected above all to energy and the pipelines transporting it to markets in Europe and East Asia. Control of pipelines has been a key component of Moscow's leverage over all the Caspian littoral states of the CIS, including Central Asia's major energy producers Kazakhstan and Turkmenistan. With the Western powers dreaming of access to the Caspian's energy riches, Brussels and Washington have aggressively promoted new pipeline deals bypassing Russia, while Moscow has responded with its own attempts to bottle up Central Asia's energy in Russian-controlled pipelines. In the scramble for Caspian energy, China has also emerged as a major player, one whose deep pockets and heavy dependence on imported energy have made it increasingly influential across Central Asia—and given the Central Asian states another option in their campaign to assert their strategic independence from Russia.

Many of the Caspian littoral states saw the courting of foreign energy companies as a way to lessen their dependence on Russia by establishing links to global markets independent of Russian control. Azerbaijan, with the BTC and BTE pipelines to Turkey, had largely escaped Russian domination by the late 1990s. Kazakhstan managed to balance between the competing demands of Russia, the West, and China by signing deals with several foreign firms to produce oil from its Caspian deposits.[91] Meanwhile Turkmenistan, which is one of the world's leading producers of natural gas, is the post-Soviet state whose relationship to the major outside powers remains the most uncertain, in part because of its exceptionally (even for the former Soviet Union) closed and mercurial leadership. Gazprom has long eyed Turkmenistan hungrily as a solution to projections of mounting postcrisis demand among Russia's customers in Europe and stagnant production inside Russia—particularly after a controversial 2008 study estimated that Turkmenistan might be sitting on as much as fourteen trillion cubic meters of gas, or more than enough to meet the demand of both Gazprom and the European companies seeking to build their own Caspian pipelines along the so-called Southern Corridor (the most well known of which is Nabucco).[92]

During the 1990s, Gazprom used its monopoly on pipelines from Turkmenistan to outside markets to tightly constrain Ashgabat's foreign policy decisions. It also paid Turkmenistan a much lower price for gas than it received for selling the same gas onward to European consumers. Yet with mounting interest from Western and Chinese energy firms, Moscow was forced to agree in early 2008 to start paying Turkmenistan (as well as the other Central Asian gas-producing countries) "European prices" for its gas, rather than the deeply discounted rate it had been paying up to that point. This decision proved costly for Gazprom as European demand plummeted during the economic crisis. A mysterious explosion along the pipeline from Turkmenistan to Russia in April 2009 freed Gazprom from this boondoggle, but increasingly poisoned relations between Moscow and Ashgabat.

Turkmenistan had used the possibility of a deal with others as a form of leverage in negotiations with the Russians, holding discussions with everyone from the Europeans and Americans, to the Iranians and Indians to explore the possibility of breaking the effective Russian monopoly on its gas exports.[93] In the event, it was cash-rich and energy-poor China that finally broke Russia's monopoly by funding the construction of a new pipeline across Turkmenistan and Uzbekistan to the western Chinese province of Xinjiang, which came online in December 2009.

Given its isolation from global markets, Central Asia's economies continue to rely heavily on Russia outside the energy sector too, a circumstance that simultaneously benefits from and underpins Moscow's continued influence in the region. Consequently, regional economic integration remains one of Russia's principal tools for enhancing its geopolitical influence in Central Asia. The importance of groups such as the Eurasian Economic Community (EurAsEC) and its trilateral Customs Union lies precisely in their contribution to creating a unified economic space across the territory of the former Soviet Union. For many Russian industrialists and oligarchs, including those at the heart of "Kremlin, Inc.," securing a guaranteed and protected market within the CIS is preferable to opening the country to foreign competition, which could eviscerate uncompetitive Russian heavy industries. For Medvedev and his supporters, conversely, post-Soviet economic integration is not necessarily antithetical to Russia's increasing participation in the global economy. Rather, as Medvedev explained, creating a larger, unified market across the region will make Russia and its neighbors "attractive to foreign partners; we become understandable, predictable countries in which a common set of regulations operates."[94]

Such post-Soviet economic ties often have security consequences too, especially in the energy sector. In the Caspian littoral region, Russian investment in energy assets has overlapped with the Kremlin's broader foreign policy goals as Russian businessmen with Kremlin connections have sought to establish cartel arrangements solidifying Russia's influence over the politics and economies of the Central Asian states and coordinating their move into Central Asia.[95] This process also coincides with the Kremlin's more direct attempts to promote political and economic integration in the region by way of multilateral organizations like EurAsEC, which some Russians view as the nucleus for some kind of future political union (much as the European Coal and Steel Community laid the foundation for the eventual formation of the EU).[96] Even in the states that are not major energy players in their own right—Kyrgyzstan, Tajikistan, and (to a lesser degree) Uzbekistan—the Kremlin has moved to establish Russia as the major supplier and pipeline operator with an eye to promoting economic integration on its own terms.

With the Western powers unable to offer sufficiently attractive proposals given the political and geographic uncertainty of operating in Central Asia (and the need to satisfy shareholders), many Central Asian leaders have looked to China as a potential hedge against overweening Russian influence. With its neighboring location and nearly insatiable appetite for foreign energy, China, rather than the West, has emerged as the most important alternative pole of attraction for the Central Asian states. Beijing has tended to see Central Asia's energy infrastructure as a strategic asset for whose acquisition it is willing to pay a premium. The most notable such example is the Chinese National Petroleum Company's August 2005 decision to purchase a controlling stake in Petrokazakhstan, the largest oil company in Kazakhstan, for well above what other competitors were offering.[97] Similarly, Beijing paid the bulk of the costs associated with the construction of the oil pipeline from Turkmenistan and Uzbekistan to China that opened in December 2009.

China's interest in Central Asia is driven to a large degree by concerns about its continued ability to control its underdeveloped western province of Xinjiang, whose Muslim, Turkic Uyghur population is closely related to the Turkic peoples making up the majority of the population in Central Asia (apart from Tajikistan). Beijing initially viewed the independence of the Central Asian states as a threat to its rule over Xinjiang. Subsequently, the Chinese leadership promoted closer ties with Central Asia both to strengthen Xinjiang's economy and to give the Central Asians an incentive to avoid irredentist activities. Economic outreach to Central Asia has been an important component of Beijing's so-called Great Western Development Drive, designed to ensure that distant Xinjiang benefits from China's rapid economic growth. Chinese trade with all five Central Asian countries has multiplied several times just since the turn of the millennium.[98]

Beijing's economic influence in Central Asia is not limited to energy; indeed, with the post-2008 economic crisis limiting Russia's capacity for new foreign investment, China increasingly stepped into the breach (not just in Central Asia, but across the CIS). China's appetite for raw materials and ability to pay for infrastructure ranging from pipelines to railroads to real estate is reshaping the region's economic geography. While the resulting diversification provides the Central Asian states with more freedom of maneuver in terms of foreign policy, it also poses a significant challenge to Russia's traditional view of the region as its own sphere of "privileged interests" since the

Chinese presence is likely to prove enduring—more so than U.S. military deployments.

Despite China's growing presence in Central Asia, one area where Moscow continues to maintain an edge is as a regional security provider in Central Asia, where local elites are most willing to see Russia as a bulwark against instability—whether democratic, populist, or Islamist. The SCO is in some ways the most visible such organization, but its lack of institutionalization (the SCO does not control any troops apart from the national forces of its members) and the presence of China limit its usefulness as a vehicle for the projection of Russian power. While the SCO's main role so far has been to manage the inevitable conflicts and disagreements between Moscow and Beijing, it is the Collective Security Treaty Organization (CSTO) that has emerged as the primary vehicle for the reestablishment of Moscow's strategic influence in Central Asia—though the Central Asian states themselves are often lukewarm about the organization and its potential to cement a Russian military presence in the region.

The CSTO, which some Russian strategists tout as a kind of Eurasian NATO, joins Russia with the Central Asian states (apart from officially neutral Turkmenistan), Armenia, and Belarus. It is one of several Russian-designed multilateral organizations in the region that took on new substance in the Putin years, along with EurAsEC and the Customs Union.[99] As its name implies, the CSTO is based on the principle of collective security, with its members committed to coming to one another's aid in the event of an outside attack. It maintains a series of joint institutions, including a general staff, though its cohesiveness and degree of independence from Moscow remain in question.

The origins of the CSTO lie in the 1992 Tashkent Treaty on Collective Security, which aimed at giving the newly independent states of the CIS some kind of overarching security framework to replace the joint structures of the Soviet Union. However, throughout the 1990s, the Tashkent Treaty was little more than a pious declaration of intent, as the various states of the CIS each pursued their own interests with little coordination. Shortly after his ascension to power in 2000, President Putin proposed revitalizing the various institutions underpinning the CIS. The immediate result was an agreement on the creation of a joint CIS Counterterrorism Center based in Kyrgyzstan. The following year, CIS states agreed to set up a joint force to promote regional stability (though these forces existed mainly on paper), and in 2002 the CSTO itself was established with the aim of becoming a mechanism for coordinating intra-CIS security cooperation.

While leaving open the possibility for the new organization to cooperate with similar blocs elsewhere in the world (specifically NATO and the SCO), Moscow made clear that the CSTO was first and foremost a regional organization and part of its broader agenda for rebuilding the ties binding Russia to its former dependencies in Central Asia. Given the vast power disparity between Russia and the other members of the CSTO (a problem that takes a different form in the SCO as a result of China's immense influence), the organization has largely served as a vehicle for expanding Russian influence over its Central Asian neighbors.

Thus the CSTO has not hesitated to follow Russia's lead in staking out positions critical of the Western powers when Moscow finds itself at odds with them—even if the Central Asian states themselves have little stake in the quarrel. For instance, the organization's members adopted a collective declaration in mid-2007 criticizing NATO and the United States for planning to establish antiballistic missile defense systems in Eastern Europe, even though Russia is the only CSTO member with a missile force that could be affected by the proposed deployment.[100] Moreover, the CSTO depends on Russia for its hardware, and the Kremlin has agreed to sell military equipment to its CSTO partners at the same subsidized rate paid by the Russian military. Unconstrained by Chinese concerns, the CSTO also took a more overtly pro-Russian stance on the 2008 Georgian war than did the Shanghai Cooperation Organization—though it, too, stopped short of extending recognition to South Ossetia and Abkhazia.[101]

As its disenchantment with the SCO has grown, Moscow has increasingly vested its hopes in the CSTO as a vehicle for its ambitions of reintegrating the post-Soviet space and establishing Russia as the region's dominant security provider. At the same time, Moscow has sought to portray the CSTO as an organization with global significance, one whose participation is indispensable to everything from the war in Afghanistan to reshaping the Euro-Atlantic security architecture. At Russia's behest, the United Nations General Assembly conferred observer status on the CSTO in 2004, while UN secretary general Ban Ki-Moon and his CSTO counterpart Nikolay Bordyuzha issued a joint statement in March 2010 affirming their shared commitment to the supremacy of the UN as a source of international legitimacy and committing the UN to help the CSTO improve its peace and security promotion capabilities.[102] Moscow has also called for the CSTO to play a greater role in Afghanistan, particularly by working with NATO to combat drug trafficking into Central Asia.[103] Medvedev's proposals for revamping the Euro-Atlantic security architecture also emphasize that the CSTO should play a role, precisely in order to constrain the "NATO-centrism" that Russia views as undermining European security.

The West has been somewhat reluctant to engage with the CSTO, and particularly to accord it a status approaching equality with NATO. In part, this reluctance is due to the West's desire to maintain a leading role for NATO in both European security and Afghanistan (where it is NATO troops, not Russian, who are fighting and dying), but it also reflects on the weaknesses of the CSTO as an organization. Not only does Russia continue to play an outsize role, but many of the organization's members—notably Uzbekistan and Belarus—are profoundly skeptical that the CSTO can be anything other than an enabler of Russian imperial ambitions, and continue to hedge against the possible emergence of an overly powerful CSTO.

Moscow too is somewhat ambivalent. While eager to promote the CSTO as a major player in international security affairs and to use the organization to legitimate its influence in the post-Soviet region, Russia also appears unwilling, or unable, to assume fully the burdens of hegemony that would come with such a status. Moscow's response to the ethnic violence that roiled Kyrgyzstan in the summer of 2010 was emblematic of this dilemma: the Kremlin demurred when Kyrgyzstan's shaky post-Bakiyev transitional government asked for Russian or CSTO troops to help contain a wave of pogroms against the country's Uzbek minority, which rogue Kyrgyz security forces may have instigated. With Russia unwilling to take the lead, none of the other CSTO members even seriously considered sending their own troops. While Moscow may have had legitimate concerns that its peacekeepers would find themselves caught in the cross fire with no peace to keep, its reluctance to seriously consider deploying troops when they were expressly requested by a fellow CSTO member under the auspices of the Tashkent Treaty's collective security provision indicated that the unity of purpose and dedication to truly collective security behind NATO's Article 5 is absent in the CSTO.

CONCLUSION

While the effects of Russia's more assertive foreign policy have been felt most strongly inside the borders of the former Soviet Union, the post-Soviet republics have, for the most part, mattered to Moscow primarily insofar as they have been a contested zone between Russia and other major power blocs—the United States and Europe on the one hand, and China on the other. From Moscow's perspective, the competitive aspect has had primarily to do with a sense that outside powers, whether East or West, were taking advantage of Russian weakness to move in and damage Russia's political, economic, and security interests in the region. In this way, Russia's relations with outside powers have turned to a great degree on how secure Moscow felt its interests in the post-Soviet space to be at different moments since 1991.

Russia possesses unique advantages in the post-Soviet space relative to other parts of the world where it has attempted to exert influence since the end of the Soviet Union. The history of Russian-Soviet control has created a series of cultural, economic, and political linkages that make reliance on

Moscow a relatively familiar strategy for the Soviet-trained elites of most CIS countries. Then again, nearly two decades of independence have trained the populations of the post-Soviet states in the habits of independence, including the benefits of maneuvering between competing suitors.

Yet for the time being, the concept of a "post-Soviet space" does connote an intellectually coherent and geographically contained region with a series of political and economic peculiarities that distinguish it from the so-called Far Abroad.[104] This post-Soviet specificity facilitates Russia's leading role in the region, insofar as Russia shares these characteristics with its neighbors. Over the longer term, the emergence of a younger generation without any memory of the Soviet Union, and in many cases without widespread knowledge of the Russian language, likely portends a gradual erosion of Moscow's position, especially in distant, culturally distinct Central Asia.

The proliferation of Russian-dominated organizations such as the CSTO and EurAsEC is largely an attempt on the part of Moscow to create new frameworks for regional integration under Russian auspices. Yet the emergence of other, more economically attractive partners for the CIS states (especially the EU in the West and China in the East) makes Moscow's task that much harder. In the post-Soviet space perhaps more than anywhere else, Russia's future influence will depend to a great extent on whether the Russian economy can generate sufficient investment capital (and demand) to keep pace with the Europeans and Chinese. The success or failure of Medvedev's modernization agenda will consequently be an important factor in this vector of Russia's foreign policy as well.

Of course, Moscow has other levers of influence available to it in the post-Soviet space, including the hard power that it deployed against Georgia in 2008. Yet as the war made clear, Russia's actions inside the CIS have consequences for its relationship with the outside world, and in contrast to the situation prevailing during the Cold War, using the military to restore Russian influence locally can negatively impact Russia's global standing. In this way, Russia confronts something of a paradox. It remains the most powerful state in the CIS by far, and has levers of influence that competing powers in both the East and the West lack. Yet the more it seeks to exert its power locally, the more difficulties it encounters globally. The CIS is thus something of a litmus test for Russian foreign policy, highlighting as it does the contradiction between Russia's desires to maintain regional hegemony and to seek deeper integration and partnerships with the rest of the world.

This contradiction between regional hegemony and global influence exists only to the extent that Moscow itself forces its neighbors to choose between Russia and the outside world. Countries such as Kazakhstan, Ukraine, and even Georgia, would like to have good relations with Russia, but not at the expense of their ability to interact with the outside world at the economic, cultural, and security cooperation levels—in other words, to be fully sovereign members of the international community. Kazakhstan, which has long-standing agreements in the Caspian with Western oil companies including ExxonMobil and Chevron, has been relatively successful in balancing these competing imperatives, while Georgia and Ukraine have seen their Western aspirations touch off serious crises with Moscow. Still, it is only because the Russian elite continues to view Russia as lying outside of and apart from the West that it regards ties between CIS countries and the West as a threat to Russian interests. The ability of Western countries and institutions to progressively engage Russia will to a great extent determine whether Moscow continues to view the struggle for influence in the former Soviet Union in essentially zero-sum terms. Indeed, one notable fruit of the U.S.-Russia "reset" has been a dramatic decrease in tension across the post-Soviet space, as Washington and Moscow have come to see a much greater degree of shared interests in the region, for example, in countering the spread of drugs and terrorism from Afghanistan and coordinating their response to the ethnic violence that roiled Kyrgyzstan in late 2010.

To be sure, Russia's attempts to maintain a zone of "privileged interests" in the former Soviet Union are intimately connected with its Great Power ambitions, but at the same time constrain efforts to transform Russia into a more modern state. Maintaining a post-imperial periphery gives Russia strategic depth, insulating it from developments beyond its borders, whether democratic revolutions or the rise of Islamist extremism. It also gives Russia a bloc of states that (for the most part) continue to follow Moscow's lead on major international issues, even if their loyalty must be purchased with cheap energy and discounted weapons.

The post-Soviet space also serves as a market for Russian goods, few of which are globally competitive, but which benefit from familiarity, not to mention protectionism, within the CIS. Corruption too flourishes across CIS borders, reinforced by personal and institutional linkages dating from the Soviet era. Nontransparent energy trading companies such as RosUkrEnergo in Ukraine funnel profits to political elites in multiple countries, creating a community of interests among corrupt politicians across the post-Soviet region. In this way, the existence of a zone of "privileged interests" reinforces the existence and power of Kremlin, Inc., which would be badly weakened by the openness that participation in European (or global) economic institutions demands. Meanwhile, democratization threatens these cozy arrangements between elites, which is one important reason Moscow has opposed uncontrolled political change in other post-Soviet countries.

To succeed, Medvedev's modernization agenda would ultimately require Russia to rethink the nature of its relationship with the rest of the post-Soviet world, especially insofar as modernization demands prioritizing ties with the developed countries of the West, a step that Medvedev's call for "modernization alliances" at least contemplates. Drawing foreign investment into Russia (especially outside the energy sector) requires openness and transparency. It also means producing higher-value-added products for sale on the global market, which implies moving away from preferential arrangements with neighboring states that benefit Russia's inefficient state and oligarchic-owned companies.

This conundrum lies at the heart of the debate in Russia over joining the WTO, with opponents pressing for regional economic integration in the context of EurAsEC, the Customs Union, or the proposed Single Economic Space as an alternative to Russia's individual membership in the global trade body. Likewise, Moscow's decision to subsidize oil and gas sales to its neighbors both serves as an inducement for those states to remain in the Russian orbit and reinforces the community of interest among corrupt elites across post-Soviet borders.

Finally, for modernization to succeed, Russia will need some degree of political liberalization, if only to create confidence in Russian judicial and administrative institutions among foreign investors. Liberalization has often proven a slippery slope, and it seems unlikely Moscow would be in a position to effectively resist the spread of democratic impulses in neighboring states if Russia itself is undergoing a process of liberalization (as happened when the *perestroika*-era Soviet Union permitted the wave of democratization that swept over Eastern Europe in the late 1980s). Conversely, as long as Russia itself remains largely authoritarian, a wave of democratization in Russia's post-Soviet neighbors represents a threat to Russian influence and indeed to the Russian political system (Moscow's aversion to Saakashvili is in part due to fears of his example). Under these circumstances, Moscow will remain starkly opposed to renewed colored revolutions, which could again become a significant source of tension with the West.

Even though Moscow sparked the war with Georgia to check the expansion of Western influence in the region and bolster its own claim to major power status, its strategy was only partially successful, given the economic turmoil and isolation that Russia itself endured afterward.[105] The war was in many ways a wake-up call to both Russia and its Western rivals that their struggle for influence was dangerously destabilizing. In the war's aftermath, the West appears to have moderated its ambitions in the post-Soviet space (for instance on NATO expansion), while Russia appears to recognize that sacrificing its ties to the West for the sake of a dubious regional hegemony does not aid Russia's campaign to be taken seriously as a powerful and respected state. Russia has not jettisoned its view of the former Soviet Union as an area where Russian influence should predominate, but it is increasingly conscious of the limits of its power in the region, as well as of the need to make itself a more attractive partner for its neighbors so that it will not have to use force to enforce its claim to a leading role.

Whether Russia and the West can work collaboratively inside the former Soviet Union will in many ways be the most important test of whether the rapprochement Medvedev appears to be pursuing with the U.S. and Europe will prove substantive and lasting. Outside powers (not only the West, but also China) are increasingly active in the post-Soviet space, a development Russia simply lacks the capacity to reverse. Along with making itself a more attractive partner, for instance by investing in modernization projects in neighboring states and establishing joint ventures that facilitate technology transfers, Russia needs to find ways of working in tandem with other powers in this most sensitive of regions if the dual promises of modernization and reconciliation are ever to be fulfilled.

Conclusion

Dealing with Russia's Foreign Policy Reawakening

The 2008 war with Georgia was a pivotal moment for Russia and Russian foreign policy. On the one hand, the war marked the culmination of long-established trends, as Russia forcefully demonstrated its claim to a zone of "privileged interests" and its capacity to act autonomously on the global stage. After years of clamoring for recognition as a Great Power, Russia's invasion and crushing victory served notice that the rest of the world (post-Soviet neighbors as well as the West) could no longer afford to ignore Russian interests. Yet the war also highlighted the limitations of both Russia's capabilities and its foreign policy vision. The war might have stopped (at least for a time) further NATO expansion, and forced the U.S. to reengage on issues Moscow considered central, including arms control and European security, but it also left Russia isolated from even its closest allies and, by contributing to economic turmoil, threatened the very growth and stability on which the country's international ambitions rested.

Just a few months later came the "reset" with the United States. The Obama administration offered Russia much of what its leadership desired: de facto acknowledgment of Russia's leading role across the former Soviet Union, an end to NATO expansion, reconfiguration of Washington's planned missile defense system (and the prospect, advanced at the November 2010 NATO-Russia Council summit in Lisbon, of collaborative missile defense), unequivocal support for membership in the WTO, and a push to deepen bilateral economic relations. The reset strategy worked in large part because Russia itself was at a far different place by early 2009 than it had been six months earlier. Having stopped NATO expansion and given substance to its claim of privileged interests in the post-Soviet space, Russia's leaders consciously rejected attempts to further extend the Russian sphere of influence, choosing instead to once again focus on the country's internal problems.[1] Washington's reset policy, which acknowledged Russia's Great Power aspirations and sought to give Moscow a greater say in global security issues, allowed the Russian leadership to make this pivot without sacrificing their commitment to ensuring that Moscow's voice was heard on a wide range of international security issues.

The war also changed the contours of the foreign policy debate within Russia, as its leaders were forced to rethink what, precisely, being a Great Power meant in the twenty-first century. While Russia's resurgence under Putin was not explicitly anti-Western, it was the cause of frequent disputes with Washington and its European allies. Though Putin's Russia generally sought good relations with the West, it also came to believe that it was powerful and influential enough to operate internationally without regard for the West if necessary. The postwar economic crisis forced Moscow to recognize the degree to which its economy was already bound to the West, and imparted a new urgency to Medvedev's message of economic modernization—a process for which Western cooperation was critical.

The attainment of Russia's Great Power ambitions requires the rest of the world to give Moscow the deference it feels is due as one of the leading world powers. The failure to give Russia the seat at the table its elite has long desired has been a leading cause of Russian resentment and revisionism toward the post–Cold War international order. Indeed, the Georgian war cannot be understood without reference to the whole series of perceived slights Moscow endured at the West's hands since the end of the Cold War, with NATO expansion and the struggle over Kosovo's independence having the most direct bearing on the conflict with Georgia. To understand Russia's foreign policy behavior, the substance—or validity—of these objections is in a sense less important than the very fact of their prominence within elite discourse. Of course, Moscow has objected to a range of policy choices undertaken by outside powers (especially the West) since the breakup of the Soviet Union. August 2008, however, was the first time Russia used force outside its own borders to challenge a key premise of the West's post–Cold War international security agenda—namely, the expansion of NATO into the former Soviet Union.

Between Moscow's hatred of Saakashvili, interest in keeping the frozen conflicts frozen, and opposition to NATO expansion—not to mention frequent signals that it would regard Georgian (or Ukrainian) membership in the alliance as a redline—the war with Georgia should not have been the complete surprise it was. The extent of Russian military preparations and the steady campaign to raise tensions in both South Ossetia and Abkhazia in the weeks leading up to the conflict also attest to a high degree of preparation on the Russian side. Moscow may not have known when

Saakashvili would try to seize the breakaway provinces, but it seemed intent on provoking him to do so—a trap about which the U.S. and other Georgian allies repeatedly cautioned him.[2] If the timing of Saakashvili's ill-conceived move into South Ossetia was contingent, the broader forces at work were not. By August 2008, many Russians had come to believe that the country's post-Soviet recovery had succeeded, and that the economic upheavals of the 1990s and the decay of Russian military power had been reversed during the period of consolidation under Putin.

Even during the 1990s, Russian elites regarded the Near Abroad as a zone of special interest and responsibility, a point Medvedev made explicitly in the aftermath of the war. Russia's temporary cession of initiative to outside powers in the region was therefore always more a result of Russian weakness than any sort of more fundamental transformation in the nature of the Russian state or the way its leadership identified its interests.

Those interests have been strongly determined by Russia's history. Lacking both natural frontiers and ethnic cohesion, Russia's borders have long expanded and contracted with the power of the state. Since Ivan the Terrible conquered the Muslim khanates of Kazan and Astrakhan in the mid-sixteenth century, Russian foreign policy has been defined by outward expansion in search of secure borders and access to trade routes. This pattern persisted into the twentieth century, which saw Russia's attempt to seize the Dardanelles and Poland during World War I, the conquest of Eastern Europe during World War II, and even the failed attempt to keep Afghanistan in the Soviet orbit in 1979.

Sometimes this drive to expand outstripped the economic, political, and military capabilities of the state, with catastrophic results. Like the Russian Empire in 1917, the Soviet Union in the mid-1980s found that its imperial commitments exceeded its capacity to sustain them. Facing rising opposition to Communist rule in Eastern Europe and military defeat in Afghanistan, Mikhail Gorbachev made the bitter but necessary decision to embark on a period of retrenchment. Gorbachev ordered Soviet troops out of Afghanistan and told his counterparts in East Germany, Poland, and elsewhere that the Red Army would no longer prop them up. Without their Soviet minders, these Communist outposts crumbled with astonishing rapidity in the summer and fall of 1989. The process of disintegration soon spread to the Soviet Union itself, and Soviet troops next found themselves called on to put down demonstrations in Tbilisi, Vilnius, and elsewhere on the USSR's fringes. But the empire, as then constituted, could not be saved.

Even without the other fourteen Soviet republics, today's Russian Federation remains a patchwork reflecting the centuries-long process of expansion that created it. To an ethnic Russian in Moscow, the distinction between North Ossetia, a constituent republic of the Russian Federation, and South Ossetia, which was part of the now independent state of Georgia, could seem somewhat arbitrary (recall too Putin's remark that "Ukraine is not even a state"). Indeed, the entire CIS, whose economy was intimately tied to that of Russia and whose populations shared a common Soviet (and largely Russophone) culture, remains bonded to Moscow by a common past, and in those states with a significant Russian population, by ties of ethnicity. Two decades after the Soviet collapse, those bonds have only partially loosened.

Establishing a new paradigm for relations between the Russian Federation and the other republics of the former USSR in many ways highlights the contradiction between Russia's imperial past and its attempts to cast itself as a Great Power in a postimperial world. Though Putin famously argued that the collapse of the USSR was "the greatest geopolitical catastrophe of the [twentieth] century," he recognized as well as anyone that restoring some semblance of the Soviet—or Russian—Empire was neither possible nor desirable from the perspective of Russia's own international ambitions.[3] Nonetheless, Russia's post-Soviet neighbors remain jealous of their sovereignty and worried that Russia has not fully internalized the permanence of their existence as independent states. The colored revolutions, especially those in Ukraine and Georgia, marked a crisis of legitimacy for Russian influence in the former Soviet Union, even as that influence was coming under pressure from the stepped-up American, European, and Chinese presence, as well as the consolidation of non-Russian (or even anti-Russian) national identities within many of the post-Soviet successor states. Moscow's decision to move to market prices for gas sales to the CIS states, a step precipitated by the fiasco of its attempts to head off the Orange Revolution, were critical in moving toward normal interstate relations between Russia and its former imperial dependencies.

Even in its conflict with Georgia, Moscow did not follow an explicitly imperial strategy. It refused calls to annex South Ossetia and Abkhazia, which were left in a kind of legal and political limbo (despite Moscow's hasty decision to recognize them as independent states). Nor did Russian forces advance on Tbilisi, much less seek to incorporate Georgia itself into the Russian state. Russian bête noire Saakashvili remained in office (though Moscow sought to undermine his authority, which was waning anyway as a result of the suffering brought on by his own rashness). For all these reasons, Georgia in 2008 was not Kazan in 1552, or even Czechoslovakia in 1968. If anything, Russia's actions in the Caucasus looked much more like the kind of interventions long undertaken by the U.S. in Latin America or France in La Francophonie, that is, the actions of a large state claiming the right to have friendly governments in its backyard, even if they must be installed or propped up by force. The real analogue to Russia's invasion of Georgia was less Kosovo (as the Russians charged) than the U.S. invasions of Grenada or Panama in the 1980s, or France's long history of intervention across Africa. What was different was Tbilisi's close ties to the U.S., and the crisis in U.S.-Russian relations that resulted from the war.

Of course, it was not just the U.S. that objected to Russia's actions in Georgia. Even China cautioned Moscow about the danger it was courting if it pushed too far. For Russia, a country with an almost insatiable desire to be taken seriously as a pillar of the international order, sacrificing relations with its most important partners merely to teach the Georgians a lesson would be a step of breathtaking rashness. Foreign diplomats, including U.S. Secretary of State Rice, cautioned Moscow that the larger goals it had sought for a decade-plus to attain were at risk because of its poorly conceived decision to attack Georgia.[4] Russia's convoluted response to such foreign pressure was an indication that strong divisions continue to exist in Moscow about whether to prioritize relations with the outside world or to emphasize Russia's special role inside the former Soviet Union.

The Medvedev-era rapprochement with the West is premised on trying to reconcile these two competing approaches. While the war in Georgia left the West more reluctant to challenge Russia's leading role in the post-Soviet space, Medvedev's Russia has also been more receptive to collaboration in the region, even if serious disputes remain. The most important collaborative efforts have focused on Afghanistan. These include joint projects in the fields of counterterrorism and counternarcotics, as well as logistical support encompassing both the NATO-operated Northern Distribution Network and a series of bilateral air transit agreements involving the major Western powers, Russia, and the Central Asian states. These agreements, which allow the U.S. and its allies to reduce their dependence on vulnerable supply routes through Pakistan, have helped change the tenor of U.S.-Russian relations in Central Asia—in part because of the revenue Russia is able to generate from transit fees, and in part because the U.S. was able to show that its involvement in Central Asia had direct security benefits for Russia itself. In consequence, Russian pressure on Kyrgyzstan to expel U.S. forces from Manas (which acts as a critical transit hub for flights into Afghanistan) faded.

The real question is whether cooperation in Afghanistan represents an exception to a still largely competitive dynamic in the post-Soviet space, or a harbinger of greater cooperation in the future. In important ways, the West and Russia continue to have incompatible visions and priorities for the region, including on the question of democratization. Russia continues to oppose OSCE efforts to conduct vigorous election monitoring, and has even sponsored a competing group of observers under the auspices of the CIS (which has repeatedly given a pass to farcical elections, such as the violence-marred presidential poll in Belarus in December 2010). On security issues, though, the picture is more positive. Beside cooperation on

Afghan transit, the Western powers and Russia are working together inside the CIS on subjects including nuclear security, counterterrorism, and counternarcotics. They are also discussing holding more joint military exercises, and potentially collaborating on missile defense. These efforts remain nascent and reversible, but if pursued diligently, could provide a foundation for further institutionalizing cooperation across the post-Soviet space and fundamentally changing the dynamic of Russia's relationship with the West, given the centrality of the post-Soviet space to Russia's strategic aims.

Nonetheless, the debate between Eurasianists and others remains very much a part of the Russian political scene. This debate is at once about the proper vector for Russian foreign policy, but at the same time, it reflects differing understandings of how to attain that which the bulk of the Russian elite desires, namely, for Russia to be acknowledged and respected as a serious international actor. For the Eurasianists, who appear to have played a key role in fomenting and propagating the conflict in Georgia (South Ossetian "president" Eduard Kokoity is a member of Dugin's International Eurasianist Movement, and Dugin himself championed both the war and Russia's decision to recognize the breakaway enclaves; he may even have drafted Medvedev's five-point speech laying out Russia's claim to "privileged interests" in the former Soviet Union), the war was a vindication of their belief that the West will take Russia seriously only when Russia stands up for itself.[5] Even after the war, Dugin favored an intensification of Russian pressure on Georgia and across the South Caucasus, which he sees as the front line in an American attempt to encircle and destroy Russia as a Great Power.[6]

The Eurasianists and their supporters in government were generally indifferent to how the West responded to the invasion of Georgia, or to attempts to reassert Russian dominance within the borders of the former Soviet Union by economic, cultural, and institutional means. They did not see integration with Western-dominated institutions like the WTO as holding any particular value to Russia anyway. Most of them would just as soon proceed with the construction of a statist, corporatist, and autarkic economic system based on a state-controlled energy sector and a series of newly created state conglomerates (many controlled by *siloviki*) in fields including weapons production, nanotechnology, high-tech exports, atomic energy, infrastructure construction, banking, and utilities.[7] An attempt to alter the geopolitical status quo, like attempting to fast-track Georgia and Ukraine for membership in NATO, would give them an opening to intensify the conflict over the fate of other parts of the CIS. Given the West's anemic response to the invasion of Georgia, the Eurasianists are confident further instability in the region would only play into their hands. Ukraine in particular could fragment if forced to decide once and for all whether to throw in its lot with Russia or with NATO, and Dugin's followers would be happy to encourage the process of fragmentation if the West gives them an opportunity to do so.[8]

For the opponents of Eurasianism, the critical imperative in the war's aftermath was to contain the fallout on Russia's broader international relationships. Putin and Medvedev did not appear to see the war as a fundamental reversal of Russia's strategy of seeking good relations with the West to the extent that doing so is in line with the broader objective of promoting Russia's claim to major power status. Arguments against the war, or at least arguments in favor of its sharp limitation, focused on the need for Russia to maintain its position as a respected member of the international community.[9]

While Russian troops appeared initially to be staying in (uncontested) Georgian territory in violation of the cease-fire agreement negotiated by French president Sarkozy, their gradual withdrawal coupled with attempts on the part of Putin and Medvedev to turn down the heat in their exchanges with the Western powers showed the limited appetite for Dugin's schemes at the top levels of power. The war notwithstanding, Putin and Medvedev made clear almost immediately that they wanted to continue cooperating with the United States in Afghanistan, where they perceived the resurgence of the Taliban as a direct threat to their own interests; that they wanted to continue making progress on the arms control agenda; and that they wanted to continue pursuing economic integration despite the suspension of some commitments made in the course of WTO ascension talks.[10] Dugin's talk of an almost apocalyptic confrontation between Russia and the United States was never realistic, as most Kremlin officials understood.[11] Indeed, the Kremlin responded enthusiastically barely six months later when U.S. Vice President Biden offered to "press the reset button" on U.S.-Russian relations.

If the conflict in Georgia was partially about vindicating Russians' belief in their special responsibility for the area of the former Soviet Union, it was also about changing the contours of Russia's relationship with the West. For nearly two decades, the fundamental challenge confronting Russian diplomacy lay in figuring out how to manage relations with a West that was at the end of the Cold War the world's dominant political, military, economic, and ideological bloc. Much of what the West stood for—prosperity, stability, and security—was appealing to Russians fresh off the tumultuous experience of the Soviet 1980s. The trade-offs that would have been necessary for Russia to truly join the West were however more than the country's political class was willing to make—in contrast to post-Communist states like Poland and Hungary, with their history of democratic rule in the interwar era, recent experiences of Russian domination, and indeed centuries of experience as part of the Catholic/Protestant West. Further complicating the strategic landscape was the fact that the

West continued expanding ever closer to Russia's borders during a period when Russia was still battling its own post-Soviet demons.

The 9/11 attacks provided Moscow with an opening to fundamentally reframe the nature of its relationship with the West, by suggesting that the Chechen conflict was part of a larger struggle between radical Islamism and a secular, pluralistic worldview shared by Russia and the Western powers. The attacks allowed Russia, with Putin in the lead, to argue that the fundamental distinction in world politics was no longer between the West and the non-West, but between those who abetted terrorists and those who did not, a framework that fit neatly with George W. Bush's famous statement that "either you are with us, or you are with the terrorists." By offering its cooperation, Moscow was aiming to, in Medvedev's words, "once and for all put an end to the division in the world that was created by the Cold War"—but in a way that maintained Russia's ability to act autonomously on the international stage and maintain its influence in the post-Soviet space.[12]

By adopting Bush's global war on terror as an organizing principle for relations with the West, Putin attempted to refashion the relationship from one based on integration to one based on the idea of a partnership of equals. Russia would not be hectored about its pummeling of Chechnya, any more than it would hector Washington about the latter's tactics in Afghanistan or indefinite detentions of prisoners at Guantanamo Bay. Moscow would cooperate with Washington's efforts to oust the Taliban—including by granting access to facilities in Central Asia—but it would do so as a matter of choice and with the right to terminate its cooperation when it no longer served Russian interests. Looking back on Primakov's promotion of multipolarity as a description of the structure of international relations, Russia would energetically assert its position as a pole.

Nonetheless, the Russian leadership was smart enough to realize that even in a multipolar world, all poles are not created equal. Only the U.S. had the capacity to be a truly global power, capable of projecting significant force far from its borders, as in Afghanistan, Iraq, and elsewhere. Russia, however well it had recovered from the ravages of the 1990s, was not in that league. Unlike the Soviet Union, it would not therefore seek to project its power and influence globally. It would, in fact, stand down from some of its more far-flung commitments, such as the military outposts it had inherited at Cam Ranh Bay, Vietnam, and Lourdes, Cuba. It would, though, proclaim its special interest in the former Soviet Union and demand that the United States, the European Union, and even China respect its primacy in that region. And since the partnership on offer after 9/11 was a classic bit of realpolitik, Moscow would not allow its new partners to intervene with their liberal democratic moralizing inside the Russian sphere of influence. Unlike the Kozyrev era, Putin's offer of partnership was not based on the idea of Russia seeking integration in the existing security architecture, but on an agreement negotiated between states with a limited range of common interests.

This post-9/11 partnership proved fleeting, both because changes in Russia's domestic political landscape moved the country further away from the value-laden Western community, and because the U.S. approach to the war on terror left little room for partners to assert their own interests. At the same time, Russia's recovery from the economic chaos sparked by the 1998 crash increasingly convinced Russia's leadership that it had other options. The roughly eight years between 9/11 and Biden's announcement of the reset were a wasted opportunity for both Russia and the West. Unwilling to offer positive inducements for cooperation or to defer to Russian priorities in the fields of arms control and international security, the West allowed its influence with Russia to dissipate. Russia, meanwhile, increasingly isolated itself by pursuing an aggressive foreign policy inside the former Soviet Union that cemented its reputation as a revisionist, rejectionist power not interested in offering practical solutions to problems of common interest. The continued sparring over the post-Soviet space and old challenges like arms control prevented the West and Russia from developing positive-sum approaches to newer problems such as climate change and the weakness of global financial markets. Still stuck in a twentieth-century mind-set, both sides missed an opportunity to work collaboratively against their common twenty-first-century challenges.

To the extent that Putin's Russia had a grand strategy, its hallmarks were state-driven economic development, the employment of Russia's new-found wealth to rebuild the foundations of national power (military, political, and economic), and a concerted effort to minimize conflicts with the other Great Powers to allow Russia time to recover from the upheavals of the 1990s. If anything, Medvedev went further down this path with his argument that foreign policy should serve the cause of economic development, not vice versa. Russia, of course, had followed a similar pattern after past catastrophes like the Crimean War or the Russo-Japanese War. It is hardly accidental then that contemporary Russian statesmen seek to emulate such prerevolutionary predecessors as Gorchakov and Stolypin.

Yet neither the tsarist nor the Soviet experience offers modern Russia a fully viable foreign policy model. The Russian Empire was an expansionary power in a largely prenationalist world. The tsars continually pushed Russia's frontiers outward, impervious to considerations of ethnicity. From the sixteenth to the nineteenth centuries, Russia's borders continually expanded, taking in groups from Poles in the west to Mongols and Evenks in the east. The emergence of modern nationalism in the second half of the nineteenth century was a development for which Imperial Russia, like the German, Austrian, and Turkish empires, was ill prepared. Unlike those states however, Russia continues to exist with some version of its imperial form in the twenty-first century (i.e., while the Magyars and Croats have long since broken away from Vienna, the Tatars, Evenks, and others remain subject to Moscow).

In the course of the nineteenth century, nationalism emerged not only among the minority peoples of the Russian Empire, but among its largest ethnic contingent, the Russians themselves. This development of nationalism as a political force among Russians and others spelled the end for the empire's traditional strategy of expansion and amalgamation on the basis of dynastic loyalty. Russian nationalism was long subsumed by the multinational Soviet Union, which downgraded the national claims of ethnic Russians in the interest of reconciling the country's non-Russian population to Soviet rule. The Soviet Union could function as an empire precisely because it claimed to be non-Russian. Despite its occasionally violent manifestations, the reemergence of Russian ethnic nationalism as a potent force in modern Russian politics and society reflects the transition away from an imperial identity in favor of belief in a self-contained national state—a development that creates its own problems in the multiethnic, multiconfessional Russian Federation.[13] If anything, the forceful assertion of Russian nationalism makes the further contraction of Russia's borders (especially in the North Caucasus) more likely than their further expansion—in general agreement with the position of the DPNI and other ethnonationalist groups.

If nationalism does not offer a viable basis for Russian foreign policy, neither does the Eurasianism of Dugin and his followers. Lacking a doctrine to replace Marxism-Leninism as an alternative to globalization, Russia cannot rally far-flung allies behind a common worldview as its Soviet predecessor did. Eurasianism as such has few adherents outside the former Soviet Union; within the former USSR, more states worry about a potential Russian threat to their independence than about alleged Western designs to contain Russia. Even countries seeking to break away from dependence on the U.S. or the West more broadly do not see Russia as a viable alternative the way members of the Communist Bloc (and much of the Non-Aligned Movement) did during the Cold War.

Globally, the most powerful challenge to liberalism and capitalism is posed by radical Islam. Though Russia has on the order of twenty million Muslim inhabitants, a country that consciously appropriates symbols of Orthodox Christianity (such as the three-barred cross impaling an Islamic crescent found atop many Russian churches) and that is more than 80 percent Orthodox cannot aspire to a leading role in an international Islamist movement merely to spite the West. And despite Samuel Huntington's worries about Orthodoxy forming the nucleus of a non-Western civilizational identity, the Orthodox world is far too fragmented and too heterogeneous to consolidate into an anti-Western bloc. Greece, Bulgaria, and Romania are already members of both the EU and NATO; Cyprus is in the EU; and Serbia, Macedonia, and Montenegro are knocking on the door of both organizations.[14]

One other possible way Russia could seek to create a counterhegemonic bloc of states is on the basis of authoritarianism itself. Some scholars have noted that as democracy becomes an increasingly important factor uniting its practitioners, nondemocratic states find they have a common interest in preventing the spread of democracy.[15] Indeed, Russia and, especially, China have found themselves on the same side of a number of critical international issues, in part for this reason. Moscow and Beijing share an aversion to the notions of humanitarian intervention and democracy promotion. Both prefer to work through the UN Security Council, which gives them the power to veto initiatives they see as threatening. Both moved to block the U.S.-led invasion of Iraq as well as intervention in Sudan's Darfur region out of a desire to preserve the veneer of absolute sovereignty protecting even the most odious regimes from interference in their internal affairs. Through organizations like the SCO, Russia and China have formed a group that to some appears the nucleus of a new authoritarian international.

Yet authoritarianism as such is hardly an idea capable of forming a broad international consensus. China, for instance, may have a political system that denies the public much in the way of meaningful participation in government. In some ways, however, China's view of the international order has more in common with that of the Western powers than with that of Russia.[16] Political upheaval, of the sort Russia unleashed with its invasion of Georgia, is inimical to the Chinese belief in order and stability as the essential factors enabling it to achieve a peaceful rise. Beijing was appalled by the hypocrisy of Russia's Georgian adventure; as the Chinese recognized, to matter as principles in international relations, state sovereignty and inviolability have to apply equally as much to Georgia as they do to Serbia or Iraq. With its own separatist dramas in Tibet and Taiwan, China had no interest in legitimating Russian-sponsored territorial revisionism.

At the same time, in contrast to China, Russia does not reject democracy as such—indeed, it argues (perhaps disingenuously) that the current semi-authoritarian political system is a temporary way station on the way to full democracy. The recognition that Russia's system of government is not viable in the long term has become more widespread within the elite during Medvedev's presidency, and particularly in the aftermath of the global economic crisis. Even in its current state, Russia counts among its closest partners several established democracies, such as Germany. Authoritarianism is in any case simply not a coherent worldview like Marxism-Leninism (and even when Marxism-Leninism still mattered, the Sino-Soviet split demonstrated how national rivalries could crop up independent of ideological affinity). And while authoritarianism as such may never disappear, individual authoritarian regimes are often fleeting, as the wave of unrest across the Middle East in early 2011 showed.

The last remaining possible partners for a Russia that seeks to challenge the prevailing global order as the Soviet Union once did are those states that have by their own behavior isolated themselves from the international mainstream. Iran under its theocratic regime is one option (and one in which Dugin places particular hopes). Still, Iran is unstable, its "mullahocracy" deeply unpopular. With his decision to support sanctions in the UN Security Council and cancel the delivery of the Russian S-300 antiaircraft system to Iran, Medvedev explicitly acknowledged that Russia's relationship with Washington mattered more than its relationship with Tehran. In a generation, Iran may in any case look much different from its present incarnation. Other rogue states, such as North Korea, are in even worse shape. Hugo Chávez's Venezuela has been happy to buy Russian weaponry, but is economically fragile and at best a third-rate power. Most importantly, a partnership with global outcasts on the basis of opposition to American, or liberal Atlanticist, hegemony would be a strange way for Russia to pursue its long-standing aim of becoming a powerful and respected member of the global community.

In short, Russia has few choices apart from seeking some kind of modus vivendi with the existing world order in which the United States is gradually losing its unquestioned dominance but is nonetheless the leading power and, in partnership with Europe, China, Japan, and others, operates an increasingly globalized economy. Autarkic fantasies may of course appeal to some Russians, but certainly those who like their bank accounts in Switzerland or Cyprus and their villas in London understand what they stand to lose were Russia to retreat from the Atlanticist world that so many of Dugin's acolytes condemn. Russia is not, and may never be, part of the West as such, but its only choice is between isolation and increasing irrelevance on the one hand, and seeking to participate, Chinese-style, in a system it did not design but from which it can nonetheless benefit on the other. In his more multilateralist moments, Putin has made clear his preference for a Russia that follows this path to prosperity and respect.

Medvedev, the lawyer, has been even more pronounced in his calls for Russia to pursue economic integration even as it seeks its own cultural, geopolitical, and institutional path.[17] Such integration must, however, occur on Russian terms. In other words, Moscow is reluctant to accept membership in organizations and regimes it had no say in designing. Even with the WTO, Moscow has frequently pressed for exceptions to the group's rules, arguing that its size entitles it to special treatment. Likewise, Medvedev has pushed insistently for Russia to play a larger role in European security, but rather than use NATO or the OSCE as a platform, insists on a new formulation that would allow Russia to be "present at the creation." Medvedev's goal has been, and remains, partnership with the West, but only on terms acceptable to Russia—which is to say on terms that Russia itself has a hand in defining.

Two interconnected dangers threaten this vision: the rise of rejectionist sentiment among important elements of the Russian elite, and a misplaced desire to punish and isolate Russia on the part of the West. The war in Georgia was dangerous precisely because it strengthened both of these tendencies. Taking advantage of the power transition in Moscow, Eurasianist hard-liners seem to have sensed an opportunity to go after Saakashvili, striking a blow at his patrons in the West at the same time. After some initial vacillation, the untested Medvedev fell into line, such that even Dugin was driven to praise the new president's tough response.[18] That even Russia's president, a man invested with enormous constitutional powers on paper, could not overawe or outmaneuver those who would embark Russia on such a perilous adventure does not speak well for the balance of forces in the Kremlin's hall of mirrors. Once the consequences of the war for Russia's international standing and economic stability had become clear, however, Medvedev actively sought to reassure the West (and Western investors) of Russia's commitment to stability, order, and progress.

Yet the Western impulse to only blame Moscow for the Georgia crisis (and other moments of tension) risks merely emboldening atavistic forces inside Russia itself while making more difficult collaboration in pursuit of common interests. To be fair, the Bush administration was relatively careful to point out Saakashvili's own poor judgment and excessive use of force against South Ossetia as factors contributing to the conflict and was very limited in its attempts to punish the Russians. The most substantive step, withdrawal of an accord on civilian nuclear cooperation (the so-called 123 Agreement) from consideration by Congress, would have affected the U.S. as much as Russia, and was quickly reversed by Barack Obama when he became president. Still, insofar as the war came in the midst of an election season in the United States, it facilitated much posturing by political candidates eager to demonstrate their toughness— American missteps in the war on terror and in Iraq having not entirely succeeded in convincing the U.S. political class that toughness and statesmanship are not always the same. Prominent among the proposed U.S. responses were suggestions to expel Russia from the G8, abolish the NATO-Russia Council, or fast-track NATO membership for Ukraine and Georgia.[19] Given the legacy of the Cold War, the U.S. in particular suffers from an unfortunate tendency to exaggerate Russian malfeasance and fall back almost reflexively on policies designed to contain and punish Russia at moments of tension. When Russian commentators complain about a Western double standard, they often have a point.

Even though most Russians were skeptical that Obama could rapidly bring about an improvement in ties between Washington and Moscow, they appreciated that his election offered an opportunity to break with many of the failed policies of the past. Indeed, with his reset policy and attempts to suffuse the U.S.-Russian relationship with substance beyond the traditional hard security agenda, Obama (along with the fallout from the war in Georgia) has played a significant role in facilitating the reorientation of Russian policy toward the West in the direction of greater collaboration. Seeking to isolate Russia, as Obama's 2008 opponent John McCain and many other U.S. politicians and academics called for (and as many congressional Republicans still favor), would indeed send a clear message to Moscow—namely, that the West is unwilling to live with and accommodate itself to a powerful Russia. The triumph of this approach in the West would only push Russia further toward the isolation and autarky favored by the likes of Dugin, while undermining stability across the wide swathes of Europe and Eurasia where Russia sees itself as having vital interests.

While it can do little to affect Russia's domestic development, the West has a much greater capacity to shape Russian international behavior—for either good or ill. NATO expansion is perhaps the most salient example from the past two decades of how, with the best of intentions, Western leaders succeeded in marginalizing Russia and succoring the most atavistic, anti-Western elements of the Russian elite. The stronger Russia of the early twenty-first century will need to be handled with much greater care than the West paid to the decrepit Russia of the 1990s. The United States and Europe need to show Russia that it can have what it most craves—respect, recognition, and responsibility for upholding order around the world—without having to resort to force or threats of force to make itself heard. A Russia that feels itself backed into a corner and in need of lashing out isolates itself (as during the war in Georgia) but also creates suffering and instability for others.

The most fundamental challenge for the West will be developing a forward-looking agenda for cooperation with Russia (i.e., moving beyond solving problems left over from the Cold War to regularly collaborating in pursuit of common interests). Leaders on both sides need to think harder about the role Russia can play in addressing global and nontraditional security threats, in areas such as climate change and the spread of radicalism in the Islamic world; Russia, after all, has the largest Muslim population in Europe, and outside of the increasingly radical North Caucasus, Russian Muslims are largely moderate and assimilated to living in a secular society. Medvedev's interest in turning Moscow into an international financial center seems highly ambitious (possibly dubious), but it nonetheless provides an opportunity for Russia to participate in the crafting of new rules governing global finance in the aftermath of the 2008 crisis.

A second major challenge will be fitting Russia into Europe's evolving institutional web. Ever since Peter the Great ordered his boyars to cut their beards and trade their caftans for suits, Russia has struggled to define its identity as a state (and a civilization) between Europe and Asia. Momentous as the end of the Cold War was, it was hardly sufficient to achieve that which Peter and his successors never fully accomplished and make Russia into a truly Western country. Yet merely by virtue of its location, Russia is inextricably linked to European security, and Europe will never be secure as long as it has a frustrated, revisionist Russia on its borders. The existing model of European security, in which NATO is the only game in town (apart from the ineffectual OSCE), cannot fully integrate Russia, and therefore fails to fulfill its most fundamental aim of ensuring the security of its members—not to mention nonmembers like Georgia.

Without abandoning its unique identity or Great Power aspirations, Russia can play a constructive role in the world. With its logistical and security assistance in Afghanistan, it is increasingly doing so. It will continue to play that role on its own terms, which for now means a rejection of norms-based institutions in favor of bilateral relationships and Great Power bargaining, and a focus on power maximization attained, for now, largely through channeling energy rents to the state.

Dealing with this Russia will require the West to reach out to Moscow, seeking to make it a partner in promoting mutual security wherever possible. It also requires the West to be firm about its own values and identity. The West's success has been as much a result of its commitment to democracy, the rule of law, and political liberalism as anything else. Western leaders should not compromise on these fundamental values, including in their dealings with Russia. Europe, for instance, should look skeptically at Gazprom's dealings on the Continent not because Gazprom is Russian, but because it is a nontransparent monopolist. There is no need for Europe to discriminate against Gazprom or other Russian companies as long as the Europeans are clear and consistent about enforcing their own laws, whether the target is Gazprom or Microsoft.

At best, the West is beginning to grope its way forward, drawing Russia into the coalition of states working to secure Afghanistan and laying the foundation for preliminary cooperation on missile defense as a basis for reshaping the European security landscape (a priority for Moscow). Still, these steps are tentative, ad hoc, and reversible, especially with a less forward leaning leader in the White House than Barack Obama. Medvedev's warning that Russia and the West will find themselves embroiled in a new arms race if the promise of missile defense cooperation proves empty deserves to be taken very seriously.[20] That development would be tragic, since the major challenges facing both Russia and the West in the twenty-first century are much broader and more geographically diffuse. Russia and the West will need to collaborate in addressing both transnational problems like climate change and more traditional security threats like the rise of China. They cannot afford to be distracted by old battles over the military balance in Europe.[21]

Having too often tried to insulate themselves from Russia's maddening complexities, the U.S. and Europe need to reach out to Moscow, seeking a model of integration that simultaneously respects Russia's stature and does not require the Western powers to sacrifice their own values. Sometimes, of course, agreement will remain out of reach no matter what. Further NATO expansion may prove to be such an issue. NATO expansion need not stop simply out of deference to Russian wishes. The countries of the former Soviet Union, like their neighbors in Eastern Europe, are fully sovereign members of the international community with a right to determine their own security orientation. Geographical considerations as well as NATO's ability and willingness to provide new members with the credible security guarantee that lies at the heart of the Atlantic Alliance will matter, too. While the prospect of membership should not be automatically foreclosed for additional post-Soviet states, neither should NATO rush into admitting new members that are not ready to undertake the burdens of collective security that membership implies or whose own publics are not strongly behind ascension, such as Ukraine. NATO's current approach to expansion—keeping the door open in theory to new members but putting off actual expansion while it works to more deeply enmesh Russia in a dialogue about European security—is probably the right one.

Medvedev's proposal for some kind of pan-European security arrangement, which was made several months before the outbreak of hostilities in Georgia, is an alternative that deserves a serious hearing. To be sure, Washington and Brussels have to be careful that any Russian approach, especially to Europe, does not come at the expense of transatlantic ties or the effective functioning of NATO. For these reasons, the treaty on European security proposed by Medvedev in July 2008 has little chance of being accepted as such.[22]

Still, allowing Russia to play a more constructive role in European security—and not basing the entire notion of European security on defending the Continent's eastern borders from Russia—is an idea to which the U.S. and its allies need to give much more thought. NATO, with its proven collective security track record, clearly has to play a central role.[23] A more active effort on the part of NATO to engage and address Russia would also help build trust between Moscow and the Atlantic Alliance, especially as NATO itself evolves in line with the ideas outlined in its 2010 Strategic

Concept. And as former U.S. ambassador to Ukraine Steven Pifer notes, a process of engagement leading to better NATO-Russian relations would be among the most effective ways of ameliorating Russian hostility to further expansion.[24] NATO-Russia cooperation on missile defense also provides an opportunity to begin refocusing threat perceptions on both sides. Yet given the technical and financial obstacles to actually deploying a functional, collaborative missile defense system in the foreseeable future, both NATO and Russia need to be careful not to put all of their eggs in the missile defense basket, and develop similar externally focused ideas in other fields.

Another area where Russia needs to be engaged is on the issue of energy security.[25] For the foreseeable future, Europe will continue to depend on Russia and Gazprom for the efficient operation of its economy. In the long run, Europe needs to develop alternatives, including non-Russian hydrocarbon sources (from the Middle East, North Africa, and Central Asia, not to mention "nontraditional" gas produced from shale, which is abundant in eastern Europe) and postcarbon sources of power such as wind. For the time being, though, Europe needs to find ways of making Russia a reliable partner in the energy market. Europe should thus develop incentives to encourage greater Russian oil and gas production and impart greater predictability to the cross-border energy trade.

Pipelines like Nord Stream and South Stream have the potential to benefit Europe as a whole. They are however potentially problematic from the standpoint of countries that would be bypassed, such as Poland. The solution is not to block the pipelines' construction or keep Russia out of European energy markets, but to ensure that Moscow does not gain untoward leverage against Poland, Ukraine, and other East European gadflies. Energy market integration (potentially including states on the EU's borders like Ukraine) is the most effective answer, albeit difficult to achieve in practice. Strong leadership from Brussels, as well as from the United States, will be needed to overcome the resistance of European energy firms as well as individual countries that benefit from the status quo. At the same time, Russian participation in European markets needs to be predicated on observance of EU rules on competition and transparency. Once again, the West needs to remain true to its own values while it seeks to engage Russia.

The idea of Russia as a major power and one of the pillars of the international system will endure no matter what happens at the top of Russian politics in 2012, when Medvedev's first term as president is up. Trying to divine whether Medvedev will win a second term or whether Putin will return to the presidency after four years as prime minister (or whether a third figure will emerge to claim the top post) is a popular parlor game among journalists in both Russia and the West. Obviously, Medvedev's presidency has coincided with a striking improvement in relations with the West, which contrasts starkly with the hostility that had built up by the end of Putin's second term in 2008. Moreover, Putin and Medvedev have at times sounded different notes about the West's importance to Russia. And whatever their own preferences, Putin and Medvedev are regarded differently by their Western interlocutors—Obama once contrasted the forward-looking Medvedev with his predecessor who had "one foot in the old ways of doing business and one foot in the new."[26] A Russia headed however nominally by Medvedev (or someone like him) will no doubt make an easier partner for the West than a Russia whose public face is Vladimir Putin.

Yet it is less the personality of the individual sitting in the Kremlin than the changing strategic landscape that Russia confronts that will play the most important role in setting the parameters for Russian foreign policy in the coming decade. With the potential for chronic instability along its southern frontier and a rapidly growing China to its east, Russia is losing the luxury of seeing the West as the principal threat to its security. Even Putin appeared to understand that reality, as when he proposed close collaboration with the U.S. against the Taliban. What Moscow saw as Washington's hubris in promoting colored revolutions and NATO expansion close to Russia's borders helped turn the tide back toward confrontation, even as rising oil prices and an economic boom fed the illusion that Russia was increasingly capable of standing up to the West. That era is over. Georgia revealed the limits of Russian military power and diplomatic heft, while the worsening economic climate (growing budget deficits and inflation) means that even if oil prices spike upward again, Moscow will not have the piles of surplus cash that fueled its adventuresome foreign policy under Putin.

Russia is neither so weak as it appeared in the 1990s or as strong as it appeared before 2008. Rather it is a middle-income country struggling to free itself from an imperial past and to define its interests in a shifting international environment. The West should do what it can to encourage Russia's transformation into a responsible stakeholder in the international system, even while standing up for its own interests and values. Above all, the West must understand that the Russians themselves will determine what kind of country they will have in the twenty-first century, and how it will interact with the rest of the world.

Notes

INTRODUCTION: THE GUNS OF AUGUST

1. OECD Stat Extracts, http://stats.oecd.org/index.aspx?queryid=350.

2. Russian Ministry of Foreign Affairs, "Obzor vneshnei politiki Rossiiskoi Federatsii," 27 Mar 2007, http://www.mid.ru/brp—4nsf/sps.

3. Among the slew of recent articles addressing Russia's foreign policy revival and attempts to cope with new challenges, see Thomas Graham, "Russia and the World," *Pro et Contra*, Jul–Oct 2010, 14(4–5); Fleming Splidsboel-Hansen and Sam Greene, "Rossiya i poiski ontologicheskoi bezopasnosti," Carnegie Moscow Center, 18 Nov 2010, http://carnegie.ru/events/?fa=3130; Andrei Tsygankov, "Russia in the Post-Western World: The End of the Normalization Paradigm?" *Post-Soviet Affairs*, Oct–Dec 2009, 25(4): 347–69; Fyodor Lukyanov, "Kremlin's Imperial Ambitions Ended in 2010," *Moscow Times*, 30 Nov 2010; Dmitri Trenin, "A New and Modern Foreign Policy," *Moscow Times*, 14 May 2010; Paul Dibb, "The Bear Is Back," *The American Interest*, Nov–Dec 2006, 2(2); Andrei P. Tsygankov, "Projecting Confidence, Not Fear: Russia's Post-Imperial Assertiveness," *Orbis*, Aut 2006: 677–90; Thomas Ambrosio, *Challenging America's Global Pre-eminence: Russia's Quest for Multipolarity* (Aldershot: Ashgate, 2005). For a more skeptical take, see S. Neil MacFarlane, "The 'R' in BRICs: Is Russia an Emerging Power?" *International Affairs*, 2006, 82(1): 41–57.

4. Daniel Kimmage, "Russian 'Hard Power' Changes Balance in Caucasus," *RFE/RI. Analysis*, 12 Aug 2008.

5. Fyodor Lukyanov, "Time for a New Foreign Policy Look," *Moscow Times*, 28 Dec 2006.

6. On the passing of U.S. hegemony, see Richard Haass, "The Age of Nonpolarity: What Will Follow U.S. Dominance?" and Kishore Mahbubani, "The Case against the West," *Foreign Affairs*, May–Jun 2008, 87(3).

CHAPTER 1: CONTOURS OF RUSSIAN FOREIGN POLICY

1. "Obretenie budushchego: Strategiya 2012," INSOR Report, 2011: 289.

2. Dmitri Trenin, "Pirouettes and Priorities," *The National Interest*, Win 2003–04 (74): 80.

3. See "Primakov on Russian Relations with the West," *OMRI Daily Digest*, 30 May 1996.

4. Russian Ministry of Foreign Affairs, "Kontseptsiya vneshnei politiki Rossiiskoi Federatsii," 2000, http://www.ln.mid.ru/ns-osndoc.nsf/0e9272befa34209743256c6 30042d1aa/fd86620b371b0cf7432569fb004872a7?OpenDocument.

5. Russian Ministry of Foreign Affairs, "Kontseptsiya vneshnei politiki Rossiiskoi Federatsii," 2000.

6. Russian Ministry of Foreign Affairs, "Kontseptsiya vneshnei politiki Rossiiskoi Federatsii," 2008, http://www.mid.ru/ns-osndoc.nsf/0e9272befa34209743256c630 042d1aa/d48737161a0bc944c32574870048d8f7?OpenDocument.

7. Fyodor Rumyantsev and Aleksandr Artemev, "Konets velikosti," *Gazeta.ru*, 15 Jul 2008.

8. Russian Ministry of Foreign Affairs, "Kontsepsiya vneshnei politiki Rossiiskoi Federatsii," 2008.

9. Russian Ministry of Foreign Affairs, "Programma effektivnogo ispol'zovaniya na sistemnoi osnove vneshnepoliticheskikh faktorov v tselyakh dolgosrochnogo razvitiya Rossiiskoi Federatsii," 11 May 2010, http://www.runewsweek.ru/country/ 34184.Doc.

10. Security Council of the Russian Federation, "Kontseptsiya natsional'noi bezopasnosti Rossiiskoi Federatsii," 2000, http://www.scrf.gov.ru/documents/decree/ 2000—24—1.shtml.

11. Security Council of the Russian Federation, "Strategiya natsional'noi bezopasnosti Rossiiskoi Federatsii do 2020 goda," Jun 2009, http://www.scrf.gov.ru/ documents/1/99.html.

12. See Keir Giles, "Russia's National Security Strategy to 2020," NATO Defense College Report, Jun 2009.

13. Celeste A. Wallander, "The Challenge of Russia for U.S. Policy," testimony to U.S. Senate Committee on Foreign Relations, 21 Jun 2005.

14. Mikhail Margelov, "Bor'ba za mnogopolyarnost'," *Nezavisimaya Gazeta*, 20 Sep 2005.

15. Dmitri Trenin, *The End of Eurasia: Russia on the Border between Geopolitics and Globalization* (Washington, DC: Carnegie, 2002), 306–8.

16. Sergei Lavrov, "Rossiya i SShA: Mezhdu proshlim i budushchim," *Mezhdunarodnik.ru*, 26 Sep 2006, http://www.mezhdunarodnik.ru/magazin/5308.html.

17. Igor Ivanov, "A New Foreign-Policy Year for Russia and the World," *International Affairs: A Russian Journal of World Politics, Diplomacy and International Relations*, 2003, 49(6): 34; Ye. Primakov, "Is the Russia-U.S. Rapprochement Here to Stay?" *International Affairs: A Russian Journal of World Politics, Diplomacy and International Relations*, 2002, 48(6): 88.

18. Primakov does deserve much of the credit for adopting the notion that Russia must remain an independent pillar of the global order. See "Primakov on Russian Relations with the West."

19. Vladimir Putin, "Poslanie Federal'nomu Sobraniyu Rossiiskoi Federatsii," The Kremlin, 10 May 2006, http://www.kremlin.ru/text/appears/2006/05/105546 .shtml. A more radical version of this idea, termed "collective neo-imperialism," was advocated around the same time by two influential Russian analysts. See Vladislav Inozemtsev and Sergei Karaganov, "Imperialism of the Fittest," *The National Interest*, Sum 2005 (80): 74–80.

20. Roderic Lyne, Strobe Talbott, and Koji Watanabe, "Engaging with Russia: The Next Phase," report to the Trilateral Commission, Triangle Papers 59, 2006: 162.

21. Irina Isakova, *Russian Governance in the Twenty-First Century: Geo-strategy, Geopolitics and Governance* (London: Frank Cass, 2005), 87–89.

22. Andrew Monaghan, "'Calmly Critical': Evolving Russian Views of U.S. Hegemony," *Journal of Strategic Studies*, Dec 2006, 29(6): 987–1013.

23. See "The New Post-Transitional Russian Identity: How Western Is Russian Westernization?" World Policy Institute/Harriman Institute Project Report, Jan 2006.

24. For instance Trenin argued that the end of Communism had finally removed any realistic basis for Russia to seek a role in the world outside the West. See Trenin, *The End of Eurasia*.

25. Jack Matlock, former ambassador to the Soviet Union, praised Putin for his "unequivocal" commitment to democracy and preference for good relations with the West. See Jack Matlock Jr., "Russia Votes: Will Democracy Win?" *New York Times*, 26 Mar 2000.

26. Lilia Shevtsova, *Putin's Russia*, trans. Antonina W. Bouis (Washington, DC: Carnegie, 2003), 4; Thomas M. Nicholas, "Russia's Turn West," *World Policy Journal*, Win 2002–2003, 19(4): 13–14. On a more philosophical level, Dmitri Trenin argued that the implosion of the Soviet Union shattered the political unity of Eurasia, leaving Russia too weak to resist the rising powers of India and, especially, China. Only by fully anchoring itself to the culture and institutions of Europe could Russia avoid the dolorous possibilities of seeking futilely to re-create the USSR or complete disintegration. According to Trenin, only the "full demilitarization of its relations with the West" and a long-term strategy of seeking to join Western institutions (including the EU and NATO) can save Russia from geopolitical marginalization. Trenin, *The End of Eurasia*, 259, 311–12.

27. See Vladimir Kuchkanov, "Demokraticheski orientirovannye perevoroty v SNG i geopoliticheskie perspektivy Rossii v regione," *Mezhdunarodnik.ru*, 28 Sep 2005, http://www.mezhdunarodnik.ru/magazin/1439.html; Janusz Bugajski, "Russia's New Europe," *The National Interest*, Win 2002–03 (74): 84–91.

28. A. Ye. Safonov, "Terrorizm apokalipsisa," *Mezhdunarodnaya zhizn'*, 2006 (5).

29. Dmitry Medvedev, "Speech at meeting with Russian ambassadors and permanent representatives in international organizations," *Russia Beyond the Headlines*, 16 Jul 2010, http://rbth.ru/articles/2010/07/16/speech_at_meeting_with_russian_ ambassadors.html.

30. See James M. Goldgeier, "The United States and Russia: Keeping Expectations Realistic," *Policy Review*, Oct–Nov 2001: 47–56. Fukuyama's notion of history's end was first stated in his "The End of History?" *The National Interest*, Sum 1989 (16). A more detailed and philosophically grounded expression of this argument can be found in Fukuyama, *The End of History and the Last Man* (New York: Free Press, 1992).

31. See especially Edward Lucas, *The New Cold War: Putin's Russia and the Threat to the West* (London: Palgrave Macmillan, 2008).

32. Dmitri Trenin, "Russia Leaves the West," *Foreign Affairs*, Jul–Aug 2006, 85(4).

33. Nodari A. Simonia, "Priorities of Russian Foreign Policy and the Way It Works," in *The Making of Foreign Policy in Russia and the New States of Eurasia*, ed. Adeed Dawisha and Karen Dawisha (Armonk, NY: M.E. Sharpe, 1995), 38–39. See also R. Craig Nation, "Beyond the Cold War: Change and Continuity in U.S.-Russian Relations," in *The United States and Russia into the 21st Century*, ed. R. Craig Nation and Michael McFaul (Carlisle Barracks, PA: Strategic Studies Institute, U.S. Army War College, 1997), 9–13.

34. Alexei G. Arbatov, "Russian National Interests," in *Damage Limitation or Crisis? Russia and the Outside World*, ed. Robert D. Blackwill and Sergei A. Karaganov (Washington, DC: Brassey's, 1994), 55. Arbatov was not alone in seeing the germ of Russia's reemergence as a Great Power in the appointment of Primakov. See, among others, Sergei A. Karaganov, "Russia's Elites," in Blackwill and Karaganov, eds., *Damage Limitation*, 54, and Uri Ra'anan and Kate Martin, eds., *Russia: A Return to Imperialism?* (New York: St. Martin's, 1995), especially the chapters by Ra'anan and Sergei Grigoriev.

35. On the role of the security services (*siloviki*), see Andrei Soldatov and Irina Borogan, "Russia's New Nobility: The Rise of the Security Services in Putin's Kremlin," *Foreign Affairs*, Sep/Oct 2010, 89(5). Also Ian Bremmer, "Who's in Charge in the Kremlin?" *World Policy Journal*, Win 2005–2006: 1–3; Ian Bremmer and Samuel Charap, "The *Siloviki* in Putin's Russia: Who They Are and What They Want," *Washington Quarterly*, Win 2006–2007, 30(1): 83–92; Olga Kryshtanovskaya and Stephen White, "Putin's Militocracy," *Post-Soviet Affairs*, 2003, 19(4): 289–306; Pavel K. Baev, "The Evolution of Putin's Regime: Inner Circles and Outer Walls," *Problems of Post-Communism*, Nov–Dec 2004, 51(6): 3–13. Of course, the term *siloviki* elides a range of distinctions among the members of this class, many of whom were already in positions of power under Yeltsin. See Brian D. Taylor, "Power Surge? Russia's Power Ministries from Yeltsin to Putin and Beyond," PONARS Policy Memo #414, Dec 2006. As Taylor points out, it is not *siloviki* as such who attained prominence under Putin, but specifically members of the FSB (*Federal'naya Sluzhba Bezopasnosti*, or Federal Security Service)—rather than the Interior Ministry, Foreign Intelligence Service, military, or other armed organizations.

36. Mariya Gamaleeva, "Formirovanie obraza Rossii kak aspekt publichnoi vneshnei politiki," *Mezhdunarodnik.ru*, 2 Aug 2006, http://www.mezhdunarodnik.ru/magazin/4812.html.

37. William Zimmerman, *The Russian People and Foreign Policy: Russian Elite and Mass Perspectives, 1993–2000* (Princeton, NJ: Princeton University Press, 2002), 14–17.

38. Gabriel Gorodetsky, "Introduction," in *Russia between East and West: Russian Foreign Policy on the Threshold of the Twenty-First Century*, ed. Gabriel Gorodetsky (London: Frank Cass, 2003), xi.

39. Timothy Snyder shows, for example, how Poland's post-Communist elites renounced their country's traditional civilizing mission to the East, in the process opening the way to membership in the Western community of nations symbolized by NATO and the European Union. Timothy Snyder, *The Reconstruction of Nations: Po-*

land, Ukraine, Lithuania, Belarus, 1569–1999 (New Haven, CT: Yale University Press, 2003), 277–93.

40. Ted Hopf, *Social Construction of International Politics: Identities & Foreign Policies, Moscow 1955 and 1999* (Ithaca, NY: Cornell University Press, 2002), 156.

41. Anastasiya Kornya, "Imperskie ambitsii ne aktual'ny," *Vedomosti*, 23 Jan 2007.

42. Putin, "Poslanie Federal'nomu Sobraniyu Rossiiskoi Federatsii," The Kremlin, 16 May 2003, http://www.kremlin.ru/appears/2003/05/16/1259—type63372type 63374type82634—44623.shtml.

43. Igor Ivanov, "The New Russian Identity: Innovation and Continuity in Russian Foreign Policy," *Washington Quarterly*, Sum 2001, 24(3): 11–12.

44. International Monetary Fund, *World Economic Outlook Database, October 2010*, http://www.imf.org/external/pubs/ft/weo/2010/02/weodata/index.aspx. According to IMF figures, Brazil's GDP in 2010 was $2.02 trillion, India's was $1.43 trillion, and China's was $5.75 trillion.

45. Stockholm International Peace Research Institute (SIPRI) Military Expenditure Database, http://www.sipri.org/databases/milex.

46. Paul Goble, "Window on Eurasia: Putin Restricts Russian Foreign Ministry's Role in CIS Countries," 14 May 2008, http://windowoneurasia.blogspot. com/2008/05/window-on-eurasia-putin-restricts.html.

47. Vyacheslav Nikonov, "The Putin Strategy," *Russia in Global Affairs*, Jan–Mar 2005, 3(1): 68–81.

48. I have chosen to use the Ukrainian spelling *Kyiv* rather than the Russian *Kiev*. Given Ukraine's history, *Kiev* has imperial overtones, which I prefer to avoid, especially when talking about relations between Ukraine and Russia.

49. Fyodor Lukyanov, "Dve Rossii," *Vedomosti*, 28 Dec 2006.

50. John D. Negroponte, "Annual Threat Assessment," testimony to U.S. Senate Select Committee on Intelligence, 11 Jan 2007; *JRL* #8, 12 Jan 2007.

51. "The U.S.-Russia Relations [sic] after the 'Reset': Building a New Agenda. A View from Russia," Report by the Russian Participants of the Working Group on the Future of the Russian-U.S. [sic] Relations, Valdai Discussion Club, March 2011.

52. Kishore Mahbubhani, *The New Asian Century: The Irresistible Shift of Global Power to the East* (New York: Public Affairs, 2008), 51–100.

53. On the ambiguity in the Russo-Chinese strategic partnership, see Bobo Lo, *Axis of Convenience: Moscow, Beijing, and the New Geopolitics* (London: Chatham House, 2008), 3–5, 41–55, 174–83.

54. A. Borodavkin, "The Asian Vector of Russia's Policy and Modernization," *International Affairs: A Russian Journal of World Politics, Diplomacy & International Relations*, 2010, 56(5): 23–30. "Going East: Russia's Asia-Pacific Strategy," *Rossiya v global'moi politke*, 25 Dec 2010.

55. Russian Ministry of Foreign Affairs, "Programma effektivnoi ispol'zovaniya."

56. Andrew E. Kramer, "Russia Claims Its Sphere of Influence in the World," *New York Times*, 31 Aug 2008. Medvedev, "Interv'yu Dmitriya Medvedeva rossiiskim telekanalam," The Kremlin, 31 Aug 2008, http://kremlin.ru/transcripts/1276.

57. "Demokraticheski orientirovannye perevoroty v SNG i geopoliticheskie perspektivy Rossii v regione," *Mezhdunarodnik.ru*, 28 Sep 2005, http://www.mezhdun arodnik.ru/magazin/1439.html.

58. It is notable, too, that in his position as head of the Russian Federation Chamber of Commerce (until early 2011), Primakov was a vocal and enthusiastic supporter of Putin's foreign policy course. Yevgeny Primakov, "Russia's Foreign Policy in 2005 Was Successful in Every Area," *International Affairs: A Russian Journal of World Politics, Diplomacy, and International Relations*, 2006, 52(2): 13–22; Fyodor Lukyanov, "Perspektiva: 2008—ne problema," *Vedomosti*, 6 Feb 2007.

59. Yury Fedorov, "Vneshnyaya politika Rossii: 1991–2000. Chast' I," *Pro et Contra*, 2001, 6(1–2).

60. A. Pravda, "Putin's Foreign Policy after 11 September," in *Russia between East and West: Russian Foreign Policy on the Threshold of the Twenty-First Century*, ed. Gabriel Gorodetsky (London: Frank Cass, 2003), 50; Andrey Kolesnikov, "Ivanov, Medvedev Seen Projecting Contrasting Facets of Russian Foreign Policy," *Gazeta.ru*, JRL #27, 4 Feb 2007.

61. "Report of the Russian Working Group," *U.S.-Russian Relations at the Turn of the Century* (Washington, DC: Carnegie Endowment for International Peace; Moscow: Council on Foreign and Defense Policy, 2000), 59.

62. Quoted in Dmitri Simes, "The Results of 1997: No Dramatic Upheavals," *International Affairs*, 1998, 44(1): 28.

63. Dmitry Shlapentokh, "Looking for Other Options: Russia's National Identity Cannot Be Based on Western Models," *Russia Profile*, 30 Oct 2006. See also Samuel Huntington, "The West and the World," *Foreign Affairs*, Nov–Dec 1997, 75(6): 37; Lawrence Freedman, "The New Great Power Politics," in *Russia and the West: The 21st Century Security Environment*, ed. Alexei Arbatov et al. (Armonk, NY: M.E. Sharpe, 1999), 22.

64. Strategicheskii kurs Rossii s gosudarstvami-uchastnikami Sodruzhestva Nezavi-simykh Gosudarstv, 14 Sep 1995. http://www.mezhizn.ru/documents/15-unity.html.

65. Andrei Kozyrev, "Partnership or Cold Peace?" *Foreign Policy*, Sum 1995 (99): 3–5.

66. See Stephen Sestanovich, "The Dinner Guest," *American Interest*, Mar/Apr 2010. Also Leon Aron, "The Foreign Policy Doctrine of Postcommunist Russia and Its Domestic Context," in *The New Russian Foreign Policy*, ed. Michael Mandelbaum (New York: Council on Foreign Relations, 1998), 29–30.

67. Michael Mandelbaum, "Introduction: Russian Foreign Policy in Historical Perspective," in *The New Russian Foreign Policy*, ed. Michael Mandelbaum (New York: Council on Foreign Relations, 1998), 1.

68. "Obzor vneshnei politiki." Even Kozyrev warned, back in 1994, that "the international order of the [twenty-first] century will not be a Pax Americana or any other version of unipolar or bipolar dominance. The United States does not have the capability to rule alone." Jeffrey Mankoff, "Russia and the West: Taking the Longer View," *Washington Quarterly*, Spr 2007, 30(2): 128; Andrei Kozyrev, "The Lagging Partnership," *Foreign Affairs*, May–Jun 1994, 73(3): 59–71.

69. Medvedev, "Interv'yu Dmitriya Medvedeva rossiiskim telekanalam," The Kremlin, 31 Aug 2008, http://kremlin.ru/transcripts/1276.

70. George Friedman, "The Medvedev Doctrine and American Strategy," *Stratfor Geopolitical Intelligence Report*, 2 Sep 2008, http://www.stratfor.com/weekly/med vedev—doctrine—and—american—strategy.

71. Bobo Lo, *Vladimir Putin and the Evolution of Russian Foreign Policy* (London: Royal Institute of International Affairs, 2003), 51–53. Primakov was, in fact, the first to make economics a central component of Russia's power projection capabilities, emphasizing Russia's capability to manipulate energy supplies to the former Soviet republics to ensure their loyalty to Moscow. Yeltsin's long-time premier, Viktor Chernomyrdin, who was also a former head of Gazprom, envisioned forcing the former Soviet republics to invest in Gazprom and other natural resource monopolies as a way of more closely tying them to Russia economically. See Andrei P. Tsygankov, *Russia's Foreign Policy: Change and Continuity in National Identity* (Lanham, MD: Rowman & Littlefield, 2006), 114–15.

72. On the reasons for the 1998 financial crisis, see Brian Pinto, Evsey Gurevich, and Sergei Ulatov, "Lessons from the Russian Crisis of 1998 and Recovery," *Managing Volatility and Crises: A Practitioner's Guide,* available at http://www1.worldbank.org/economicpolicy/documents/mv/pgchapter10.pdf.

73. Putin, "Vstupitel'noe slovo na zasedanii Soveta Bezopasnosti, posvyashchennom meram po realizatsii Poslaniya Federal'nomu Sobraniyu," The Kremlin, 20 Jun 2006, http://www.kremlin.ru/text/appears/2006/06/107450.shtml.

74. Putin, "Poslanie Federal'nomu Sobraniyu Rossiiskoi Federatsii," The Kremlin, 8 Jul 2000, http://www.kremlin.ru/appears/2000/07/08/0000—type63372type 63374type82634—28782.shtml.

75. Putin, "Poslanie Federal'nomu Sobraniyu Rossiiskoi Federatsii," The Kremlin, 26 Apr 2007, http://www.kremlin.ru/appears/2007/04/26/1156—type63372type 63374type82634—125339.shtml.

76. Clifford Gaddy and Fiona Hill, "Putin's Agenda, America's Choice: Russia's Search for Strategic Stability," Brookings Institution Policy Brief #89, May 2002. See also Opening Statement of Senator Joseph R. Biden Jr. to Senate Committee on Foreign Relations hearing on "U.S. Policy toward Russia," 21 Jun 2005. According to Biden, capital flight in 2005 may have reached the equivalent of $7 billion.

77. Jeffrey Mankoff, "The Russian Economic Crisis," Council on Foreign Relations Special Report, no. 53, Apr 2010: 4–5, http://www.cfr.org/publication/21803/russian_economic_crisis.html.

78. Medvedev, "Speech at meeting with Russian ambassadors."

79. "Russia 'to Pay Paris Club Early,'" BBC News, 3 Feb 2005, http://news.bbc.co.uk/2/hi/business/4233547.stm.

80. Carlos Pascual, "The Geopolitics of Energy: From Security to Survival," Brookings Institution, Jan 2008, http://www.brookings.edu/papers/2008/01—energy—pascual.aspx.

81. Stockholm International Peace Research Institute (SIPRI), Military Expenditures Database, 2011, http://milexdata.sipri.org. Publicly, Kremlin and military officials have called for spending to rise even faster. See Aleksei Nikol'skii and Maksim Tovkailo, "Rossiya ukhodit v oboronu," *Vedomosti,* 30 Jul 2010. Christian Neef, "Russian Bear Roars: Why Is Moscow Risking a New Cold War?" *Der Spiegel* online, 25 Jun 2008, http://www.spiegel.de/international/world/0,1518,562073,00.html.

82. Fred Weir, "With Russia's $650 Billion Rearmament Plan, the Bear Sharpens Its Teeth," *Christian Science Monitor,* 28 Feb 2011.

83. Putin, "Poslanie federal'nomu sobraniyu," The Kremlin, 10 May 2006, http://www.kremlin.ru/appears/2006/05/10/1357—type63372type63374type82634—105546.shtml.

84. See Lyne, Talbott, and Watanabe, "Engaging with Russia," 65.

85. Anders Åslund, *Russia's Capitalist Revolution: Why Market Reform Succeeded and Democracy Failed* (Washington, DC: Peterson Institute, 2007), 247–59.

86. Wallander, "Challenge," testimony to U.S. Senate Foreign Relations Committee.

87. Alexander Koliandre, "Russia Keeps China Energy Options Open," BBC News, 21 March 2006, http://news.bbc.co.uk/2/hi/business/4830768.stm.

88. See Thomas Graham, "Russia and the World," *Pro et Contra*, Jul–Oct 2010, 14 (4–5). Also Fyodor Lukyanov, "Kremlin's Imperial Ambitions Ended in 2010," *Moscow Times*, 23 Dec 2010. On the transformation and diffusion of power in the twenty-first century, see Joseph S. Nye Jr., *The Future of Power* (New York: Public Affairs, 2011), 3–24.

89. See Mikhail Delyagin, "Energeticheskaya politika Rossii," *Svobodnaya mysl'*, 2006 (9–10): 5–14.

90. Rajan Menon and Alexander J. Motyl, "Why Russia Is Really Weak," *Newsweek*, Sep 2006.

91. For figures on xenophobic attitudes and incidents, see the annual reports published by the SOVA Center. The most recent is Galina Kozhevnikova, "Pod znakom politicheskogo terrora: Radikal'nyi natsionalizm v Rossii i protivodeistvie emu v 2009 goda," SOVA Center, Feb 2010, http://www.sova-center.ru/racism-xenophobia/publications/2010/02/d17889/.

92. Preliminary results of the 2010 census according to the Russian State Statistics Committee (Goskomstat), http://www.perepis-2010.ru/message-rosstat.php.

93. Nicolas Eberstadt, "The Russian Federation at the Dawn of the Twenty-first Century: Trapped in a Demographic Straightjacket," *National Bureau of Asian Research (NBR) Analysis*, Sep 2004, 15(2): 7.

94. Judyth Twigg, "Differential Demographics: Russia's Muslim and Slavic Populations," Center for Strategic and International Studies PONARS Policy Memo No. 338, Dec 2005: 136–37. Twigg notes that births among Russia's Slavic population began increasing around 1999 while Muslim births started declining shortly thereafter. The percentage of Muslim conscripts will thus peak around 2016–2017—assuming conscription has not been abolished by then.

95. On Russian/Soviet messianism, see Daniel B. Rowland, "Moscow—the Third Rome or the New Israel?" *Russian Review*, 1996, 55: 594–95.

96. Mankoff, "Russia and the West," 127–29.

97. Gorchakov's diplomacy, which aimed at rebuilding and reintegrating Russia into the European Concert following the Crimean War, has in particular been invoked as a model for what Russia today requires. Both former foreign minister Igor Ivanov and his successor Sergey Lavrov consciously identified with Gorchakov, while Putin has often cast himself as heir to Stolypin's legacy. See Igor Ivanov, *The New Russian Diplomacy* (Washington, DC: Nixon Center/Brookings Institution, 2002), 26–28. Putin, "Polsanie Federal'nomu Sobraniyu," 8 Jul 2000, The Kremlin, http://archive.kremlin.ru/appears/2000/07/08/0000_type63372type63374type82634_28782.shtml. Putin, "Predsedatel' Pravitel'stva Rossii V.V. Putin predstavil v Gosudarstvennoi Dume otchët o deyatsel'nosti Pravitel'stva Rossiiskoi Federatsii za 2010 god," 20

Apr 2011, http://premier.gov.ru/events/news/14898/multiscripts.html. See also Flemming Splidsboel-Hansen, "Past and Future Meet: Aleksandr Gorchakov and Russian Foreign Policy," *Europe-Asia Studies*, 2002, 54(3): 377–96. Abraham Ascher, *P.A. Stolypin: The Search for Stability in Late Imperial Russia* (Palo Alto, CA: Stanford UP, 2002), 4–5.

98. As Pursianinen points out, current debates about the relative importance of power and ideology in framing the outlines of Russian foreign policy are in many ways reminiscent of similar debates that long simmered over the Soviet Union. See Christer Pursianinen, *Russian Foreign Policy and International Relations Theory* (Aldershot: Ashgate, 2000), 48.

99. Kenneth N. Waltz, *Theory of International Politics* (Reading, MA: Addison Wesley, 1979), 102–28.

100. Alexander Wendt, *Social Theory of International Politics* (New York: Cambridge University Press, 1999), 1–7, 103–19.

101. On this point see Richard Rosencrance and Arthur A. Stein, "Beyond Realism: The Study of Grand Strategy," and Michael W. Doyle, "Politics and Grand Strategy," in *The Domestic Bases of Grand Strategy*, ed. Richard Rosencrance and Arthur A. Stein (Ithaca, NY: Cornell University Press, 1993), 3–21, 22–47; David A. Lake and Robert Powell, "International Relations: A Strategic Choice Approach," in *Strategic Choice and International Relations*, ed. David A. Lake and Robert Powell (Princeton, NJ: Princeton University Press, 1999), 3–38.

102. Lo, *Vladimir Putin and the Evolution of Russian Foreign Policy*, 13–14. See also Andrei Kozyrev, *Preobrazhenie* (Moscow: Mezhdunarodnye otnosheniya, 1995), 221.

103. Tsygankov, *Russia's Foreign Policy*, 26.

CHAPTER 2: BULLDOGS FIGHTING UNDER THE RUG: THE MAKING OF RUSSIAN FOREIGN POLICY

1. Dmitri Trenin, "Russia: Back to the Future?" testimony to U.S. Senate Committee on Foreign Relations, 29 Jun 2006.

2. William Zimmerman, *The Russian People and Foreign Policy: Russian Elite and Mass Perspectives, 1993–2000* (Princeton, NJ: Princeton University Press, 2002), 1–3, 11–13. Zimmerman identifies elites as "those who controlled the instruments of coercion or persuasion, dominated key parts of the economy, had specialized knowledge, or occupied key formal political positions." Sergei A. Karaganov, "Russia's Elites," in *Damage Limitation or Crisis? Russia and the Outside World*, ed. Robert D. Blackwill and Sergei A. Karaganov (Washington, DC: Brassey's, 1994), 41–42. See also Harold Lasswell et al., *The Comparative Study of Elites* (Stanford, CA: Stanford University Press, 1952).

3. Constitution of the Russian Federation, Chapter 4, Article 86. An English-language text of the constitution is available at http://www.constitution.ru/en/10003000–01.htm.

4. Under the reform scheme introduced by President Putin in 2004, members of the Federation Council are chosen by the heads of administration from each of

Russia's eighty-three juridical regions (*oblast, krai,* autonomous *okrug,* and autonomous *oblast* governors; republic presidents; and the mayors of Moscow and St. Petersburg). Most of these officials, in turn, are now appointed by the Kremlin.

5. In the December 2007 parliamentary elections, United Russia officially received 64.30 percent of votes cast, while among the opposition, only the Communists (11.57 percent), the Liberal Democrats (8.14 percent), and the Just Russia coalition (7.74 percent) surpassed the 7 percent threshold to receive seats in parliament. Foreign observers strongly criticized the conduct of the vote for depriving opposition parties of access to the media and opportunities to campaign. Official results are available at the website of the Central Election Commission of the Russian Federation, "Svedenie o provodyashchikhsya vyborakh i referendumakh," http://www.vybory.izbirkom.ru/region/region/izbirkom?action-show&root-1&tvd-1001 00021960186&vrn-100100021960181&region-0&global-1&sub—region-0&prver-0 &pronetvd-null&vibid-100100021960186&type-242.

6. Karaganov, "Russia's Elites," 43; Bobo Lo, *Vladimir Putin and the Evolution of Russian Foreign Policy* (London: Royal Institute of International Affairs, 2003), 33–34. As Lo points out, MID's role is much more central at the working level, where it continues to maintain a high level of technical expertise, in contrast to the political level, where weak leadership has increasingly shunted MID aside as an incubator of new foreign policy ideas. The same is true of the Duma, which has largely lost its role as an initiator of policy but continues, in its Foreign Affairs Committee, to analyze international problems and Russia's response to them. The Putin-Medvedev-era Duma is not the rubber stamp that the old USSR Supreme Soviet was, but neither is it a real parliament with fully developed legislative powers. See B. Makarenko, "Rossiiskii politicheskii stroi: Opyt neoinstitutsional'nogo analiza," *Mirovaya ekonomika i mezhdunarodnye otnosheniya,* Feb 2007 (2): 32–42.

7. Andrei P. Tsygankov, *Russia's Foreign Policy: Change and Continuity in National Identity* (Lanham, MD: Rowman & Littlefield, 2006), 83.

8. Robert H. Donaldson and Joseph L. Nogee, *The Foreign Policy of Russia: Changing Systems, Enduring Interests,* 2nd ed. (Armonk, NY: M.E. Sharpe, 2002), 141–49. The Security Council's importance in coordinating foreign policy was at its apex during the first Chechen war, when it was headed by Yeltsin's close associate Oleg Lobov. As Donaldson and Nogee note, the formation of the Security Council in 1992 was widely perceived at the time as an attempt to rein in the overly Atlanticist tendencies of Kozyrev's Foreign Ministry.

9. Amina Azfal, "Russian Security Policy," *Strategic Studies,* Spr 2005, 25(1): 68. Under Yeltsin, the Security Council was subject to repeated turnover and was often ignored on key issues by Yeltsin and his administration. See "Report of the Russian Working Group," *U.S.-Russian Relations at the Turn of the Century* (Washington, DC: Carnegie Endowment for International Peace/Moscow: Council on Foreign and Defense Policy, 2000), 59; Aleksandra Samarina et al., "Sovbezu khotyat vernut' deesposobnost'," *Nezavisimaya Gazeta,* 20 Oct 2004. The two Ivanovs are not related. The appointment of another technocrat, Vladimir Sobolev, to replace Igor Ivanov in July 2007 did nothing to upgrade the Security Council's role.

10. "Ot redaktsii: Gorizontal'nyi razmen," *Nezavisimaya Gazeta,* 6 Jun 2008.

11. Keir Giles, "Russia's National Security Strategy to 2020," NATO Defense College report, Jun 2009: 3–4.

12. Such is one official justification for the state's growing role in the strategic energy sector. See "News Conference of Presidential Aide Vladislav Surkov, Deputy Head of the Presidential Administration," press conference at the July 2006 G8 summit in St. Petersburg, http://en.g8russia.ru/news/20060704/1168817.html. Also see the discussion of Vladislav Surkov's worldview below.

13. See Lo, *Vladimir Putin*, 39–40.

14. Vladimir Kvint, "The Internationalization of Russian Business," lecture at Kennan Institute, 16 Oct 2006, *JRL* #237. With the 2008 war in Georgia, Moscow announced it was ending (at least for a time) its attempts to join the WTO.

15. Yury Baluevsky, "Struktura i osnovnye soderzhanie novoi Voennoi doktriny Rossii," 20 Jan 2007, http://www.mil.ru/847/852/1153/1342/20922/index.shtml; "Sergey Ivanov: 'U Rossii nyet voenno-politicheskikh vragov,'" *Izvestiya*, 11 Feb 2007.

16. Voennaya doktrina Rossiiskoi Federatsii, Section II, 5 Feb 2010, http://news.kremlin.ru/ref_notes/461.

17. Gregory White, "Russia's Sechin Defends Investment Climate," *Wall Street Journal*, 22 Feb 2011. "Igor Sechin vyshel v informatsionnoe pole," *Kommersant*, 13 Dec 2007. Sechin is also reputed to have been a leading figure in the campaign against Khodorkovsky and Yukos and to have blocked attempts to make Gazprom more open and transparent. See "Sechin, Igor," *Lentapedia* (*Lenta.ru*), http://lenta.ru/lib/14160890/full.htm.

18. Irina Isakova, *Russian Governance in the Twenty-First Century: Geo-strategy, Geopolitics and Governance* (London: Frank Cass, 2005), 38–39; Karaganov, "Russia's Elites," 48–50.

19. Dmitri Trenin, "Russia's Security Integration with America and Europe," in *Russia's Engagement with the West: Transformation and Integration in the Twenty-First Century*, ed. Alexander J. Motyl, Blair A. Ruble, and Lilia Shevtsova (Armonk, NY: M.E. Sharpe, 2005), 283–92; Nikolai Poroskov, "Pushka chesti ne otdast: V Rossii gotovitsya novaya voennaya doktrina," *Vremya Novostei*, 1 Feb 2007; "Oboronnaya politika Rossii," SVOP report, 14 Oct 2003, http://www.svop.ru/live/materials.asp?m—id-7271&r—id-7272.

20. See Vladimir Shlapentokh, "Serdiukov as a Unique Defense Minister in Russian History: A Sign of Putin's Absolute Power," comment on *JRL* #76, 1 Apr 2007; Stephen Blank, "Russia's Serdyukov and His Generals," *RFE/RL Endnote*, 11 Dec 2007.

21. Dale R. Herspring and Peter Rutland, "Russian Foreign Policy," in *Putin's Russia: Past Imperfect, Future Uncertain*, ed. Dale R. Herspring (Lanham, MD: Rowman & Littlefield, 2005), 261. Jeffrey Checkel, "Structure, Institutions, and Process: Russia's Changing Foreign Policy," in *The Making of Foreign Policy in Russia and the New States of Eurasia*, ed. Adeed Dawisha and Karen Dawisha (Armonk, NY: M.E. Sharpe, 1995), 45–47. As a result of the institutional chaos of the Yeltsin years, foreign policy was increasingly politicized, in contrast to the more centralized and consensual approach of the Putin team.

22. Stephen White and Olga Kryshtanovskaya, "Russia: Elite Continuity and Change," in *Elites, Crises, and the Origins of Regimes*, ed. M. Dogan and J. Higley (Lanham, MD: Rowman & Littlefield, 1998), 127. See also Richard Rose, *New Russia Barometer III: The Results* (Glasgow: Strathclyde University Press, 1994), 28.

23. Odobrenie deyatel'nosti gosudarstvennykh institutov, VTsIOM, Mar 2011, http://wciom.ru/index.php?id=172.

24. Zimmerman, *Russian People and Foreign Policy*, 16. Jack Snyder, "Democratization, War, and Nationalism in the Post-Communist States," in *The Sources of Russian Foreign Policy After the Cold War*, ed. Celeste A. Wallander (Boulder, CO: Westview, 1996), 36. Snyder argues that, as an unstable society with weak political institutions, Russia in the mid-1990s was liable to fall victim to the pressures of nationalism, popular upheaval, and an aggressive foreign policy in the pattern described by Alexander Gerschenkron, Karl Polanyi, and Barrington Moore in the mid-twentieth century.

25. Angus Reid Global Monitor Poll, "Russians Reject Army's Intervention Abroad," *JRL* #220, 1 Dec 2008.

26. The role of domestic political institutions in shaping foreign policy outcomes is a topic somewhat neglected in the international relations literature, which largely focuses on system-level variables or looks at questions of state identity apart from the question of institutions. For a clear statement of the thesis that domestic institutions affect foreign policy in meaningful ways, see Ronald Rogowski, "Institutions as Constraints on Strategic Choice," in *Strategic Choice and International Relations*, ed. David A. Lake and Robert Powell (Princeton, NJ: Princeton University Press, 1999), 115–36. More generally, see Richard Rosencrance and Arthur A. Stein, eds., *The Domestic Bases of Grand Strategy* (Ithaca, NY: Cornell University Press, 1993).

27. "Russians Appreciate Putin's Foreign Policy Efforts—Opinion Poll," *Interfax*, 27 Mar 2007, *JRL* #73.

28. Anastasiya Kornya, "Imperskie ambitsii ne aktual'nye: Grazhdane ne khotyat chtoby Rossiya stala energeticheskoi sverkhderzhavoi," *Vedomosti*, 23 Jan 2007; "Russians Want to See Their Country as a Superpower—Poll," *Interfax*, 25 Jan 2007, *JRL* #18.

29. Angela E. Stent, "America and Russia: Paradoxes of Partnership," in *Russia's Engagement with the West: Transformation and Integration in the Twenty-First Century*, ed. Alexander J. Motyl, Blair A. Ruble, and Lilia Shevtsova (Armonk, NY: M.E. Sharpe, 2005), 272; Dmitri Trenin, "Russia Leaves the West," *Foreign Affairs*, Jul–Aug 2006, 85(4): 87–96.

30. Medvedev, "Poslanie Federal'nomu Sobraniyu," 12 Nov 2009, http://kremlin.ru/transcripts/5979.

31. Of course, even within the most tightly controlled regimes, such as the pre-perestroika Soviet Union, elites are by their nature somewhat heterogeneous, based in differences in background, occupation, and a variety of personal factors. See Mattei Dogan and John Higley, "Elites, Crises, and Regimes in Comparative Analysis," in *Elites, Crises, and the Origins of Regimes*, ed. Mattei Dogan and John Higley (Lanham, MD: Rowman & Littlefield, 1998), 14–19; Douglas A. Borer and Jason J. Morrissette, "Russian Authoritarian Pluralism: A Local and Global Trend?" *Cambridge Review of International Affairs*, Dec 2006, 19(4): 571–88.

32. For example, Margot Light and others talk about "liberal Westernizers," "pragmatic nationalists," and "fundamentalist nationalists." See Margot Light, John Löwenhardt, and Stephen White, "Russia and the Dual Expansion of Europe," in *Russia between East and West: Russian Foreign Policy on the Threshold of the Twenty-First Century*, ed. Gabriel Gorodetsky (London: Frank Cass, 2003), 63–64. This three-way division (often with slightly different names for the different tendencies) is employed by many analysts. See, for example, A. G. Arbatov, *Rossiiskaya natsional'naya ideya i vneshnyaya politika (mify i realnosti)* (Moscow: Moskovskii obshchestvennyi nauchni fond, 1998),

48–50; Ilya Prizel, *National Identity and Foreign Policy: Nationalism and Leadership in Poland, Russia, and Ukraine* (Cambridge: Cambridge University Press, 1998), 240; James Richter, "Russian Foreign Policy and the Politics of National Identity," in *The Sources of Russian Foreign Policy After the Cold War*, ed. Celeste A. Wallander (Boulder, CO: Westview, 1996), 70. Trenin employs a similar scheme implicitly. See Dmitri Trenin, *The End of Eurasia: Russia on the Border between Geopolitics and Globalization* (Washington, DC: Carnegie Endowment, 2002), 206–8. Andrei Tsygankov, who has written the most comprehensive account of the intra-elite foreign policy debate, offers a slight variation, in that he identifies four camps, termed "New Thinking" (mostly associated with Gorbachev-era reformists), "Integration with the West," "Great Power Balancing," and "Great Power Pragmatism." See Andrei Tsygankov, *Russia's Foreign Policy*, 26. Irina Isakova also identifies four schools, which she terms "Westernism," "Eurasianism" (geographic determinism of the kind advocated by Communist leader Gennady Zyuganov or Liberal Democratic leader Vladimir Zhirinovsky), "Neo-Eurasianism" (extremist anti-Americanism, as advocated by Dugin in the 1990s), and "Pragmatism." See Isakova, *Russian Governance*, 16–17. Bobo Lo, meanwhile, suggests quite rightly that "the ultimate goal [of the liberal Westernizers] differed little from that of the *derzhavniki* and quasi-imperialists." See Lo, *Vladimir Putin*, 13–14. A slightly different approach is adopted by the social constructivist Ted Hopf, who portrays the different foreign policy orientations in terms of competing "discursive formations" that he labels "New Western Russia," "New Soviet Russia," "Liberal Essentialist," and "Liberal Relativist." See Ted Hopf, *Social Construction of International Politics: Identities & Foreign Policies, Moscow 1955 and 1999* (Ithaca, NY: Cornell University Press, 2002). Because he is interested in broader social discourses, Hopf understands these categories as all-encompassing worldviews that structure perceptions of self-identity and relations with an internal or external "Other." The most nuanced outline of the competing approaches to foreign policy in Putin's Russia is provided by Yury Fedorov of the Moscow State Institute of International Relations (MGIMO), who refers to "hard traditionalists" (or "buffoons"), "neo-imperialists," and "pragmatists." See Yury Fedorov, "'Boffins' and 'Buffoons': Different Strains of Thought in Russia's Strategic Thinking," Chatham House Russia and Eurasia Program Briefing Paper, Mar 2006.

33. This scheme most closely approximates the one employed by Irina Isakova. The designation of "Pragmatism," which Fedorov, Isakova, and Tsygankov all employ in some form as a separate ideological tendency, appears overly deterministic. The pragmatists, by and large, have been those in power who do not have the luxury of ideological purity but are forced to employ a range of sometimes incompatible policies. Saying that Putin is a pragmatist is a rather banal observation. Determining which areas of his foreign policy are influenced by pro-Western liberals and which by extreme Eurasianists provides a more nuanced picture of actual policy. It should be kept in mind, of course, that Kozyrev himself called for a "geopolitical" foreign policy in 1992, in contrast to what he termed the "ideological" approach of the Soviet Union. Jonathan Valdez, "The Near Abroad, the West, and National Identity in Russian Foreign Policy," in *The Making of Foreign Policy in Russia and the New States of Eurasia*, ed. Adeed Dawisha and Karen Dawisha (Armonk, NY: M.E. Sharpe, 1995), 89.

34. The breakdown of elite ideologies and their relative strength looked quite similar in late 1993. See Alexei G. Arbatov, "Russia's Foreign Policy Alternatives,"

International Security, Aut 1993, 18(2): 5–43. Arbatov predicted at the time that "Russian foreign policy most probably will shift . . . to a centrist or moderate-conservative position" that would place greater emphasis on protecting Russian prestige and national interests, especially within the CIS.

35. Dmitri Trenin, "Russia's Security Integration with America and Europe," in *Russia's Engagement with the West: Transformation and Integration in the Twenty-First Century*, ed. Alexander J. Motyl, Blair A. Ruble, and Lilia Shevtsova (Armonk, NY: M.E. Sharpe, 2005), 289. Some scholars, particularly Tsygankov, see a significant discontinuity between the foreign policy views of Primakov and Putin. Tsygankov labels Primakov's approach "Great Power Balancing" in contrast to Putin's "Great Power Pragmatism." The distinction between the two appears more subtle, however, especially since Primakov has been a firm supporter of Putin's foreign policy.

36. See Steven Lee Myers, "Anti-Immigrant Views Catching on in Russia," *New York Times*, 22 Oct 2006.

37. Nabi Abdullaev, "Nationalists Step Forward to Make Political Claims," *St. Petersburg Times*, 22 Nov 2005. The YeSM leader later complained about the DPNI's use of xenophobic rhetoric during the march, charging St. Petersburg police with complicity.

38. Paul Goble, "Russian Anti-Immigrant Group to Collaborate with German Neo-Nazis," Window on Eurasia (blog), 26 Sep 2008, http://windowoneurasia.blogspot.com/2008/09/window-on-eurasia-russian-anti.html.

39. Paul Goble, "Russians Attack Ethnic Georgians Inside the Russian Federation," Window on Eurasia (blog), 14 Aug 2008, http://windowoneurasia.blogspot.com/2008/08/window-on-eurasia-russians-attack.html.

40. Fred Weir, "Putin Taps into a Growing Anti-Minority Fervor," *Christian Science Monitor*, 10 Oct 2006.

41. Sergei Mulin, "Natsi-Proekt," *Novaya Gazeta*, 19 Dec 2007. More broadly, see also Alexander Zaitchik and Mark Ames, "Skinhead Violence Rising in Russia," *The Nation*, 29 Aug 2007; and Jeffrey Mankoff, "Generational Change and the Future of U.S.-Russian Relations," *Journal of International Affairs*, Spr/Sum 2010, 63(2): 10–11.

42. Victor Yasmann, "Red Religion: An Ideology of Neo-Messianic Russian Fundamentalism," *Demokratizatsiya*, Spr 1993, 1(2): 22–24; Donaldson and Nogee, *The Foreign Policy of Russia*, 125–26.

43. H. J. Mackinder, *Democratic Ideals and Reality* (London: Constable, 1919). See also Mackinder, "The Geographical Pivot of History," *Geographical Journal*, Apr 1904, 23(4): 421–37.

44. Zbigniew Brzezinski, *The Grand Chessboard: American Primacy and Its Geostrategic Imperatives* (New York: Basic Books, 1997); Brzezinski, *Game Plan: A Geostrategic Framework for the Conduct of the U.S.-Soviet Contest* (Boston: Atlantic Monthly Press, 1986). See also Francis P. Sempa, *Geopolitics: From the Cold War to the 21st Century* (New Brunswick: Transaction, 2002), 100–114.

45. Yasmann, "Red Religion," 25–28. See also Vladimir Malashenko, "The Russian-Eurasian Idea (Pax Rossica)," *Russian Analytica*, Sep 2005 (6): 5–14.

46. Andreas Umland, "The Rise of Integral Anti-Americanism in the Russian Mass Media and Intellectual Life," History News Network, 26 Jun 2006, http://hnn.us/articles/26108.html.

47. See A. Dugin, "Kondopoga: A Warning Bell," *Russia in Global Affairs*, 2006, 4(4): 8–13.

48. Leonid Ivashov, "Vpolzanie v 'myatezhevoinu,'" *Nezavisimaya Gazeta*, 13 Nov 2002. Marlène Laruelle, *Russian Eurasianism: An Ideology of Empire* (Washington, DC: Woodrow Wilson Center Press, 2008), 115–20.

49. Laruelle, *Russian Eurasianism*, 65–70, 74–83. Yasmann, "Red Religion," 25–31.

50. John B. Dunlop, "Aleksandr Dugin's *Foundations of Geopolitics*," *Demokratizatsiya*, Win 2004, 12(4): 41–42; A. G. Dugin, *Osnovy geopolitiki: Geopoliticheskoe budushchee Rossii* (Moscow: Arktogeya, 1997).

51. Dunlop, "Foundations," 49–52; Dugin, *Osnovy*, 248–60, 367, 377.

52. Fred Weir, "Moscow's Moves in Georgia Track a Script by Right-Wing Prophet," *Christian Science Monitor*, 20 Sep 2008.

53. Laruelle, *Russian Eurasianism*, 155–62. Dunlop, "Foundations," 43–46. The MYeD's website is http://evraziya.info.

54. Aleksandr Dugin, "The Conservator's Balance," Evraziya.org, 8 Aug 2008, http://evrazia.org/article.php?id=577. See also Andrei P. Tsygankov, "Misreading Putin," comment on *JRL* #45, 23 Feb 2007. For Dugin's take on Medvedev, see Aleksandr Chalenko, "Aleksandr Dugin: 'Medvedev povyshaet ugrozu raspada Rossii,'" *Segodnya* (Ukraine), 28 Oct 2010.

55. See L. N. Klepatskii, "The New Russia and the New World Order," in *Russia between East and West: Russian Foreign Policy on the Threshold of the Twenty-First Century*, ed. Gabriel Gorodetsky (London: Frank Cass, 2003), 9; Dmitry Polikanov and Graham Timmins, "Russian foreign policy under Putin," in *Russian Politics under Putin*, ed. Cameron Ross (Manchester: Manchester University Press, 2004), 223–28; Prizel, *National Identity and Foreign Policy*, 269–71; Arbatov, *Rossiiskaya natsional'naya ideya*, 7–8. See also S. N. Baburin, *Territoriya gosudarstva: Pravovye i geopoliticheskie problemy* (Moscow: Izd-vo MGU, 1997), 407–8. A 2001 report by the U.S. National Intelligence Council argues that this trend is essentially power maximizing and nonideological, though arguments about Russia's civilizational identity are by their nature ideological. See "Russia in the International System," Conference Report of the National Intelligence Council, 1 Jun 2001, http://www.dni.gov/nicconfreports—russiainter.html.

56. Aleksandr Lukin, "Litsom k Kitayu: Rossiyane nikak ne otvyknut' smotret' na soseda svysoka," *Kommersant*, 9 Nov 2006.

57. SVOP, "Novye vyzovy bezopasnosti i Rossiya," 11 Jul 2002, http://www.svop.ru/live/materials.asp?m—id-6729&r—id-6758.

58. Sergei Karaganov, "Russia Pulled East and West," trans. Project Syndicate, Feb 1997, http://www.project-syndicate.org/commentary/kar5.

59. Sergei Karaganov, "The NATO Summit," *RFE/RL Newsline*, 19 Nov 2002. See also Mette Skak, "The Logic of Foreign and Security Policy Change in Russia," in *Russia as a Great Power: Dimensions of Security under Putin*, ed. Jakob Hedenskog et al. (London: Routledge, 2005), 91–95.

60. Sergei Karaganov, "Russia and the West After Iraq," trans. Project Syndicate, Jun 2003, http://www.project-syndicate.org/commentary/karaganov8.

61. Sergei Karaganov, "Russia and the International Order," *Military Technology*, Jan 2006: 221–26; Vladislav Inozemtsev and Sergei Karaganov; "Imperialism of the

Fittest," *The National Interest*, Sum 2005 (80): 74–80; Sergey Karaganov, "Farsovaya 'Kholodnaya voina,'" *Rossiiskaya Gazeta*, 26 Dec 2006.

62. Vladimir Lukin, "Our Security Predicament," *Foreign Policy*, Aut 1992 (88): 57–58. See also V. P. Lukin and A. I. Utkin, *Rossiya i Zapad: obshchnost' ili otchuzhdenie?* (Moscow: Yabloko, 1995), 7–9.

63. Vladimir Lukin, "New Century, Greater Concerns," *International Affairs: A Russian Journal of World Politics, Diplomacy and International Relations*, 2002, 48(2): 49.

64. G. A. Zyuganov, "Kak vernut'sya Rossii doverie i uvazhenie mezhdunarodnogo soobshchestva," *Pravda*, 6 Sep 2006. In the mid-1990s, a major struggle broke out within the KPRF over the party's foreign policy orientation. Zyuganov then stood for an aggressive Eurasianist position, emphasizing the Russian people's role in reconstituting a powerful Eurasian state capable of challenging the West's supremacy. His opponents in the party adhered to a traditional Marxist internationalist approach that was no less anti-West but that emphasized the Communist Party's commitment to the international proletariat, without Russia per se occupying any special position in the global division of labor. See Vladimir Bilenkin, "The Ideology of Russia's Rulers in 1995: Westernizers and Eurasians," *Monthly Review*, Oct 1995.

65. Russian Ministry of Foreign Affairs, "Programma effektivnogo ispol'zovaniya na sistemnoi osnove vneshnopoliticheskikh faktorov v tselyakh dolgosrochnogo razvitiya Rossiiskoi Federatsii," 11 May 2010.

66. E. G. Solov'ëv, *Natsional'nye interesy i osnovnye politicheskie sily sovremennoi Rossii* (Moscow: Nauka, 2004), 15.

67. Of course, even Sergey Ivanov, the former intelligence operative once identified as Putin's most likely successor, described himself as "liberal enough" on economic policy, while expressing a fair degree of skepticism regarding Western-style democracy and little interest in Russia's political and security integration with the West. See Neil Buckley and Catherine Belton, interview with Sergey Ivanov, *Financial Times*, 18 Apr 2007.

68. "Medvedev Calls for Strengthened Fight against Corruption in Russia," *International Herald Tribune*, 22 Jan 2008.

69. Eduard Solov'ev, "The Foreign Policy Priorities of Liberal Russia," *Russian Politics and Law*, May–Jun 2006, 44(3): 52–53.

70. A. B. Chubais, "Missiya Rossii v XXI veke," *Nezavisimaya Gazeta*, 1 Oct 2003. Yu. Arkhangel'sky and P. Yermolaev, "Politicheskaya elita i strategicheskie prioritety RF: Mezhdu 'metologicheskim idealizmom' i 'naivnym realizmom,'" *Mirovaya ekonomika i mezhdunarodnye otnosheniya*, Nov 2006 (11): 100. Chubais's idea is similar to the "superimperialism" advocated by Karaganov and Vladislav Inozemtsev. See Inozemtsev and Karaganov, "Imperialism of the Fittest."

71. Yegor Gaidar, "The Collapse of the Soviet Union: Lessons for Contemporary Russia," address to the American Enterprise Institute, 13 Nov 2006, http://www.aei.org/events/filter.all,eventID.1420/transcript.asp. Also see Gaidar, *Gibel' imperii: Uroki dlya sovremennoi Rossii* (Moscow: ROSSPEN, 2006).

72. "Rossiya XXI veka: Obraz zhelaemogo zavtra," INSOR Report, Jan 2010, http://insor-russia.ru/files/Obraz_gel_zavtra_0.pdf.

73. Petr Ovrekhin and Evlaliya Samedova, "Korporatsiya 'Kreml' uspeshno porabotala," *Nezavisimaya Gazeta*, 26 Jul 2005.

74. *Vlast'-2010: 60 biografii* (Moscow: Panorama, 2010), 5–11, 190–93, http://scilla.ru/works/knigi/vlast2010.pdf.

75. Neil Buckley and Arkady Ostrovsky, "Back in Business—How Putin's Allies Are Turning Russia into a Corporate State," *Financial Times,* 19 Jun 2006.

76. News conference of presidential aide Vladislav Surkov, Deputy Head of the Presidential Administration.

77. Philip Hanson and Elizabeth Teague, "Big Business and the State in Russia," *Europe-Asia Studies,* Jul 2005, 57(5): 657–80.

78. Dmitri Trenin, "Russia Redefines Itself and Its Relations with the West," *Washington Quarterly,* Spr 2007, 30(2).

79. Medvedev, "Speech at meeting with Russian ambassadors and permanent representatives in international organizations," 16 Jul 2010, *Russia Beyond the Headlines,* http://rbth.ru/articles/2010/07/16/speech_at_meeting_with_russian_ambassadors .html.

80. Stefan Wagstyl, "Medvedev Clashes with Putin," *Financial Times,* 10 Jul 2009.

81. "Na troikh ne vkhoditsya," *Kommersant,* 11 Jul 2009.

82. *Vlast'-2010,* 163–67. Russian Agency for Youth Affairs (RosMolodëzh), "Vladislav Surkov vstretil'sya s molodymi liderami Ameriki," 15 Mar 2011.

83. Elina Bilevskaya, "Teksty Surkova vozvrashchayutsya," *Nezavisimaya Gazeta,* 9 Aug 2010.

84. Andrew E. Kramer, "Russian Stock Market Fall Is Said to Imperil Oil Boom," *New York Times,* 12 Sep 2008.

85. Dmitry Medvedev, "Vystuplenie na vstreche s predstavitelyami politicheskikh, parlamentskikh i obshchestvennykh krugov Germanii," The Kremlin, 5 Jun 2008, http://www.kremlin.ru/appears/2008/06/05/1923—type63374type63376 type63377—202133.shtml.

86. Bobo Lo, "The Securitization of Russian Foreign Policy under Putin," in *Russia between East and West: Russian Foreign Policy on the Threshold of the Twenty-First Century,* ed. Gabriel Gorodetsky (London: Frank Cass, 2003), 12–15.

87. Matthew Schmidt, "Is Putin Pursuing a Policy of Eurasianism?" *Demokratizatsiya,* Win 2005, 13(1): 92.

88. Putin, "Poslanie Federal'nomu Sobraniyu Rossiiskoi Federatsii," The Kremlin, 25 Apr 2005, http://www.kremlin.ru/appears/2005/04/25/1223—type63372type 63374type8263487049.shtml.

89. Putin, "Poslanie Federal'nomu Sobraniyu Rossiiskoi Federatsii," The Kremlin, 16 May 2003, http://www.kremlin.ru/appears/2003/05/16/1259—type63372 type63374—44623.shtml.

90. James Collins, foreword to *Putin's Russia: Past Imperfect, Future Uncertain,* ed. Dale R. Herspring (Lanham, MD: Rowman & Littlefield, 2005), xiv–xv.

91. Mark N. Katz, "Primakov Redux? Putin's Pursuit of 'Multipolarism' in Asia," *Demokratizatsiya,* Win 2006, 14(1): 148–49.

92. Isakova's argument that Putin sought both economic and security integration with Western institutions is somewhat overstated. See Isakova, *Russian Governance,* 40. As Lo points out, security engagement and integration are sharply limited and remain subordinate to the larger goal of Russia reasserting itself as a central global player. See Lo, *Vladimir Putin,* 111–13.

93. Schmidt, "Pursuing," 93.

94. "Nachalo vstrechi s prezidentom Gruzii Mikhailom Saakashvili," The Kremlin, 6 Jun 2008, http://www.kremlin.ru/appears/2008/06/06/1618—type63377—202182.shtml.

95. Ellen Barry, "Russian President Dismisses Georgia's Leader as a 'Political Corpse,'" *New York Times*, 2 Sep 2008.

CHAPTER 3: RESETTING EXPECTATIONS: RUSSIA AND THE UNITED STATES

1. Eugene Rumer and Angela Stent, "Russia and the West," *Survival*, Apr/May 2009, 51(2): 91–104. See also James Goldgeier, "A Realistic Reset with Russia," *Policy Review*, Aug/Sep 2009 (156): 15–26.

2. Russian Ministry of Foreign Affairs, "Obzor vneshnei politiki Rossiiskoi Federatsii," Mar 2007: 48–49, http://www.mid.ru/brp—4.nsf/sps.

3. Thomas Graham, statement to "Russia: Today, Tomorrow—and in 2008" Conference, American Enterprise Institute, 14 Oct 2005, http://www.aei.org/events/eventID.1119,filter.all/event—detail.asp.

4. Sergey Rogov, "Strategicheskoe partnerstvo vsë eshchë vozmozhno," *Nezavisimaya Gazeta*, 19 Mar 2007.

5. See Irina Isakova, *Russian Governance in the Twenty-First Century: Geo-strategy, Geopolitics and Governance* (London: Frank Cass, 2005), 87–89.

6. See Andrew Monaghan, "'Calmly Critical': Evolving Russian Views of U.S. Hegemony," *Journal of Strategic Studies*, Dec 2006, 29(6): 987–1013.

7. Yevgeny Primakov, "Superderzhavy perestali sushchestvovat' s okonchaniem 'kholodnoi voiny,'" interview with *Rossiiskaya Gazeta*, 20 Oct 2006.

8. See, for instance, Sergey Lavrov, "Rossiya i SShA: Mezhdu proshlym i budushchim," *Mezhdunarodnik.ru*, 26 Sep 2006, http://www.mezhdunarodnik.ru/magazin/5308.html.

9. "Lavrov prokommentiroval otnosheniya Rossii s SShA," *Izvestiya*, 21 May 2007.

10. Alex Pravda, "Putin's Foreign Policy after 11 September: Radical or Revolutionary?" in *Russia between East and West: Russian Foreign Policy on the Threshold of the Twenty-First Century*, ed. Gabriel Gorodetsky (London: Frank Cass, 2003), 50–51.

11. Revelations of pervasive corruption and double-dealing, for example, on the part of the Harvard Institute for International Development (HIID)—which was successfully sued by the U.S. government and then shut down in response to the scandal—did nothing to allay Russian suspicion of U.S. motives in aiding the transition from Communism. On the HIID scandal, see David McClintick, "How Harvard Lost Russia," *Institutional Investor*, Feb 2006, http://www.dailyii.com/article.asp?ArticleID-1020662.

12. On this point see especially Dmitri Simes, "Losing Russia," *Foreign Affairs*, Nov–Dec 2007, 86(6).

13. Yevgeny Gal'tsov, "Kosmicheskaya oborona dlya zemnogo shara," *Nezavisimaya Gazeta*, 21 Mar 2003; Petr Polkovnikov, "Okno uyazvimosti," *Nezavisimaya Gazeta*, 21 Feb 2003.

14. "Gosdep SShA prosit Rossiyu ne obol'shchat'sya svoei voennoi mosh'yu," *Izvestiya*, 20 Apr 2007. U.S. diplomats are of course aware of how U.S. actions are perceived in Russia but have had less success in changing those perceptions. See William J. Burns, "Coffee Break at the State Department: U.S. Ambassador to Russia," *JRL* #8, 12 Jan 2007.

15. See Council on Foreign Relations, "Russia's Wrong Direction: What the United States Can and Should Do," Independent Task Force Report #57, Mar 2006.

16. See especially James M. Goldgeier and Michael McFaul, *Power and Purpose: U.S. Policy toward Russia after the Cold War* (Washington, DC: Brookings, 2003), 157–60.

17. Goldgeier and McFaul, *Power and Purpose*, 158–59.

18. Yevgeni Primakov, "Turning Back over the Atlantic," *International Affairs: A Russian Journal of World Politics, Diplomacy and International Relations*, 2002, 48(6): 65–74.

19. Alan Russo, "Mir v Yugoslavii: Komu eto vygodno?" Carnegie Moscow Center Briefing, Jun 1999, 1(6), http://www.carnegie.ru/ru/print/48347-print.htm. True, the bombing of Serbia was not technically unilateral since Washington's NATO allies were involved. Still accustomed to thinking in terms of power blocs, though, Moscow perceived the attack as a fundamentally U.S. policy in which the West Europeans acquiesced.

20. Derek Averre, "From Pristina to Tskhinvali: The Legacy of Operation Allied Force in Russia's Relations with the West," *International Affairs*, 2009, 85(3): 585–7.

21. Sean Kay, "What Is a Strategic Partnership?" *Problems of Post-Communism*, May–Jun 2000, 47(3): 15–24.

22. On the international response to the October 1999 invasion of Chechnya, see Strobe Talbott, *The Russia Hand: A Memoir of Presidential Diplomacy* (New York: Random House, 2002), 165–68; "EU Calls for Dialogue between Moscow, Grozny," *RFE/RL Newsline*, 8 Oct 1999.

23. On SORT and opposition to it, see Anatoly Dyakov and others, "Ratifitsirovat' nel'zya otklonit': Chto delat' s Dogovorom o strategicheskikh nastupatel'nykh potentsialakh Rossii i SShA?" *Nezavisimoe voennoe obozrenie*, 20 Sep 2002. Lacking verification measures and not mandating the destruction of decommissioned warheads, SORT was criticized by arms control advocates as lacking substance. Precisely this feature induced the Bush administration to submit it to the Senate for ratification. See Donald Rumsfeld, "Prepared Statement to Senate Foreign Relations Committee," 17 Jul 2002, http://www.defenselink.mil/speeches/speech.aspx?speechid-269.

24. Amy F. Wolf and Stuart D. Goldman, "Arms Control after START-II: Next Steps on the U.S.-Russian Agenda," Congressional Research Service Report for Congress, 22 Jun 2001.

25. Wolf and Goldman, "Arms Control."

26. Pavel K. Baev, "The Trajectory of the Russian Military," in *The Russian Military*, ed. Steven E. Miller and Dmitri V. Trenin (Cambridge, MA: American Academy of Arts and Sciences, 2004), 57–59; Robert H. Donaldson and Joseph L. Nogee, *The Foreign Policy of Russia: Changing Systems, Enduring Interests*, 2nd ed. (Armonk, NY: M.E. Sharpe, 2002), 333–37.

27. This connection was made explicit, for instance, in Putin's 2003 address to the Federal Assembly. Putin, "Poslanie Federal'nomu Sobraniyu Rossiiskoi Federatsii,"

The Kremlin, 16 May 2003, http://www.kremlin.ru/appears/2003/05/16/1259—type 63372type63374type82634_44623.shtml.

28. See "Bush and Putin: Best of Friends," BBC News, 16 Jun 2001, http://news .bbc.co.uk/2/hi/europe/1392791.stm.

29. Dmitri K. Simes, "A View from Russia: Grading the President," *Foreign Policy*, Jul–Aug 2003 (137): 36.

30. Condoleezza Rice, "Campaign 2000: Promoting the National Interest," *Foreign Affairs*, Jan–Feb 2000, 79(1).

31. Igor Ivanov, "The New Russian Identity: Innovation and Continuity in Russian Foreign Policy," *Washington Quarterly*, Sum 2001, 24(3): 7–13.

32. See James M. Goldgeier, "The United States and Russia: Keeping Expectations Realistic," *Policy Review*, Oct–Nov 2001: 47–65.

33. Timothy J. Colton and Michael McFaul, "America's Real Russian Allies," *Foreign Affairs*, Nov–Dec 2001, 80(6): 46–58.

34. Paul J. Murphy, *Wolves of Islam: Russia and the Faces of Chechen Terror* (Washington, DC: Brassey's, 2004), 89–91; Dale Herspring and Peter Rutland, "Putin and Russian Foreign Policy," in *Putin's Russia: Past Imperfect, Future Uncertain*, ed. Dale Herspring (Lanham, MD: Rowman & Littlefield, 2005), 272–73.

35. Vladimir Putin, "Vstupiel'noe slovo na zasedanii Soveta bezopasnosti," 3 Dec 2003, http://www.kremlin.ru/appears/2003/12/03/1821—type63374type63378—56602.shtml.

36. "Joint Statement by U.S. President George Bush and Russian Federation President V. V. Putin Announcing the Global Initiative to Combat Nuclear Terrorism," *Joint Communiqué of 2006 G8 Summit*, http://en.g8russia.ru/docs/5.html. See also Daniel Fried, "Statement before Senate Foreign Relations Committee," 21 Jun 2007.

37. Igor Ivanov interview, "Otvety Ministra inostrannykh del Rossiiskoi Federatsii I. S. Ivanova na voprosy zhurnala 'Kosmopolis,'" *Kosmopolis*, Aut 2002 (1).

38. See James Sherr, "Russia's Current Trajectory," *Russia in the International System*, Conference Report of the U.S. National Intelligence Council, 1 Jun 2001, http://www .dni.gov/nic/confreports—russiainter.html. Sherr believed in 2001 that Russian saber rattling in Afghanistan was in reality designed to intimidate Uzbekistan, which had recently joined the anti-Russian GUUAM grouping, into returning to the Russian fold.

39. Gennady Charodeev, "My raskroem amerikantsam afganskie tainy," *Izvestiya*, 14 Sep 2001.

40. Vladimir Putin, "Zayavlenie Prezidenta Rossii," The Kremlin, 24 Sep 2001, http://www.kremlin.ru/appears/2001/09/24/0002—type63374type63377—28639.shtml.

41. Vladimir Mukhin, "Vashington i Moskva uzhe planiruyut poslevoennoe ustroistvo mira," *Nezavisimaya Gazeta*, 21 Sep 2001.

42. Vladimir Mukhin, "SShA ishchut voennye bazy v SNG," *Nezavisimaya Gazeta*, 15 Sep 2001. His choices were also constrained by the willingness of Central Asia's leaders (especially Uzbekistan's Islam Karimov) to grant the U.S. basing rights regardless of Russian sensibilities.

43. Milrad Fatullaev, "Voina idët v Rossiyu," *Nezavisimaya Gazeta*, 11 Oct 2001.

44. Bobo Lo, *Vladimir Putin and the Evolution of Russian Foreign Policy* (London: Royal Institute of International Affairs, 2003), 118–20; Herspring and Rutland, "Putin and Russian Foreign Policy," 273–74. On Russian aid to the Northern Alliance, see

Igor Korotchenko, "Lend-liz ot Sergeya Ivanova," *Nezavisimaya Gazeta*, 4 Oct 2001. On the other hand, the strategy of supporting the U.S. in Afghanistan also proved popular with the Russian public, as even Putin's opponents acknowledged. Grigory Yavlinsky, "Domestic and Foreign Policy Challenges in Russia," speech to Carnegie Endowment for International Peace, 31 Jan 2002, http://www.cdi.org/russia/johnson/6061-1.cfm.

45. See the roundtable discussion "Russia's Place in the World after September 11," *International Affairs: A Russian Journal of World Politics, Diplomacy, and International Relations*, 2002, 48(2): 78–91.

46. Yevgeny Primakov, "Is the Russia-U.S. Rapprochement Here to Stay?" *International Affairs: A Russian Journal of World Politics, Diplomacy, and International Relations*, 2002, 48(6): 87–88.

47. Karimov's demand was made in the name of the Shanghai Cooperation Organization, in which Russia (as well as China) plays a key role. See Lionel Beehner, "Severing of U.S.-Uzbek Ties over Counterterrorism," *Council on Foreign Relations Backgrounder*, 30 Sep 2005, http://www.cfr.org/publication/8940/severing—of—usuzbek—ties—over—counterterrorism.html.

48. Andrew C. Winner, "The Proliferation Security Initiative: The New Face of Interdiction," *Washington Quarterly*, Spr 2005, 28(2): 129–43.

49. Council on Foreign Relations, "Russia's Wrong Direction," 24–25.

50. See especially Thomas Nichols, "Russia's Turn West," *World Policy Journal*, Win 2002–2003, 19(4): 13–22.

51. Vladimir Putin, "Poslanie Federal'nomu sobraniyu," The Kremlin, 18 Apr 2002, http://www.kremlin.ru/appears/2002/04/18/0000—type63372type63374type82634—28876.shtml.

52. See Tor Bukkvoll, "Putin's Strategic Partnership with the West: The Domestic Politics of Russian Foreign Policy," *Comparative Strategy*, 2003 (22): 222–42.

53. Ariel Cohen, "Bringing Russia into an Anti-Saddam Coalition," Heritage Foundation Executive Memorandum #812, 29 Apr 2002, http://www.heritage.org/Research/RussiaandEurasia/EM812.cfm.

54. Robin Wright and Keith B. Richburg, "Rice Reaches Out to Europe: Paris Speech Urges 'New Chapter' in U.S. Alliance," *Washington Post*, 9 Feb 2005.

55. Russian Ministry of Foreign Affairs, "Obzor vneshnei politiki," 49.

56. Andrew Kuchins, "A Turning Point in U.S.-Russian Relations?" Carnegie Endowment for International Peace (originally published in *Vedomosti*, 20 Nov 2006), http://www.carnegiendowment.org/publications/index.cfm?fa-view&id-18872&prog-zru.

57. Yuri Ushakov, "From Russia with Like," *Los Angeles Times*, 1 Feb 2007.

58. "Doktrina formirovaniya Strategicheskogo Soyuza Rossii i SShA," *Nezavisimaya Gazeta*, 29 Oct 2003.

59. Nikita Ivanov and Vladimir Frolov, "Dogovor o strategicheskoi druzhbe," *Izvestiya*, 11 Sep 2003.

60. Yevgeny Verlin, "Vashingtonu predlozhili strategicheskii soyuz," *Nezavisimaya Gazeta*, 29 Sep 2003.

61. Robert Legvold, "All the Way: Crafting a U.S.-Russian Alliance," *The National Interest*, Win 2002–2003: 21–31; Robert MacFarlane, "What's Good for Russia Is Good for America," *New York Times*, 26 Sep 2003.

62. "Remarks by the President and Russian President Putin in Press Availability Camp David," 27 Sep 2003, http://moscow.usembassy.gov/bilateral/transcript.php?record—id-18.

63. Roderic Lyne, Strobe Talbott, and Koji Watanabe, "Engaging with Russia: The Next Phase," report to the Trilateral Commission, Triangle Papers 59, 2006: 40–44.

64. Janusz Bugajski, "Russia's New Europe," *The National Interest*, Win 2003–2004 (74): 84–91.

65. Putin, "Vystuplenie i diskussiya na Myunkhenskoi konferentsii po voprosam politiki bezopasnosti," The Kremlin, 10 Feb 2007, http://www.kremlin.ru/appears/2007/02/10/1737—type63374type63376type63377type63381type82634—118097.shtml.

66. "Fact Sheet: U.S.-Russia Strategic Framework Declaration," 6 Apr 2008, http://www.whitehouse.gov/news/releases/2008/04/20080406–5.html.

67. James Marson, "Putin to the West: Hands Off Ukraine," *Time*, 25 May 2009.

68. John McCain, "We Are All Georgians," *Wall Street Journal*, 14 Aug 2008.

69. William Kristol, "Will Russia Get Away With It?" *New York Times*, 10 Aug 2008. McCain's call for international peacekeepers seemed to imply a leading role for NATO in policing the cease-fire, a move which would have been equally provocative.

70. "Official Statements on Russia-Georgia Conflict," http://www.sras.org/official_statements_on_russia_georgia_conflict.

71. Konstantin Remchukov, "Medvedev protiv konflikta s Zapadom," *Nezavisimaya Gazeta*, 18 Nov 2008.

72. Michael McFaul, "Testimony to House Committee on International Affairs," 9 Sep 2008, http://iis-db.stanford.edu/pubs/22223/MCFAUL-Testimony-9-9-2008-FINAL.pdf.

73. Craig Whitlock, "'Reset' Sought on Relations with Russia, Biden Says," *Washington Post*, 8 Feb 2009. Obama had used the term "reset" somewhat earlier, during his 7 December 2008 appearance on *Meet the Press*, but it was Biden's imagery of the reset button that gave the image traction.

74. Medvedev, "Poslanie Federal'nomu Sobraniyu," The Kremlin, 5 Nov 2008, http://www.kremlin.ru/transcripts/1968.

75. Sergei Lavrov, "Russia and the World in the 21st Century," *Russia in Global Affairs*, 2008, (3): 14.

76. "Medvedev-Obama: Perezagruzka," RIA-Novosti, 1 Apr 2009, http://www.rian.ru/politics/20090401/166744761.html.

77. Matthew Rojansky, "Indispensible Institutions: The Obama-Medvedev Commission and Five Decades of U.S.-Russia Dialogue," Carnegie Endowment for International Peace, 2010. U.S.-Russia Bilateral Presidential Commission Fact Sheet, 9 Jul 2009, http://www.america.gov/st/texttrans-english/2009/July/20090706131018xjsnommis0.5159418.html.

78. Olga Allenova, "Rossiya pomozhet SShA s afganskim tranzitom," *Kommersant*, 6 Jul 2009.

79. Andrei Terekhov, "Obama vykhodit iz igry pri svoikh," *Nezavisimaya Gazeta*, 18 Sep 2009.

80. Marc Champion and Peter Spiegel, "Allies React to U.S. Missile U-Turn," *Wall Street Journal*, 18 Sep 2009.

81. Medvedev, "Poslanie Prezidenta Federal'nomu Sobraniyu," The Kremlin, 30 Nov 2010, http://www.kremlin.ru/transcripts/9637.

82. Lavrov, "Stenogramma vystupleniya i otvetov Ministra inostrannykh del Rossii S.V. Lavrova na voprosy SMI v khode press-konferentsii po itogam telefonnogo razgovora Prezidenta Rossii D.A. Medvedeva i Prezidenta SShA B. Obamy," Russian Ministry of Foreign Affairs, 26 Mar 2010.

83. "Key Facts about the New START Treaty," White House Office of the Press Secretary, 26 Mar 2010, http://www.whitehouse.gov/the-press-office/key-facts-about-new-start-treaty.

84. "Treaty Between the United States of America and the Russian Federation on Measures for the Further Reduction and Limitation of Strategic Offensive Arms," 8 Apr 2010, http://www.state.gov/documents/organization/140035.pdf.

85. Lavrov, "Stenogramma interv'yu Ministra inostrannykh del Rossii S.V. Lavrova programme 'Vesti v subbotu,' telekanala 'Rossii,'" Russian Ministry of Foreign Affairs, 10 Apr 2010.

86. Lavrov, "Stenogramma vystupleniya i otvetov Ministra inostrannykh del Rossii S.V. Lavrova na voprosy SMI v khode press-konferentsii po itogam telefonnogo razgovora Prezidenta Rossii D.A. Medvedeva i Prezidenta SShA B. Obamy," Russian Ministry of Foreign Affairs, 26 Mar 2010.

87. U.S. Census Bureau, Foreign Trade Statistics 2009, http://www.census.gov/foreign-trade/balance/c4621.html#2009.

88. "Programma effektivnogo ispol'zovaniya na sistemnoi osnove vneshne-politicheskikh faktorov v tselyakh dolgosrochnogo razvitiya Rossiiskoi Federatsii," Russian Ministry of Foreign Affairs, 11 May 2010, http://www.runewsweek.ru/country/34184.

89. "Rossiya i mir: 2011: Ekonomika i vneshnyaya politika, Yezhegodny prognoz," INSOR, 2010: 88–90. Also see Samuel Charap, "The Transformation of US-Russia Relations," *Current History*, Oct 2010, 109(729): 281–7; Sergey Karaganov, "Posle 'perezagruzki,' Novaya povestka dnya dlya rossiisko-amerikanskikh otnoshenii," *Rossiiskaya Gazeta*, 30 Sep 2010.

90. Ray Takeyh and Nicolas Gvosdev, "Why Rice's Moscow Visit Failed," *Moscow Times*, 20 Oct 2005.

91. Robert O. Freedman, "Putin, Iran, and the Nuclear Weapons Issue," *Problems of Post-Communism*, Mar–Apr 2006, 53(2): 39–48.

92. Peter Finn, "Iran, Russia Reach Tentative Nuclear Deal," *Washington Post*, 27 Feb 2006.

93. Steven Erlanger and Mark Landler, "Iran Agrees to Send Enriched Uranium to Russia," *New York Times*, 1 Oct 2009.

94. "Russia's Medvedev raps US, EU sanctions against Iran," BBC News online, 18 Jun 2010, http://news.bbc.co.uk/2/hi/world/us_and_canada/10348630.stm.

95. "Senior Russian lawmaker blames Iran for Russia's S-300 sale ban," RIA-Novosti, 27 Sep 2010.

96. Clifford J. Levy and Thom Shanker, "In Rare Split, Two Leaders in Russia Disagree on Libya," *New York Times*, 21 Mar 2011.

97. Most notably, this charge was leveled by former Communist Party central committee secretary and Soviet ambassador to West Germany Valentin Falin and retired Lt. General Gennady Yevstafiev of the SVR in a report leaked to the press in December 2006. The report was designed in part to discredit former prime minister Mikhail Kasyanov, who had become a leading critic of Putin, by charging him with being a U.S. agent and the likely beneficiary of a Russian colored revolution. See

Yulia Petrovskaya, "Izolyatziya i revolyutsiya: V Vashingtone rasschityvayut na prikhod k vlasti v Moskve levogo politika, podderzhannogo liberal'nymi silami," *Nezavisimaya Gazeta*, 21 Sep 2006. Also see "Der Kalte Krieg ist nicht zu Ende," interview with Valentin Falin, *Russland.ru*, http://russland.ru/kapitulation1/morenews .php?iditem-39.

98. "Russia's Lavrov Slams Bush Statement on S. Ossetia," RIA-Novosti, 13 Aug 2008, http://en.rian.ru/russia/20080813/116020741.html.

99. See S. Oznobishchev, "Russia and the United States: Is 'Cold Peace' Possible?" *International Affairs: A Russian Journal of World Politics, Diplomacy, and International Relations*, 2004, 50(4): 55.

100. Of course, one should be careful about generalizing from these cases. The Baltic states never accepted their incorporation in the USSR at the start of World War II, while Georgia's anti-Russian inclinations were strengthened by Moscow's two-decade-long encouragement of the Abkhazian and South Ossetian separatists. It might be more accurate to say that Russian meddling in the domestic politics of these states strengthens anti-Russian sentiment (such was the case in Ukraine leading up to the 2004 Orange Revolution). It is also worth noting that Saakashvili's Georgia has hardly turned into a paragon of democracy, though Saakashvili has maintained a pro-Western foreign policy orientation and expressed serious interest in bringing Georgia into NATO.

101. "Crisis in Georgia: Frozen Conflicts and U.S.-Russian Relations," Carnegie Endowment for International Peace meeting summary, 11 Oct 2006, *JRL* #237.

102. Mikhail Zigar, "Dik Cheini proshchupal dno Kaspii," *Kommersant*, 6 May 2006.

103. "In Tbilisi, Clinton Raps Russia Over Bases," *Moscow Times*, 6 Jul 2010.

104. "Joint Statement of the Presidents of the United States and the Russian Federation in Connection with the Situation in the Kyrgyz Republic," 24 Jun 2010, http:// www.whitehouse.gov/sites/default/files/US-Russia%20Joint%20Statement% 20on%20Kyrgyzstan.pdf.

105. David J. Kramer, "U.S. Abandoning Russia's Neighbors," *Washington Post*, 15 May 2010.

106. Medvedev, "Interv'yu Dmitriya Medvedeva telekanalam 'Rossiya', Pervomu, NTV," The Kremlin, 31 Aug 2008, http://www.kremlin.ru/appears/2008/08/31/ 1917—type63374type63379—205991.shtml.

107. Ilya Azar and Aleksandr Artemeyev, "Zaryadka mirovoi napryazhennosti," *Gazeta.ru*, 29 Jul 2008.

108. Andrew E. Kramer, "Putin Likens U.S. Foreign Policy to That of Third Reich," *International Herald Tribune*, 9 May 2007.

CHAPTER 4: EUROPE: BETWEEN INTEGRATION AND CONFRONTATION

1. Of the former Warsaw Pact states that were not onetime constituent republics of the USSR, only Albania—which left the pact in 1968—remains outside the EU. Albania is also the only ex–Warsaw Pact member outside of NATO (all of the Yugo-

slav successor states apart from Slovenia also remain outside one or both organizations, but because of the Tito-Stalin rift, Yugoslavia never joined the Warsaw Pact). The former Soviet republics of Lithuania, Latvia, and Estonia are also members of both NATO and the EU.

2. See Dov Lynch, "Russia's Strategic Partnership with Europe," *Washington Quarterly*, Spr 2004, 27(2): 100. The 2009 Treaty of Lisbon created the CFSP, which in its previous incarnation was known as the Common Foreign Policy (CFP) and operated separately from the European Security and Defense Policy (ESDP).

3. Yevgeny Primakov, "Intervention at the North Atlantic Cooperation Council ministerial," 11 Dec 1996, http://www.nato.int/docu/speech/1996/s9612115.htm.

4. Putin mentioned this promise in his widely covered 2007 Munich Security Conference speech. Vladimir Putin, "Vystuplenie i diskussiya na Myunkhenskoi konferentsii po voprosam politiki bezopasnosti," 10 Feb 2007, http://www.kremlin.ru/appears/2007/02/10/1737—type63374type63377type63381type82634—1181097.shtml. For diverging takes on this promise, see Mark Kramer, "Russian Policy Toward the Commonwealth of Independent States: Recent Trends and Future Prospects," *Problems of Post-Communism*, Nov/Dec 2008, 55(6) and Charles Kupchan, "NATO's Final Frontier: Why Russia Should Join the Atlantic Alliance," *Foreign Affairs*, May/Jun 2010, 89(3).

5. Daniel Fried, "The Future of NATO: How Valuable an Asset?" testimony to House of Representatives Committee on Foreign Affairs, 22 Jun 2007, http://foreignaffairs.house.gov/110/fri062207.htm.

6. Lúcio Vinhas de Souza, "Foreign investment in Russia," ECFIN Country Focus, Nov 2008, 5(1).

7. On discussions concerning Russian membership in the EU, see Vitaly Merkushev, "Relations between Russia and the EU: The View from across the Atlantic," *Perspectives on European Politics and Society*, 2005, 6(2): 360–62. Alexander Kramarenko, "5 Reasons Why Russia Could Join NATO," *Moscow Times*, 9 Dec 2010. Angela Charlton, "Putin Says Russia Could Join NATO," Associated Press, 5 Mar 2000.

8. Vladimir Putin, "50 Years of the [sic] European Integration and Russia," *JRL* #72, 26 Mar 2007. See also Putin, "Poslanie Federal'nomu sobraniyu," The Kremlin, 16 May 2003, http://www.kremlin.ru/appears/2003/05/16/1259—type63372type63374type82634—44623.shtml.

9. Sergei Lavrov, "Russia and the World in the 21st Century," *Russia in Global Affairs*, 2008 (3): 10.

10. Merkushev, "Relations between Russia and the EU," 366.

11. "Ministr inostrannykh del Rossii Sergei Lavrov: 'Setovaya diplomatiya' seichas vostrebovana kak nikogda," *Izvestiya*, 28 Dec 2006.

12. Putin, "Vystuplenie na soveshchanii rukovodyashchego sostava sotrudnikov diplomaticheskoi sluzhby Rossii," The Kremlin, 26 Jan 2001, http://www.kremlin.ru/appears/2001/01/26/0000—type63374type63377type63378—28464.shtml.

13. Angela Stent, "Berlin's Russia Challenge," *The National Interest*, Mar–Apr 2007: 47.

14. European Union External Relations Directorate-General, "Russia: Country Strategy Paper, 2007–2013," 7 Mar 2007, http://ec.europa.eu/external—relations/russia/csp/index.htm. The "frozen conflicts" refer to the unresolved disputes between

Georgia and Abkhazia/South Ossetia, between Moldova and Transnistria, and the three-way dispute among Armenia, Azerbaijan, and the Nagorno-Karabakh enclave.

15. Angela Stent and Eugene Rumer, "Russia and the West," *Survival*, Apr–May 2009, 51(2): 95.

16. Russia did not sign any agreements with the EC proper until 1988. See Merkushev, "Relations between Russia and the EU," 357–58.

17. Nadezhda Arbatova, "L'échéance de 2007 et l'état des relations politiques entre la Russie et l'UE," Institut Français des Relations Internationales (IFRI), Russie.Nei.Visions (20): 7.

18. Mette Skak, "The Mismatch of Russia and the EU as Actors in a Globalized World," presentation to the "Russia and the European Union after Enlargement: New Prospects and Problems" conference, *JRL* #9265, 11 Oct 2005.

19. During the second Chechen war, the Council of Europe's Parliamentary Assembly (PACE) briefly suspended Russia's voting rights in April 2000.

20. Russian Ministry of Foreign Affairs, "Medium-term Strategy for Development of Relations between the Russian Federation and the EU," 22 Oct 1999, http://presidency.finland.fi/netcomm/News/showarticle1610.html.

21. Russian Ministry of Foreign Affairs, "Medium-term Strategy for Development."

22. Angela Stent and Lilia Shevtsova, "America, Russia, and Europe: A Realignment?" *Survival*, Win 2002–2003, 44(4): 121–34.

23. European Council, "Conclusions and Plan of Action of the Extraordinary European Council Meeting on 21 September 2001," http://www.eurunion.org/partner/EUUSTerror/ExtrEurCounc.pdf.

24. European Council, "A Secure Europe in a Better World," 12 Dec 2003, http://www.consilium.europa.eu/uedocs/cms—data/docs/2004/4/29/European%20Security%20Strategy.pdf.

25. On the European Union's expanded defense capability, see Bastian Giegerich and William Wallace, "Not Such a Soft Power: The External Deployment of European Forces," *Survival*, Sum 2004, 46(2): 163–82.

26. Alexander Nikitin, "Russian Perceptions of the CFSP/ESDP," European Institute for Security Studies Analysis, May 2006, www.iss-eu.org/new/analysis/analy145.pdf.

27. "Russia Warns EU over Ex-Soviet Sphere of Influence," *JRL* #30, 7 Feb 2007.

28. "EU Must Give Kiev Ascension Hope," *Financial Times*, 28 Aug 2008. "Gazeta Wyborcza: Ukraine's EU Membership Is a Matter of Time, Ukraine's Foreign Minister Says," *Kyiv Post*, 22 May 2010.

29. Vladimir Avdonin, "Rossiiskaya transformatsiya i partnërstvo s Yevropoi," *Kosmopolis*, Win 2003–2004, 4(6).

30. Nikitin, "Russian Perceptions," 7.

31. Celeste A. Wallander, "The Challenge of Russia for U.S. Policy," testimony to Senate Committee on Foreign Relations, 21 Jun 2005. See also Jeffrey Mankoff, "Russian Foreign Policy in the Putin Era," Yale University International Security Studies Working Papers, Jan 2007, http://www.yale.edu/macmillan/iac/mankoff.pdf.

32. Uwe Klussmann, Christian Neef, and Matthias Schepp, "Russland: Annähern und verflechten," *Der Spiegel*, 2 Oct 2006; Stent, "Berlin's Russia Challenge."

33. Katrin Bastian and Roland Götz, "Deutsch-russische Beziehungen im europäischen Kontext: Zwischen Interessenallianz und strategischer Partnerschaft,"

Stiftungs Wissenschaft und Politik Berlin (SWP-Berlin) Diskussionspapiere, May 2005: 5–6.

34. This policy was particularly associated with Merkel's first foreign minister, Frank-Walter Steinmeier, a Social Democrat who was also a close adviser to Schröder. See Stent, "Berlin's Russia Challenge."

35. Russian Ministry of Foreign Affairs, "Obzor vneshnei politiki Rossiiskoi Federatsii," 27 Mar 2007: 45.

36. Stent, "Berlin's Russia Challenge."

37. "Declaration by the Presidency on Behalf of the European Union on the Deterioration of the Situation in South Ossetia (Georgia)," 11 Aug 2008, http://europa.eu/rapid/pressReleasesAction.do?reference-PESC/08/99&format-HTML&aged-0&language-EN&guiLanguage-en.

38. Steven Erlanger, "E.U. Treads Gingerly in Georgia Crisis," *New York Times*, 25 Aug 2008; Judy Dempsey, "Diplomatic Memo—A Role for Merkel as Bridge to Russia," *New York Times*, 24 Aug 2008.

39. "EU Must Be United and Firm on Russia," *Financial Times*, 31 Aug 2008.

40. "Russia-EU Agreement on Partnership and Cooperation," 1 Dec 1997, http://eur-lex.europa.eu/LexUriServ/LexUriServ.do?uri-CELEX:21997A1128(01):EN:HTML. Although signed in 1994, the PCA was not ratified until 1997—for a period of ten years.

41. Katrin Bastian and Rolf Schuette, "The Specific Character of EU-Russia Relations," in *Russia versus the United States and Europe*, ed. Hannes Adomeit and Anders Åslund (Berlin: SWP Berlin, 2005), 85–88.

42. Jakub Kulhánek, "EU and Russia in search of a new modus operandi: Time is running out," Czech Association for International Affairs, 12 Apr 2010, http://www.amo.cz/publications/eu-and-russia-in-search-of-a-new-modus-operandi-time-is-running-out.html?lang=en.

43. Nadezhda Arbatova, "'Problema-2007': Chto dal'she?" *Rossiya v global'noi politike*, Jan–Feb 2006 (1).

44. Ariel Cohen, "The North European Gas Pipeline Threatens Europe's Energy Security," Heritage Foundation Backgrounder #1980, 26 Oct 2006: 2.

45. T. A. Romanova, "Rossiya i YeS: Dialog na raznykh yazykakh," *Rossiya v global'noi politike*, Nov–Dec 2006 (6).

46. According to the Russians, lax quality control and inspections in Poland allowed substandard meat to enter the Russian market, including Indian buffalo that was labeled as beef. See George Parker, "EU-Russia Meat Talks End in Deadlock," *Financial Times*, 22 Apr 2007.

47. Ahto Lobjakas, "EU Suspects Political Motives in Russia-Poland Meat Row," *RFE/RL Newsline*, 22 May 2007; Marc Champion, "Russian Energy Grip Splits EU," *Wall Street Journal*, 13 Nov 2006.

48. European Commission, "The Policy: What Is the European Neighborhood Policy?" http://ec.europa.eu/world/enp/policy—en.htm.

49. Putin, "50 Years."

50. Thomas Gomart, "Predstavlenie pri polupustovom zale," *Nezavisimaya Gazeta*, 11 May 2005; Avdonin, "Rossiiskaya transformatsiya."

51. "EU's New Eastern Partnership Draws Ire from Russia," *Deutsche Welle*, 21 Mar 2009.

52. In 1943, German occupation authorities announced the discovery of mass graves containing the remains of thousands of Polish officers in the Katyń Forest region of what had been eastern Poland. The Germans blamed the Soviet NKVD for the massacres, which took place in the spring of 1940 when prewar Poland had been overrun and divided by German and Soviet troops under the secret protocol to the Molotov-Ribbentrop Pact. Rejecting calls for an international investigation, the Soviet government claimed the massacres had been carried out by the Nazis. Despite overwhelming evidence to the contrary, Moscow maintained this position until 1990.

53. Steven Lee Meyers, "No Cold War, But Big Chill," *New York Times*, 16 Aug 2008.

54. Russian Ministry of Foreign Affairs, "Interv'yu ofitsial'nogo predstavitelya MID Rossii A.A. Nesterenko *RIA-<Novosti>* v svyazi s predstoyashchim rabochim vizitom v Moskvu Ministra inotrannykh del Pol'shi R. Sikorskogo," 30 Apr 2009.

55. Russian Ministry of Foreign Affairs, "Stenogramma vystupleniya i otvetov na voprosy SMI Ministra inostrannykh del Rossii S.V. Lavrova na sovmestnoi press-konferentsii po itogam peregovorov s Ministrom inostrannykh del Pol'shi R. Sikorskim i pyatogo zasedaniya Komiteta po voprosam strategii rossiisko-pol'skogo sotrudnichestva," 6 May 2009.

56. Putin, "V.V. Putin vystupil na sostoyavshcheisya v Gdanske tseremonii, posvyashchennoi 70-oi godovshchine nachala Vtoroi mirovoi voiny," Government of the Russian Federation, 1 Sep 2009, http://premier.gov.ru/visits/world/6130/events/8206/.

57. Judy Dempsey, "Tragedy as a Catalyst for Change," *New York Times*, 15 Apr 2010.

58. Kupchan, "NATO's Final Frontier." Jeffrey Mankoff, "Reforming the Euro-Atlantic Security Architecture: An Opportunity for U.S. Leadership," *The Washington Quarterly*, 33(2): 65–83.

59. Robert E. Hunter, "Solving Russia: Final Piece in NATO's Puzzle," *Washington Quarterly*, Win 2000, 23(1): 118–23.

60. James M. Goldgeier, "NATO Expansion: The Anatomy of a Decision," *Washington Quarterly*, Win 1998, 21(1): 88.

61. NATO Topics, "The Partnership for Peace," http://www.nato.int/issues/pfp. On the political background to the development of PfP, see Goldgeier, "NATO Expansion," 86–92.

62. Sergey Oznobishchev, "Rossiya-NATO: Realisticheskoe partnerstvo ili virtual' noe protivostoyanie?" *Mirovaya ekonomika i mezhdunarodnye otnosheniya*, Jan 2006 (1): 15–16.

63. John Vinocur, "Historic Expansion Is Approved with Some Discord at Summit: Alliance Votes to Accept Poland, Hungary and Czech Republic," *International Herald Tribune*, 9 Jul 1997; Gary Hart and Gordon Humphrey, "Creating a Cold Peace by Expanding NATO," Cato Institute brief, 20 Mar 1998, http://www.cato.org/pub—display.php?pub—id-5929.

64. James M. Goldgeier and Michael McFaul, *Power and Purpose: U.S. Policy toward Russia after the Cold War* (Washington, DC: Brookings, 2003), 183–85.

65. "Opposition to NATO Expansion," open letter to Bill Clinton signed by fifty leading figures in U.S. foreign policy, 26 Jun 1997, http://www.armscontrol.org/act/1997—06-07/natolet.asp.

66. Goldgeier and McFaul, *Power and Purpose*, 183–85.

67. Hunter, "Solving Russia," 123.

68. Andrei Kozyrev, "The Lagging Partnership," *Foreign Affairs*, May–Jun 1994, 73(3).

69. Quoted in Andrei P. Tsygankov, *Russia's Foreign Policy: Change and Continuity in National Identity* (Lanham, MD: Rowman & Littlefield, 2006), 100–101.

70. Russian representatives had participated in NATO activities since 1991 as part of the North Atlantic Cooperation Council, and since 1994 in the context of the Partnership for Peace. The PJC for the first time institutionalized relations at the political level and provided a regular schedule for discussion.

71. "Founding Act on Mutual Relations, Cooperation and Security between NATO and the Russian Federation," 27 May 1997, http://www.nato.int/docu/basic-txt/fndact-a.htm.

72. Goldgeier and McFaul, *Power and Purpose*, 247–48.

73. Ira Straus, "NATO: The Only West Russia Has?" *Demokratizatsiya*, Spr 2003, 11(2).

74. Dmitri Trenin, "Russia's Foreign and Security Policy under Putin," Carnegie Moscow Center, 24 Jun 2005, http://www.carnegie.ru/en/pubs/media/72804.htm.

75. Dmitri Trenin and Bobo Lo, *The Landscape of Russian Foreign Policy Decision Making* (Moscow: Carnegie Moscow Center, 2005), 4.

76. A. I. Voronin, "Russia-NATO Strategic Partnership: Problems, Prospects," *Military Thought*, 2005, 14(4): 20–21.

77. "NATO-Russia Relations: A New Quality," declaration by Heads of State and Government of NATO Member States and the Russian Federation, 28 May 2002, http://www.nato-russia-council.info/htm/EN/documents28may02—1.shtml.

78. Jaap de Hoop Schaeffer, "Opening Statement by the Secretary General [to] Informal Meeting of the NATO-Russia Council and the Level of Foreign Ministers," 26 Apr 2007, http://www.nato-russia-council.info/htm/EN/documents 26apr07.shtml.

79. Tuomas Forsberg, "Russia's Relationship with NATO: A Qualitative Change or Old Wine in New Bottles?" *Journal of Communist Studies and Transition Politics*, Sep 2005, 21(3): 342.

80. Clifford J. Levy, "Russia Adopts Blustery Tone Set by Envoy," *New York Times*, 27 Aug 2008.

81. NATO Riga Summit Declaration, 29 Nov 2006, http://www.nato.int/docu/pr/2006/p06-150e.htm#eapc—pfp.

82. R. Nicholas Burns, "The NATO-Russia Council: A Vital Partnership in the War on Terror," U.S. Department of State, 4 Nov 2004, http://www.state.gov/p/eur/rls/rm/38244.htm.

83. Forsberg, "Russia's Relationship with NATO," 337.

84. Besides the question of Russian soldiers stationed in Georgia and Moldova, the dispute has to do with the large quantities of heavy weapons Moscow provided to separatist groups in these countries. The CFE Treaty places limitations on the possession of such weaponry by states; at issue is whether the agreement also covers weapons in the possession of nonstate actors with political ties to a state (in this case, Russia). See Vladimir Socor, "Moscow Confronts the West over CFE Treaty at OSCE," *Jamestown Foundation Eurasia Daily Monitor*, 25 May 2007.

85. Sergei Ivanov, Speech at the 42nd Munich Conference on Security Policy, 5 Feb 2006, http://www.securityconference.de/konferenzen/rede.php?id-171&sprache-en&.

86. Voronin, "Russia-NATO," 21–22; Irina Isakova, *Russian Governance in the Twenty-First Century: Geo-strategy, Geopolitics and Governance* (London: Frank Cass, 2005), 47–52. The Russian government suspended participation in the CFE Treaty in July 2007 in protest at U.S. plans to build antimissile systems in Eastern Europe.

87. Sergei Lavrov, "Speech at MGIMO University, Moscow, 3 Sep 2007," *JRL* #188, 4 Sep 2007.

88. Isabel Gorst and Jan Cienski, "Missile Shield Accord Draws Russian Fire," *Financial Times*, 15 Aug 2008.

89. Andrew Tully, "US: What Is Strategy for Bases in Former Soviet Bloc?," *RFE/RL Newsline*, 7 Dec 2005.

90. "Moscow wants answers from U.S. on Romania missile shield plan," RIA-Novosti, 5 Feb 2010. Nicholas Kulish and Ellen Barry, "Romania Accepts U.S. Plan for Basing of Missiles," *New York Times*, 4 Feb 2010.

91. Charles Grant, "A More Political NATO, a More European Russia," in *Europe after September 11*, ed. Howard Bannerman, et al. (London: Centre for European Reform, 2001), 50; A. V. Kelin, "Spokoino negativnoe otnoshenie k rasshireniyu NATO," *Mezhdunarodnaya zhizn'*, 31 Dec 2003.

92. Forsberg, "Russia's Relationship with NATO," 345.

93. "Russia Condemns NATO's Expansion," BBC News, 1 Apr 2004, http://news.bbc.co.uk/2/hi/europe/3587717.stm.

94. Yulia Petrovskaya and Lyudmila Romanova, "Sblizhenie—da, smyagchenie—nyet," *Nezavisimaya Gazeta*, 3 Oct 2001.

95. Voennaya doktrina Rossiiskoi Federatsii, 5 Feb 2010.

96. "Putin Says Moscow May Change View of NATO Expansion If NATO Changes Itself," *RFE/RL Report*, 4 Oct 2001, http://www.rferl.org/newsline/2001/10/041001.asp.

97. On the expansion of NATO's role, see especially Ivo Daalder and James Goldgeier, "Global NATO," *Foreign Affairs*, Sep–Oct 2006, 85(5): 105–13.

98. Russian Ministry of Foreign Affairs, Obzor vneshnei politiki, 44–45.

99. NATO-Russia Council Joint Statement, 20 Nov 2010, http://www.nato.int/cps/en/natolive/news_68871.htm.

100. Vadim Solov'ëv and Vladimir Ivanov, "Shankhaiskii dogovor vmesto Varshavskogo," *Nezavisimaya Gazeta*, 10 Aug 2007.

101. "Ministr inostrannykh del Rossii Sergei Lavrov: 'Setovaya diplomatiya' seichas vostrebovana kak nikogda," interview with Yevgeny Umerenkov, *Izvestiya*, 28 Dec 2006. Also see Polikanov, "U-Turns," 78.

102. Nikitin, "Russian Perceptions," 2, 8–9.

103. For a more comprehensive analysis, see Jeffrey Mankoff, "Reforming the Euro-Atlantic Security Architecture: An Opportunity for U.S. Leadership," *The Washington Quarterly*, Apr 2010, 33(2): 65–83; Michael Mandelbaum, "America, Russia, and Europe," lecture at the Kennan Institute, Woodrow Wilson Center, October 17, 2008, http://www.wilsoncenter.org/news/docs/Michael_Mandelbaum_on_US-Russia_Relations.pdf; and "Obretenie budushchego: Strategiya 2012," INSOR Report, 2011: 299–301.

104. Lavrov, "Vystuplenie i otvety Ministra inostrannykh del S.V. Lavrova na voprosy SMI na press-konferentsii po itogam deyatelnosti Rossiiskoi diplomatii v 2010 godu," Russian Ministry of Foreign Affairs, 13 Jan 2011.

105. European Commission, "EU Energy in Figures 2007/2008," http://ec.europa .eu/dgs/energy_transport/figures/pocketbook/doc/2007/2007_energy_en.pdf.

106. Yevlaliya Samedova and Oksana Gavshina, "Neft' i gaz iz odnikh ruk," *Nezavisimaya Gazeta*, 22 Nov 2005; Martha Olcott, "Vladimir Putin i neftyanaya politika Rossii," Carnegie Moscow Center Working Paper, 2005 (1): 10–13.

107. Zeyno Baran, "EU Energy Security: Time to End Russian Leverage," *Washington Quarterly*, Aut 2007, 30(4): 130–31; Lionel Beehner, "Energy's Impact on EU-Russian Relations," Council on Foreign Relations Backgrounder, Jan 2006, http:// www.cfr.org/publication/9535/energys—impact—on—eurussian—relations.html.

108. Marcin Sobczyk, "U.S. Giants Bet on Shale Gas in Poland," *Wall Street Journal*, 8 Apr 2010. See also John Deutsch, "The Good News about Gas," *Foreign Affairs*, Jan/Feb 2011, 90(1).

109. Roland Götz, "Europa und das Erdgas des kaspischen Raums," SWP-Berlin Diskussionspapiere, Aug 2007: 10. Nikolai Scevola and Dmitry Zhdannikov, "Corrected—Gazprom, Eni Plan Big Gas Pipeline Bypassing Turkey," Reuters, 23 Jun 2007.

110. Baran, "EU Energy Security," 138–39. Russia had initially asked to be allowed to participate in the consortium to build Nabucco. After its offer was refused, presumably because of U.S. opposition, Gazprom moved forward with negotiations on building South Stream.

111. Stern, *The Future of Russian Gas*, 139.

112. Daryna Krasnolutska and Kateryna Choursina, "Ukraine Agrees New $14.9 Billion IMF Loan Arrangement," *Business Week*, 3 Jul 2010.

113. See Peter Havlik, "European Energy Security in View of Russian Economic and Integration Prospects," Wiener Institut für Internationale Wirtschaftsvergleiche Research Report No. 362, May 2010: 27–28.

114. See for instance Jackson Diehl, "An Explosive Gas Deal: Putin's Hard Bargain Could Undermine Democracy in Europe," *Washington Post*, 27 Feb 2006.

115. European Commission, "The January 2009 Gas Supply Disruption to the EU: An Assessment," Commission Staff Working Document, 16 Jul 2009: 3–4, 15–16.

116. Paul Abelsky, "Russian Foreign Direct Investment Fell 17.6% in First Quarter," *Business Week*, 21 May 2010. V. Belov, "Russia-Germany: Partnership for Modernization," *International Affairs: A Russian Journal of World Politics, Diplomacy & International Relations*, 2010 56(5): 108–19.

117. Judy Dempsey, "Russia Seeks Tighter Trade Ties With Germany," *New York Times*, 4 Jun 2010.

118. Russian Ministry of Foreign Affairs, "Programma effektivnogo ispol'zovaniya na sistemnoi osnove vneshnepoliticheskikh faktorov v tselyakh dolgosrochnogo razvitiya Rossiiskoi Federatsii," 11 May 2010, http://www.runewsweek.ru/country/ 34184/.

119. Medvedev, "Speech at a meeting with Russian ambassadors and permanent representatives in international organizations," 16 Jul 2010, *Russia Beyond the Headlines*.

120. "Joint Statement on the Partnership for Modernization, EU-Russia Summit," 1 Jun 2010, http://www.consilium.europa.eu/uedocs/cms_Data/docs/pressdata/en/er/114747.pdf.

121. Dempsey, "Russia Seeks Tighter Trade Ties With Germany."

CHAPTER 5: RISING CHINA AND RUSSIA'S ASIAN VECTOR

1. Igor Ivanov, *The New Russian Diplomacy* (Washington, DC: Nixon Center/Brookings Institution Press, 2001), 122.

2. Sergei Blagov, "Russia moves into trade surplus with China," *Asia Times Online*, 18 Feb 2010, http://www.atimes.com/atimes/Central_Asia/LB18Ag01.html.

3. Some scholars and commentators see Russia and China as exemplars of a new "authoritarian capitalism" that seeks to combine economic openness with tightly controlled political and social life. See Azar Gat, "The Return of Authoritarian Great Powers," *Foreign Affairs*, Jul–Aug 2007, 86(4); Andrew Kuchins, "État Terrible," *The National Interest*, Sep–Oct 2007, (91); *Russia Profile* Weekly Experts Panel: "The Russian Model: Do Russia and China Provide an Alternative to Liberal Democracy?" 5 Oct 2007, http://www.russiaprofile.org/page.php?pageid-Experts%27+Panel&articleid-a1191582534; Gordon G. Chang, "How China and Russia Threaten the World," *Commentary*, Dec 2006. For more skeptical assessments, see Francis Fukuyama, "The Kings and I," *The American Interest*, Sep–Oct 2007, 3(1) and Wang Jisi, "China's Search for a Grand Strategy," *Foreign Affairs*, Mar/Apr 2011, 90(2): 68–79.

4. Dmitry Medvedev and Hu Jintao, "Zayavleniya dlya pressy po itogam rossi-isko-kitaiskikh peregovorov," The Kremlin, 23 May 2008, http://www.kremlin.ru/appears/2008/05/23/1933—type63377type63380—201233.shtml.

5. Vladimir Putin, "Interv'yu kitaiskim gazetam 'Wenmin Jiabao,' 'Yuzhnyi korrespondent Kitaya' i Tsentral'nomu televideniyu Kitaya," The Kremlin, 13 Oct 2004, http://www.kremlin.ru/text/appears/2004/10/77852.shtml.

6. Andrey Piontkovsky, "At the Edge of the Middle Kingdom," *Moscow Times*, 15 Aug 2005.

7. While Russia is cutting back its nuclear force in line with the START New accord with the U.S., China (which is not a party to the START agreement) is rapidly modernizing and expanding its own nuclear forces and will likely reach parity with Russia within the next decade. Dmitri Trenin, *Russia's China Problem* (Washington, DC: Carnegie Endowment for International Peace, 1999) 9–10, 27–31.

8. Aleksandr Khramchikhin, "A ne vse pro vse—vsego 85 brigad postoyanoi boevoi gotovnosti," *Nezavisimoe Voennoe Obozrenie*, 16 Oct 2009.

9. Simon Saradzhyan, "The Role of China in Russia's Military Thinking," International Relations and Security Network, 4 May 2010, http://belfercenter.ksg.harvard.edu/publication/20129/role_of_china_in_russias_military_thinking.html and Saradzhyan, "Russia's War Games: Preparing for Conflict with the East," International Relations and Security Network, 26 May 2010, http://oilprice.com/Geo-Politics/International/Russias-War-Games-Preparing-for-Conflict-with-the-East.html.

10. The Chinese National Petroleum Company won a tender in August 2005 to take control of Petrokazakhstan, the largest oil company in Kazakhstan, by paying far

above market price, following a pattern of "overpay[ing] for assets; it's more of a security issue for them than the absolute price." See Keith Bradsher and Christopher Pala, "China Ups the Ante in Its Bid for Oil," *New York Times*, 22 Aug 2005: C1.

11. E. Wayne Merry, "Moscow's Retreat and Beijing's Rise as Regional Great Power," *Problems of Post-Communism*, May–Jun 2003, 50(3): 25–26.

12. Vadim Solov'ëv and Vladimir Ivanov, "Shankhaiskii dogovor vmesto varshavskogo," *Nezavisimaya Gazeta*, 10 Aug 2007. Also see "The Shanghai Cooperation Organization: Is It Undermining U.S. Interests in Central Asia?" U.S. Commission on Security and Cooperation in Europe hearing, 26 Sep 2006.

13. Alexei Bogaturov, "International Relations in Central-Eastern Asia: Geopolitical Challenges and Prospects for Political Cooperation," Brookings Institution Center for Northeast Asian Policy Studies (CNAPS), Jun 2004: 9.

14. Russian Ministry of Foreign Affairs, "Obzor vneshnei politiki Rossiiskoi Federatsii," Mar 2007: 53.

15. Li Jingjie, "From Good Neighbors to Strategic Partners," in *Rapprochement or Rivalry? Russia-China Relations in a Changing Asia*, ed. Sherman W. Garnett (Washington, DC: Carnegie Endowment, 2000), 94.

16. See Paradorn Rangsimaporn, "Russian Elite Perceptions of the Russo-Chinese 'Strategic Partnership' (1996–2001)," *Slovo*, Aut 2006, 18(2): 129–45.

17. Stephen Kotkin, "The Unbalanced Triangle," review of *Axis of Convenience* by Bobo Lo, *Foreign Affairs*, Sep/Oct 2009, 88(5).

18. Dmitri Trenin and Vitaly Tsygichko, "Kitai dlya Rossii: Tovarishch ili gospodin?" *Indeks bezopasnosti*, 82(2).

19. Andrey Kozyrev, "Riski svoi i chuzhie," *Moskovskie novosti*, 1 Aug 2000. See also Alexander Lukin, "Russia's Image of China and Russian-Chinese Relations," Brookings Institution CNAPS Working Paper, May 2001, http://www.brookings.edu/fp/cnaps/papers/lukinwp—01.pdf.

20. Dmitri Trenin, "Natsional'naya bezopasnost': Bol'shaya vostochnaya strategiya," *Vedomosti*, 14 Feb 2005.

21. For the most eloquent statement of this position, see Dmitri Trenin, *The End of Eurasia: Russia on the Border between Geopolitics and Globalization* (Washington, DC: Carnegie, 2002). See also Robert Kagan, *The Return of History and the End of Dreams* (Washington, DC: Knopf, 2008).

22. See Eduard Lozansky, "Pragmatizm v politike—velenie vremeni," *Nezavisimaya Gazeta*, 25 May 2010. Also Bobo Lo, *Axis of Convenience: Moscow, Beijing, and the New Geopolitics* (London: Chatham House, 2008) 50–5, 163–73.

23. Russian Ministry of Foreign Affairs, Programma effektivnogo ispol'zovaniya na sistemnoi osnove vneshnopoliticheskikh faktorov v tselyakh dolgosrochnogo razvitiya Rossiiskoi Federatsii, 11 May 2010, http://www.runewsweek.ru/country/34184.

24. See Chandler Rosenberger, "Moscow's Multipolar Mission," *ISCIP Perspective*, Nov–Dec 1997, 8(2), http://www.bu.edu/iscip/vol8/Rosenberger.html. Primakov's victory culminated in the sacking of then-defense minister Igor Rodionov, who had publicly identified China as a common foe of the CIS states.

25. Roger McDermott, "Reflections on Vostok 2010: Selling an Image," *Jamestown Foundation Eurasia Daily Monitor*, 13 Jul 2010. See also Saradzhyan, "Russia's War Games: Preparing for Conflict with the East."

26. Jeanne L. Wilson, "Strategic Partners: Russian-Chinese Relations and the July 2001 Friendship Treaty," *Problems of Post-Communism*, May–Jun 2002, 49(3): 3–13.

27. Lo termed the warming of Russo-Chinese ties "arguably the greatest Russian foreign policy success of the post-Soviet era." See Bobo Lo, "The Long Sunset of Strategic Partnership: Russia's Evolving China Policy," *International Affairs*, 2004, 80(2): 296.

28. Sherman Garnett, "Limited Partnership," in *Rapprochement or Rivalry? Russia-China Relations in a Changing Asia*, ed. Sherman W. Garnett (Washington, DC: Carnegie Endowment, 2000), 7–15.

29. "Russian-Chinese Joint Declaration on a Multipolar World and the Establishment of a New International Order," 23 Apr 1997, http://www.fas.org/news/russia/1997/a52—153en.htm.

30. U.S. Open Source Center Analysis, "Russia: Foreign Policy Thinkers Undaunted by Rising China," *JRL* #191, 7 Sep 2007.

31. Ye. Primakov, "Opening Statement by H. E. Mr. E. Primakov, Minister of Foreign Affairs of Russia," ASEAN, May 1997, http://www.shaps.hawaii.edu/security/arf/primakov-arf-9707.html.

32. Primakov, "Yevgeny Primakov: Nam nuzhny stabil'nost' i bezopasnost'," *Rossiiskaya Gazeta*, 19 Jan 2006.

33. Lukin, "Russia's Image."

34. Lanxin Xiang, "China's Eurasian Experiment," *Survival*, Sum 2004, 46(2): 112–13.

35. Lyle Goldstein and Vitaly Kozyrev, "China, Japan, and the Scramble for Siberia," *Washington Quarterly*, Spr 2006, 48(1): 168–69.

36. Sabrina Tavernise, "Gazprom Sees Room to Grow after Russian-Chinese Treaty," *New York Times*, 9 Aug 2001.

37. Sherman Garnett, "Challenges of the Sino-Russian Strategic Partnership," *Washington Quarterly*, Aut 2001, 24(4): 142–43. Garnett cites a figure of $3.3 billion for the value of Chinese purchases of Russian arms in the period 1995–1999.

38. Russian Ministry of Foreign Affairs, "O peregovorakh Prezidenta Rossii V. V. Putina s Predsedatelem KNR Khu Tsintao," 21 Mar 2006. In July 2008, Russia agreed to cede what it terms Tarabarov Island to China and divide Bolshoi Ussuriisky Island between the two countries. See "China, Russia: An End to an Island Dispute," Stratfor, 17 Jul 2008, http://www.stratfor.com/analysis/china—russia—end—island—dispute.

39. "Russia and China End 300 Year Old Border Dispute," BBC News, http://news.bbc.co.uk/1/hi/world/analysis/29263.stm.

40. Vladimir Skosyrev, "Granitsa s Podnebesnoi yuridicheski oformlena," *Nezavisimaya Gazeta*, 25 Oct 2004; Sergei Blagov, "Russia Hails Border Agreement with China Despite Criticism," *Jamestown Foundation Weekly Monitor*, 25 May 2005.

41. Miriam Lanskoy, Jessica Stern, and Monica Duffy Toft, "Russia's Struggle with Chechnya: Implications for the War on International Terrorism," Kennedy School of Government/Belfer Center Report, Caspian Studies Program, 26 Nov 2002. For the most comprehensive analysis of Islamism's role in the Chechen conflict, see Paul J. Murphy, *The Wolves of Islam: Russia and the Faces of Chechen Terror* (Washington, DC: Potomac, 2004).

42. Xiang, "China's Eurasian Experiment," 112; John Daly, "'Shanghai Five' Expands to Combat Islamic Radicals," *Jane's Terrorism & Security Monitor*, 19 June 2001; Ariel Cohen, "The Russia-China Friendship and Cooperation Treaty: A Strategic Shift in Eurasia?" 18 Jul 2001, Heritage Foundation Backgrounder #1459, http://www.heritage.org/Research/RussiaandEurasia/BG1459.cfm.

43. Garnett, "Challenges," 44–46. The initiative for the treaty came from the Chinese side, which was eager for a resolution of its outstanding disputes with Russia. See V. Putin, "Zayavlenie dlya pressy i otvety na voprosy na sovmestnoi press-konferentsii s Predsedatel'em Kitaiskoi Narodnoi Respubliki Jiang Zeminem," The Kremlin, 16 Jul 2001, http://www.kremlin.ru/appears/2001/07/16/0003—type63377 type63380—28588.shtml.

44. "China, Russia Sign Good-Neighborly Friendship, Cooperation Treaty," *People's Daily*, 17 Jul 2001. The text of the treaty is available from the Chinese Foreign Ministry at http://www.fmprc.gov.cn/eng/wjdt/2649/t15771.htm.

45. Robert Marquand, Ilene Prusher, and Fred Weir, "US Quickens China, Russia Thaw," *Christian Science Monitor*, 3 May 2001, 93(111).

46. Svetlana Babaeva and Ekaterina Grigorieva, "Prostranstvo svobody," *Izvestiya*, 16 Jul 2001. The 2001 treaty was supplemented by a joint agreement on implementation signed by Putin and new Chinese leader Hu Jintao in May 2003.

47. Russian Ministry of Foreign Affairs, "Interv'yu zamestitel' Ministra inostrannykh del Rossii A. P. Losyukova agenstvu 'Interfaks' po rossiisko-kitaiskim otnosheniyam," 16 Jul 2001.

48. Patrick E. Tyler, "Russia and China Sign 'Friendship' Pact," *New York Times*, 17 Jul 2001.

49. "Russia's Isolation Plays into China's Hands," *International Herald Tribune*, 30 Aug 2008.

50. Kuchins, "État Terrible."

51. See Joshua Cooper Ramo, *The Beijing Consensus* (London: The Foreign Policy Centre, 2004).

52. Russian Ministry of Foreign Affairs, "Stat'ya ofitsial'nogo predstavitelya MID Rossii A. V. Yakovenko po voprosam rossiisko-kitaiskikh otnoshenii," 29 Jun 2005.

53. The Kremlin, "Plan deistvii po realizatsii polozhenii o Dogovore o dobrososedstve, druzhbe i sotrudnichestve mezhdu Rossiiskoi Federatsiei i Kitaiskoi Narodnoi Respublikoi (2005–2008g.)," 14 Oct 2004.

54. "Threats and Responses; In Their Words: The Security Council," *New York Times*, 6 Feb 2003.

55. An overview of Russian and Chinese interests in the "axis of evil" countries is available in Oleksandr Gladkyy, "American Foreign Policy and U.S. Relations with Russia and China after 11 September," *World Affairs*, Sum 2003, 166(1): 3–24.

56. Natalya Melikova, "Putinu pokazhut chudo sveta," *Nezavisimaya Gazeta*, 14 Oct 2004.

57. Dmitri Trenin, "After the Empire: Russia's Emerging International Identity," in *Russia between East and West: Russian Foreign Policy on the Threshold of the Twenty-First Century*, ed. Gabriel Gorodetsky (London: Frank Cass, 2003), 43–45.

58. Lukin, "Russia's Image."

59. "China to become Russia's Largest Trading Partner," *Russia Briefing,* 10 Mar 2011, http://russia-briefing.com/news/china-to-become-russias-largest-trading-partner.html/.

60. Mikhail Dmitriev, "Strategiya dlya nebol'shogo gosudarstva," *Kommersant,* 21 Nov 2006.

61. Richard Lotspeich, "Perspectives on the Economic Relations between China and Russia," *Journal of Contemporary Asia,* 2006, 36(1): 63.

62. Lotspeich, "Perspectives," 63.

63. Sergei Blagov, "Russia moves into trade surplus with China," *Asia Times Online,* 18 Feb 2010, http://www.atimes.com/atimes/Central_Asia/LB18Ag01.html; "Russia-Chinese trade up 55.8% in May y-o-y," RIA-Novosti, 10 Jun 2010.

64. "China to raise investment to Russia: Russian ministry," Xinhua, 2 Jun 2010.

65. Chen Yun, "Kitai i Rossiya v sovremennom mire," *Svobodnaya Mysl',* 2006 (3): 47.

66. Melikova, "Putinu pokazhut chudo sveta."

67. Hsiu-Ling Wen and Chien-Hsun Chen, "The Prospects for Regional Economic Integration between China and the Five Central Asian Countries," *Europe-Asia Studies,* Nov 2004, 56(7): 1062–65.

68. Stephen J. Blank, "The Eurasian Energy Triangle: China, Russia, and the Central Asian States," *Brown Journal of World Affairs,* Win–Spr 2006, 12(2).

69. British Petroleum, "Statistical Review of World Energy, 2010."

70. Goldstein and Kozyrev, "China, Japan, and the Scramble for Siberia," 169.

71. A thorough account of the Kremlin maneuvering over Yukos and the Daqing pipeline deal can be found in Leszek Buszynski, "Oil and Territory in Putin's Relations with China and Japan," *Pacific Review,* Sep 2006, 19(3): 289–93. See also Danila Bochkarev, *Russian Energy Policy during President Putin's Tenure: Trends and Strategies* (London: GMB, 2006).

72. Khodorkovsky's fall resulted at least in part from his role in pushing for the construction of the Daqing pipeline. See Stephen Blank, "China Makes Policy Shift, Aiming to Widen Access to Central Asian Energy," EurasiaNet.org, 13 Mar 2006, http://www.eurasianet.org/departments/business/articles/eav031306.shtml. On Sakhalin, see James Brooke, "Russia Rattles Asia with Attack on Shell's Sakhalin-2," Bloomberg News, 19 Oct 2006, *JRL* #235.

73. Blank, "The Eurasian Energy Triangle."

74. Buszynski, "Oil and Territory," 290. See also Aleksandr Blinov, "Ven poprosil verit' Kitayu," *Nezavisimaya Gazeta,* 27 Sep 2004.

75. Under pressure from environmental groups and the Ministry of Environment, the Russian cabinet agreed to move the starting point of the pipeline from Angarsk (due west of Lake Baikal) to Taishet, some 500 kilometers farther north. The Taishet-Nakhodka route would pass well north of the lake rather than skirting along its shores as foreseen in the initial plan. Eventually the pipeline's endpoint was moved for environmental reasons as well, from Perevoznaya Bay to Kozmino Bay, several kilometers southeast of Nakhodka in Russia's Maritime Province (Primorskii Krai).

76. Sergei Blagov, "Russia's Pacific Pipeline Seen as Double Edged Sword," *Jamestown Foundation Eurasia Daily Monitor,* 12 Jan 2005.

77. Natalya Melikova, "Severo-Yevropeiskii gazoprovod po-kitaiski," *Nezavisimaya Gazeta,* 22 Mar 2006.

78. Konstantin Simonov, "Vostochnyi ekspress pribudet po raspisaniyu," *Nezavisimaya Gazeta*, 18 Nov 2006.

79. "Neftyaniki dobili kitaiskii kredit," *Kommersant*, 18 Feb 2009.

80. Oliver Bullough, "Russian Arms Sales: A Rising Worry," *International Herald Tribune*, 21 Jun 2006.

81. For a breakdown of the hardware sold to China, see Alexander Shlyndov, "Military Technical Collaboration between Russia and China: Its Current Status, Problems, and Outlook," *Far Eastern Affairs*, 2005, 33(1): 2–6.

82. Cohen, "The Russia-China Friendship and Cooperation Treaty."

83. Chen Yun, "Kitai i Rossiya v sovremennom mire," 49.

84. Paradorn Rangsimaporn, "Russia's Debate on Military-Technological Cooperation with China: From Yeltsin to Putin," *Asian Survey*, May–Jun 2006, 46(3): 478. Figures taken from Center for Analysis of Strategies and Technologies, "Identified Contracts for Russian Arms Deliveries Signed in 2003," Moscow Defense Brief #2.

85. Pavel Felgenhauer, "Billions Down the Drain," *Moscow Times*, 1 Jun 2004. Felgenhauer points out that because military research and development is tax exempt in Russia, firms have an incentive to claim to be doing military research without ever producing anything.

86. David Lague, "Russia and China Rethink Arms Deals," *International Herald Tribune*, 2 Mar 2008.

87. Stephen Blank, "Turning a New Leaf in Relations: Russia's Renewed Arms Sale to China," Jamestown China Brief, 28 Jan 2011.

88. Ariel Cohen, "Washington Ponders Ways to Counter the Rise of the Shanghai Cooperation Organization," *Eurasia Insight*, 15 Jun 2006, http://www.eurasianet.org/departments/insight/articles/eav061506—pr.shtml.

89. "Deklaratsiya o sozdanii Shankhaiskoi organizatsiya sotrudnichestva," 15 Jun 2001, http://www.sectsco.org/html/00651.html. The six countries who combined to form the SCO also signed the so-called Shanghai Convention on the Struggle against Terrorism, Separatism, and Extremism during the June 2001 Shanghai summit.

90. Analysts taking a particularly negative view of the SCO's intentions include Ariel Cohen and William Odom. Others, including Daniel Kimmage, Martha Brill Olcott, Carlos Pascual, and Stephen Blank are more sanguine, arguing that the SCO's focus is increasingly economic and that in any case, Russo-Chinese tensions remain too serious for the SCO to evolve into a real military-political bloc akin to NATO. For an overview, see Lionel Beehner, "The Rise of the Shanghai Cooperation Organization," Council on Foreign Relations Backgrounder, 12 Jul 2006, http://www.cfr.org/publication/10883/.

91. Carlos Pascual, "Russo-Chinese Ties Need Not Worry U.S.," Reuters, 27 Mar 2007.

92. Evan A. Feigenbaum, "The Shanghai Cooperation Organization and the Future of Central Asia," U.S. Department of State, 6 Sep 2007, http://www.state.gov/p/sca/rls/rm/2007/91858.htm. Also see Caitlin B. Doherty, "Inside Track: The SCO and the Future of Central Asia," *The National Interest*, 7 Sep 2007.

93. Jao Huashen, "Kitai, Tsentral'naya Aziya i Shankhaiskaya Organizatsiya Sotrudnichestva," Carnegie Moscow Center Working Paper No. 5, 2005: 17.

94. "Dushanbe Declaration of Heads of SCO Member States," 28 Aug 2008, http://www.sectsco.org/news—detail.asp?id-2360&LanguageID-2.

95. "Here There Be Dragons: The Shanghai Cooperation Organization," Center for Defense Information China Report, 26 Sep 2006; Daly, "'Shanghai Five' Expands to Combat Islamic Radicals."

96. "Moscow hosts conference on Afghanistan," RIA-Novosti, 27 Mar 2009.

97. For the SCO's agenda in Afghanistan, see "Plan of Action of the Shanghai Cooperation Organization Member States and the Islamic Republic of Afghanistan on combating terrorism, illicit drug trafficking, and organized crime," Russian Ministry of Foreign Affairs, 27 Mar 2009.

98. See Alexander Cooley, "Cooperation Gets Shanghaied: China, Russia and the SCO," *Foreign Affairs*, 14 Dec 2009, http://www.foreignaffairs.com/articles/65724/ alexander-cooley/cooperation-gets-shanghaied.

99. Merry, "Moscow's Retreat," 25–26; Alexei Bogaturov, "International Relations in Central-Eastern Asia: Geopolitical Challenges and Prospects for Political Cooperation," Report of the Brookings Institution Center for Northeast Asian Policy Studies, Jun 2004: 9.

100. Aleksandr Dugin, "Zapad-Vostok: Velikii shans Rossii," *Vedomosti*, 13 Jul 2005.

101. Edited transcript of Putin remarks to Valdai Discussion Club, 9 Sep 2006, http://en.valday2006.rian.ru/materials/20060910/52329444.html.

102. Jao Huashen, "Kitai, Tsentral'naya Aziya i Shankhaiskaya Organizatsiya Sotrudnichestva," 11–12. Chinese general secretary Hu Jintao went out of his way to assure the U.S. that the SCO was not an anti-American bloc during a summit meeting with U.S. president Bush in April 2006. See "Predsedatel' KNR: ShOS ne yavlyaetsya antamerikanskoi organizatsiei," IBK.ru News, 21 Apr 2006, http://www.ibk.ru/news/ predsedatel—knr—shos—ne—yavlyaetsya—antiamerikanskoi—organizatsiei-16946.

103. Medvedev, "Vstupitel'noe slovo na zasedanii Soveta glav gosudarstv—chlenov Shankhaiskoi organizatsii sotrudnichestva v rasshirënnom sostave," The Kremlin, 16 Jun 2009, http://kremlin.ru/transcripts/4464.

104. Russian Ministry of Foreign Affairs, "Vystuplenie zamestitelya Ministra inostrannykh del Rossii A.V. Yakovenko na 'kruglom stole' na temu <Rol' Rossii v Shankhaiskoi organizatsii sotrudnichestva>," 22 Mar 2010. See also Lo, *Axis of Convenience*, 104–12.

105. Lavrov, "Vystuplenie Ministra Inostrannykh Del Rossii S. V. Lavrova na zasedanii MID ShOS, Bishkek," Russian Ministry of Foreign Affairs, 7 Jul 2007; Putin, "Otvety na voprosy rossiiskikh i inostrannykh zhurnalistov po okonchanii sammita Shankhaiskoi organizatsii sotrudnichestva," Russian Ministry of Foreign Affairs, 16 Jun 2005.

106. Both Beijing and Moscow had previously conducted maneuvers with the militaries from the Central Asian states (in the Russian case, under the auspices of the CSTO as well as the SCO). Previous exercises, however, were much smaller in scale and more focused on specifically local threats. In contrast, Peace Mission 2005 was held on China's Shandong Peninsula and involved land, air, naval, and amphibious forces from both Russia and China. Though portrayed as providing operational training in antiterrorist tactics, the scale of the exercises and the use of heavy

weaponry (including naval/amphibious forces and Russian Tu-22 strategic bombers) belied such claims.

107. "Exercise of Power," *Financial Times* editorial, 19 Aug 2005; Stephen Blank, testimony to U.S. Commission on Security and Cooperation in Europe, 26 Sep 2006; Dmitri Trenin, "ShOS i vybor za mir," *Yezhednevnyi zhurnal*, 29 Aug 2007.

108. Vladimir Mukhin, "Mirnaya missiya za dva milliarda," *Nezavisimaya Gazeta*, 7 Aug 2007.

109. Medvedev, "Vystuplenie na zasedanii Soveta glav gosudarstv—chlenov Shankhaiskoi organizatsii sotrudnichestva," The Kremlin, 28 Aug 2008.

110. Marina Selina et al., "Dal'nyi Vostok dolzhen stat' blizhnim," *RBK Daily*, 26 Sep 2008. More broadly, see Lo, *Axis of Convenience*, 56–72.

111. Goldstein and Kozyrev, "China, Japan and the Scramble for Siberia," 168. Already the Kremlin has agreed to allocate $13.8 billion (358 billion rubles) for Far Eastern development until 2013. Sergei Blagov, "Balancing China in the Russian Far East," *JRL* #77, 2 Apr 2007.

112. Veniamin Gotvansky, "Tikhaya ekspansiya Kitaya," *Nezavisimaya Gazeta*, 23 Sep 2010. Also Igor Naumov, "V rossiisko-kitaiskoi druzhbe usililas' syrëv'aya privyazannost'," *Nezavisimaya Gazeta*, 23 Sep 2009.

113. Gabriel Gatehouse, "Russia's Far East Looks to China," BBC News, 5 Jun 2007, http://news.bbc.co.uk/2/hi/europe/6713509.stm; David Wall, "Kremlin Fears for Its Far East," *Japan Times*, 21 Dec 2006.

114. Rajan Menon, "The Sick Man of Asia: Russia's Endangered Far East," *The National Interest*, Aut 2003.

115. Clifford G. Gaddy, "As Russia Looks East: Can It Manage Resources, Space, and People?" *Gaiko Forum*, Jan 2007. Also see Clifford G. Gaddy and Fiona Hill, *The Siberian Curse: How Communist Planners Left Russia Out in the Cold* (Washington, DC: Brookings Institution, 2003).

116. Russian Ministry of Foreign Affairs, "Interv'yu direktora Pervogo departamenta Azii MID Rossii K.V. Vnukova po problematike rossiisko-kitaiskikh otnohenii, opublikovannoe v zhurnale 'Itogi'," 12 Mar 2007. For the range of estimates, see Maria Repnikova and Harley Balzer, "Chinese Migration to Russia: Missed Opportunities," Woodrow Wilson International Center for Scholars, Kennan Institute Eurasian Migration Papers, 2009, (3): 13–15.

117. Harley Balzer and Maria Repnikova, "Chinese migration to Russia," *Post-Soviet Affairs*, 2010, 26(1).

118. Menon, "The Sick Man of Asia;" Trenin and Tsygichko, "Kitai dlya Rossii."

119. Quoted in "Ugroza po sosedstvu: Pered rossiiskim Dal'nem Vostokom vstaet real'naya ugroza 'polzuchei' kitaiskoi ekspansii," *Vzglyad*, 4 Aug 2005, http://www.vzglyad.ru/politics/2005/8/42962.html. On the whole, there is little discussion, polemical or otherwise, in the Russian press regarding the immigration of non-Chinese East Asians. Trenin has called for Moscow to encourage the immigration of a range of ethnicities to populate the Far East (including Koreans, Thais, and other Southeast Asians) precisely as a way to ensure that the region does not pass under Chinese hegemony. Balzer and Repnikova make the same argument.

120. "BBC Monitoring: Russia's Putin Sees No Threat from China's Economic Expansion," *JRL* #2010–165, 31 Aug 2010.

121. See Gilbert Rozman et al., eds., *Russian Strategic Thought toward Asia* (New York: Palgrave Macmillan, 2006), 32–36.

122. For an overview of Russian participation in ASEAN structures, see Lavrov, "Vystuplenie Ministra Inostrannykh Del S. V. Lavrova na Postministerskoi Konferentsii Rossiya-ASEAN, Manila, 1 avgusta 2007 g.," Russian Ministry of Foreign Affairs, 1 Aug 2007. Also see Natalya Melikova, "Zavoevanie Azii," *Nezavisimaya Gazeta,* 14 Dec 2004.

123. Lavrov, "Stenogramma vystupleniya Ministra inostrannykh del Rossii S.V. Lavrova na voprosy SMI po itogam dvustoronnykh vstrech <na pol'yakh> Postministerskoi-konferentsii Rossiya-ASEAN," Russian Federation Ministry of Foreign Affairs, 22 Jul 2010.

124. Medvedev, "Stenograficheskii otchët o soveshchanii po sotsial'no-ekonomicheskomu razvitiyu Dal'nego Vostoka i sotrudnichestvu so stranami Aziatsko-Tikhookeanskogo regiona," The Kremlin, 2 Jul 2010, http://kremlin.ru/transcripts/8234.

125. "Moscow Says Japan-Russia Diplomacy 'in a State of Catastrophe,'" AFP News, *JRL* #255, 13 Nov 2006. For a comprehensive history of the Kurils dispute up to the mid-1990s, see James E. Goodby, Vladimir I. Ivanov, and Nobuo Shimotomai, eds., *"Northern Territories" and Beyond: Russian, Japanese, and American Perspectives* (Westport, CT: Praeger, 1995).

126. Jonathan Eyal, "Russia-Japan Relations Set to Improve with Visits," *Straits Times,* 26 Jan 2007.

127. For a comprehensive account of Russia's policy toward North Korea, see Alexander Vorontsov, "Current Russia-North Korea Relations: Challenges and Achievements," Brookings Institution, CNAPS Working Paper, Feb 2007.

128. Jo Johnson and Neil Buckley, "Russia and India Seek to Remodel Partnership," *Financial Times,* 25 Jan 2007.

129. "Ne otdeli Moskvu ot Deli," *Kommersant,* 25 Jan 2007.

130. Nayanima Basu, "India, Russia aim for $20 bln bilateral trade by 2015," *Business Standard,* 19 Jun 2010.

131. For a list of achievements in the Russo-Indian relationship, see S. Lavrov, "Russia and India: Mutually Beneficial Cooperation and Strategic Partnership," *International Affairs: A Russian Journal of World Politics, Diplomacy, and International Relations,* 2007, 53(3): 24–29; A. Mantyskii and V. Khodzhaev, "New Vistas of Russia-India Cooperation," *International Affairs: A Russian Journal of World Politics, Diplomacy, and International Relations,* 2005, 51(1): 49–55.

CHAPTER 6: PLAYING WITH HOME FIELD ADVANTAGE? RUSSIA AND ITS POST-SOVIET NEIGHBORS

1. De facto, the CIS includes all the former republics of the USSR except for the Baltic states (which never joined) and Georgia (which withdrew in 2009). De jure, Ukraine is not an official member because it never ratified the CIS Charter (though it fully participates in CIS functions), while Turkmenistan is an "associate member" in keeping with its officially neutral, non-aligned status.

2. Putin, "Poslanie Federal'nomu Sobraniyu Rossiiskoi Federatsii," 25 Apr 2005, http://www.kremlin.ru/appears/2005/04/25/1223_type63372type63374type 82634_87049.shtml. Putin, "V pryamom efire telekanalov 'Rossiya,' 'Rossiya24,' radiostantsii 'Mayak,' 'Vesti FM,' i 'Radio Rossii' vyshla spetsial'naya programma 'Razgovor s Vladimirom Putinym. Prodolzhenie," Government of Russia (Premier), 16 Dec 2010, http://www.premier.gov.ru/events/news/13427/.

3. Ariel Cohen, "Putin's Foreign Policy and U.S.-Russian Relations," Heritage Foundation Backgrounder #1406, 18 Jan 2001, http://www.heritage.org/Research/ RussiaandEurasia/BG1406.cfm. The locations of Russian troop deployments and a full order of battle are available at the Russian Armed Forces website, http://www .geocities.com/pentagon/9059/RussianArmedForces.html. Russian troops withdrew from Georgia (excepting South Ossetia and Abkhazia) by the end of 2007, before temporarily returning to Georgia proper in the course of the August 2008 war.

4. Roy Allison, "The Military and Political Security Landscape in Russia and the South," in *Russia, the Caucasus and Central Asia: The 21st Century Security Environment*, ed. Rajan Menon, Yuri E. Fedorov, and Ghia Nodia (Armonk, NY: M.E. Sharpe, 1999), 42–55; Dmitri Trenin, "Southern Watch: Russia's Policy in Central Asia," *Journal of International Affairs*, Spr 2003, 56(2): 120–22.

5. Andrey Ryabov, "Zapadnyi uklon Kremlya," *Gazeta.ru*, 17 May 2010.

6. According to the 2001 census, 67.5 percent of the inhabitants of Ukraine listed Ukrainian as their native language, versus 29.6 percent who listed Russian. Such statistics require context, however, since most Ukrainians understand Russian, and a large number (including ex-president Yushchenko) speak Russian or a mixed dialect known as *surzhyk* in everyday life. See "Chislennost' i sostav naseleniya Ukrainy po itogam Vseukrainskoi perepisi naseleniya 2001 goda," http://ukrcensus.gov.ua/rus/ results/general/language.

7. GUAM (an acronym of its members' names: Georgia, Ukraine, Azerbaijan, Moldova) was formed in 1994 and aimed at (in the words of the organization's charter) "promoting democratic values, ensuring rule of law and respect of human rights; ensuring sustainable development; strengthening international and regional security and stability." See "Charter of Organization for Democracy and Economic Development GUAM [sic]," 23 May 2006, http://www.guam.org.ua/267.0.0.1.0.0.phtml. GU(U)AM has often been seen as a counterweight against Russian influence, even though all of its members are also members of the Commonwealth of Independent States. From 1999 to 2004, the organization was known as GUUAM, reflecting Uzbekistan's decision to join, then leave the group.

8. On the formation and significance of GU(U)AM for Ukraine, see John A. Armstrong, "Ukraine: Evolving Foreign Policy in a New State," *World Affairs*, Sum 2004, 167(1): 34–38. Also see Armstrong, "Independent Ukraine in the World Arena," *Ukrainian Quarterly*, Spr–Sum 1998, 54(1–2): 5–15.

9. See especially Taras Kuzio, "Neither East nor West: Ukraine's Security Policy under Kuchma," *Problems of Post-Communism*, Sep–Oct 2005, 52(5): 59–68.

10. Michael Wines, "Report of Arms Sale by Ukraine to Iraq Causes Consternation," *New York Times*, 7 Nov 2002; Tatyana Ivzhenko, "Kuchme grozit arest," *Nezavisimaya Gazeta*, 18 Nov 2005.

11. Russian Ministry of Foreign Affairs, "Stenogramma vystuplenii Ministrov inostrannykh del Rossii S. V. Lavrova i Ukrainy K. I. Grishchenko po itogam sovmest-

nogo zasedaniya Kollegii Ministerstv inostrannykh del Rossii i Ukrainy," 28 May 2004.

12. Taras Kuzio, "Russian Policy toward Ukraine during Elections," *Demokratizatsiya*, Aut 2005, 13(4): 492.

13. Adrian Karatnycky, "Ukraine's Orange Revolution," *Foreign Affairs*, Mar–Apr 2005, 84(2): 38–42.

14. For a detailed examination of the Kremlin's participation in the dirty tricks campaign against Yushchenko, see Kuzio, "Russian Policy toward Ukraine during Elections," 493–99. Pavlovsky admitted in a 2007 interview that he had come to Ukraine in 2004 under an agreement between Putin and Kuchma. See "Russian Spin Doctor Views Moscow's Relations with Ukraine, Georgia," *Ukrainska Pravda*, JRL #241, 21 Nov 2007.

15. See Karatnycky, "Ukraine's Orange Revolution," 35–37.

16. Robert Coalson, "Analysis: Kremlin Wary of New Ukrainian President," *RFE/RL Feature*, 24 Jan 2005; Askold Krushelnycky, "Ukraine: Russian President Stops Short of Openly Endorsing Yanukovych During Visit," *RFE/RL Newsline*, 27 Oct 2004.

17. V. Putin, "Vstupitel'noe slovo i otvety na voprosy v khode sovmestnoi press-konferentsii po itogam sammita Rossii-YeS," The Kremlin, 25 Nov 2004, http://www.kremlin.ru/appears/2004/11/25/2239—type63377type63380—80195.shtml.

18. Colin Powell, State Department Briefing, 24 Nov 2004, http://www.state.gov/secretary/former/powell/remarks/38738.htm. Notably, though, President Bush was more circumspect, refraining from direct criticism of Russia's role.

19. Tatyana Ivzhenko, "'Oni khotyat delat' iz nashikh lyudei idiotov,'" *Nezavisimaya Gazeta*, 24 Dec 2004.

20. Richard L. Armitage, interview with Oleksandr Tkachenko, Novy Kanal TV, 8 Dec 2004.

21. Matt Kelley, "U.S. Money Has Helped Opposition in Ukraine," *San Diego Union-Tribune*, 11 Dec 2004. According to Kelley, the U.S. government spent $65 million on promoting democracy in Ukraine.

22. The video is posted on Medvedev's official Kremlin blog: *V otnosheniyakh Rossii i Ukrainy dolzhny nastupit' novye vremena*, 11 Aug 2009, http://blog.kremlin.ru/post/30.

23. World Bank, "Ukraine Economic Update," 1 Jul 2010, http://siteresources.worldbank.org/INTUKRAINE/Resources/MacroUpdate1007EngFinal.pdf.

24. Dale Peleschuk, "Ukraine's Yanukovych Seeks Balance Between Russia and EU," *World Politics Review*, 27 Jul 2010.

25. Jan S. Adams, "Russia's Gas Diplomacy," *Problems of Post-Communism*, May–Jun 2002, 49(3): 18–19.

26. On Kyiv's charge that Moscow was violating existing agreements, see Mykhailo Krasnyanskiy, "Who Is Blackmailing Whom?" *Ukrayinska Pravda*, 12 Dec 2005, http://pravda.com.ua/en/news/2005/12/12/4919.htm. Moscow also signed a new deal in December 2005 to buy more gas from Turkmenistan, the major supplier in Central Asia, thus reducing the amount of non-Russian gas available to the Ukrainians.

27. A detailed overview of the events leading up to the January 2006 gas cutoff is provided in Nikolai Sokov, "Alternative Interpretations of the Russian-Ukrainian Gas Crisis," Center for Strategic and International Studies, PONARS Policy Memo No. 404, Jan 2006. The cutoff affected not only gas produced inside Russia but also gas originating in Turkmenistan and Uzbekistan that flowed to Ukraine through Russian pipelines.

28. Russian Ministry of Foreign Affairs, "Zayavlenie MID Rossii o situatsii v ros-siisko-ukrainskikh otnosheniyakh v gazovoi sfere," 1 Jan 2006.

29. Additionally, the agreement specified that Russian gas would be sold to Ukraine through the joint company RosUkrEnergo, which would pay $230 per thousand cubic meters, then mix the Russian gas with cheaper gas from Central Asia before selling it to Naftohaz Ukrainy at $95. The deal also resolved a related Russo-Ukrainian dispute over tariffs paid by Gazprom for the use of Ukraine's pipeline network for moving its gas to Europe. See "Russia: Moscow, Kyiv Announce End of Gas Dispute," *RFE/RL Newsline*, 4 Jan 2006.

30. See among others Marshall I. Goldman, "Moscow's New Economic Imperial-ism," *Current History*, Oct 2008: 322–29; Khatuna Salukvadze, "Russia's New Doc-trine of Neo-Imperialism," *Central Asia-Caucasus Institute Analyst*, 8 Feb 2006; Edward Lucas, *The New Cold War: Putin's Russia and the Threat to the West* (New York: Palgrave Macmillan, 2008) 163–89.

31. Tatyana Ivzhenko, "Kiev ugrozhaet Putinu," *Nezavisimaya Gazeta*, 23 Dec 2004.

32. See, for example, Ariel Cohen, "Russia's Gas Attack on Ukraine: An Uneasy Truce," Heritage Foundation Web Memo #954, 4 Jan 2006, http://www.heritage.org/Research/RussiaandEurasia/wm954.cfm; Torbakov, "Kremlin Uses Energy."

33. Judy Dempsey, "Russia Tells Ukraine Gas Price Could Triple," *International Herald Tribune*, 1 Aug 2005.

34. "Dvoinoi standarty 'gazovoi voiny,'" *Izvestiya*, 3 Jan 2006.

35. Ivanna Gorina, "Finskii proval," *Rossiiskaya Gazeta*, 30 Oct 2006.

36. Oleg Gavrish and Natalya Grib, "Tsena Oprosa," *Kommersant*, 20 Oct 2006.

37. Yanukovych termed this linkage a completely natural result of the close eco-nomic integration between Russia and Ukraine. See Aleksandr Martynenko, inter-view with Viktor Yanukovych, *Rossiiskaya Gazeta*, 20 Oct 2006.

38. Simon Pirani, Jonathan Stern, and Katja Yafimava, "The Russo-Ukrainian Gas Dispute of January 2009: A Comprehensive Assessment," Oxford Institute for Energy Studies, Feb 2009, http://www.oxfordenergy.org/pdfs/NG27.pdf.

39. Pirani, Stern, and Yafimava, "The Russo-Ukrainian Gas Dispute."

40. Anatoly Medetsky, "Deal Struck on Gas, Black Sea Fleet," *Moscow Times*, 12 Apr 2010.

41. Roman Olearchyk and Stefan Wagstyl, "Russia Cuts Gas Prices to Ukraine," *Financial Times*, 22 Feb 2010. Also see Kateryna Choursina, "Ukraine Unions Seek to Block Gas Price Increase Pledged to Gain IMF Loan," Bloomberg, 27 Jul 2010.

42. See Andrey Terekhov, "Demokraticheskaya missiya Kondolizy," *Nezavisimaya Gazeta*, 19 Apr 2005.

43. "Shevardnadze Accuses Soros of Financing Coup d'Etat in Georgia," *Pravda.ru* (English), 1 Dec 2003, http://newsfromrussia.com/world/2003/12/01/51582.html.

44. See Pavel Zarifullin, "Pri chem zdes' Saakashvili?" *Russkii Kur'yer*, 6 Nov 2006.

45. Sergey B. Ivanov, "International Security in the Context of the Russia-NATO Relationship," speech to Fortieth Munich Conference on Security Policy, 7 Feb 2004, http://www.securityconference.de/konferenzen/rede.php?menu—2005-&menuekonferenzen-&sprache-en&id-126&. Russia did suspend implementation of the CFE Treaty in 2007, though its reasons for doing so were more complex.

46. Mikheil Saakashvili, "The Way Forward: Georgia's Democratic Vision for the Future," *Harvard International Review*, Spr 2006, 71–72.

47. Alexander Y. Skakov, "Russia's Role in the South Caucasus," *Helsinki Monitor*, 2005, (2): 121.

48. Ahto Lobajakas, "CIS: Referendums Seen as Kremlin's Master Plan," *RFE/RL Feature*, 20 Sep 2006. The South Ossetian and Abkhaz conflicts have also influenced the debate in the U.S. government about backing Georgia's candidacy for membership in these organizations. See "Background Briefing by Senior Administration Officials on the NATO Summit," 29 Nov 2006, http://www.whitehouse.gov/news/releases/2006/11/20061129-4.html.

49. Stephen Erlanger, "Yeltsin Voices Russia's Anger at Ethnic Wars Roiling the Old Soviet Empire," *New York Times*, 22 Jun 1992. The International Crisis Group estimates 180,000–200,000 ethnic Georgians fled Abkhazia in the course of the 1991–1992 conflict. Almost none has returned.

50. On the dispute over Russian peacekeepers, see Aleksandr Gol'ts, "Voennoe mirotvorchestvo Rossii," *Pro et Contra*, Sep–Dec 2006: 65–74; Christine Ben Bruusgaard, "Budushchee rossiiskikh mirotvortsev," Moscow Carnegie Center Briefing, Jun 2007, 9(2). The South Ossetian peacekeepers were dispatched in 1992 with the assent of both Tbilisi and Tskhinvali, although the Georgian side began calling for their withdrawal in 2000. See M. Mayorov, "South Ossetia: Conflict Zone," *International Affairs: A Russian Journal of World Politics, Diplomacy, and International Relations*, 2002, 48(2): 117.

51. On the Russian response to Kosovo's independence, see Lavrov, "Stenogramma press-konferentsii Ministra inostrannykh del Rossii S. V. Lavrova, Zheneva, Russian Ministry of Foreign Affairs, 12 fevralya, 2008 goda," 12 Feb 2008.

52. Arkady Dubnov, "Razmorozhennaya druzhba," *Vremya Novostei*, 12 Feb 2004.

53. "Press-konferentsiya po okonchanii vstrechi s Prezidentom Gruzii Mikhailom Saakashvili."

54. Ariel Cohen, "Saakashvili Visits Washington amid Heightening Geopolitical Tension in the Caucasus," *EurasiaNet Insight*, 24 Feb 2004, http://www.eurasianet.org/departments/insight/articles/eav022404.shtml.

55. Oleg Zorin and Gennady Sysoev, "Moskva podstraivaetsya pod Mikhaila Saakashvili," *Kommersant*, 19 Jan 2004.

56. When Chechen fighters sought refuge in Kodori in mid-2001, Moscow accused the Georgian government of aiding the separatists. Russian troops, along with pro-Russian Abkhaz militiamen, drove the Chechens out militarily while Tbilisi protested the Russian incursion as a violation of its sovereignty. After the Chechens left, Shevardnadze's government deployed Georgian forces to the area over the opposition of Moscow (and the Abkhaz leadership in Sukhumi). The UN eventually negotiated a withdrawal agreement in the spring of 2002, though Russian forces made an abortive attempt to return later that year, nearly starting a firefight with the Georgians. See Keti Bochorishvili, "Georgia: Fear and Poverty in the Kodori Gorge," Institute for War & Peace Reporting, 31 May 2002, http://iwpr.net/?p-crs&s-f&o-160838&apc—state-henicrs2002.

57. Andrey Ryabov, "Gruzino-abkhazskii tupik." *Pro et Contra* (Sep–Dec 2006): 33–34.

58. Jean-Christophe Peuch, "Caught between Russia and Georgia, South Ossetia Rift Widens," *RFE/RL Feature*, 14 Nov 2007.

59. The Georgian Foreign Ministry linked the arrest of the Russian officers with the participation of both South Ossetian and Abkhaz leaders in a Russian-sponsored economic forum in Sochi. See Vladimir Solov'ëv, "Zapad na vorot," *Kommersant*, 2 Oct 2006.

60. See Yury Simonyan et al., "Tbilisi proshel tochku vozvrata," *Nezavisimaya Gazeta*, 29 Sep 2006.

61. "Putin Fury at Georgia 'Terrorism,'" BBC News, 2 Oct 2006, http://news.bbc .co.uk/2/hi/europe/5397102.stm. The sociopathic Beria was an ethnic Mingrelian from Abkhazia (which was then part of the Georgian SSR). Putin's remark thus carried the implication that in political terms Saakashvili was Beria's descendant.

62. "Georgia: Hundreds Left Stranded after Deportations from Russia," *RFE/RL Feature*, 17 Oct 2006.

63. "Vnutrenyaya diplomatiya," *Kommersant*, 6 Oct 2006.

64. Claire Bigg, "Is Moscow Behind Georgian Unrest?" *RFE/RL Feature*, 14 Nov 2007; Sergey Lavrov, interview with *Rossiiskaya Gazeta*, 28 Sep 2007.

65. Sergey Lavrov, "Zayavlenie Ministra inostrannykh del S. V. Lavrova na press-konferentsii dlya rossiiskikh i zarubezhnykh SMI v svyazi s situatsiei v Yuzhnoi Ossetii," Russian Ministry of Foreign Affairs, 8 Aug 2008.

66. Dmitry Medvedev, "Zayavlenie v svyazi s situatsiei v Yuzhnoi Ossetii," The Kremlin, 8 Aug 2008, http://www.kremlin.ru/appears/2008/08/08/1522—type63374type 63378type82634 205027.shtml.

67. By and large, the looting and attacks on civilians appear to have been the work of the irregular South Ossetian militias rather than the Russian military, which in places worked to stop the depredations (and in others did nothing). Sabrina Tavernise, "Signs of Ethnic Attacks in Georgia Conflict," *New York Times*, 14 Aug 2008.

68. Andrew E. Kramer, "Peace Plan Offers Russia a Rationale to Advance," *New York Times*, 13 Aug 2008. The cease-fire agreement negotiated by Sarkozy was ambiguous on the question of troop withdrawals. While calling on both Tbilisi and Moscow to withdraw their forces to prewar positions, it permitted Russia to station peacekeepers in designated regions abutting South Ossetia and Abkhazia, where they were allowed to take unspecified "additional security measures." Moscow refused Sarkozy's attempts to modify this provision of the cease-fire. It eventually withdrew forces from Georgia proper but kept them in the "independent" enclaves of South Ossetia and Abkhazia.

69. Nauru recognized Abkhazia, but not South Ossetia. For background, see Ellen Barry, "Abkhazia Is Recognized—by Nauru," *New York Times*, 15 Dec 2009.

70. Russia and Abkhazia signed an agreement in February 2010 allowing Moscow to upgrade and expand existing military and naval facilities in the region, while authorizing a Russian military presence until 2059. Russia already had more than four thousand troops in Abkhazia at the time of the signing. See "Russia Gains Military Base in Abkhazia," *RFE/RL*, 17 Feb 2010.

71. Wolfgang Zellner, "Can This Treaty Be Saved? Breaking the Stalemate on Conventional Forces in Europe," Arms Control Association, Sep 2009, http://www. armscontrol.org/act/2009_09/Zellner#18.

72. Obama's Republican opposition frequently charged him with abandoning Georgia and other allies in Europe and the CIS in pursuit of his "reset" with Moscow.

See especially David J. Kramer, "U.S. Abandoning Russia's Neighbors," *Washington Post*, 15 May 2010.

73. Vladimir Paromonov and Aleksei Strokov, *The Evolution of Russia's Central Asia Policy* (Shrivenham: UK Defense Academy, 2008). See also Scott G. Frickenstein, "The Resurgence of Russian Interests in Central Asia," *Air & Space Power Journal*, Spr 2010, 68.

74. Dina Malysheva, "Konflikty u yuzhnykh rubezhei Rossii," *Pro et Contra*, 2000, 5(3): 7–32; Roy Allison, "Strategic Reassertion in Russia's Central Asia Policy," *International Affairs*, 2004, 80(2): 285–86.

75. Adeeb Khalid, *Islam After Communism: Religion and Politics in Central Asia* (Berkeley, CA: University of California Press, 2007), 153–58.

76. Jeronim Perovic, "From Disengagement to Active Economic Competition: Russia's Return to the South Caucasus and Central Asia," *Demokratizatsiya*, Win 2005, 13(1): 62.

77. Trenin, "Southern Watch," 121–22. See also Putin's autobiography. Vladimir Putin, *Ot pervogo litsa: Razgovory s Vladimirom Putinim* (Moscow: Vagrius, 2000), 135–37.

78. Khattab, nom de guerre of the Saudi-born leader of the Chechens' Arab sympathizers (born Samir Saleh Abdullah al-Suwailem), was poisoned by the Russian security services in March 2002. Maskhadov, the relatively moderate president of the Republic of Ichkeria (Chechnya), was killed in murky circumstances in March 2005. Basaev, by far the most notorious of the Chechen field commanders and the man responsible for the most spectacular acts of terrorism in the Chechen conflict (including the 1995 Budyennovsk hospital seizure, the 1999 invasion of Dagestan, the 2002 Dubrovka theater siege, and the 2004 Beslan school seizure), died in an explosion in July 2006. The FSB claims its agents detonated a truck full of explosives driving next to Basaev's car, while Chechen rebel sources claim the truck explosion was an accident. See Sergey Mashkin, "Shamilya Basaeva ubila firmennaya bomba," *Kommersant*, 13 Jul 2006.

79. On the significance of these visits, see Lena Jonson, *Vladimir Putin and Central Asia: The Shaping of Russian Foreign Policy* (London: I. B. Tauris, 2004), 65.

80. For an overview of the IMU's 1999 invasion of Kyrgyzstan and firsthand reporting of the event, see Aleksandr Kim, "Batkenskaya voina 1999: Kak eto bylo na samom dele," *TsentrAziya.ru*, 30 Aug 2002, http://www.centrasia.ru/newsA .php4?Month-8&Day-30&Year-2002. See also Igor Rotar, "The Islamic Movement of Uzbekistan: A Resurgent IMU?" *Jamestown Foundation Terrorism Monitor*, 18 Dec 2003, 1(8).

81. Jonson, *Vladimir Putin and Central Asia*, 70–71.

82. "Kremlin Adviser Explains Putin's Decision to Ally with West," *RFE/RL Report*, 10 Oct 2001.

83. Leonid F. Ryabikhin, "Rossiya i Zapad: Soderzhanie i perspektivy vzaimootnoshenii," in *Rossiya i Zapad posle 11 sentyabrya*, materials from roundtable sponsored by Russian Academy of Sciences European Institute (Moscow: RAN-Institut Evropy, 2002), 68–69.

84. Alan Kasaev and Armen Khanbabyan, "Den' velikogo peredela," *Nezavisimaya Gazeta*, 20 Sep 2001. See also Jonson, *Vladimir Putin and Central Asia*, 85–86.

85. For a brief history of the IMU in its early years, see Mark Burgess, "In the Spotlight: Islamic Movement of Uzbekistan (IMU)," CDI Terrorism Project, 25 May

2002, http://www.cdi.org/terrorism/imu.cfm. Also see Khalid, *Islam After Communism*, 141–44, 155–60.

86. Catherine A. Fitzpatrick, "Is the U.S. Violating Turkmenistan's Neutrality with the NDN?" Eurasianet.org, 1 Aug 2010, http://www.eurasianet.org/node/61652.

87. "Russia to Establish Air Base in Kyrgyzstan, Deals Blow to U.S. Strategic Interests in Central Asia," *EurasiaNet Eurasia Monitor*, 3 Dec 2002, http://www.eurasianet.org/departments/insight/articles/eav120302.shtml.

88. Roger McDermott, "CSTO in Crisis as Moscow Secures Second Military Base in Kyrgyzstan," *Eurasia Daily Monitor*, 4 Aug 2009.

89. Viktoriya Panfilova, "<Manas> smenil vyvesku," *Nezavisimaya Gazeta*, 24 Jun 2009.

90. M. K. Bhadrakumar, "US reaps bitter harvest from 'Tulip' revolution," *Asia Times*, 10 Apr 2010.

91. Adam N. Stulberg, *Well-Oiled Diplomacy: Strategic Manipulation and Russia's Energy Statecraft in Eurasia* (Albany, NY: State University of New York Press, 2007).

92. "Turkmeniya nashla gaz v obkhod Rossii," *Kommersant*, 15 Oct 2008.

93. "Indiya voznamerilas' 'peresest' na turkmenskuyu gazovuyu trubu," *Izvestiya*, 10 Nov 2007; "Turkmenistan Threatens Gas Cutoff to Russia After Talks Fail," *RFE/RL Newsline*, 29 Jun 2006.

94. Medvedev, "Press-konferentsiya po itogam zasedanii Vysshego organa Tamozhennogo soyuza i Mezgosudarstvennogo soveta Yevraziiskogo ekonomicheskogo soobshchestva," 9 Dec 2010, http://kremlin.ru/transcripts/9764.

95. "'LUKOIL' i 'Gazprom' budut rabotat' v Kazakhstane, Uzbekistane, i Ukraine ruka ob ruku," *Izvestiya*, 16 Nov 2004.

96. "Strategicheskie interesy Rossii na postsovetskom prostranstve (po materialam Uchennogo soveta IMEMO)," *Rossiya i novye gosudarstva Yevrazii*, 2010 (3): 5–21. See also A.N. Spartak, "Rossiya i postsovetskoe prostranstvo," *Mirovaya ekonomika i mezhdunarodnye otnosheniya*, 2010 (8).

97. See Keith Bradsher and Christopher Pala, "China Ups the Ante in Its Bid for Oil," *New York Times*, 22 Aug 2005.

98. Henryk Szadziewski, "How the West was Won: China's Expansion into Central Asia," *Caucasian Review of International Affairs*, Spr 2009, 3(2): 210, 214.

99. "Korotko: Yevraziiskii NATO," *Nezavisimaya Gazeta*, 17 May 2002.

100. CSTO, "Zayavlenie Parlamentskoi Assemblei Organizatsii Dogovora o Kollektivnoi Bezopasnosti ob Izmenenii Konfiguratsii Voennogo Prisutstviya NATO v Yevrope," 30 Mar 2007.

101. "CSTO Condemns Georgia's Actions in S. Ossetia, Backs Russia," RIA-Novosti, 5 Sep 2008.

102. CSTO, "Sovmestnaya deklaratsiya o sotrudnichestve mezhdu sekretariatami Organizatsii Ob"edinennykh Natsii i Organizatsii Dogovora o kollektivnoi bezopasnosti," 18 Mar 2010.

103. "NATO should cooperate with CSTO in Afghan drug crackdown—Rogozin," RIA-Novosti, 9 Jun 2010.

104. Christopher Marsh and Nikolas K. Gvosdev, "The Persistence of Eurasia," Carnegie Council Policy Innovations, 5 Nov 2009, http://www.policyinnovations.org/ideas/commentary/data/000152.

105. See Ronald D. Asmus, *A Little War that Shook the World* (New York: Palgrave Macmillan, 2010) 215–34.

CONCLUSION: DEALING WITH RUSSIA'S
FOREIGN POLICY REAWAKENING

1. See Fyodor Lukyanov, "Kremlin's Imperial Ambitions Ended in 2010," *Moscow Times*, 23 Dec 2010.

2. For a discussion of these provocations and the Georgian reaction, see Daniel Fried, "U.S.-Russia Relations in the Aftermath of the Georgia Crisis," testimony to U.S. House Committee on Foreign Affairs, 9 Sep 2008.

3. Putin's remark was made during his 2005 annual address to parliament. Putin, "Poslanie Federal'nomu Sobraniyu Rossiiskoi Federatsii," The Kremlin, 25 Apr 2005, http://www.kremlin.ru/appears/2005/04/25/1223—type63372type63374 type82634—87049.shtml.

4. Condoleezza Rice, "Secretary Rice Addresses U.S.-Russia Relations at the German Marshall Fund," U.S. Department of State, 18 Sep 2008, http://www.state.gov/secretary/rm/2008/09/109954.htm.

5. Fred Weir, "Moscow's Moves in Georgia Track a Script by Right-Wing Prophet," *Christian Science Monitor*, 23 Sep 2008.

6. Marlène Laruelle, "Neo-Eurasianist Alexander Dugin on the Russia-Georgia Conflict," *Central Asia-Caucasus Analyst*, 3 Sep 2008.

7. Clifford Gaddy, "How Not to Punish Moscow," *Newsweek*, 23 Aug 2008; Dmitry Butrin, "Tsarevye dary," *Kommersant Vlast'*, 24 Dec 2007; Ilya Amladov and Polina Ivanova, "'Oboronprom' poshel v nastuplenie," *Kommersant*, 27 Dec 2007.

8. Aleksandr Dugin, "Russian Nationalist Advocates Alliance against the U.S.," interview with *Los Angeles Times*, 4 Sep 2008.

9. Megan K. Stack, "Russia Sees Georgia Outcome as Proof of Its Dominance," *Los Angeles Times*, 25 Aug 2008.

10. "Russia Still Seeks WTO Membership, Broader Ties with EU," RIA-Novosti, 2 Sep 2008.

11. "What the Russian Papers Say," RIA-Novosti, 19 Sep 2008.

12. Dmitry Medvedev, "Vystuplenie na Konferentsii po mirovoi politike," The Kremlin, 8 Oct 2008, http://www.kremlin.ru/text/appears/2008/10/207422.shtml.

13. Eduard Solovyev, "Russian Geopolitics in the Context of Globalization," in *Russia and Globalization: Identity, Security, and Society in an Era of Change*, ed. Douglas W. Blum (Washington, DC: Woodrow Wilson Center, 2008), 303.

14. In his well-known book on the clash of civilizations, Huntington sees Orthodoxy as one of the civilizational blocs that will emerge in the twenty-first century as the world increasingly fragments along cultural lines. See Samuel Huntington, *The Clash of Civilizations and the Remaking of World Order* (New York: Touchstone, 1996), 72–80, 163–67.

15. See especially Robert Kagan, *The Return of History and the End of Dreams* (Washington, DC: Carnegie Endowment for International Peace, 2008). Also Joshua Cooper Ramo, *The Beijing Consensus*, (London: Foreign Policy Centre, 2004).

16. See Anne-Marie Slaughter's statement to *The Economist*'s online debate over the consequences of the Georgian war, http://www.russiablog.org/2008/09/the—economist—hosts—oxfordstyl.php.

17. See especially Dmitry Medvedev, "Vystuplenie na V Krasnoyarskom ekonomicheskom forume 'Rossiya 2008–2020. Upravlenie rostom,'" 15 Feb 2008, http://www.medvedev2008.ru/performance—2008—02—15.htm.

18. Dugin, "Russian Nationalist."

19. For several months after the end of active hostilities, the U.S. blocked meetings of the NATO-Russia Council, a move denounced by Moscow as unhelpful. "U.S. Blocks NATO's Activities—Russian Envoy," *Russia Today*, 23 Sep 2008.

20. Medvedev, "Poslanie Federal'nomu Sobraniyu," 30 Nov 2010, The Kremlin, http://www.kremlin.ru/transcripts/9637.

21. See Alexander Kramarenko, "5 Reasons Why Russia Could Join NATO," *Moscow Times*, 9 Dec 2010.

22. Judy Dempsey, "Russian Proposal Calls for Broader Security Pact," *New York Times*, 28 Jul 2008.

23. Steven Pifer, "What Does Russia Want? How Do We Respond?" Lecture at Texas A&M University, 11 Sep 2008, http://www.brookings.edu/speeches/2008/0911—russia—pifer.aspx.

24. Pifer, "What Does Russia Want?"

25. See Jeffrey Mankoff, "Eurasian Energy Security," Council on Foreign Relations Special Report, (43), Feb 2009.

26. Chris McGreal and Luke Harding, "Barack Obama: Putin Has One Foot in the Past," *The Guardian*, 2 Jul 2009.

Index

About the Author

Jeffrey Mankoff was a 2010–11 Council on Foreign Relations International Affairs Fellow based in the Bureau of European and Eurasian Affairs at the U.S. Department of State. From 2008 to 2010, he was Associate Director of International Security Studies at Yale University and adjunct fellow for Russia studies at the Council on Foreign Relations. Previously, he was a John M. Olin National Security Fellow at the Olin Institute for Strategic Studies, Harvard University; Henry Chauncey Fellow in Grand Strategy, Yale University; and a fellow at Moscow State University. His areas of functional expertise include Russian/Eurasian affairs, great power relations, foreign policy decision making, ethnic conflict, and energy security. Dr. Mankoff has also taught classes at Yale on Russian foreign policy, Central Asia, and modern diplomatic and military history.

He received his Ph.D. and M.Phil. in history and his M.A. in political science from Yale, and his B.A. in international studies and Russian from the University of Oklahoma.